BUSINESS ETHICS AND CORPORATE GOVERNANCE

BY THE SAME AUTHOR

- Boost Your Professional Career: Total Solutions (2003)
- Business Ethics and Managerial Values (2004)
- Constructive Industrial Relations and Labour Laws (2004)
- International Practices in Industrial Relations (2003)
- Management of Change and Organisation Development (2003)
- Managing Cultural Diversity in Globalisation (2003)
- New Compensation Management in Changing Environment (2003)
- Principles and Techniques of Personnel Management
  Co-author (Nirmal Singh) (2001)
- Management of Absenteeism
- Industrial Relations and Collective Bargaining (2000)
- Training and Development: Concepts and Practices (In Press) (2004)

BUSINESS ETHICS AND CORPORATE GOVERNANCE

Concepts, Issues, Practices and Dilemmas in Shaping Ethical Culture for Competitive Advantage of Organisations

S.K. BHATIA

Director
Human Resource Management Foundation, New Delhi
and, Senior Faculty, Business Management Institutes

Formerly:
- Director (Personnel), Oil India Ltd.
- Director (Pers. and PR), Mekaster Group Co's.
- Add. General Manager (Pers. and Admn.) Bharat Heavy Electricals India Ltd.

Foreword by

DR. ABAD AHMAD

Professor of Management and Former Pro-Vice-Chancellor,
University of Delhi, Delhi

DEEP & DEEP PUBLICATIONS PVT. LTD.

F-159, Rajouri Garden, New Delhi-110027

BUSINESS ETHICS AND CORPORATE GOVERNANCE

First Published : 2007
Reprinted : 2009
Reprinted : 2010

ISBN 81-7629-593-0
(PAPERBACK EDITION)

Typeset by ASHISH TECHNOGRAPHICS,
3190, Mohindra Park, Shakur Basti, Delhi - 110 034.

Printed in India at MAYUR ENTERPRISES
WZ Plot No. 3, Gujjar Market, Tihar Village, New Delhi - 110 018.

Published by DEEP & DEEP PUBLICATIONS PVT. LTD.,
F-159, Rajouri Garden, New Delhi - 110 027
Phones : 25435369, 25440916
E-mails : ddpubs@gmail.com • ddpbooks@yahoo.co.in
Showroom :
2/13, Ansari Road, Daryaganj, New Delhi - 110 002 • Telefax : 23245122

Dedicated to

my wife Kusum Bhatia,

who is an epitome of high values and ethics

in her life.

CONTENTS

PART IV

SHAPING AND MAINTAINING THE ETHICAL CULTURE (PROGRAMMES)

PART V

PROFESSIONALS AND ETHICS

PART VI

ETHICAL VALUES

PART VII

INDIAN ETHOS IN MANAGEMENT

PART VIII

CORPORATE GOVERNANCE AND PROFESSIONAL ETHICS

PART IX

CULTURE

PART X

CORPORATE SOCIAL RESPONSIBILITY

PART XI

PROTECTION OF STAKEHOLDERS

FOREWORD

There are, at present, three approaches having a similar focus in protecting various interests, i.e. corporate social responsibility, business ethics and corporate governance. These subjects have, however, developed separately during different periods.

The first approach, CORPORATE SOCIAL RESPONSIBILITY has its origin in USA about seven decades ago. It is an obligation of decision-makers to take actions which protect and improve the welfare of society as a whole along with their own interests. Such decisions may affect environment, consumers and community. It was Peter Drucker who later emphatically argued that management should assume social responsibility. Management should consider the impact of every business policy and action upon society. It has to consider the actions that are likely to promote the public good and to advance the basic beliefs of society, and to contribute to its stability, strength and harmony. He laid emphasis on "Quality of product and customer service".

Later on Sandra Holmes in her study of 540 top executives emphasised that in addition to making profit, business should help solve special problems whether or not business creates these problems.

The second concept, BUSINESS ETHICS with its social values and social concerns came to focus in 1970's in USA, which forced companies to abstain their policies that violate consumer protection and environmental problems. Business ethics safeguards business practices relating to different stake-holders or constituencies (i.e. internal and external constituencies). Business ethics are rules of business conduct, by which propriety of business activities may be judged. Business ethics equally relates to the behaviour and responsibilities of managers and ethical obligations of business professionals. Here focus is on people, how individuals should conduct themselves in fulfilling the ethical requirements of business. There is a growing realisation all over the world that ethics is vitally important for any business and for progress of any society. Ethical leadership can attain this by standing the test of environmental performance and development of corporate social performance (CSP) as recently highlighted by Clarkson. Ethics and profits go together in the long-run and it can protect the society. In fact experience convincingly shows that good ethics is the foundation of good business.

The third approach is CORPORATE GOVERNANCE which advocates enhancing the accountability of the board of directors to shareholders, more transparent auditing and more responsibilities of independent directors, and a division of roles of chairman and chief executive, etc. The importance of good corporate governance can hardly be over-emphasised, specially after witnessing the shocking corporate failures like that of Enron recently, and many such crises caused earlier by inadequacies and malpractices in corporate governance.

I am happy to note that Shri Bhatia has exhaustively covered all these approaches in his book. Another aspect of vital importance is the role of ethical leadership in providing direction and communicating the values and beliefs that influence and shape the organisation culture and behavioural norms. The moral environment of an organisation depends on the moral calibre and integrity of the leader. The author has touched this aspect in great detail in chapters highlighting critical role of leadership. In addition, chapters in Section XI have been specifically devoted to protection of stake-holder's interests.

In my opinion the book, besides being educative on various concepts, practices and dilemmas, will provide a thrust on practical implementation and development of ethical practices in organisations. It is a practical tool for enhancing integrity in the organisations. The book has been written in simple and easily understandable language.

I am confident this will be a valuable addition to the management literature in India. It will serve as a teaching and learning resource for corporate managers and students of business ethics and corporate governance who want to improve reputation, image and enhance competitive advantage of their organisations by following a principled approach with awareness of duties and obligations.

Delhi

DR. ABAD AHMAD
Professor of Management, and
Former Pro-Vice Chancellor,
University of Delhi, Delhi

PREFACE

Important of Subject

Business ethics and corporate governance have become topics of worldwide importance in present times. These have become top concerns at international business community and financial institutions. In recent years we have media filled with shocking stories of corporate misconduct and wrong doing by individual business people. It is difficult to imagine areas of study that have greater importance to business, managerial leaders and society at large.

Business Ethics relates to the behaviour and obligations of business professionals. Here the focus is on people, how individuals should conduct themselves in fulfilling the ethical requirements of business. Business ethics requires managers to be honest with stakeholder's interests, society, environment and themselves. It is vitally important for any business, for progress of society and efficient economy. It is ethics alone, not government laws and regulations, which can protect society. Business ethics and profits go together in the long-run, for sustenance of organisations. If a company wants to survive and grow, it has to discharge its obligations to the society. So corporates have to pave the way for a stronger ethical foundations.

Corporate Governance stipulates parameters of accountability, control and reporting functions of the board of directors of the corporation. It also calls for establishing a proper and a viable relationship amongst the various participants of a corporation, the board, the management team, auditors, shareholders and other stakeholders. Corporate governance is a set of systems and processes to ensure that company is managed to suit the best interests of all stakeholders. The philosophy of corporate governance hinges on total transparency, integrity and accountability of the management which includes non-executive directors. The importance of corporate governance lies in its contribution to business prosperity. It means implementing the philosophy of corporate governance in letter and in spirit. It is an important tool for shareholders' protection and maximisation of their long-term values.

Another concept which is aimed similar in approach to protect various interest is *social responsibility* of business. It means the obligation of business enterprise to make decision and follow lines of action which are desirable in terms of the objectives and values of society. Decisions may affect environment, employees, consumers and community. Social responsibility is thus an obligation of decision-makers to take actions which protect and improve the welfare of society as a whole along with their own interest.

Aim of the Book

Business ethics now occupies a centre stage in management education in India and is a topic of public concern. The objective of this book is to:

(a) Share knowledge, build skills and develop minds of the young entrepreneurial managers of tomorrow,

(b) Provide clarity and insights into concepts of business ethics and corporate governance so that young managers avoid business misconduct,

(c) Inculcate high level of integrity and create moral and social awareness so that they can decide when faced with business dilemma,

(d) Help in fostering ability to reason when applying ethical principles, and

(e) Help realise their social responsibility and values, wisdom and way of life.

Contents

The book covers all the major concepts and approaches on the topics of:

- Business ethics,
- Indian ethos in management,
- Corporate governance,
- Social responsibility of business,
- Some vital subjects such as: corruption, sexual harassment at work place, work-life balance, wisdom management, spirituality and humanism, work ethics, professional ethics and managerial values.

I hope readers—students as well as practicing managers will find the book comprehensive and useful. It reflects contemporary developments in the field.

Suggestions for improvement of this text, which is for educational purpose, will be highly appreciated.

New Delhi S.K. BHATIA

ACKNOWLEDGEMENTS

I express my immense gratitude to many sources that have been consulted in the preparation of this book. It is both my pleasure, and bounden duty to acknowledge, with all humility, my grateful thanks and indebtedness to various scholars, authors, their publishers from whose distinguished works and writings, I gained so much, whose ideas and valuable contributions to the vast subject of business ethics and corporate governance, have been of great help to me in completion of this volume. As far as possible, I have tried to include their names and publications at the close of each chapter and list of references. If, however, there has been any omission, inadvertently, I crave their indulgence.

I take this opportunity to congratulate the editors of "Chartered Secretary" who brought out two special separate issues on "Business Ethics" and"Corporate Governance in September and November, 2003 which incorporated enlightened views of competent professionals in various articles. 1 gratefully acknowledge their contribution to vast subject and their ideas have been great help to me. I have attempted to include their names in each chapter as a source of reference. If, however, there has been any omission, inadvertently, I crave their indulgence.

I am immensely thankful to Prof. S.A. Sherlekar for his inspiring insight into ancient Indian wisdom. His monumental work"Ethics in Management" which is based on two ideals: (i) Human values-spiritual, ethical and moral values, and (ii) Holism-oneness, unity, cooperation,. has been a great source of education and enlightenment to me. This has enabled me to include a separate Part VII titled "Indian Ethos in Management." I owe him personal debt of gratitude for his eminent ideas and concepts which I have incorporated in this volume.

Some articles were collected from various sources—newspapers, magazines and text books during long years of service and used as teaching material. Unfortunately, these sources were not noted and it is impractical to offer acknowledgement. I express my thanks to those who contributed anonymously to this book.

Text-books for educational purpose are a team project. While my name is on the cover of this book, literally, it is combined contribution of the writings of so many scholars and authors. Their names and publications are given in each chapter. Every effort has been made to contact them and gratefully acknowledged, but if any have been inadvertently overlooked, I shall be pleased to make necessary arrangement at the first opportunity.

I am immensely grateful to my son, Neeraj Bhatia and daughter-in-law Pulkit Bhatia, in USA, who not only arranged my study visit to USA, but also helped in arranging the literature on the subject, from various sources. Company of little Arunika and Arjun made my study tour more lively and interesting.

I also thank the publisher for his expediting and nice get up of the book.

New Delhi S.K. BHATIA

Contributions Acknowledged

Carter McNamara, "Complete Guide to Ethics Management", St. Paul, Minesota, USA.

Joseph H. Boyett and Jimmie T. Boyett, "The Guru Guide to the Knowledge Economy", 2001, USA.

R.N. Kanungo and M. Mendonca, Journal of Human Values, 1998, Sage Publications, Thousand Oaks.

Stephen P. Robbins, "Organisation Behaviour", Prentice-Hall of India Pvt. Ltd.

Peter Pratley, "The Essence of Business Ethics."

Azhar Kazmi, Department of Business Administration, Aligarh Muslim University.

Patricia Hayes Andrews and Richard T. Herschel.

Barbara Key Toffler, "Though Choices Managers Talk Ethics."

G. Anjaneya, "Organisation with a Heart."

Thomas Donaldson, "Ethics in Business: A New Look."

Sorab Sadri, "Business Ethics", McGraw Hill.

Tom Mcewan, "Managing Values and Beliefs in Organisation", Financial Times, Prentice Hall, Harlow.

Nan Demars, "You Want To Do What", Simon and Schuster, USA.

S.A. Sherlekar, "Ethics in Management."

Editors, "Chartered Secretary", New Delhi.

Raja Achanta, "The Work-Life Balance", HRM Review, March 2004.

PART I

BUSINESS ETHICS, NATURE, IMPORTANCE IN ORGANISATIONS

CHAPTER

1

BUSINESS ETHICS

There is no agreement as to what the term business ethics means. Let us remember story of a boy who went to a priest and said, "I will give you an apple if you tell me where God is!"? Priest replied, "But I will give you two apples if you tell me where he is not?"

It is much the same with business ethics. One can hardly say where it is not. It is a discipline which addresses numerous issues, problems and dilemmas.

SCOPE OF BUSINESS ETHICS

Ethical issues are there everywhere, at all levels of business activity. Business ethics concern the ground rules of individual company and societal behaviour.

(a) Societal Level

- Concern for poor and down-trodden.
- No discrimination against any particular section or group.
- Concern for clean environment.
- Preservation of scarce resources for posterity.
- Contributing to better quality of life.

(b) Stakeholder's Level

(i) Employees

- Security of job.
- Better working conditions.
- Better recommendation.
- Participative management.
- Welfare facilities.

(ii) Customers

- Better quality of goods.
- Goods and services at reasonably price.
- Not to corner stocks and create securities.
- Not to practice discriminatory pricing.
- Not to make false claims about products in advertisements.

(iii) Shareholders

- Ensure capital appreciation.
- Ensure steady and regular dividends.
- Disclose all relevant information.
- Protect minority shareholders' interests.
- Not to window dress balance sheets.
- Protect interests in times of mergers, amalgamations and takeovers.

(iv) Banks and other Lending Institutions

- Guarantee safety of borrowed funds.
- Prompt repayment of loans.

(v) Government

- Complying with rules and regulations.
- Honesty in paying taxes and other dues.
- Acting as partner in the progress of the country.

(c) Internal Policy Level

- Fair practices relating to recruitment, compensation, lay-offs, perks, promotion, etc.
- Transformational leadership to motivate employees to aim at better and higher things in life.
- Better communication at all levels.

(d) Personal Policy Level

- Not to misuse others for personal ends.
- Not to indulge in politics to gain power.
- Not to spoil promotional chances of others.
- Not to use office car, stationery and other facilities for personal use.
- Not to fall prey to shortcuts and easy money.
- Promise keeping.
- No violence, i.e. preventing or not causing physical harm to others.
- Mutual help.
- Respect for persons and property.

NATURE OF BUSINESS ETHICS

Ethical issues occur frequently in management and extend for beyond the commonly discussed problems of bribery, collusion and theft, reaching into area such as corporate acquisitions, marketing policies and capital investments. For example, after the merger of two firms, ethical question arises whether to demote or fire the employees those who have been serving honestly for so many years.

Ethics requires a manager to be honest with himself and society. The manager's performance and quality reflect in the success of a business. Sometimes ethical issues occur as managerial dilemmas because they represent a conflict between an organisation's economic performance (measured by revenues, costs and profits) and its social performance (stated in terms of obligation to persons both inside and outside the organisation).

ETHICAL BASE OF BUSINESS

Now, what is the relevance of ethics for business? A business, regardless of its organizational structure, is manned only by human beings. And so, business too cannot and shall not be immune to ethics. The goal of business is to provide goods and services to customers and clients and earn profits or income. If business has ethics, it will ensure that the goods and services are of reasonable equality and are offered at reasonable prices to earn reasonable profits, as distinguished from profiteering.

More importantly, the interests of the stakeholders shall receive care and consideration at the hands of business. The stakeholders include customers, suppliers, creditors, government employees, shareholders and the community. Business has to promote its growth with fairness and truth in its advertisements. This is broadly known as social responsibility of business. As an extension of this concept, business is also expected to share a part of its prosperity with the community in the midst of which it is located by offering amenities and services not otherwise available to the needy in that community.

The new concept of "Maximising shareholder value" is being touted as the be all and end all of business in recent times. This concept assumes that the investors (promoters and large shareholders) are the most valuable constituents of business and all others are peripheral ones. If a company can enhance the value of its shares in the stock market, its market capitalization goes up. In many cases, speculative reports, creative accounting and other manipulative methods also achieve this even without proven fundamentals. Thus, this theory is not one without flaws. "Ethics is a matter of developing good habits, and it doesn't happen overnight. It happens through repetition and a long process of development." (P.T. Rangamani)

A TWO-FOLD OBJECTIVE

According to Peter Pratley (The Essence of Business Ethics) business ethics has a two-fold objective: "it evaluates human practices by calling upon moral standards; also it may give prescriptive advice on how to act morally in a specific kind of situation.

(i) The first aim implies *analysis and evaluation*. It leads to an ethical diagnosis of past actions and events. The analysis consists of clarifying standards and lines of argument. Here ethics can be useful, as one is often unaware about most moral values and habits of thought. The basic assumptions behind our moral actions and judgements are mainly taken for granted.

Normative ethics sets itself a second and more curative purpose. Ethics develops rational methods for answering the present and future issues. In order to achieve this second objective one has to be well informed. *Balanced judgements* are based on the careful assessment of relevant information; also one has to be quite specific when deciding upon appropriate normative standards. If both these conditions are met, ethical thought may lead to valid prescriptions.

(ii) So, the second objective is to provide *therapeutic advice*. It suggests solutions and policies when facing the present dilemmas and future dangers, based on well-informed opinions. This especially requires an identification of relevant stakeholder and a clear understanding of the vital issues at stake."

ETHICS

To begin with, let us understand, what is 'Ethics'? The word "Ethics" has origin in Greek word "Ethics" means character; norms, morals and ideals prevailing in a group, society.

Ethics may be referred to as some standardised form of conduct/ behaviour of individuals understood and accepted in a particular field of activity, or

Ethics is a mass of moral principles or sets of values about what conduct ought to be. They give an idea what is right or wrong, true or false, fair or unfair, just or unjust, proper or improper, e.g. honesty, obedience, equality, fairness, etc. and respect and then doing the right thing.

Ethics is a fundamental, personal trait which one adopts and follows as a guiding principle or basic Dharma in one's life. It implies moral conduct and honourable behaviour on the part of an individual. Ethics in most cases runs parallel to law and shows due consideration of others' rights and interests in a civilized society. Compassion on the other hand may induce a person to give more than what ethics might demand.

Even while rendering a service for a *quid pro quo*, the individual is expected to ensure that his services do not militate against public good, are not morally indefensible or are not prohibited or punishable by law. Those placed in positions of trust and recognised for their knowledge and expertise shall perform their duty with integrity, independence, sincerity and honesty. That is the basic norm of professional ethics. A professional cannot justify his failure, negligence of compromise, with excuses and explanations.

Every rational human being practices ethics for his own and others' welfare and safety.

BUSINESS ETHICS

Different meaning is given to business ethics by various people. Business ethics are rules of business conduct, by which the propriety of business activities may be judged. Ethical principles are dictated by the society and underlie broad social policies. These principles when known, understood and accepted, determine generally the propriety or impropriety of business activities.

Business ethics also relates to the behaviour of manager. It can be defined as an attempt to ascertain the responsibilities and ethical obligations of business professionals. Here the focus is in people, how individuals should conduct themselves in fulfilling the ethical requirements of business?

One writer (Deepak Parekh, CMO HDFC in his J.R.D. Tata Corporate Leadership Award lecture in 27.2.1997) has given one line definition of ethics: "Do not do something that you would be ashamed of, if it becomes public." It is not too difficult to achieve this reality. There is no pillow as soft as a clear conscience.

Carter McNamara has defined: "Business ethics is generally coming to know what is right or wrong in the work place and doing what is right—this is in regard to effects of products/services and in relationships with stakeholders." "Attention to ethics in the work place sensitizes managers and staff to how they should act so that they retain a strong moral compass. Consequently, business ethics can be strong preventive medicine."

BUSINESS ETHICS IS NOW A MANAGEMENT DISCIPLINE

McNamara further states that "Business ethics has come to be considered a management discipline, especially since the birth of the social responsibility of business." Business owed responsibility to work to improve society, e.g. environmental protection, equal rights, public health and improving education. Business operations have replaced the word "stockholder" with "stakeholder", meaning to include employees, customers, suppliers and the wider community.

According to Robert Kreitner in his book, "Management", "Highly publicized accounts of corporate misconduct in recent years have led widespread cynicism about business ethics. And when a 1992 Gallup Poll asked Americans to rate the ethical standards of various professions, only 18 per cent scored business executives either high or very high on honesty and ethical standards. Other professions rated as follows: druggists/pharmacists, 66 per cent; medical doctors, 52 per cent; police officers, 42 per cent; funeral directors, 35 per cent; journalists, 27 per cent; stock brokers, 13 per cent; members of Congress, 11 per cent; and car salespeople, 5 per cent." Fortunately, the subject of ethics is receiving serious attention in management circles these days.

THE IMPORTANCE OF ETHICS

Patrica Hayes Andrews and Richard T. Herschel, 'Organisation Communication' (pp. 309-10) have excellently summarised the importance of ethics as under: "Unfortunately, in recent years an alarming number of "unethical" situations have arisen in American organizations. For example, the Ford Motor Company refused to alter the dangerous gas tank on its Pinto model because changing it would have cost the company $ 11 per car. In the end, the flaw cost Ford millions of dollars in lawsuits—and cost many people their lives.

Equity Funding tried to hide 64,000 phony insurance claims but went bankrupt when the truth came out. Ivan Boesky engaged in "insider trading", an illegal practice for investment counsellors. A number of directors of savings and loan associations defrauded depositors, in many cases depriving people of their life savings. It is little wonder that a large majority of the public think executives are dishonest, overly profit-oriented, and willing to step on other people to get what they want (Andrews, 1989)."

In India also there are numerous cases of scams and cheating the small investors of their hard earned money. To name few—MS Shoes East Ltd. for misleading investing public, Manu Chabra Group for wrecking the fortunes of about half-a-dozen companies and facing investigations on FERA violations, the Harshad Mehta Epic Stock Scam, claims of the Sterling Group and a host of other engaged in teak plantations, ITC's violation of excise laws and the recent one UTI scam where they have left crores of investors high and dry. This is all to point how managements out of greed to make more money and achieve goals, take the various constituents of the company for a ride in the most unfair ways.

Whether or not everyone would agree that the behaviours described above are equally unethical, when considered together, they lead to a critical question: Why is ethical behaviour important? There are several compelling reasons.

First, *ethical behaviour is usually associated with important positive consequences.* Honesty in one's professional dealings promotes trust and establishes the foundation for relationship development and positive future interactions. Business in particular depends on the acceptance of rules and expectations, mutual trust and fairness. Thus, ethical business is good business. In contrast, unethical behaviour can cause serious damage affecting both the persons committing the behaviour and the people touched by it. In the cases described above, innocent people suffered serious financial losses, injury, or loss of life, and in some cases the perpetrators were sentenced to jail. But beyond that, the people and organisations that were involved lost credibility. Once an organisation's image is so tarnished that people are no longer willing to put their faith in it or its leaders, it is almost certain to fail. Nothing is more dangerous to business, than a tarnished public image—the fact is that a tarnished image has direct consequences, for sales, for profits, for morale, for the day-to-day running of the business. Distrust of a company can quickly drive it to bankruptcy.

Second, from a personal perspective, *ethical errors end careers more quickly* than any other mistakes in judgment and accounting. Lying, stealing, cheating, on contracts, and so on undermine the very foundation upon which the business and professional world is built. Ethical behaviour is especially important for organizational leaders because they influence the ethical climate for everyone else. Leaders are role models. When they make ethical blunders, they are held especially accountable. No one can excuse immorality. The US House of Representatives in July, 2002 expelled Democratic legislator James Traficant of Ohio, making the former sheriff turned convicted felon the second House member since the Civil War to be tossed out of Congress. On a vote of 420-1, law-makers booted the nine-term Traficant for ethics violations stemming from his April conviction on federal charges of bribery, kickbacks and tax evasion. Gene Green, a Texas Democrat, said, "If we can't remove a Congressman convicted of 10 felony counts . . . we risk losing the faith and trust of the American people." (*Reuters*)

Third, *ethical behaviour is empowering for all parties*. The manager who behaves ethically establishes an organisational climate of supportiveness, honesty, and trust. This climate in turn empowers employees to try out new ideas, take risks, express dissent, and generally assume enhanced responsibility.

Finally, *ethical behaviour is intrinsically valuable*. Those who know that they are honest, who behave humanely in their dealings with others, who are fair in their evaluations of others, and who are concerned for the welfare of the organization as a whole and the society it serves are rewarded with a peace of mind that carries no price tag.

Ultimately, managers who treat other people with unimpeachable integrity thereby *earn those people's trust and make them more willing to support the organization*. Conversely, managers who lack integrity promote mistrust among those with whom they deal and make their employees ashamed of their organization and the products and services they provide. Since workers feel their work is unworthy, they stop caring.

Andrew Sigler, "The Business Roundable", *New York Times*, February 1981 has highlighted that "*Ethics provides the broader framework within which business life must be understood*, there may be few people for whom business is all of life, for whom family and friendship are irrelevant. For them money means only more investment potential and has nothing to do with respect or status or enjoying the good life. But most successful executives understand that *business is part of life. Corporations are part of a society*."

"Executives are *most effective and successful* when they retain their "real life" view of themselves, their positions and the human world outside as well as inside the corporation. Business ethics, ultimately, is just business in its larger human context."

"A Corporation's responsibilities includes its impact of its actions on all, from shareholders, customers, employees and to the society at large. Its business activities must make business sense."

ETHICS PLAYS KEY ROLE IN BUSINESS

Another writer Thomas Donaldson (Ethics in Business: A New Look) has observed that "There are three key reasons why business ethics is not a fad and why ethics plays a key role in business.

First, it is crucial that *ethics have a considerable influence* if we want an efficient, smoothly operating economy. Ethics helps the market to its best. For example, the economist, Alfred Marshall remarked in 1925, that a score of Tata's might well do more for India than any Government, British or local could accomplish—the emphasis is that history of Tata evolution is not just on any kind of capitalism but on ethically-based management.

Second, the *government, laws and lawyers cannot resolve certain key problems of business and protect the society: ethics can.* Ethics can only resolve futuristic issues such as technology races ahead much faster than the government. Regulations almost always lag behind. That companies social responsibility extends beyond what the law strictly requires.

Third, *ethical activity is valuable in itself,* for its own sake, because it *enhances the quality of lives* and the work we do—business has an ethical responsibility for fairness for humanity, e.g. employee."

TO SUM UP—IMPORTANCE OF BUSINESS ETHICS

Thomas Donaldson (Ethics in Business: A New Look) sums up that "There is a growing realisation all over the world that ethics is vitally important for any business and for the progress of any society. Ethics makes for an efficient economy; ethics alone, not government or laws, can protect society; ethics is good in itself; ethics and profits go together in the long-run. An ethically responsible company is one which has developed a culture of caring for people and for the environment; a culture which flows downwards from the top managers and leaders."

CONCEPTUAL MODEL FOR BUSINESS ETHICS

Madsen in his book, "Essentials of Business Ethics", explains business ethics can broadly be divided into separate areas:

THREE "C's" OF BUSINESS ETHICS

1. The need for *compliance* of rules, including—

- Laws,
- Principles of morality, the customs of community, and
- Policy of the company and fairness.

Business Ethics

Managerial Mischief | *Moral Problems* Manager's Face in Decision-making

1. Managerial Mischief

Concerning:

(i) Illegal acts.

(ii) Unethical or questionable practices of individual managers, its causes, and remedial measures to eradicate them.

Examples:

(i) Fraud, kickbacks, bribery, improprieties, illegal disposal of hazardous materials, intentional violations of work place safety, stealing expense account cheating.

(ii) Dumping of pesticides banned in USA to other countries, providing money or sexual favour to buyers.

Causes of Misconduct:

1. Individual monitory gain to commit illegalities.
2. Organisation pressures due to composition and desire to succeed with emphasis on short-term profits. Fosters improprieties.
3. Corporate values and peer pressure influence individual's business conduct. Success at any cost leads to managerial mischief.

2. Moral Problems

Manager's Face in Decision-Making

1. Micro-Level Problems

Individual front line managers while dealing, e.g.

- Fairness in performance appraisals.
- Confidentiality of company.
- Accepting gifts.
- Confronting expense account cheating.
- Treatment of problem employees.
- Continuing harmful environmental practices and failing or exceeding in managerial role.

2. Macro-issues dealt by top management

- Corporate Social Responsibility.
  By laying corporate mission/objectives, purpose. For example, a pharma company laying objective of promoting better health and saving life.
- Laying Ethical Standards, e.g.
  codes of conduct,
  statement of corporate responsibility, and
  laying polices and practices for ethical decision-making.

2. The *contribution* business can make to society through—

- The core values,
- Quality of one's products and services,
- By providing jobs to employees,
- Usefulness of activities to surrounding community, and
- QWL (Quality of Work Life) influenced by ethical and moral values.

3. The *consequences* of business activity—

- Towards environment inside the plant and outside the organisation and community, e.g. Bhopal Gas Leaking Tragedy.
- Social responsibility towards shareholders, bankers, suppliers, customers and employees of organisation.
- Good public image. Sound business practices so that public image is not tarnished.

Reference

1. P.T. Rangamani, "Ethics, Business and Professions", *Chartered Secretary*, November 2003.

CHAPTER

2

WHY BUSINESS ETHICS IS VITAL FOR MANAGERS/STUDENTS/ORGANISATIONS?

Apart from the hard skills, tools and management techniques like just-in-time, total quality management, business process re-engineering, etc., adequate attention must be paid to the relatively softer skills like business ethics and business practices. As a training ground of professional managers, the effort must first start in the management schools. In the west, a course on business ethics, cross-cultural variance with respect to values, corporate social responsibility, forms an integral part of the MBA curriculum.

BENEFITS FOR STUDENTS

Some benefits for the student young managers are:

(i) Young managers should understand and be aware of the reasons that underlie moral principles. These are helpful in fostering *ability to reason* when applying these principles. It is vital part of ensuring compliance by managers with company standards for conduct.

(ii) Knowledge of business ethics will help managers in *resolving ethical issues/dilemmas* as they arise.

(iii) Knowledge will help managers in setting highly *responsible tone for the organisation*—in individual judgements and decisions whether ethical or not.

(iv) The study of business ethics will *provide conscientious managers* with morally responsible approach to business. The need for responsible managers is acute as questions of business ethics cannot wholly be determined by law or government regulations, but must remain the concern of individual manager.

(v) It helps *managers to realise their social responsibility.* Many organisations find it wise to go beyond their primary mission and take into account needs of the community. Business ethics makes managers more accountable for social responsibility.

(vi) The study of business ethics *inculcates high level of integrity in managers.* Goal of ethics education is to share knowledge, build skills and develop minds. It helps to gain clarity and insight into business ethics and avoid business misconduct in organisations. The study of business ethics helps manager arrive at a decision that he feels to be "right and proper" 'just'. It facilitates individual's to understand their moral standards and ethical norms, beliefs and values so that they can decide when faced with business dilemma.

(vii) Business ethics *creates awareness of social and moral values* through education (value education) because erosion of essential values and increasing cynicism in society is leading to violence, superstition and fatalism.

In view of aforesaid benefits, majority of business management institutes in India have now introduced a separate course on business ethics for management students. Knowledge and awareness of the concepts and practices of business ethics is equally helpful to practicing managers in managerial conduct and decision-making. Business ethics improve the skills of reflective managers both in analyzing concrete moral issues and in deliberating and deciding upon strategies for solving moral dilemmas. The study of cases by students reminds them the importance of precise and accurate judgements that take into account the concrete facts and issues. Business ethics contributes by highlighting basic principles in a systematic manner.

In nutshell, business ethics provides a basic outlook to the training of a business manager. He would enter the bad word with fortified set of values and less of doubts.

Peter Pratley, in "The Essence of Business Ethics" cautions against one particular erroneous expectation: People with immoral habits will not change by reading a book on business ethics. He states that "Behaving with a sense of moral responsibility *require practice, it is reflective activity. Ethics can guide our reflection* on such matters, but cannot actually reorient and shape the qualities of our character, commitment and mind. This is a matter of education, giving the right example, and learning to practice moral behaviour in honest dialogue."

It has to be realised that business cannot do without ethics. Sound ethics pay-off in the long-run. Much neglect of ethics occurs out of incompetence, cowardice and myopia.

Azim Prem Ji, recently said that in his journey from tiny business of Rs. 5 crores to Wipro's net worth today touching some Rs. 3500 crores, everything in Wipro but *for values and integrity*, has undergone a drastic change. He cautioned the emerging breed of entrepreneurs and business managers to *desist from temptation of shortcuts and windfall gains.*

BENEFITS OF MANAGING ETHICS IN THE ORGANISATION

Carter McNamara describes various (ten) benefits from managing ethics in the work place as under:

(i) Attention to Business Ethics has Substantially Improved Society

A few decades ago, children in USA worked 16 hours day. Workers' limbs were cut-off in accidents and disabled workers were condemned to poverty and often to starvation. Employees were terminated based on personalities. Then society reacted and demanded that businesses place high value on fairness and equal rights. Anti-trust laws were instituted. Government agencies were established. Unions were organised. Laws and regulations were established.

(ii) Ethics Programmes Help Maintain a Moral Course in Turbulent Times

Wallace and Pekel explain that attention to business ethics is critical during times of fundamental change—times much like those faced now by businesses. During times of change, there is often no clear moral compass to guide leaders through complex conflicts about what is right or wrong. Continuing attention to ethics in the work place sensitizes leaders and staff as to how they should act—consistently.

(iii) Ethics Programmes Cultivate Strong Teamwork and Productivity

Ethics programmes align employee behaviours with those top priority ethical values preferred by leaders of the organisation. Ongoing attention and dialogue regarding values in the work place builds openness, integrity and community—critical ingredients of strong teams in the work place. Employees feel strong alignment between their values and those of the organization. They react with strong motivation and performance.

(iv) Ethics Programmes Support Employee Growth and Meaning

Attention to ethics in the work place helps employees face reality, both good and bad—in the organization and themselves. Employees feel full confidence they can deal with whatever comes their way. Bennett explains that a consulting company tested a range of executives and managers. Their most striking finding: the more emotionally healthy executives, as measured on a battery of tests, the more likely they were to score high on ethics tests. *Ethics is necessary for human survival and existence.* In fact, one's own survival is linked with survival of others and this is ethics. The six main characteristics of ethics are—patience, tolerance, forgiveness, consideration, humility and compassion. These are *intertwined with the purpose of life.* Living a life of peace and happiness is the goal of everyone.

(v) Ethics Programmes are an Insurance Policy—They Help Ensure that Policies are Legal

Ethical principles are often state-of-the-art legal matters. These principles are often applied to current, major ethical issues to become legislation. Attention to ethics ensures highly ethical policies and procedures in the work place. It's far better to incur the cost of mechanisms to ensure ethical practices now than to incur costs of litigation later. A major intent of well-designed personnel policies is to ensure ethical treatment of employees, e.g., in matters of hiring, evaluating, disciplining, firing, etc.

(vi) Ethics Programmes Help Avoid Criminal Acts "Of Omission" and can Lower Fines

Ethics programmes tend to detect ethical issues and violations early on so they can be reported or addressed.

(vii) Ethics Programmes Help Manage Values Associated with Quality Management, Strategic Planning and Diversity Management—This Benefit Needs for More Attention

Ethics cannot be imbibed by laws alone, but by people and their systems. People have to understand ethical values. Ethics programmes *identify preferred values* and ensure organizational behaviours are aligned with those values. This effort includes recording the values, developing policies and procedures to align behaviours with preferred values, and then training all personnel about the policies and procedures. This overall effort is very useful for several other programmes in the work place that require *behaviours to be aligned with values,* including quality management, strategic planning and diversity management. Total Quality Management includes high priority on certain operating values, e.g., trust among stakeholders, performance, reliability, measurement, the feedback.

(viii) Ethics Programmes Promote a Strong Public Image

Attention to ethics is also strong public relations, frankly, the fact that an organization regularly gives attention to its ethics can portray a strong positive impression to the public. People see those organizations as valuing people more than profit, as striving to operate with the utmost of integrity and honour. Aligning behaviour with values is ethical to effective marketing and public relations programmes. Consider how Johnson and Johnson handled the Tylenol crisis *versus* how Exxon handled the oil spill in Alaska. "Ethical values, consistently applied, are the cornerstones in building a commercially successful and socially responsible business."

(ix) Overall Benefits of Ethics Programmes

Donaldson and Davis, in "Business Ethics? Yes, But What Can it Do for the Bottom Line?" (*Management Decision*, Vol. 28, No. 6, 1990) explain that managing ethical values in the work place legitimizes managerial actions, strengthens the coherence and balance of the organization's culture, improves trust in relationships between individuals and groups, supports greater consistency in standards and qualities of products, and cultivates greater sensitivity to the impact of the enterprise's values and messages.

(x) Last—and Most—Formal Attention to Ethics in the Work place is the Right Thing to do

(xi) Ethics Programmes to Uncover Values

In fact, ethics should a compulsory subject not just in B-schools, but in primary schools as well. These values need to be inculcated from childhood. But that alone will not help, "Parents need to set an example at home. Teachers too need to be active role models. Finally, the finishing touches should come from the employers themselves." Ethically-oriented managers are smarter, more alert with a stronger drive and they will take over the managers with the old school of thought. This will help in reducing the generation gap and should bring a revolutionary change in the way corporates are being run today.

The qualities we seek are already a part of us, not apart from us. We wouldn't yearn for them if they weren't already there. *Our risk is to uncover.*

ESSENTIAL PRINCIPLES OF A HIGHLY ETHICAL ORGANIZATION

Mark Pastin, in the "Hard Problems of Management: Gaining the Ethics Edge (Jossey-Bass, 1986)", provides the following four principles for highly ethical organizations:

1. They are at *ease interacting with diverse internal and external stakeholder groups*. The ground rules of these firms make the good of these stakeholder groups part of the organizations' own good.
2. They are *obsessed with fairness*. Their ground rules emphasize that the other persons' interests count as much as their own.

3. *Responsibility is individual* rather than collective, with individuals assuming personal responsibility for actions of the organization.
4. *They see their activities in terms of purpose.* This purpose is a way of operating that members of the organization highly value. And purpose ties the organization to its environment.

Doug Wallace asserts the following characteristics of a high integrity organization:

1. There exists a *clear vision* and picture of *integrity* throughout the organization.
2. The *vision is owned* and embodied by top management, over time.
3. The *reward system is aligned with the vision* of integrity.
4. *Policies and practices* of the organization are aligned with the vision, no mixed messages.
5. It is understood that every significant management *decision has ethical value* dimensions.
6. Everyone is expected to *work through conflicting-stakeholder value perspectives.*

THREE CONCEPTS

(a) Corporate Social Responsibility,

(b) Business Ethics, and

(c) Corporate Governance.

Three major concepts which are almost similar in approach in protecting various interests. These are:

(a) *Corporate Social Responsibility,* which has its origin in USA and Government had passed Anti-Trust Act against monopolistic practices, so as to protect and improve the welfare of society.

(b) *Business Ethics,* which highlighted social values and society's concerns in the 1970s and forced corporates in the USA to abstain in their policies which violated consumer protection and environmental protection, etc.

(c) *Corporate Governance* commenced in the UK for improved accountability of directors to shareholders, emphasised for more transparent auditing and increased responsibilities of independent directors, division of rules of chairman and managing directors for safeguarding interests of shareholders.

SOCIAL RESPONSIBILITY MODEL

Here we present Carroll's four-part social responsibility model which clarifies distinction in various responsibilities, i.e. economic, legal, ethical and discretionary of business.

Economic Responsibilities	Legal Responsibilities	Ethical Responsibilities	Discretionary Responsibilities

Carroll's Four-Part Model

(i) The model suggests that business is basically an economic entity and primary responsibility is *economic*, i.e. produce goods and services that society wants and sell them at profit.

(ii) Legal responsibilities are also basic firms must *operate within laws* of the land.

(iii) Ethical responsibility refers to *behaviour by the firm* that is expected by the society—but not codified in a law. For example, until the passage of Foreign Corrupt Practices Act in 1977 it was not illegal in USA to bribe foreign officials. But there was public indignation to such practice.

(iv) Discretionary responsibility is *purely voluntary obligation* that an organisation assumes, e.g. providing philanthropic contributions to institutes etc. Few people expect organisations to fulfil discretionary responsibilities, but all expect a firm to satisfy ethical obligations.

However, ethical and discretionary together constitute social responsibilities of business.

Discretionary responsibility of today may become the ethical responsibility of tomorrow, e.g. day care facilities for children is moving from discretionary to an ethical responsibility.

Carroll suggests that company's to undertake both activities voluntarily otherwise society will assert to make it legal.

CURRENT ISSUES IN CORPORATE ETHICS

These problems can be mentioned in 4 categories as under:

(i) Equity

Equity includes fairness apart from established legal human rights. For example, sometimes top directors' salary scales are inequitable—there is often controversy on such matters.

(ii) Rights

Rights are treatments to which a person has just claim—through legislation. The rights defend individual autonomy from encroachment. The rights keep a check on hire and fire, equal employment opportunity, etc.

(iii) Dignity

Dignity is sub-category of rights, e.g. employee privacy, protection from sexual harassment. There are lot of court decisions on these topics but no absolute formula is there to guide. Similarly, screening of employees for drug abuse to maintain safe work place is debatable issue.

(iv) Honesty

Honesty in corporate ethics relates to integrity and truthfulness of company policies, e.g. misleading advertising, gifts for foreign officials, fraud in government contracts are labelled as dishonest.

WHICH ETHICAL ISSUES ARE MOST IMPORTANT?

Some current important issues which are ethical in nature are as under:

- Environmental issues.
- Product and work place safety.
- Security of company records.
- Employee health screening.
- Shareholder interests.

CHAPTER

3

UNDERSTANDING ETHICS

It is appropriate to understand and clarify ideas regarding meaning of various terms used as under:

1. Moral.
2. Ethical.
3. Ethics.
4. Personal ethics.
5. The stages of moral development.
6. Difference between corporate social responsibility and business ethics.
7. Difference between office and business ethics.

1. Moral

Moral implies conformity with the generally accepted standards of goodness or rightness in conduct or character; moral is generally used to describe who people are, e.g. a moral person.

In other words, our morals are those principles and values that have internalized. Our morals are automatic responses to situation. They are a part of who we are and our unique personality. We make moral decisions without a lot of thought because they are based on the principles and values we believe in most deeply. We learn our morals from our parents, teachers, religious leaders, friends, and experiences, and they provide the context or framework for our moral actions.

2. Ethical

Ethical implies conformity with an elaborated, ideal code of moral principles. Ethical is generally used to describe how people behave, act and conduct themselves, i.e. an ethical lawyer or an ethical secretary.

3. Ethics

Ethics is our code of conduct. Ethics are a set of rules and standards that guide our behaviour. Ethics may or may not be written down. We have personal ethics, which guide our personal behaviour ("I will not lie to a friend"), and we have professional ethics, which guide our professional conduct ("I will do everything in my power and support my supervisor"). Ethics are rooted in our morals, but they are modified by group decisions, peer pressure and circumstances. Hopefully, our ethics are an extension and expression of our morals.

When an action is in harmony with our morals, we say that the action is ethical. When it is not, it is unethical. In an ideal office, a set of shared ethical standards coincide with our personal morals and ethics. When the ethics in the office conflicts with our personal morals and ethics, we are confronted with the classic ethical dilemma: The gap between our morals and the prevailing office ethical standards. The larger the gap, the greater the stress.

4. Personal Ethics

Most people at some times in their lives pause to reflect on what morals and principles they have or should have and what moral standards are the best justified. When a person accepts a moral principle and then it becomes a part of a moral code to such an extent that he is highly motivated towards the conduct required by the principle and against behaviour that conflicts with that principle. The guilt feeling occurs whenever his or her own conduct violates that particular principle.

Our conscience evolved as we internalised the moral instruction of the parents or other authority figures who raised us. Seeking reward or avoiding punishment motivates small children to do what is expected of them. As we grow, we are able to reflect on and understand the moral lessons we were taught.

Sometimes doing what we believe would be morally right and doing what would best satisfy our own interest may be two different things. Morality serves to restrain our purely self-interested desires so we can all live together. There must be an excellence that we can achieve simply as human beings and to attain this, we have to develop our truly human capacities. Corporations are a particularly relevant example of an environment that can potentially damage individual integrity and responsibility.

During a survey, it has been found that managers at all levels experience role conflicts because of pressures from the top to meet corporate goals. Managers today feel under pressure to compromise personal standards to achieve company goals.

5. The Stages of Moral Development

The good aspect is that we know quite a bit about how people mature morally. As they develop morally, their code of conduct—their ethics—mature, too.

Extensive research has taught us that moral development follows the same pattern as cognitive development. It proceeds in an invariant sequence of development stages. The stages of growth occur in order, from lower to higher stages, and no stages are skipped over.

Lawrence Kohlberg provided this breakthrough understanding of moral development in the early 1960s. Briefly, his research consisted of presenting moral dilemmas to many people with different backgrounds. During the course of extensive interviews with these people, he was able to sample their systems of reasoning, thinking and judging ethical decisions. In analyzing these interviews, Kohlberg formed the six-stage category system shown below (see at next page).

The stages are defined by the major set of assumptions a person uses to think through and justify an important ethical decision. Each higher stage is "better" than the one that preceded it; and each higher stage takes into account an increasingly broader perspective, more complex and abstract thought, and more personal empathy. The higher the stage of development, the moral accommodation there is to values and ethics based on principles of justice. At the lowest stages are the self-centred, relatively immature codes of ethical conduct; at Stage 6, we see the likes of Joan of Arc, Gandhi, Madame Curie, Sister Kenny, Martin Luther King, Jr., Florence Nightingale, Albert Schweitzer, Abraham Lincoln, Eleanor Roosevelt, Henry David, Thoreau, Socrates, Mother Theresa and other moral leaders.

This 6-stage category system from Kohlberg explains in Table why some people see some ethical issues as simple black or white choices. That's also why it is possible for you to have a personal morality that is not perfectly aligned with your office's generally accepted ethics.

No one is totally in just one stage of development. Again, like cognitive development, moral development is in a continual process of evolution.

TABLE

Kohlberg's Six-Stage Category System of Understanding Moral Development

	Focus of Concern	*Characterized by*	*Motivation*	*Sounds like*
Stage 1:	Self	Obedience to powerful authority	Fear of punishment	"I must do what my supervisor tells me to do, or he'll fire me."
Stage 2:	What another person can do for me	"Looking out for number one"	Satisfaction of my own needs	"You scratch my back and I'll scratch yours (but I want to come out a little bit ahead whenever we exchange favours)," and "It's all right to steal, especially if you get away with it."
Stage 3:	Meeting the expectations of groups of people, performing "good" and "the right" roles and conformity to group norms	"Going along to get along"	Acceptance as "a nice guy/gal." Affection plays a strong role	"Let's be good to each other so we look good as a group."
Stage 4:	Preserving the social order	"Doing what is expected"	Desire to follow the social rules	"On my honour I will do my duty to uphold the rules. . ."
Stage 5:	Free arguments and social contracts	"What is right is what the whole society decides. Society can change the standards if everyone agrees"	Desire to achieve the greatest good for the greatest number of people; there are no legal absolutes	"Where the law is not affected, what is right is a matter of personal opinion and agreement between persons."
Stage 6:	Universal ethical principles	Principles that are general ("All persons are created equal") instead of rules that are specific ("Thou shall not kill")	What is right is a decision of one's conscience, based on ideas about rightness that apply to everyone (all nations, people, etc.). These are general ethical principles, not specific rules	"The most important ethical principles deal with justice, equality, and the dignity of all people." These principles are *higher* than any given law.

6. Difference between Corporate Social Responsibility and Business Ethics

Michael J.D. Hopkins makes the following distinction in his book "Corporate Social Responsibility Come of Age."

Corporate social responsibility goes much further than business ethics. Social responsibility encompasses good business ethics. This is the reason, one normally thinks of business ethics applying to what business does within its walls, that is to four of its stakeholders—(i) managers, (ii) consumers, (iii) investors/owners, and (iv) employees.

Less concern is placed on other three stakeholders, e.g. (a) the natural environment, (b) the community, and (c) its suppliers and their conditions of work.

Thus, social responsibility encompasses good ethics, both within the walls of the company and outside. It encourages enterprises to be involved in social issue, such as community improvement, improving under-developed working conditions and so on; that are outside the walls of the enterprise.

It is argued that corporations are so powerful, they have an obligation to assume social responsibilities. Corporations should be managed for the benefit of their stakeholders, i.e. the customers, suppliers, managers, employees, and local communities, as well as their owners. Corporate leaders bear fiduciary responsibility to all stakeholders.

7. Difference between Office and Business Ethics

The author in her monumental book, "You Want Me to do What", has given the difference between office and business ethics. We quote her views, "Broadly speaking, discussions of business ethics refer to the "big picture

	Offices Ethics	*versus*	*Business Ethics*
(i) Chief characteristics	• focus is on personal conduct (office ethics guide our individual behaviour and interpersonal relationships at work) • based on long-held personal beliefs and values, which are not likely to change		• focus is on corporate conduct (business ethics guide corporate strategies, decisions, policies and culture) • based on the organization's customs and culture that have been successful in the past; these are easy to describe, but difficult to change
(ii) Time reference	• short-term decisions; office ethics guide personal choices on a case-by-case, tactical basis ("Do I or don't I?" and "What am I going to do about this?")		• sustained mid- and long-term efforts; business ethics build corporate culture and guide strategic decisions ("What is the company going to do about our environmental problems?" and "How can we improve our customer service?")
(iii) Typical application	• generally reactive		• generally proactive
(iv) Who can influence these ethics?	• each and every one of employees		• the leaders and decision-makers in the organization who:

		(a) establish the expectations for performance (e.g., How much will the company tolerate in order to achieve its goals?) (b) write the rules for others to follow (c) lead by their example, thereby creating the climate for the company's ethical conduct
(v) Who is affected by these ethics?	• every person we have personal contact with, e.g. co-workers, customers, vendors	• employees, customers, vendors, competitors, other organizations, community leaders, media, shareholders and others within the sphere of influence of the organization.
(vi) Questions asked of ethical dilemmas	• How am I going to handle this? • How do I feel about this? • What's the right thing to do?	• How should the company handle this? • What's our policy? • What have we done in the past? • What's the right thing to do?
(vii) Examples of dilemmas where these ethics can help guide conduct	• harassment • lying to supervisor or co-worker • challenges tampering with files or documents • use and misuse of company resources • knowledge of schemes or practices that take advantage of the company • requests for confidential information • sharing and withholding information • rumors and gossip • contributing or withholding support to the office team • time card reports • gifts, gratuities, entertainment • security, theft • outside interests • expense reports • quality, testing, financial reports • failure to follow through • selling, marketing practices • conflicts of interest • substance abuse • inside information	• goals that create pressure leading to misconduct • downsizing • recruitment • community relations, public safety • compliance with the spirit and letter of environmental, employment, and safety laws • responses to whistle-blowing • customer relations • vendor relations • gifts, gratuities, entertainment • political contributions • pricing • substance abuse • selling, marketing practices • immigration • food, drug laws • fraud, deceit • tax laws • racketeering • corruption of public officials • antitrust
(vii) How do I know when I/we have an ethical office and/or an ethical business?	• "My co-workers and I am a real team. We support each other without whining, and we trust each other to be fair and honest." • "I'm proud of my company." • "I'm proud of what I accomplish." • "I respect my boss's integrity." • "I know my manager values my work and my input." • "I can talk to my supervisor about any ethical concerns I have, and I have confidence they will be taken seriously and addressed."	• The company has earned a reputation for honest communication with all its constituencies. • Sales growth is above average. • Customer and employee retention is above average. • Subordinates trust their managers, and *vice versa*. • Concerns about ethics are listened to seriously. • We back up the company's statements of values with meaningful action. • People who leave the company, for whatever reasons, are treated fairly. We listen to our neighbours in the community. We give something back. We have learned to manage our business profitably while complying with the spirit and the letter of relevant laws. We strive to be a responsible corporate citizen."

Source: "You Want Me To Do What."

decisions" affecting the management of our organizations. Discussions of office ethic, on the other hand, focus on the "small picture choices" that comprise our personal and interpersonal conduct at work. I believe it is the day-to-day exercise of a person's office ethics that make business ethics possible and meaningful throughout an organization. Here are some of the ways these two views of ethics are inter-related.

CHAPTER

4

Ground Rules of Ethics—Pillars of Character

ETHICAL VALUES

Ethical principles are the rules of conduct that are derived from ethical values, which are known as six pillars of character, viz. trustworthiness, respect, responsibility, fairness, caring and citizenship. These values are inseparable from one another and are closely interwoven and interlinked with each other. A number of scientific and research studies have amply proved that the aforesaid ethical values enhance one's own judgment to take right and good decisions to benefit all sections of civil society.

Anywhere and everywhere a person of character and integrity is immensely loved, respected, admired and emulated by others because he is always accessible, straight forward in his dealings, humble and simple. Naturally Vedanta lays great emphasis on humility. Admirably Sri Ramakrishna says, 'To become great, one must be humble.'

PROFESSIONAL ETHICS

There is no difference between the tenets of ethics applicable to an individual and that of a professional, the only difference being a professional, is having a higher responsibility and accountability to his action or inaction to all segments of society on account of his status and position. Every professional has to discharge his responsibility with a reasonable degree of care and skill to benefit the entity or person using his professional service. Naturally, any violation or abdication or abandonment of his prime responsibility or misuse of his power and position to the detriment of the community is taken seriously.

GROUND RULES OF ETHICS

Let us, therefore, make a brief study of these ground rules of ethics, which can be identified as *universal virtues* which every human being should imbibe, develop and practise. In fact, it is of immense relevance and importance to a good professional who is required to serve the society well and he must, therefore, try to acquire or develop such virtues.

Trustworthiness

The first ground rule says when others trust us to the core and hold us in high esteem, they believe we have the competence, knowledge, skills and ability to guide them suitably and the capacity to take care of their rights and interests properly by our ethical action. Naturally, every professional should constantly live up to the expectation of others by good performance and refrain from doing anything remotely that will harm or affect that trust. Incidentally trustworthiness involves possessing a number of sterling qualities such as honesty (in communication and conduct), integrity (acting on firm beliefs and not according to expediency), reliability (promise keeping) and loyalty (allegiance, fidelity and devotion).

Respect

The second rule provides that while dealing with others one should show proper civility, courtesy, decency, dignity, tolerance, freedom to express their viewpoints and agree or disagree with our view points. A good professional always gives a patient hearing to his client to express his/her views frankly and freely to understand the intensity of a problem. A heart to heart talk on a vexed problem provides a lot of emotional relief to a person who is affected by it.

Responsibility

The third rule which is more relevant to all professionals makes it clear that if we get involved in handling any professional work or rendering any professional advice or opinion to others on any matters, we are accountable for all our action and resulting consequences. An accountable person when something goes wrong with his advice or opinion does not shift the blame on others' shoulders or claim credit for the work done by others. Needless to say every professional has a moral duty to carry out the assigned tasks entrusted to him by his clients to the best of his ability based on information obtained, collected, gathered, collated, studied, searched and verified with adequate preparation and involvement in a most efficient and cost effective manner with due diligence, reliability and carefulness.

Fairness

The fourth rule emphasizes that every professional must pay close and proper attention on every issue or problem presented to him by his client for solution with equality, openness, impartiality without any sort of bias, favouritism or prejudice and adherence of a balanced standard.

Caring

The fifth rule is the heart of ethics as every human being is expected to take care of the interest and well-being of others in society by his attitude and approach and it is the basis for establishing a durable and everlasting personal relationships with others. Every professional in the course of his professional work establishes a long lasting and durable relationship with a number of people who matter in every organisation at a personal level. Needless to say a satisfied client will always take the initiative to recommend a good professional for others' engagement.

Citizenship

The sixth and final rule touches upon civil virtues and duties that we all owe as a responsible socially committed member of the community to make the world we live in as a happy place now and for future generations. It covers among other things conservation of ecological environment, preservation of natural resources, taking care of public hygiene, health care, education, housing, sanitation, and providing physical and financial assistance to less fortunate, infirm and aged citizens to make the world as a better place to live in. Society expects every knowledgeable professional not only to share his knowledge and expertise for the benefit of mankind but allocates his precious time for any sort of social work to improve the lot of under-privileged sections of society.

Reference

S. Krishnamoorthy, Professional Ethics and Social Commitment, *Chartered Secretary*, November 2003. Gretefully acknowledged.

PART II

SOME MISCONCEPTIONS ABOUT BUSINESS ETHICS

CHAPTER

5

Myths about Business Ethics

Carter McNamara has emphasised that "Business ethics at work place is about prioritizing moral values for the work place and ensuring that behaviours are aligned with those values—its values management." He has highlighted certain myths which arise from notion of ethics as well as views of ethical dilemmas as under:

1. "Myth: Business ethics is a more matter of religion than management. This is not true. Diane Kirrane asserts that "Altering people's values or souls is not the aim of an organisation ethics programme—managing values and conflict among them is . . ."

2. "Myth: Our employees are ethical so we don't need attention to business ethics—most managers face complex ethical dilemmas at work place and most people realise there's a wide "Grey area" when trying to apply ethical principles."

3. "Myth: Business ethics is a discipline best led by philosophers, academics and theologians who treat it as philosophical debate or a religion. However, business ethics is a management discipline with practical approach in all areas of management."

4. "Myth: Business ethics (i.e., code of ethics and ethical values) are superfluous—they only assert the obvious: "Do Good." However, the value of a codes of ethics to an organisation is its priority and focus regarding certain ethical values in that work place. For example, if an organisation is struggling around continuing occasions of deceit in the work place, a priority on honesty is very timely—and honesty should be listed in that organisation's code of

ethics."

5. "Myth: Business ethics is a matter of the good persons preaching to bad persons. However, top management's realise that good people can take bad actions. Managerial ethics requires us to help each other manager to remain ethical while handling, stressful ethical dilemmas."

6. "Myth: Business ethics is the new police-person in organisations and it is recent phenomenon. However, business ethics was written about 2000 years ago. Business ethics has gotten more attention recently because of social responsibility movement started in the 1960s."

7. "Myth: Ethics cannot be managed. Actually, ethics is always managed—But, too often, indirectly—for example, behaviour of the organisation's founder is a strong influence on behaviour of employees. Laws, regulations and rules directly influence behaviours to be more ethical to minimise harm to the community. Similarly, 'Codes of Ethics' have great influence in moulding manager's value system."

8. Myth: Business ethics had social responsibility are same thing. No—the social responsibility is one aspect of overall discipline of business ethics. Madsen and Shafritz refine the definition of business ethics to be:

(i) An application of ethics to be corporate community,

(ii) A way to determine responsibility in business dealings,

(iii) The identification of important business and social issues, and

(iv) A critique of business.

Items (iii) and (iv) are often matter of social responsibility writings. About social responsibility often do not address practical matter of managing ethics in the work place, e.g. developing codes, updating policies and procedures, approaches to resolving ethical dilemmas, etc.

9. Myth: Our organisation is not in trouble with the law, so we are ethical. One can often be unethical, yet operate within the limits of the law, e.g. withhold information from superiors, fudge on budgets, etc. However, breaking the law often starts with unethical behaviour that has gone unnoticed.

10. Myth: Managing ethics in the work place has little practical relevance. Managing ethics in the work place involves identifying and prioritising values to guide behaviours in the organisation, and establishing associated policies and procedures to ensure those behaviours are conducted. One might call this "values management." Values management is also highly important in other management practices, e.g. managing diversity, total quality management and strategic planning.

CHAPTER

6

MYTH BUSTING ABOUT OFFICE ETHICS

Another renowned author Nan Demars in her monumental book, "You Want Me To Do What", has highlighted some common beliefs/myths about office ethics as untrue:

Myth 1: "I can trust my boss to always be fair." Wrong, your supervisor is a human being capable of mistakes in judgement.

Myth 2: "I can trust my company to always be fair." Wrong: The company has no feelings or conscience. However, the decision-makers who direct the company can go wrong. They try to stay out of court, stay out of media's limelight and consider it is good practice to cover up things.

Myth 3: "I have to do what I am told to do my job." As an illustration—

Boss: I want you to do this thing and do it like this.

Employee: I disagree or I have a better idea or I object to doing this thing.

Boss: Look, I am the boss. Do what I say, or I will replace you with someone who will do.

The coercion is not that blunt, but many of us have gotten the same message. This is a reality. People take this defence in scandles that boss wanted me to do this. It is better to spear up/initiate with your best ideas and alternative approaches.

Myth 4: "What others do is none my concern." Yes, it is! Leaking confidential salary information, slipping office by a colleague.

Myth 5: "An action is either right or wrong." There is no middle ground. No. "It depends" in case of ethical dilemmas.

Myth 6: "It is not my job to police my boss." Yes, it is. It is your job to tactfully keep your boss from getting careless and taking shortcuts.

Myth 7: "I cannot change this place." Yes, you can.

Myth 8: "You are born with your morality—you believe what you believe, and you will cling to it throughout your life. Wrong again. People grow up. They mature because of their experiences and opportunity to reflect an example in their decisions.

Myth 9: Women have a more developed sense of ethics; they are more moral and more principled. Wrong. Moral development is similar in both sexes.

Myth 10: People just naturally "Do the right thing" when presented with a moral dilemma.

Coleman sees three types of people:

Type I: Ethical people who strive to always "Do the right thing."

Type II: Unethical people who are willing to intentionally do the wrong thing, because it serves their interests, sometimes at the expense of others and the risk of their reputation.

Type III: Non-ethical people who may not ever think about the ethical implications of a decision or action these people are completely unfamiliar with an environment that builds personal character and/or challenges principles and values.

Myth 11: Good employees do not do bad things. People act unethical because they are selfish or bad. Most reasons for unethical performance are:

(a) Pressure to meet deadlines, slipping dates, schedules.

- To financial target,
- As a response to peer pressure,
- To accomplish a task within time and money constraints,
- To accomplish unrealist goals,
- To alter data so that it looks good to boss, and
- To meet perceived expectations of superiors.

(b) Ambition—personal gain.

(c) Doing it for the company—A misplaced sense that anything is O.K. as long company gets ahead.

(d) This is what is rewarded—This is the "Go along to get along" justification.

(e) Path of least resistance.

(f) Office politics—Image issues, must win attitude.

(g) No one will notice.

(h) No body cares.

(i) Everybody does it. I deserve it too. He did it. Why should not I? I did it for the good of the company. I did not know it was wrong.

Myth 12: Ethical management means ethical organisations. Codes of conduct do not guarantee ethical behaviour as lower employees hold negative views about ethics.

We should encourage employees to have discussions among them about ethical dilemmas. The more employees discuss what is to be done in specific situations the better prepared are employees to meet such dilemmas.

Reference: Nan Demars, You Want To Do What, Simon and Schuster, USA.

CHAPTER

7

AMBIGUITY OF BUSINESS ETHICS—LIGHTER SIDE

PERSONAL ETHICS—LIGHTER SIDE

1. Joke. It is OK, Son, Everybody does it—Jack Griffin

When Johnny was 6 years old, he was with his father when they were caught speeding. His father then handed the officer a twenty dollar bill with his driver's licence. "It is OK, son", his father said as they drove-off, "Everybody does it."

When he was 8, he was present at a family council presided over by Uncle George on the surest means to shave points-off the income tax return. "It is OK, kid", his uncle said, "Everybody does it."

When he was 9, his mother took him to his first theatre production. The box office man couldn't find any seats until his mother discovered an extra $ 5 in her purse. "It is OK, son", she said, "Everybody does it."

When he was 12, he broke his glasses on the way to school. His aunt Francine persuaded the insurance company that they had been stolen and they collected $ 75. "It is OK, kid", she said, "Everybody does it."

When he was 15, he was made right guard on the high school football team. His coach showed him how to block and at the same time, grab the opposing end by the shirt so that the official couldn't see it. "It is OK, kid", the coach said, "Everybody does it."

When he was 16, he took his first summer job at a supermarket. His assignment was to put the overripe strawberries in the bottom of the boxes and the good ones on the top where they would show. "It's OK, kid", the manager said, "Everybody does it."

When he was 18, Johnny and a neighbour applied for a college scholarship, Johnny was a marginal student. His neighbour was in the upper three percent of his class, but could not play right guard. Johnny got the scholarship. "It's OK, son", his parent said, "Everybody does it."

When he was 19, he was approached by the upperclassman who offered test answers for $ 50, "It's OK, kid", he said, "Everybody does it."

Johnny was caught and sent home in disgrace. "How could you do this to your mother and me?" His father said, "You never learned anything like this at whom." His Aunt and Uncle were also shocked.

If there is one thing that the adult world can't stand, it's a kid who cheats. . .

2. The book from Thomas Donaldson ("Ethics in Business: A New Look") narrates jokes on Business Ethics

"To begin the article in a lighter vein, the author would begin it with a couple of jokes that reflect on "ethics" in business."

"Two people, one a Catholic Pope and the other a businessman, die and go to the Christian *heaven* and they are met by St. Peter. St. Peter meets the Pope very warmly and says, "I am so glad to have you here. We would like you to stay about three streets down. Please take your things and go there; you will find a modest bungalow on the right; that is where you are to stay." He then turns to the businessman and says, "I am so happy to have you here. You see the large mansion upon the hill with 24 columns, that is where we want you to stay." "What do you means", asks the businessman, "You want the Pope to stay in the modest bungalow and me to stay in this incredibly lavish house? I don't understand." St. Peter says: "It is all very simple. We have had 422 Popes here already, but you are the first businessman to show up."

The second joke is a definition of a Corporate Ethics Committee. "A Corporate Ethics Committee is a committee consisting of 12 people who, for some reason, *didn't get picked* to serve on any important committee."

These jokes are an expression of the ambiguity that we feel, both in the United States and in India, when we talk about subjects such as Business Ethics. The aim of this discussion is to relieve some of that ambiguity by answering two questions.

The first question has to do with whether or not business has an ethical responsibility. The answer to that is in the affirmative and there are a number of reasons for the affirmative answer. The second question has to do with identifying the areas of special importance in this matter that we call business ethics.

Source: "Power of Ethical Management" by Kenneth Blanchard and Norman Vincent Peale

PART III

MANAGING ETHICAL DILEMMAS

CHAPTER

8

WHAT IS ETHICAL DILEMMA?

MEANING OF ETHICAL DILEMMA

There are situations when there is not simple choice between right or wrong. (It is not like situations whether or not to lie, steal, cheat, break terms of contract. For these answers are obvious). Dilemmas are complex when managers have no clear guidelines either in law or in religion. Managers are in fix, predictament, mess, perplexity, difficulty. Choice one is faced is clearly of the right *versus* right sort.

Ethical dilemma are complex judgements on the balance between the economic performance and the social performance of an organisation.

Doug Wallace, consultant explains, "An ethical dilemma exists when one is faced with having to make a choice among following alternatives—

(a) Significant value conflicts among differing interests,

(b) Real alternatives that are equally justiciable, and

(c) Significant consequences on "stakeholders" in the situation.

According to Rushworth Kidder, in Ethical Dilemma, the toughest choices are Right *versus* Right. P. Kidder further adds that "They are genuine dilemmas precisely because each side is firmly rooted in one of our basic, core values. Four such dilemmas are so common to our experience that they stand as models, patterns, or paradigms. They are:

- Truth *versus* loyalty.

- Individual *versus* community.
- Short-term *versus* long-term.
- Justice *versus* mercy."

To understand ethical dilemma some examples are given:

(i) A Boss tells his supervisor that one of supervisor's employee is among the several persons to be retrenched by the company. Boss informs supervisor not to tell the employee yet or he might tell the whole organisation which may create an uproar. In the meantime, supervisor learns from the employee that he is taking new house near the office to avoid long travel. What should Supervisor Do?

(ii) A customer asked for purchase of television set from your store. After you told the price, he said it is too high. You know he could get cheaper from competitor. Should you tell about the drawbacks in competitor product. Or let him go without getting what he needs? What should you do?

(iii) Your colleague Ram Nath told you in confidence that he is leaving the company in a month and take up new job some where else. However, your boss tells you that he is not promoting you and he is giving elevation to Ram Nath. What should you do?

(iv) It is right to support the principle of creative and aesthetic freedom for the curator of a photography exhibition—and right to uphold the community's desire to avoid displaying pornographic or racially offensive works.

METHODS OF RESOLVING ETHICAL DILEMMAS

Normally management's should set-up procedure for dealing with ethical dilemmas and constitute a committee of senior managers to resolve dilemmas. Some methods are:

(i) An ethical *checklist* (by Doug Wallace and Jon Pekel) to do good ethical analysis.

(ii) Another method is *ten step method* of decision-making (also by Wallace and Pakel).

(iii) Third method is *twelve questions* to address ethical dilemmas (by Laura L. Nash).

(iv) Another method is *nine steps for dealing ethical dilemma* by Rushworth Kidder (extract from "How Good People make Choices—Resolving the Dilemmas of Ethical Living", William/Morrow, New York, 1995). The steps are as under:

(1) Recognise that there is a moral issue and define the problem accurately.

(2) Determine the actor who will be affected by the decision. Also determine your role.

(3) Gather the facts how events happened. Analysis helps us to cut through mystery, complexity and confusion. This will reduce dilemmas to common patterns which are ultimately manageable.

(4) Test for right *versus* wrong issues. Is it illegal? What does your gut tell you? Would your Mom do it? How would you define the problem if you stood on the other side of fence.

(5) Test for right *versus* right paradigms such as, Truth *versus* Loyalty, self *versus* community, short-term *versus* long-term, justice *versus* mercy.

(6) Apply the resolution principles. Work through all *three approaches to resolving the dilemma*—end-based thinking (utilitarianism, i.e. do whatever produces the greatest good for the greatest number). Rule-based thinking (i.e. follow only) and care-based (putting love for others first. Do to others what you would like them to do to you. In other words, it asks you to test your actions by putting yourself in another's shoes and imagining how it would be if you were the recipient of your actions.) Your goal is to find the line of reasoning that seems most persuasive.

(7) Investigate if there is any third way out of the situation.

(8) Make decision and take action.

(9) Revisit and reflect on the decision.

(v) Yet another method, there is *eleven steps to ethical problem-solving* by Charles Steels (CEO and Chairman, Deloitte, Haskins and Sells) as under:

(1) Define the problem.

(2) Determine whether it is an ethical problem or "just a business decision."

(3) Isolate the ethical dimensions of the problem.

(4) Ask yourself if it is a case of conflicting interests or a question of rights and fairness.

(5) Who can help? Distinguish technical from ethical aspects.

(6) Ask yourself whose problem it is. Is it a personal problem, a role-defined problem, a company problem, an industry problem, or a

social problem?

(7) Who is affected? The party with the ethical problem is very often not the party who may be the victim of the problem.

(8) Reduce the number of alternatives to a manageable two or three; don't flounder all over the place.

(9) Weigh the alternatives.

(10) Given each alternative, ask yourself is there a law against it? Is it a violation of a clear moral rule ("Don't cheat", "Don't steal")? Is it an offense to local customs or mores?

(11) Ask yourself how it makes you look? Does it accurately reflect the kind of person/company you are or want to be? ("Can we get away with it" is not a step in ethical reasoning).

(vi) Finally, we give Hosmer's views on making dilemmas issues more simpler.

"These ethical problems or issues are complex because of extended consequences, multiple alternatives, mixed outcomes, uncertain occurrences and personal implications. These ethical issues are very complex to deal with but according to Hosmer managers should keep in mind the five following things to make these issues more simpler:

1. The decision of managers have an impact upon others—both within the organisation and within the society—that is beyond their control. So utmost care should be taken while making any decision.
2. Common belief is that a yes or no choice exists for any ethical issue but that is not true always. Most ethical issues have multiple alternatives.
3. Most ethical decisions have mixed outcome. Social benefits and costs as well as financial revenues and expenses are associated with almost all of the alternatives in ethical choices.
4. Ethical issues in management have got uncertain consequences. It is commonly thought that ethical issues in management are free of risk or doubt, with a known outcome for each alternative.
5. Most ethical decisions have personal implication. It is commonly thought that ethical issues in management are largely impersonal, separated from the lives and careers of the managers."

APPROACHES TO RESOLVING ETHICAL DILEMMAS

We have observed there are three classical approaches in resolving ethical dilemmas—(a) *ends-based thinking* (also called utilitarianism), (b) *rule-based thinking* (Kantian Theory), and (c) *care-based thinking* (Care-based approach says that you have an obligation to care for those with whom you have valuable and close relationships). However, critics of the care-based approach to ethics argue that it can degenerate into unjust favouritism and sacrifice of own needs to care for children, parents, spouse and friends with whom you have valuable close relationship.

However, Joseph H. Boyett and Jimmie T. Boyett in their latest treatise, "The Guru Guide to the Knowledge Economy" has observed that "No single approach to ethics is appropriate in all situations. They suggest in addition to (a), (b), (c) above the *fourth approach* (d) *virtue ethics*. This is an alternative to applying end-based, rule-based or care-based thinking to ethical situation. In virtue ethics, an action is considered morally right if in carrying out the action the person performing the action exercises, exhibits or develops a morally virtuous character."

According to Peter Pratley, *The Essence of Business Ethics*, "virtue ethics can be represented as a mental construction with prudence. More exactly, this mental construction has two ceilings—one is crowned by private prudence and the other by public prudence. This image describes how we can distinguish two spheres of excellence, public and private well-being. One should make every effort to gain a wider *understanding of corporate, private and social well-being.*"

CHAPTER

9

CHARACTERISTICS OF ETHICAL DILEMMAS IN MANAGEMENT

Ethical dilemmas have following features:

1. Most ethical decisions *have extended consequences.* The results of managing dilemma and actions do not stop with first level consequences. These results extend throughout society and the extension constitutes the essence of the ethical argument.

The decisions of managers have an impact upon others—both within the organisation and within the society. That is beyond their control and therefore should be considered when decisions are made, e.g. bribes change government processes, pollution affects environmental health, unsafe products destroy individual lives.

2. Most ethical decisions *have multiple alternatives and have to be considered.* It is commonly thought that ethical issues in management have two choices—a "yes" or a "no", but no other alternative. Should a manager pay a bribe or not? Should a factory pollute air or not? However, it does not accurately reflect managerial dilemma.

3. Most ethical decisions *have mixed outcomes.* It is generally thought that ethical issues in management are opposed to each other, i.e. financial returns *versus* social costs, for example cause some air pollution, but avoid the costs of installing pollution control equipment, and for example design a slightly unsafe product but reduce the material and labour costs of manufacture.

Social benefits and costs as well as *financial revenues and expenses* are associated with almost all the alternatives in ethical choices.

4. Most ethical decisions *have uncertain consequences.* It is not clear what consequences will follow from most ethical choices, e.g. invest in pollution control equipment and emissions will be reduced "X" at "Y" cost of operation does not simplify managerial dilemma.

5. Most ethical decisions *have personal implication.* Individual benefits and cost as well as financial and social benefits are associated with most of the alternatives in ethical decisions, e.g. many people believe that ethical decisions may reduce the profits of the company but not the executive salary or opportunity for promotion. However, managerial controls are meant for financial results and most incentive systems are based upon these controls.

Ethical decisions are *easy to make when a person is not directly involved.* From a distance, it is easy to review other people's actions and say, "yes", that is right, or "no", that is wrong.

Ethical decisions are much more difficult to make when a person is directly involved in the situation. Put yourself in the position of the purchasing agent in the automobile company who had to lie to a supplier, could you do it? If you did not do it, could you continue to work for that company?

Suppose your immediate superior wants you to cheat the company when purchasing air tickets, and pass along the benefits to him. Would you do it. This is a case of managerial dishonesty. But your career is at risk if you "blow the whistle" on your boss. At some time in future, an auditor may find out about this practice and list you one of the participants.

To conclude, ethical decisions are not simple choices between right and wrong. They are complex judgements on the balance between the economic performance and the social performance of an organisation.

CHAPTER

10

IMPROVING ETHICAL DECISION-MAKING—ETHICAL REASONING

STEPS IN DECISION-MAKING

Every management school teaches its students, how they should take decisions such as:

(i) Identify the problem,

(ii) Generate alternative solutions,

(iii) Evaluate alternatives,

(iv) Selection of solution, and

(v) Implement the chosen solution.

However, the alternatives would be constrained by ethical considerations. As ethical considerations should be important criteria in organisation decision-making, there are three different ways to frame decisions and look at the factors that shape an individual's ethical decision-making behaviour.

FOUR ETHICAL DECISION-MAKING CRITERIA OR PRINCIPLES OF ETHICS

An individual may use different criteria in making ethical choices, but no single criteria is adequate to judge:

1. Utilitarian Criterion

Decisions are made solely on the basis of their outcomes or consequences. The goal of utilitarian is to provide greatest good for the greatest number. This view tends to dominate business decision-making. For instance, by maximising profit, a business executive can argue he is securing the greatest good for greatest number—as he hands out termination notices to 10% of his employees. This promotes efficiency and productivity.

Raising prices, selling products with questionable effect on consumer health, closing down plants, laying-off large number of employees and similar decisions can be justified in utilitarian terms.

Decision-makers, tend to feel safe when they use utilitarianism. A lot of questionable actions can be justified as in best interests of "the organisation." But many argue that this perspective needs to change. Increased concern in society about individual rights and social justice suggests the need for managers to develop ethical standards based on non-utilitarian criteria.

2. Rights Criteria

Another ethical criteria is to focus on rights. This calls on individuals to make decisions consistent with fundamental liberties and privileges as laid in the constitution. It means decisions to respect and protect the basic rights of individuals, e.g. right to speech and due process.

For instance, use of this criteria would protect Whistle-Blowers when they report unethical or illegal practices by their organisation to press or government agencies on grounds of right to speech.

3. Focus on Justice Criteria

This requires individuals to impose and enforce rules fairly and impartially so there is equitable distribution of benefits and costs. It justifies paying the same wages for a given job and using seniority as the main determination in making retrenchment decision.

It looks at issues from the perspective of the other person's or affected parties. The questions to be asked are:

(i) Have you defined the problem accurately?

(ii) Would you define in the same way if you stood on the other side?

(iii) To whom and what is your loyalty as a person and as a member of the organisation.

(iv) Whom will the decision injure?

(v) Can you discuss with affected party?

(vi) Will the decision stand the test of time?

4. Ethics of Care

We mention fourth criteria advocated by Manuel G. Velasquez, i.e. Ethics of Care. This is based on the claim that individual cannot exist in isolation from caring relationships with others. I need others to feed and care for me when I am born, I need others to educate me and care for me as I grow. I need others as friends and lovers to care for me as I mature. Always I must live in a community on whose language, tradition, culture and other benefits I depend and that come to define me. *Relationships* are necessary for self to exist and should be maintained and nurtured.

Ethics of care means that we have an obligation to exercise special care toward those *particular persons* with whom we have *valuable close relationships,* particularly *relations of dependency*—A key concept in an "Ethic of Care." (advocated by feminst ethicists recently)—compassion, concern, love, friendship, and kindness are all sentiments or virtues that normally manifest this dimension of morality. The ethics of care emphasizes two moral demands:

(a) We exist in a web of relationships and should *preserve and nurture* those concrete relationships *with specific persons,* and

(b) We should *exercise special care* for those whom we are *concretely related* by *attending to their needs,* values, well-being by *responding* positively who are dependent on our care.

However, demands of caring are sometimes in conflict with demands of justice. For example, suppose one day a supervisor catches her friend stealing from company. Should she confront her friend as company policy requires from her. The demands of ethics of care would require that manager favour her friend. How conflicts of this sort be resolved.

Manager has certain role as duties of position. She has promised to protect the resources of the company and abide by company policy and uphold. We have to pay attention to impartial justice. If we want to favour friend then we relinquish, the institutional role—resign the job.

Then What is Alternative?

Increased concern in society about individual rights and social justice suggests the need for managers to develop ethical standards based on non-utilitarian criteria. This presents a challenge to managers to use criteria such as individual rights and social justice involves more ambiguities than using utilitarian criteria—such as effects on profits and efficiency. This helps to explain why managers are criticised for their actions.

But that may no longer be a single criteria by which good decisions should be judged.

INTEGRATING ETHICAL CRITERIA OF UTILITY, RIGHTS, JUSTICE AND CARING

Our morality contains four kinds of basic moral considerations—utilitarian standards, basic rights of individuals, standards of justice, standards of caring. But no one principle captures all the factors that must be taken into account in making moral judgements.

One simple strategy for ensuring that all four kinds are incorporated into one moral reasoning is as in Figure 1.

Moral Standards:		Factual Information:		Moral Judgement:
1. Maximise social utility 2. Respect moral rights 3. Distribute benefits and burdens justly 4. Exercise caring	→	Concerning the policy or deduction under consideration	→	On the rightness or wrongness of policy or decision

One might, ask a series of questions about an action that one is considering:

(a) Does the action, as far as possible, *maximise* social benefits and *minimise* social injuries?

(b) Is the action consistent with moral *rights* of those whom it will affect?

(c) Will the action lead to a *just* distribution of benefits and burdens?

(d) Does action exhibit *appropriate care* of those who are closely related or dependent on oneself?

In fact, we have no comprehensive moral theory capable of determining precisely when utilitarian considerations become sufficiently large to outweigh narrow infringements on a conflicting right, a standard of justice, or demands of caring. There is no universal rule.

Hence, these are rough criteria that can guide our thinking. However, these criteria remain rough and intuitive. This ethics can guide on moral reasoning.

TYPES OF ETHICALLY QUESTIONABLE MANAGERIAL RULE-RELATED ACTS

These are given as under:

Type	*Direct effect*	*Examples*
1. Non-managerial role	The firm	• Expense account creating • Embezzlement • Stealing supplies
2. Managerial role failure	-do-	• Superficial performance appraisal • Not confronting expense account cheating • Palming of poor performer to other department • Omission or commission of accounts
3. Managerial role distortion	For the firm advantage	• Bribery • Price fixing • Manipulation of suppliers
4. Managerial role—over-exertion	-do-	• Unauthorised high-risk investments • Continuing harmful environmental practices • Failure to cooperate with regulatory agencies.

Managers can unwittingly engage in wide range of types of role-related acts that are regarded as ethically questionable and need improvement in decision-making. 1st and 4th type acts are usually spotlighted and addressed. 2nd and 3rd type receive little attention as a form of proactive management control. Most of acts fall in these types. Senior management ignores/neglects/condones.

FACTORS INFLUENCING ETHICAL DECISION-MAKING BEHAVIOUR

What accounts for unethical behaviour in organisations? Is it immoral individuals or a work environment that promote unethical activity? The answer is both. Ethical or unethical actions are largely a function of both the individual's characteristics and the environment in which he works.

Following model explains ethical or unethical behaviour, i.e. factors affecting decision-making behaviour:

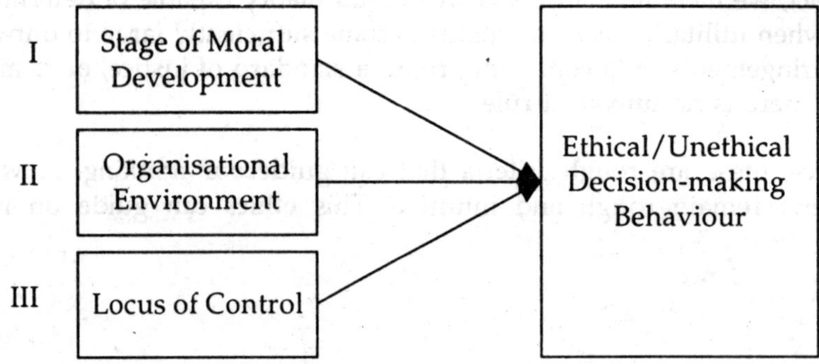

1. Stage of Moral Development

It is an assessment of a person's capacity to judge what is morally right. The highest one's moral development, the less dependent he is on outside influences and hence more he will be ethically high. For instance, adults are at middle level of moral development—they are strongly influenced by peers and will follow an organisation's rules and procedures. Those individuals who have progressed to higher stages of moral development place increased value on the rights of others. Regardless of majority's opinion, they are likely to challenge organisation practices they believe are personally wrong.

2. Locus Control

It is a personality characteristic that taps the extent to which people believe they are responsible for the events in their lives.

People with external locus control (believe what happens to them in life is due to luck or chance) are less likely to take responsibility for their behaviour and are more likely to rely on external influences.

People with internal control are more likely to rely on their own internal standards of right or wrong to guide their behaviour.

3. Organisation Environment

It refers to an employee's perception of organisation expectations. Does the organisation encourage and support ethical behaviour by rewarding it or discourage unethical behaviour by punishing it?

Examples: Written codes of ethics, high moral behaviour by senior management, performance appraisal that evaluate means as well as ends, visible recognition and promotions for individuals who display high moral behaviour and visible punishment for those who act unethically are some examples of organisation environment that is likely to foster high ethical decision-making.

In summary, people who lack a strong moral sense are much less likely to make unethical decision if they are constrained by an organisational environment that frowns on such behaviour. Conversely, very righteous individuals can be corrupted by an organisational environment that permits or encourages unethical practices.

Thus, managers at senior level can influence the employee's work environment. Managers should overtly convey high ethical standards to employees through their actions. By what managers 'say', 'do', 'reward', 'punish' and 'overlook', they set the ethical tone for their employees. Manager's can weed out ethically undesirable applicant at the time of recruitment in the selection process by learning about an individual's level of moral development and locus of control. Managers can identify individuals whose ethical standards might be in conflict with those of organisation or who are vulnerable to negative external influences.

FACTORS THAT GUIDE MANAGERS TO MAKE ETHICAL DECISIONS

Some factors are summarised below:

1. A man's personal code of ethics—i.e. what one considers moral. It is felt older a businessman becomes, the more ethical is his attitude.
2. The company's formal policies are values and culture.
3. The ethical climate in the industry.
4. Government regulations. It is morality that transcends conformity to law. Deep belief to abide the laws.
5. Behaviour of a man's associates and superiors in the company. People look their actions/attitudes, and emulate them how honestly they prepare travelling bills, medical bills, sanction overtime to staff, etc.
6. Professional managers are more ethical. Ethical standards are deep-seated in them and they refuse to compromise.
7. As corporations become larger, their standards of ethical conduct tend to rise because of greater public exposure/image.

Reference

Manuel G. Vecasquez, Business Ethics, Prentice Hall of India, New Delhi, 2003. Four Basic Principles in Business Ethics.

CHAPTER

11

ETHICAL ISSUES AND DILEMMAS IN ORGANISATIONS

Joseph H. Boyett and Jimmie T. Boyett has cited ethically questionable situations in business as either practices involving out-right illegal activities; such as the application of personal expenses to contract budgets, the stealing of company products, or practices which compromise a recognised corporate code or policy like gift-giving or practices like dumping of toxic wastes into a local river. These practices deal with the breaking of laws and rules or causing harm. Thus, these situations offer a clear choice between doing right and doing wrong. Infact, ethical concerns in business are more pervasive and complex than is generally recognised. In fact, ethical concerns are part of the routine practice of management, they are characterised less frequently by legal issues (deal with right and wrong decision) than concerns about relationships and responsibility; they involve factors that make the right and wrong less than patently clear.

A study carried out by leading expert Barbara Ley Toffler, Harvard Business School in book titled, "Tough Choices Managers Talk Ethics" indicated the following areas in which most of ethical problems arise:

Area	*Percentage of Cases*
(a) Managing human resources and processes (e.g. performance evaluation, hiring, firing, promotions, administering personnel systems, managing relationship on-the-job).	66

(b) Managing external constituents. 17
(e.g. customer and suppliers, purchasing, sales, etc.).

(c) Managing personal risks *versus* company loyalty 12
(e.g. pressure from a superior to act against one's own values and beliefs, making a personal scarifices for the good of the company, managing the work/home conflicts).

(d) Others 5

THE FORM OF ETHICAL PROBLEMS/DILEMMAS

When we talk of ethical problems, we refer to dilemmas, situations in which we are faced with difficult choices and where no clear-cut right answer existed. These dilemmas contrast with the way ethical concerns (issues) are voiced at the organisational level, both in the writing of formal policy and in the formal expression of company values. At the policy level, ethical concerns are appropriately expressed as issues where the right course of action is prescribed such as bribery, fair treatment of employees, worker safety, environment pollution. So it is appropriate to mention in Table 1 characteristics of "issues and dilemmas."

TABLE 1

Characteristics of "Issues and Dilemmas"

Issues	*Dilemmas*
1. Issue is easy to name.	1. It is hard to name/identify.
2. It is conceptual notion. It is not specific in a setting.	2. It is embedded in a specific context/circumstance and situation factors.
3. There is general agreement that issue is ethical.	3. Disagreement as to whether or not the case in point involves ethics.
4. Decision addresses the claims of a single stake-holder (individual or group).	4. Decision addresses the claims of multiple, often competing stakeholders (such as closing the plant).
5. Addresses the right and wrong, good or bad of one value. (e.g. bribery, polluting environment is bad).	5. Addresses multiple, often competing values not simple right or wrong (e.g., it is right to close the plant and other to be honest with employees).
6. Assumes that individual can do the "right thing" if they want to and have intention.	6. Assumes that individuals want to do the "right thing" but (a) do not know what it is, or (b) do not have the capacity to do it. Regardless of how well-intentioned the manager, the "right" course of action is often not clear.

HOW MANAGERS REACT TO DILEMMAS—PERSONAL BACKGROUND AND CHARACTERISTICS OF MANAGERS HAS IMPACT

How managers react to dilemmas—ethical and other—is affected by factors in their background and by personal characteristics and traits. A manager brought up by a successful, domineering father may react to authority differently from one whose parent struggled in a clerical job.

Some factors affecting the emergence and management of ethical dilemmas in organisations are as under.

Organisational Factors	*Individual Factors*
1. Policies, rules, procedures 2. Culture 3. Systems 4. "The way we do things around"	1. Manager's perception of job— • Task requirements • Implicit and explicit roles • Availability of choice • Dependency/utility of job • Likes and dislikes 2. Personal background and characteristics

CONCEPT OF CAPACITY RESPONSIBILITY

Joseph H. Boyett and Jimmie T. Boyett have highlighted the point of "Capacity Responsibility." *Capacity responsibility* means that one has a responsibility to deal with a situation if one has the capacity of doing so. If one has the capacity to handle a situation, one must be willing to accept the responsibility. For an example if person 'A' is standing at the water's edge and he sees another person 'B' drowning 100 meters from shore, 'A' does not know how to swim and no cellular telephone around. Does 'A' have a responsibility to save the drowning victim 'B'? The answer must be no, because 'A' does not have the capacity to do so. If on the other hand 'A' was a good swimmer, the situation would be different. 'A' might be presumed to have the capacity to take responsibility; the more critical question would be whether or not 'A' willing to assume responsibility—capacity responsibility is the most subtle form.

Let us take another illustration and notice that the use of real capability on the part of all employees of an organisation can be a productive force, and one that can counter potentially unethical activity. It does require that the organisation and its leadership allow employees the flexibility to use their capabilities. A worker was sent by a boss to work on a broken machine. Regardless of whose fault it may be (boss or worker), unless something or someone intervenes, an injury is likely to occur. Suppose a co-worker on the same shop floor knows that machine is broken. There is responsibility on the co-worker. But the co-worker knows of the problem and has the capability of telling the worker, the shop floor supervisor, or someone that the machine is dangerous. Therefore, he has capacity responsibility to prevent an injury.

Of course, the use of capacity responsibility raises a number of questions about the consequences to individuals assuming such responsibility. The ongoing debate about whistle-blowing is really an argument about the exercise of one kind of capacity responsibility and is very much a microcosm of the pros and cons of assuming responsibility out of one's appointed role. Depending on the environment in which it is operating, the talking of capacity responsibility can create ethically sticky situations or provide energy and creativity toward their resolution.

HOW TO ANSWER ETHICAL DILEMMAS?

There are no easy answers to ethical dilemmas. We reproduce here what a learned author Scott W. Ventrella (*Executive Excellence*, July 2001) provides a "Platinum Standard" of ethics for dealing with ethical dilemmas.

We face many ethical dilemmas regularly. Consider the following situations:

(i) Taking office supplies home for personal use;

(ii) Searching the Web for job opportunities on company time;

(iii) Going to a pornographic Web site during your lunch break;

(iv) Using the phone for personal use on company time;

(v) Calling in sick when you are healthy;

(vi) Putting a personal item in your expense report as a business expense; and

(vii) Having your assistant tell someone that you're in a meeting when you're not.

Do you consider these activities:

(a) wrong—anyone caught doing this should be asked to leave the company immediately;

(b) borderline—not terribly wrong, but something doesn't seem right either; or

(c) totally acceptable behaviour—everybody does it.

For some the choice (or decision) is a matter of interpretation. Others would say that it depends on circumstances. But for those who work in companies with established policies, the choice is clear.

While there are no easy answers to ethical dilemmas, I suggest that we adopt a "platinum standard" of ethics—truths we can turn to when we are confronted with ethical issues.

1. Question your Motives

In *The Power of Ethical Management*, Norman Vincent Peale and Ken Blanchard ask:

(i) Is it legal and in line with policy? If what you are doing or about to do is illegal or against policy, don't do it!

(ii) Is it fair to all concerned? If it's exclusionary or benefits only certain people, don't do it! and

(iii) "In the end, how will I feel about myself? Would I like it if my actions were broadcast for all to hear?"

2. Practice what you Preach

Does your character match your actions? Do not ask others to do anything that you would not do. Know what you believe in.

3. Be your own Investigative Reporter

Imagine a reporter accompanies you to work and on business trips—listening to your phone conversations, sharing your mail, and observing your actions. What story would the reporter write?

4. Keep your Commitments

When you say you will do something, do your associates believe you will, or do they doubt? If you make promises lightly, they will be taken lightly.

5. Learn to say "no" to things for which you have no Time, Talent, or sincere Interest

By saying "no" to such things, you can say "yes" to what matters most.

6. Build and maintain your Integrity

The two most sought-after qualities of a top executive are honest and loyalty. Integrity is acting on a personal commitment to honesty, openness, and fairness—living by and for our standards. The word "integrity" is derived from the Latin word *integer*, meaning "whole." Integrity is a centering power. It provides us with the navigational tools to guide us through the fuzzy ethical landscape.

"We show integrity each time we use consistent and appropriate criteria to measure our own behaviour and performance; use ethics, morals, and principles to guide our activities; do not undermine or criticize others behind their backs; acknowledge our own weaknesses; recognise others' efforts and give them credit; strive to create "win-win" outcomes with others; and do what is right, even though there may be easier, more expedient solutions.

Integrity is acting on personal commitment. It's not merely holding a moral or principled idea or position."

Source: Joseph H. Boyett and Jimmie T. Boyett, "The Guru Guide to the Knowledge Economy,"

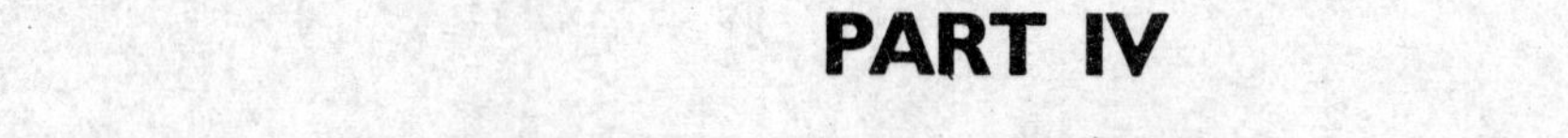

PART IV

SHAPING AND MAINTAINING THE ETHICAL CULTURE (PROGRAMMES)

CHAPTER

12

BUILDING COMPANY'S COMMITMENT TO ETHICS MANAGEMENT: AN OVERVIEW

It is mistake to think that unethical behaviour in business is just a matter of bad individuals—wrong doers.

To a large degree it is behaviour of descent people who normally would not think of doing anything illegal or immoral and but they get backed into doing some thing unethical by systems and practices of their own firms.

Unethical behaviour in business arises when firms fail to pay attention to ethical risks that are created by their own systems and practices.

FACTORS WHICH CREATE UNETHICAL BEHAVIOUR

Factors that create pressures from above for unethical behaviour:

(i) Managements deviate when they are trying to meet goals and have to cut corners to do it. Competition; or

(ii) Pressures of budget system; or

(iii) Promotion system or merit pay system under which they work; or

(iv) They feel that management wants them to save money even at the price of unethical behaviour; or

(v) They follow the orders of someone, who himself may not know what is going on; or

(vi) They take poor decision without thinking of implications; or

(vii) Ambiguous situations create problems in integrity. However, ethical codes can satisfy this need for guidelines.

Example: USA electrical companies, i.e. GE, Westing-house and others in industry. Managers of these concerns gave reasons—to meet budget sales, increase profit, to get ahead in career.

So creating corporate commitment to ethics is vital and it is a most valuable asset a firm can possess. It requires self-sacrifice, foregoing gains and bearing costs and burdens. It pays in the long-run.

For example:

(i) IBM cultivated a tradition of ethical treatment of employees. So employees are loyal to company. They are not likely to engage in thefts and fraud. IBM management do not have monitoring and keeping watch on them.

(ii) Hewlett-Packard maintains high ethical standards in their treatment of customers. This has helped them to get more business share and raise in prices. They provided high quality of product and service.

(iii) Johnson & Johnson: Several persons died after consuming Tylenol capsules contaminated with poison. Their manager felt to protect the public and took over all capsules from all places world-over. A corporate commitment to health and safety of consumers has deep-rooted in J & J and influenced the managers. A crisis incident that might have destroyed the company, became a catalyst that boosted its image in eyes of millions of consumers.

DEVELOP COMMITMENT TO ETHICS

Commitment to ethics is most valuable asset firm can possess, it is most difficult to acquire and maintain. Several companies have developed programmes and institutionalised them.

A call for action—It is relevant to quote from "Management" by Robert Kreitner as under: Corporate misconduct underscore the importance of the following call to action. It comes from Thomas R. Horton, president and chief executive officer of the American Management Association:

> "In my view, this tide can be turned only by deliberate and conscious actions of management at all levels. Each manager needs to understand his or her own personal code of ethics: what is fair; what is right; what is wrong? Where is the ethical line that I draw, the line beyond which I shall not go? And where is the line beyond which I shall not allow my organisation to go?"

"Horton's call is personal. His words suggest each of us can begin the process of improving business ethics by looking in a mirror.

A survey of 2,856 college students from twenty-eight schools across the United States revealed that female students were more concerned about business ethics than were their male counterparts. In view of the proportional growth in the number of female managers in recent years, this finding might foretell a needed boost for business ethics. Managers—women or men—who have a well-developed value system are better equipped to confront tough ethical questions."

PERSONAL VALUES AS ETHICAL ANCHORS

Personal values play a pivotal role in managerial decision-making and ethics. Contemporary social observers complain that many managers have turned their backs on ethical values such as honesty. But others, detect a change in the wind: "I think we're going back to basic, fundamental values—issues of trust, respect, dignity, commitment, integrity and accountability."

ELEMENTS OF PROGRAMMES FOR BUILDING COMMITMENT TO ETHICS

1. Commitment of Top Management

- Top management to ensure adequate resources are invested in programmes for building commitment to ethics.
- Ethical behaviour is truly supported by the top management.
- Top management to provide leadership through example.
- Top management to ensure ethics is folded into every aspect of corporate life—including strategic planning process. One CEO personally saw to programmes and its integration in company, planning and management procedures, e.g. (i) strategic management, (ii) HRM, (iii) participative management, (iv) quality management, and (v) ethical decision-making.
- The chairman of the company must fully support ethics programme and also announce it and ensure its implementation.
- An ethics committee at board of director's level, if established, will oversee development and operation of ethics programme.

2. Assignment of Responsibility for Implementation of Ethics Programme

Some top level manager is to be responsible for development, coordination and implementation of programme. He is to be assisted by full time manager to implement and is a business ethics specialist. He can function as ombuds person. He can also have ethics management committee of senior officers for administering policies and procedures. The most important aspect is the process of reflection and dialogue while preparing codes, policies and procedures, etc. The Ethics Management Committee becomes decisions in groups, which should be cross functional teams. These code of ethics can avoid the occurrence of ethical dilemmas.

3. Clarifying the Company's Ethical Standards

In written statement or ethical code or credos, "code of ethics", this includes:

(i) Company's mission, purpose or beliefs.

(ii) Main stockholders, employees, suppliers, consumers, community, etc. are stakeholders to whom company is obliged. Specific obligations to above groups or behaviours required or permitted are to be laid.

(iii) Penalties for violation of obligations of the management.

(iv) An organisational code of ethics is to be firmly supported by top management and equitably enforced through the reward and punishment system. Selective or uneven enforcement is the quickest way to kill the effectiveness of an ethical code according to Robert Kreitner.

4. Building Systems that Support Ethical Behaviour

(a) Ensuring that systems are established, e.g. audit is done to monitor and enforce the ethical behaviour.

- *New employees are being informed of ethical standards.*
- Annual performance appraisal includes observance of standards and deviations noted in files. Corrective actions that managers have taken to remedy deviations.
- GTE Corporation of USA states in ethical guidelines that "personal integrity and moral fibre are as important to advancement as technical competence."

(b) *Communicating the company's values,* to all employees plays a vital role.

- Employees should alert the company about any unethical behaviour that is—"Internal whistle-blowing" made higher management aware of violations in time.

5. Constructive Steps to be taken by the Management

The challenge for today's management is to create an organisational climate in which the need to blow the whistle is reduced. Constructive steps include the following:

- Encourage the free expression of controversial and dissenting viewpoints.
- Streamline the organisation's grievance procedure so that problems receive a prompt and fair hearing.
- Find out what employees think about the organisation's social responsibility policies and make appropriate changes.
- Let employees know that management respects and is sensitive to their individual consciences.
- Recognise that the harsh treatment of a whistle-blower will probably lead to adverse public opinion.
- Company to provide advisory service in case doubts/clarification.

6. Ethics Training

To arrange workshops for employees regularly and to make aware of company commitment to ethics. Such 1/2 day workshops are lead by the line managers. Thus concerted and systematic attention to ethics will reduce and eliminate such risks. Carefully designed and administered ethics training programmes can make a positive contribution. According to Robert Kreitner key features of effective ethics training programmes include the following:

- Top management support.
- Open discussion in resolving of realistic cases/dilemmas.
- A clear focus on ethical themes in all training.
- A mechanism for anonymously reporting ethical violations.
- An organisation climate that rewards ethical conduct.
- Supplying all staff a copy of code of ethics/code of conduct. Also explain all employees how these work and what is their role in it.

7. In the final analysis, individual behaviour makes organisations ethical or unethical. The organisational forces can help bring out the best in people by clearly identifying and rewarding ethical conduct.

CHAPTER

13

Organisation Ethics Development System (OEDS)

Some important elements of Organisation Ethics Development System (OEDS) are as under:

1. *Moral leadership* and ethical influence to raise higher levels of motivation and morality. Right leadership, integrity, proficiency, commitment to social values of a manager can change the expected behaviour of individuals.
2. *Regular assessment* is to be conducted of ethical work culture and ethics needs. This can be used to direct ongoing improvement efforts.
3. Ethics in organisation is long-term *strategy and structure* so as to promote development of resources with decentralised, participative authority.
4. Setting up of *ethics steering committee* for ethics policy formulation, guidance, coordination and updating policy.
5. Laying down formal statement of priority values and *written code of conduct* to ensure integrity, character development and external reputation for self-respect.
6. Bringing out *ethics policy handbook* and procedure manual for self-governance and responsible conduct and integrity. Business ethics must be reflected in the philosophy and policies of business organisation and recognised by top management.

7. To take *preventive steps to ensure integrity* in Human Resources selection, performance appraisal, recognition, reward, incentive and promotion, etc. Also *identifying wrong doers.* Organisation to provide for commendation for moral excellence and integrity.

8. Focusing on *ethics in communication* (formal or informal) that encourages integrity. Top management commitment, leadership, examples are crucial to corporate ethics/culture. This commitment is communicated in many ways—speeches, directives, company publications, policy statements and most important actions. Top management should establish clear policies that encourage ethical behaviour.

9. Providing *ethics training* and education programmes for responsible conduct to follow legal and ethical decision-making as well as company's codé of ethics. By offering course in business ethics in MBA programmes helps in creating conscientious (diligent) managers with morally responsible approach.

10. Adherence to *ethics in decision-making process* for promoting participative, cooperative and personal accountability.

11. *Nominating ethics officer* and/or establishing decentralised authority. Integrity through the investigation, analysis, resolution of ethical disputes and enforcement of ethical standards.

12. *Laying ethics reporting and conflict resolution process* for disciplining wrong doers, such as: contacting ethics officer to report questionable ethical practices and solicit ethical advice prior to decision-making. This will protect and reward whistle-blowers for constructive loyalty.

    Enforcement of fair and just system to punish unethical conduct is vital. Any employee becomes aware of unethical behaviour be encouraged to report incident to their superior.

13. *To perform ongoing ethics audit and evaluation process* to assess individual ethical performance and organisation integrity systems by bench-marking. This will ensure public accountability for ethical and social responsibility performance.

CHAPTER

14

Organisation Culture—The Tool to Promote Ethical Corporate Behaviour

Organisational culture is the tool to promoting ethical corporate behaviour. The practice of good ethics in various operational areas of business does not happen on its own. In companies where organisation culture is strong in terms of the top management's commitment to good business practices, open communication, shared values, beliefs and norms for the good of all, ethics obviously takes center stage in influencing the organisational behaviour.

FOSTERING CORE VALUES BASED ON ETHICS

As per Mordsjo, the global quality manager for Volvo Trucks, which is setting up a plant in Bangalore, puts it: "Even if we have a truck which is 99 per cent assembled and just one tiny part with a quality problem is holding up its full assembly, we will not use that part just to keep our delivery schedule." Such pronouncements from the top functionaries of any organisation obviously signify the company's commitment. Success in organisations comes from developing and fostering core values based on ethics and involving all employees in their implementation.

FOCUS ON DOMINANT BELIEFS

Culture in the organisational context refers to the set of values, dominant beliefs and guiding norms of a people. It denotes 'mental programmes' shared by the members of an organisation. A strong culture provides a basis for the productive ethos of an organisation. Excellent companies rich in legends, anecdotes, a sense of pride, excitement and achievement orientation and a unique corporate folklore provide the basis for a strong culture.

Such a culture spearheads the company's commitment in respect to quality, reliability, customer service, employee welfare, etc. The concern for the values, the company holds dear, is diffused throughout the organisation.

Kilmann, one of the prominent writers on organisational culture, views culture in terms of 'right' or 'wrong'—i.e., he holds that culture governs people's behaviour in their right or wrong direction. As organisations are viewed as systems composed of ideas, metaphors, myths, rituals and ceremonies, rich networks of legends and parables of all sorts pervade effective organisation.

GUIDING POWER OF CULTURE AND ETHICS

Thomas Donaldson (Ethics in Business: A New Look) narrates one of the most striking case studies showing the power of the culture—is the story of Johnson & Johnson. It is interesting to know the Johnson & Johnson story, the case where it was discovered that some capsules of Tylenol had been laced with poison. There was a question whether the company should recall the product or not. It is a classic case study of how to handle a business crisis and if one talks with the people, who were there at the time and asks them the secret to their handling of that management crisis. They are unanimous in saying that it was their culture of values that came forth at a time when everything else was hazy and the national spotlight was focussed exclusively on Johnson & Johnson. And if one talks to managers afterwards, they say thing like, "you know why it worked; all that time we spent talking about the Johnson & Johnson credo, we really meant it."

Having understood the interface between corporate ethics and culture, let us examine the ways in which conducive culture can be fostered in an organisation to promote acceptable ethical behaviour.

TOP MANAGEMENT'S INITIATIVE

Top managers have to serve as exemplary role models for the young as the latter draw meanings easily from the behaviour of their bosses. The 'superiors' through pronouncements, decisions, interpretations and communication, should demonstrate their disposition towards ethical business practices. Their role is crucial in developing and institutionalising culture. They shape culture through the creation of symbols, ideologies, language, beliefs, rituals and myths.

A summary of the research findings in this area made by Kao indicates how top management build a strong culture by:

- Creating, diffusing and sharing a vision of the organisation's mission and purpose;

- Communicating openly, clearly and persuasively towards securing and sustaining shared perceptions;
- Providing an environment for supportive interpersonal relationships;
- Exhorting and coaching towards high standards of ethical behaviour; and
- Praising and recognising accomplishments of good behaviour through symbols, rituals and ceremonies.

Note: For details on organisation culture refer to chapters in Part IX.

Source: "Organisation with a Heart" by Dr. G. Anjaneya Swamy.

CHAPTER

15

Managers can Influence their Organisation Climate

COMMUNICATING ETHICAL VALUES

As organisations attempt to grapple with ethics, they increasingly seek varied routes for communicating their values. For instance, they may *develop corporate mission statements* to tell employees what the organisation is about and where it is going. These statements may serve to separate an organisation from its competitors and provide it with a sense of identity, legitimacy and direction.

The mission statement may be accompanied by a *code of ethics* (a general code, as well as one that is technology-focussed), which speaks to activities that cannot be closely supervised by management, like honesty in dealing with clients or mutual respect among employees.

Now adopted by more than 200 of the **Fortune 500** companies, ethical codes contribute to long-term organisational success only to the extent that they are upheld by both employers and employees; that is, they depend upon voluntary cooperation.

Finally, and most important, management behaviours remain the real key to developing organisational ethics.

Managers can influence their organisation's ethical climate in several ways:

(i) They may, for instance, emphasize and discuss ethics continually. A code of ethics becomes real only when a manager talks about it by *encouraging subordinates* to *raise ethics-related issues*, doubts or concerns; by referring to it when answering questions or making decisions; and by keeping others' attention focussed on it.

(ii) Managers must also develop and *articulate realistic goals*.

(iii) Employees who are confronted with goals they *cannot achieve are tempted* to cut corners, sacrificing ethics for achievement.

(iv) By *identifying areas that are vulnerable to unethical* practices, managers may also avoid ethical problems by discussing with employees the sorts of temptations that might arise.

(v) Finally, by encouraging *reporting of unethical activities*, managers let all employees know that each of them has an important role in enforcing ethical standards; at the same time, they indicate their serious intent to ensure ethical behaviour (Dolcheck, 1989).

(vi) Ultimately, values cannot be taught; they must be lived. *People emulate what they see*, not what they are told. If they see that unethical behaviours are practiced or tolerated, they will pay little attention to written codes of ethics or mission statements. Richard Zimmerman, Chairman and CEO of Hershey Foods Corporation, refers to his company's value system as an "anchor" for the organisation and asserts, "Each *manager must have a grip on those clearly defined values* and be able to demonstrate them through their own behaviour to employee groups" (Blank, 1986, p. 33).

(vii) Andrews (1989) argued that *ethical decision-making* is the key to effective management, maintaining that ethical decisions require three qualities of those making them:

(a) Competence to recognise ethical issues and to think through the consequences of alternative resolutions.

(b) *Self-confidence* to seek out different points of view and then to decide what is right at a given time and place in a particular set of relationships and circumstances.

(c) *Tough-mindedness* or the willingness to make decisions when all that needs to be known cannot be known and when the questions that press for answers have no established and incontrovertible solutions.

(viii) *Role of Top Management is Critical*: Maya Reddi (in her article on "Ethical Organisation: Role of Top Management" states that the role of top management becomes critical to the setting of standards of business behaviour. Senior management is often perceived to have double standards, at least that's the general perception, which is: one rule for themselves and another for the rest of the corporation. And, invariably when one goes around talking to people, they always say, "Yah, all that is fine, it is all accepted but what is the real story among the top management? Do you really pay your taxes; do you really produce vouchers for payments you claim; do you really follow the rules when travelling or do you get additional perks?" These are the kinds of questions one has to answer which really imply people's belief that there is one rule for the top management and another rule for the rest of the employees.

(ix) *Integration of Ethics in Personal Life and Business Life*: Business ethics has to be preached, practised and shouted from the roof tops, in both, one's personal and one's official life. Before setting business standards, *ethics and morality have to be internalized*, so that they become a part of the blood stream. This is rather a strong statement; but there really is this sort of *integration between personal life and business life*, so that it is not done one thing to slip a transistor through customs just as it is not right to evade customs duty when one has a large system being imported. What one does when one goes up to the customs officer as an individual and later when one is talking inside the organisation, these are both one and the same thing; they are not two different stories.

When this happens, values will permeate the organisation and get translated into business standards and practices. *Top management must stand out like a light and be able to pass the test of intense scrutiny*. And, the penalty for not conforming to accepted ethical behaviour must be severe, whoever may be involved."

Source: Patricia Hayes Andrews and Richard T. Herschel.

CHAPTER

16

Creating Capacity Responsibility in Managers for Ethical Decision-making

"... I felt that if you are really going to run an ethical institution, and set high standards, you have to set them from top." (Smith)

"Our institution has an unstructured environment with unwritten rules and regulations. In order to ethically perform in this organisation, a lot is left to chance."

The organisation is responsible for shaping the way things are done. Top management has to take and accept its own accountability and responsibility to ethical management.

STEPS IN CREATING CAPACITY RESPONSIBILITY

Some steps involved are as under:

1. Management to Create an Environment

For ethical conduct of business, the organisations must develop formal and informal policies and guidelines which unambiguously state the values of the organisation, while reflecting an awareness of the dilemmas of implementation.

2. Building Effective Processes

The finest policies and designs will be limited in their effect if organisations do not develop process that are essential for implementation and allow concerns, problems, and disagreement to be raised and responded to. To do this requires attention to two things: making ethics a legitimate topic of discussion, and developing and supporting effective communication at all levels of the organisation.

Managers at all levels and employees must learn to express their ethical concerns and to listen to and hear each other as they do so. This is necessary for effective implementation.

3. Education and Training

Education and training is required to help employees to think about ethics and training to help them incorporate it into their activities.

4. Manager to Act with Integrity

The manager as individual must act with integrity. In the face of pressures from many stakeholders, they must work for the benefit of the organization. However, one of the biggest problems in managers is cowardice.

Taking responsibility and being an ethical and effective manager requires more than simply good character. Effective manager normally recognise that time is a basic and necessary tool of dealing effectively with competing claims. Knowing where to draw the line is essential to responsible and effective management.

However, beware of rationalisation of the decision we have made or action we have taken, we give reasons why we have done it, for self-protection. Any manager seeking to contribute to creating an ethically responsible organisation must control rationalisation.

5. Promoting Ethical Management

Organisations must bear the burden of *creating environments* in which ethical management can be carried out. Managers in their capacity as designers, builders and guides of organisations take a major share of responsibility for promoting ethical business management.

6. Capacity to Act with Integrity

This does not mean instructions should be ignored or superiors challenged, etc. Although it may sometimes come to that—standing firm, to questioning, to challenging—it means simply pausing before doing—"What we always do in cases like this" and rethinking and reflecting. The creativity should be contributing to keeping their organisations alert and ethically aware and capable of providing an environment in which all employees have the *capacity to act with integrity*.

And that requires never just setting for "the way we do things around here" it will be appropriate to quote from Kenneth R. Andrews, "Ethics in Practice", *Harvard Business Review*, 1989. Making ethical decisions is easy when the facts are clear and the choices black and white, but it is a different story when the situation is clouded by ambiguity, incomplete information, multiple points of view, and conflicting responsibilities. In such situations—which managers experience all the time—ethical decisions depend on both the decision-making process itself and on the experience, intelligence and integrity of the decision-maker."

Source: Barbara Ley Toffler, "Tough Choices Manager Talk Ethics", 1986, John Wiley & Sons, USA.

CHAPTER

17

DEVELOPING CODES OF ETHICS

Ethical codes are statements of the norms and beliefs of an organisation. These norms and beliefs are generally proposed, discussed, and defined by senior executives in the firm and then published and distributed to all the members. A code of ethics specifies the ethical rules of operation.

Most important thing is *developing and continuing dialogue* around codes and values. Occasionally, employees react to codes with suspicion, believing code and values are window dressing. But Carter McNamara points out "that when managing a complex issue, especially in a crisis, having code is critical." He further highlights that "continued dialogue and reflection around ethical values produces ethical sensitivity and consensus."

Also *update the code periodically*—all ethical values are attractive to include in a code; however, we should include those that provoke behaviours needed in the organisation.

CONDITIONS FOR MAKING CODES EFFECTIVE

In a recent Dutch study Kaptein and Klamer (1991) list six conditions for effective codes of ethics:

(i) *A valid motivation for its introduction*: It should insist on important benefit for adopting and complying with the code. An 'us too' attitude is not enough.

(ii) *Broad acceptance within the company*: Involve representatives from all departments in the process of elaborating the code. The code should be discussed, checked and redefined before it is finally laid down.

(iii) *Continuous feedback*: Difficulties occur during the implementation of the code, and also norms on how to act in specific situations change. This calls for feedback. Living up to a code is not simply a matter of blindly applying rules, it is part of a process.

(iv) *Verification and control*: Any inconsistencies between rules and practice should be disclosed. One method of achieving this is peer discussions. New guidelines should be drawn up if the rules prove inadequate in any way.

(v) *Integration into a broad company philosophy on corporate services and responsibilities*: The set of rules should be part of a wider ethical mission statement. This may involve staff training programmes, a company ethical committee or discussions with external stakeholders.

(vi) *Sanctions and control*: Compliance with codes needs enforcement—both positive and negative. In order to become effective, some system of sanctions must exist. Free-wheeling permissiveness would only lead to lip service. Many companies do now have severe sanctions against, for example, bribery.

ESTABLISHING PRIORITY BETWEEN NORMS AND BELIEFS

However, the basic difficulty with codes of ethics is that they do not establish priority between norms and beliefs. The priorities are true values of a firm and they are not included. As an example, one division in a firm is faced with declining sales and profits; the question is whether to reduce employment and cut over head costs (the classic downsizing decision).

Norms are, of course, are standards of behaviour; they are the ways the senior people in the organisation want the others to act when confronted with a given situation. An example would be, "employees of this company will not accept personal gifts with a monetary value over Rs. 400 in total, from any business friend, and they are expected to pay their full share of the costs for meals or other entertainment (theatre, sporting events, etc.) that have a value above Rs. 400 per person."

The *norms* in an ethical code are generally expressed as a series of negative statements (list of thing a person should not do).

The *beliefs* in an ethical code are standards of thought. They are the ways that senior people want others to think. It is to encourage ways of thinking and patterns of attitudes that will lead towards wanted behaviour. Beliefs in ethical code are generally expressed in a positive form. *Examples*:

(i) "Our first responsibility is to our customers."

(ii) "We wish to be good citizens of every community in which we operate."

ILLUSTRATION OF CODES OF ETHICS

Some illustrations of corporate codes of ethics are given in Annexure I to this chapter.

Code of conduct or ethics of some professional bodies are contained in Annexure II of this chapter.

DIFFICULTIES IN IMPLEMENTING CODES OF ETHICS

However, the basic difficulty with codes of ethics is that they do not establish priority between norms and beliefs. The priorities are true values of a firm, and they are not included:

(a) As an example, one division in a firm is faced with declining sales and profits; the question is whether to reduce employment and cut overhead costs (the classic downsizing decision), but code of ethics says in one section that we respect our employees and in another section that we expect "fair" profits. How do we decide? The code of ethics does not tell us.

(b) Another example, whether direct distribution from factory "to retailer would be economical" when our code of ethics says "we will work closely with distributors, for they too deserve a profit." But we can reduce our prices to our customers and gain a competitive advantage for ourselves, if we eliminate the wholesalers and ship directly. The code does not tell us to choose.

(c) Are ethical codes—effective at ensuring that the moral standards of senior executives are known and followed throughout the organisation. If yes, then some events can be just anomalies such as—for years, GE has been regarded in USA as one of the examplarly companies, a breed ground for managerial excellence, a good corporate citizen. But unfortunately GE was convicted 3 times of crimes, i.e. price fixing, bribery and fraud. GE pleaded guilty of charges of defrauding the government on missile-warhead contracts.

In such a case we have to examine causes of unethical actions in individual cases. In this connection an example of code of ethics of Johnson & Johnson, Inc. helped managers in time of crisis. Johnson & Johnson spent over $ 100 million removing Tylenol from shelves of every store after non-prescription drug was found to have been deliberately poisoned in Chicago area during 1982, causing death of 4 individuals. James Burke, Chairman of Johnson & Johnson, credits that code with guiding the actions of his company. "This document of code of ethics spells out our responsibilities to all our constituencies: consumers, employees, community, stock-holders. It served to guide all of us during the crisis, when hard decision had to be made. All our employees world-wide were able to watch the process of Tylenol, withdrawal and subsequent reintroduction in temper-resistant packaging." "There was a great sense of shared pride in the knowledge that the credo was being tested and it worked." "I think we can agree that the employees of J & J should be proud of the response of the firm which put consumer safety ahead of company profits."

ECONOMICS MIXES WITH ETHICS

Thus, ethical dilemmas are *conflicts between economic performance and social performance*. The social performance being expressed as obligations to employees, customers, distributors and the general public. In J & J case, ethical code helped managers to choose between economic and social performance, as such codes can be effective.

In case, codes of ethics (or ombudsmen) cannot ensure that the moral standards selected by the president and board of directors of a firm will be followed by all the members of the firm. Then we have to *look to the causes of unethical behaviour*. This can be due to structural causes of unethical behaviour within organisations, e.g. planning systems—may rank your unit below average. The problem is that ethics in management represents a conflict between the economic and the social performance of an organisation. If that *conflict is not specifically addressed and resolved by the senior executives,* the natural tendency of middle operating level managers will be to favour the economic side of the balance, why? Because under current managerial systems, their performance is measured by economic criteria and their future is dependent upon economic results.

THE ETHICAL RESPONSIBILITIES OF SENIOR MANAGEMENT

How can the *conflict between economic and social performance be resolved by senior executives. This has to be done as part of the strategic planning process (SPP).*

(i) Ethical issues have to be made a *part of SPP,* and no longer ignored or pushed down onto operating levels. Hard ethical questions have to be asked by the managers in the units, and specific answers to be supplied by corporate executives, e.g. "We can substantially increase our bank revenues by charging Rs. 10 per month for all accounts below a minimum balance, but this will place burden on many older, retired customers, should we make a charge?"

"We can reduce our costs by replacing the wholesale distributors who helped us in building the market, should we start direct sales?"

(ii) Managers in units also *ask themselves hard questions*, e.g., "What are the residues of this chemical process and how are those waste materials being handled?"

"What is the failure rate of this product, and are these failures being satisfactorily repaired?"

Now *how these ethical questions to be answered*? With *character and courage*. This is the character to face issues that have adverse social impacts. Associated with each of the alternatives and the courage to evaluate each of these alternatives following economic, legal and moral forms of reasoning and then arrive at a decision.

This is *the character* to recognise that personal costs may be associated with the choice, due to the biased nature of the planning, control and motivation systems, and the courage to bear those costs.

Those who differ with this approach is due to their differences in their perspectives or in their beliefs in the importance of economic outcomes, under moral values of justice and liberty. We make ethical decisions based on our sense of responsibility to others; it is a test of our character and a measure of our courage.

Source: Carter McNamara.

ANNEXURE I

CORPORATE CODES OF ETHICS CATEGORIES FOUND IN ORGANISATIONS

Category I

"Be a *dependable organisation citizen*":

1. Demonstrate honesty and fairness in relationships with customers, suppliers and employees.
2. Comply with safety, health and security regulations.
3. Dress in business-like attire.
4. Be reliable in attendance and punctuality.

Category II

"Don't do *anything unlawful or improper that will harm the organisation*":

1. Maintain confidentiality of customer, employee and corporate records and information.
2. Avoid outside activities which conflict with or impair the performance of duties.
3. Make decisions objectively without regard to friendship or personal gain.
4. Acceptance of any form of bribes is prohibited.
5. Conduct personal and business dealings in compliance with relevant laws, regulations.
6. Do not use company property or resource for personal benefit.
7. Do not provide false or misleading information to corporation or government agency.

Category III

"Be *good to our customers*":

1. Strive to provide products and services of highest quality.
2. Convey true claims for products.

Category IV (Unclustered)

1. Exhibit standards of personal integrity and professional conduct.
2. Racial, religious or sexual harassment is prohibited.
3. Protect quality of environment.

ANNEXURE II

CODE OF CONDUCT OF ETHICS FOR PROFESSIONAL GROUPS

Professional Associations lay down code of ethics for their members—behaviour required or expected of its members, Doctors, Personnel Managers, etc.

These codes give clue to what type of response is expected in given situation. It comprises of norms and standards of discipline, honesty and integrity and professional ethics to be followed and enforced by association.

As an illustration extracts from some codes of conduct of professional bodies are mentioned.

A. Codes of the Medical Council of India

The codes cover 33 principles:

(i) General principles.

(ii) Duties to patients.

(iii) Duties to profession.

(iv) Doctor to doctor relationship.

Example: They should educate public on correct and ethical use of drugs.

List of misconduct as well given, e.g. refusing to perform a sterilisation operation on religious grounds.

B. Ethics for Chartered Accountants in Chartered Accountant's Act

Some misconducts are:

(i) If he allows any person to practise as C.A. if he is not one.

(ii) If he advertises or solicits work.

(iii) If he accepts a position held by another C.A. without communicating with him.

(iv) If he discloses confidential information about his client.

(v) He certifies a statement without adequate scrutiny.

C. The Engineers' Code

The National Society of Professional Engineers has a code, which requires professionals to:

1. Dissociate themselves from organisations that are of a questionable character.
2. Further the cause of public good.
3. Avoid engineeringly unsafe ventures.
4. Maintain confidentiality.
5. Advise clarity, the consequences, if a technical opinion is overruled by a non-technical person.

D. Code for Marketing Managers

A code of ethics for marketing managers is issued by the American Marketing Association. It includes:

1. *Basic guidelines*: Not doing harm knowingly, accurate representation of their education and training, following the laws in letter and spirit.
2. *Honesty and fairness*: Serving customers, clients, employees, distributors and public, avoid conflict of interest, employ equitable fee schedules of payments or receipt.
3. *Follow the well-understood principles of rights and duties in the process of exchange*: Products should be safe, communications not deceptive in good faith, adequate processes for redressal of grievances.
4. *Product development*: Safety standards, any component substitution to be advised to the customer, extra cost and added features.
5. *Promotion*: Avoid false, misleading, high pressure and manipulative tactics.
6. *Distribution*: No coercion, ensuring free channels, etc.
7. *Pricing*: Neither predatory nor rigged.
8. *Market research*: Prohibit selling under the guise of market research, research integrity, confidentiality and privacy of respondents.
9. *Organisational*: Avoid adverse organisational behaviour.

E. Code of Ethics of Public Relations Practitioners

1. The core philosophy of the code is to uphold the Universal Declaration of Human Rights of the UNO.
2. It upholds the free flow of information.
3. It requires behaviour, in a manner, as to develop the confidence of those, with whom they come in contact, whether clients or employers.

4. The practitioners must avoid ambiguous language and maintain loyalty to the clients and employers.
5. They must protect the interests of the organisation they serve and the general public.
6. They must never compromise on the truth due to other requirements.
7. They must never manipulate to create sub-conscious motivations.
8. They must never impair human dignity and integrity.

F. Code of Ethics of the Association for Computer Machinery (ACM)

The ACM has five canons. An ACM member should:

1. Act with integrity at all times.
2. Strive to increase his own competence and the competence and prestige of the profession.
3. Accept responsibility for his work.
4. Act with professional responsibility.
5. Use his knowledge and skills for the advancement of human welfare.

G. Code of Advertisers issued by the Advertisement Council of India

1. Moral and religious sentiment should not be offended.
2. Advertisements should not directly and adversely compare products with those of the competitors.
3. Rhetoric like offering to refund money, if the product is not good should be avoided.

H. The ICSI Code of Conduct

In order to evoke the necessary interest and awareness among the members and to create the necessary climate for laying down the right type of conduct which should govern the profession; the ICSI organised in February 1976 a National Convention primarily to evolve the necessary framework for a code of conduct. After the conclusion of that Convention, the Council of the Institute appointed a Code of Conduct Committee with the task of formulating a model code of conduct. The Council of the Institute accepted the recommendations of the Code of Conduct Committee which *inter alia* prescribed:

(a) rules applicable to all members; and

(b) rules applicable to members in service or practice.

In formulating the code of conduct, the Committee and the Council adopted a certain normative approach or value judgement. The codes evolved were rooted in the principles of Dharma stating positively what the profession stands for, what it expects from the members and what it cherishes as valued ideals of the society. The code also negatively laid down what may or may not constitute a breach of the code in any given situation and the penal consequences for any violation or misconduct.

The ICSI code of conduct acquired statutory status with the conversion of the Institute into a statutory body under the Company Secretaries Act, 1980, with effect from 1st January, 1981. The First and the Second Schedules to the Act enumerate in detail, various instances of professional misconduct on the part of the members of the Institute in practice as well as in service.

In view of the development of the profession during the last decade, the ICSI has brought out revised edition of the Guidance Note on Code of Conduct to focus the attention of the members in general and those in practice in particular, to the various provisions of the code of conduct to enable them to uphold the professional values.

I. Code of Ethics of Automotive Service Association (USA)

Code of Ethics

The owners and managers of automotive service businesses that belong to the Automotive Service Association (ASA) agree to adhere to a Code of Ethics. ASA's Code of Ethics is the automotive service industry's standard for professional business practices—

- To perform high quality repair service at a fair and just price.
- To use only proven merchandise of high quality distributed by reputable firms.
- To employ the best skilled technicians obtainable.
- To furnish an itemized invoice for fairly priced parts and services that clearly identifies any used or remanufactured parts.
- Replaced parts may be inspected upon request.
- To have a sense of personal obligation to each customer.
- To promote goodwill between the motorist and members of the association.
- To recommend corrective and maintenance services, explaining to the customer which of these are required to correct existing problems and which are for preventive maintenance.

- To offer the customer a price estimate for work to be performed.
- To furnish or post copies of any warranties covering parts or services.
- To obtain prior authorization for all work done, in writing, or by other means satisfactory to the customer.
- To notify the customer if appointments or completion promises cannot be kept.
- To maintain customer service records for one year or more.
- To exercise reasonable care for the customer's property while in our possession.
- To maintain a system for fair settlement of customer's complaints.
- To cooperate with established consumer complaint mediation activities.
- To uphold the high standards of our profession and always seek to correct any and all abuses within the automotive industry.
- To uphold the integrity of all members of the Automotive Service Association.

CHAPTER

18

DEVELOPING CODES OF CONDUCT

"*Codes of conduct* specify actions in the work place and *codes of ethics* are general guides to decisions about those actions", explains Graig Nordlund, of Hewlett Packard. He suggests that codes of conduct contain examples of appropriate behaviour to be meaningful. Codes of conduct are focussed at lower levels in companies.

While developing a code of conduct Carter McNamara lays following guidelines:

"1. *Identify key behaviours* needed to adhere to the ethical values proclaimed in your code of ethics."

"2. *Include wording* that indicates all employees are expected to conform to behaviours specified in the code of conduct."

"3. *Obtain review* from key members of the organisation and not confined to legal or human resource department. Such reviews to ensure these policies are in accordance with laws and regulations."

Some topics covered in codes of conduct are: e.g. following instructions of superiors, maintaining confidentiality, · not accepting costly gifts from stakeholders as a result of company role, complying with laws and regulations, not using company's property for personal use, etc.

We would like to elaborate first point, i.e. identify key behaviours needed to adhere to the ethical values mentioned in code of ethics. We quote views of Karen Trisko in her paper titled, "Power of Integrity" (*Executive Excellence*, July 2001). Many organisations include "integrity" in their values and in their marketing communications to prospects and customers. Naturally, most people want to do business with people and organisations with integrity. So, explicitly claiming your organization has integrity seems useful for attracting customers, employees and suppliers.

Declaring integrity has many impacts, mostly positive. The positive impacts include setting expectations for behaviour and communicating a desirable image. Yet, it is difficult to remain in a state of integrity because of the many people and processes involved. Every breach of integrity—and there are many each day—hurts the level of trust and the self-esteem among employees, not to mention damaging relationships with customers and suppliers.

Integrity has many meanings: living one's word, delivering on promises, alignment of beliefs and actions, wholeness, honesty, sincerity and authenticity. There are hundreds of opportunities in anyone's workday where a break in integrity can occur. For example, the company misses a delivery commitment to a customer or supplier; someone arrives late to a meeting; a salesperson exaggerates the company's experience; a sales proposal includes incorrect data; managers don't conduct performance reviews; a worker explains a mistake in a way that makes him or her appear blameless.

Some might argue that some of these examples are not breaches of integrity, but the results of mistakes. They all represent broken commitments or promises. Eliminating these breaks yields a higher level of integrity.

Breaks in integrity by leaders have very high negative impact. People develop trust in others based on their actions more than their words. Furthermore, employees tend to emulate their leaders' behaviour or that of people who appear to be valued. Breaks in integrity that go unacknowledged also cause damage because they breed more mistrust. Companies that publicly acknowledge product safety problems and take positive actions to correct them fare better in regaining market share after the incidents than companies that try to cover up problems.

If you say your organisation has integrity or you are people of integrity, you must live up to your word with extraordinary effort—or the loss of trust will be even greater than if you never claimed integrity at all. Leaders who value integrity and publicly declare it must understand the meaning of integrity; recognise integrity breakdowns when they occur; admit when they break integrity; apologize for the impact on others; provide processes and training that assure promises to customers, employees, and suppliers can be met; continually reinforce the value of integrity; and reward behaviour that shows integrity.

Don't assume everyone understands the meaning of integrity. Your interpretation of integrity, aligned with your values and mission, needs to be made explicit.

Karen Trisko once worked for a CEO who said he would help or make time to talk with anyone who asked. He kept his word almost perfectly over seven years. What a wonderful role model he was, and what a refreshing culture his behavoiur created because employees emulated him.

Apology is a powerful way to repair breaks in integrity and regain trust—if it is not overused. A colleague of mine was chronically late to meetings. He apologized almost every time, but ultimatley his apologies were received with cynicism.

In a high-trust environment, employees, customers and suppliers genuinely want to be part of the organization and eagerly refer others as potential employees and customers. Warren Bennis notes: "Integrity is the basis of trust, which is not as much an ingredient of leadership as it is a product. It is the one quality that cannot be acquired, but must be earned. It is given by co-workers and followers; without it, the leader can't function."

The intentional pursuit of integrity satisfies a basic human need for trust in relationships and breeds higher employee and customer loyalty, which lead to improved profitability.

CONDUCT, DISCIPLINE AND APPEAL RULES

Majority of corporations both in the private and public sector in India have laid down elaborate rules often termed as "Conduct, Discipline and Appeal Rules." These lay down do's and don'ts for codes of behaviour.

Note: An illustration in abstract form is contained in Annexure A of this chapter.

Anneuxre A

CONDUCT, DISCIPLINE AND APPEAL RULES

Salient Features of such rules are:

- Employees to maintain absolute integrity, devotion to duty and do nothing unbecoming of in employee.
- Acts and omissions constituting misconduct.
  - Such acts are mentioned as illustrative in nature.
- Certain Do's and Don'ts:
  - Unauthorised communication of information.
  - Employment of relatives of employees in firms enjoying company's patronage.
  - Private trade or employment.
  - Bigamous marriage.
  - Inventions.
  - Movable, immovable and valuable property.
  - Gifts acceptance.
- Suspension rules.
- Penalties and procedure for imposing penalties.
- Special procedure in certain cases:
  - Conviction on criminal charge.
  - Cases where it is not practicable to hold an inquiry.
  - In the interest of security of company, not expedient to hold an enquiry.
- Appeals.
- Review.

CHAPTER

19

DEVELOPING POLICIES AND PROCEDURES

Policies and procedures are laid covering the areas of code of ethics such as job descriptions, performance appraisal forms, budget report formats.

For managing values in the code of ethics companies also prescribe policies and procedures, e.g. a high value on responsiveness to customers might be implemented by instituting policies to return the phone calls or to repair defective equipment within a certain period of time.

Policies and procedures are also to be laid to address ethical dilemmas.

CHAPTER

20

Ethical Use of Power— Guidelines

It is appropriate to quote from Stephen P. Robbins *"Organisation Behaviour"* as under:

> "It is true that power corrupts and absolute power corrupts absolutely? These concerns beg this question: Is it unethical for organisational members to use power? Many contemporary behavioural scientists would argue it isn't. They note that power is a natural part of human interactions—"we influence, or try to influence, other people every day under all sorts of conditions"—that carries into organisational life.
>
> Power really has two faces: one negative and the other positive. The negative side is associated with abuse—when, for example, power-holders exploit others or use their power to merely accumulate status symbols. The positive side is characterised by a concern for group goals, helping the group to formulate its goals, and providing group members with the support they need to achieve those goals."

THE ETHICAL USE OF POWER

The question is not whether power tactics are or are not ethical; rather, the question is which tactics are appropriate and which are not. The use of power in groups and companies is a fact of organizational life that all employees must accept. In doing so, however, all employees have a right to know that the exercise of power within the organization will be governed by ethical standards that prevent abuse or exploitation.

Several guidelines for the ethical use of power can be identified. These

EXHIBIT I

The Ethical Use of Power

Basis of Power	*Guidelines for Use*
Referent power	• Treat subordinates fairly • Defend subordinates' interests • Be sensitive to subordinates' needs, feelings • Select subordinates similar to oneself • Engage in role modelling
Expert power	• Promote image of expertise • Maintain credibility • Act confident and decisive • Keep informed • Recognize employee concerns • Avoid threatening subordinates' self-esteem
Legitimate power	• Be cordial and polite • Be confident • Be clear and follow-up to verify understanding • Make sure request is appropriate • Explain reasons for request • Follow proper channels • Exercise power regularly • Enforce compliance • Be sensitive to subordinates' concerns
Reward power	• Verify compliance • Make feasible, reasonable requests • Make only ethical, proper requests • Offer rewards desired by subordinates • Offer only credible rewards
Coercive power	• Inform subordinates of rules and penalties • Warn before punishing • Administer punishment consistently and uniformly • Understand the situation before acting • Maintain credibility • Fit punishment to the infraction • Punish in private

Source: From Gary A. Yukl, *Leadership in Organizations*, 1981, pp. 44-58. Adapted by permission of Prentice-Hall, Inc., Englewood Cliffs, N.J.

can be arranged according to five bases of power, as shown in Exhibit I. As will be noted, several techniques are available that accomplish their aims without compromising ethical standards. For example, a manager using reward power can verify subordinate compliance with work directive, ensure that all requests are both feasible and reasonable, make only ethical or proper requests, offer rewards that are valued by employees, and ensure that all rewards for good performance are credible and reasonably attainable.

Even coercive power can be used without jeopardizing personal integrity. For example, a manager can make sure that all employees know the rules and penalties for rule infractions, provide warnings before punishing, administer punishments fairly and uniformly, and so forth. The point here is that managers have at their disposal numerous tactics that they can employ without crossing over into questionable managerial behaviour. In view of the increasing number of lawsuits filed by employees for harmful practices, it seems wise for a manager to consider his behaviours before acting; this will help ensure the highest ethical standards.

In final analysis it can be concluded that power is inevitable in today's organisations. How power is used and what type of power is used can vitally affect human performance and organisational goals.

USE OF POWER IN PRACTICE: ETHICAL CHALLENGE—INVESTIGATING THE CHALLENGER DISASTER

The January 1986 explosion of the space shuttle *Challenger*, at a cost of seven lives, has been analyzed from several managerial standpoints: poor decision-making, poor management control, and poor leadership have all been blamed. We can also see in this tragedy an example of the unethical use of organizational power.

It has been determined that the explosion that doomed the space shuttle was caused by poorly designed seals on the booster rockets. The boosters were manufactured by Morton Thiokol, a major defence contractor. When the U.S. Congress initiated its investigation of the causes of the disaster, it found several disturbing facts. To begin with, several Morton Thiokol engineers had warned that the boosters were unsafe early in the design stage, but no one listened. Once the boosters were in production, engineers again warned of possible problems, but to no avail. The company kept the information quiet.

Equally disturbing was the fact that after two company engineers testified in the congressional hearing, they were abruptly transferred to undesirable assignments elsewhere in the company. When asked by Congress whether they thought their transfers were in retaliation for their "whistle-blowing", both engineers responded yes. One noted, "I feel I was set aside so I would not have contact with the people from NASA." The company had, in effect, used its power to try to isolate those who talked freely with the congressional investigators. In its defense, Morton Thiokol responded that it had *demoted* no one as a result of the investigation. "We've changed a lot of duties . . . because we're reorganizing", a management representative said.

Source: Stephen P. Robbins, Organisation Behaviour, Prentice Hall of India Pvt. Ltd.

CHAPTER

21

Employee's Role in Maintaining Ethical Office

Ethics is the set of good rules that determine how we relate and conduct ourselves with others. Some keys to maintaining ethical office are mentioned:

1. Lead by setting an example of good ethical conduct and good ethical problem-solving skills. One should share, communicate and discuss these with colleagues.
2. Never give the impression that you do not care that improper actions are taking place. We cannot control others, but we can control how we react to other's conduct. One should commit to being involved in the process of doing right things. Establish language of ethics with those in your office.
3. Support your boss's efforts to uphold high standards for ethical conduct. Communicate about ethics and solve ethical dilemmas.
4. Be consistent and be predictable in dependability.
5. Pay attention to details how you act.
6. Ask lot of clarifications when in doubt.
7. Avoid unethical traps of others. Remember that virtue is its own reward.
8. Protect your key assets:
   - Good health (healthy eating, exercise),

- Strong self-esteem (achieving something),
- Good communication skills, and
- Your reputation as a person of integrity.

A consistently ethical office features a climate that promotes fairness, mutual respect, decisions that are extensions of personal beliefs and values.

To build a more ethical office is not a quick or easy assignment to take oneself. One will encounter resistance because change makes people uncomfortable. But the productivity, profitability and ultimately well-being of your organisation depends upon you consistently deciding to do the thing for the right reasons.

Your colleagues may help you for building an ethical and honourable enterprise. You have an important role to play and you can make a real difference. So never give up.

CHAPTER

22

ETHICAL LEADERSHIP IS CRITICAL FOR AN ORGANISATION

True and effective leadership is one in which leader's behaviour and the exercise of the leadership influence processes are consistent with ethical and moral values. Such leadership should include three dimensions approach. A leadership is the ability to influence a group towards achievement of goals.

IMPORTANCE AND NEED OF ETHICAL LEADERSHIP TODAY

Leadership is the most important aspect of human behaviour. It give a positive direction and brings out the best in man. It has tremendous influence or ethical human performance.

(i) Leadership has never been such a hot topic in corporate world as now. It ranks at the top of the list of developmental programmes. Organisations are investing large sums of money on training in leadership. Why, because there is need for more effective and ethical leadership in our ailing companies.

A few years ago a scientist was asked what he considered to be ten dangers to society. First, he named some kind of nuclear war or accident that can destroy human race. Second, danger is world-wide epidemic. Third, that could bring destruction to society is quality of leadership.

(i) As such leadership makes real *difference between success and failure,* whether in a war, a business or games or family or society.

(ii) Leadership is where *all progress begins.* Without proper ethical leadership, all our institutions are in serious trouble.

(iii) There are increasing *societal concerns* that are unacceptable for organisational leaders—to be indifferent to moral responsibility, much less engage in unethical behaviour.

True leadership *assesses the followers' needs* and expectations and inspires them to realise a vision which best serves the followers and the organisation. The leader's vision informs and expresses the organisation's mission; provides the direction and rationale for organisation's objectives and goals. He communicates the beliefs and values which influence and shape organisation's culture and behaviour norms, and lays the foundation for organisation's strategies, policies and procedures.

(iv) It is the leader's moral principles and integrity which impart legitimacy and *creditability to the vision and sustain it*. Without ethical leadership, the organisation is soulless structure. Ethical leadership exists in the organisation when moral intent and principles infuse and guide the leader's actions in achieving.

For example, we see reports of widespread bribery by Italian, Indian and Japanese government officials, exorbitant executive salaries in USA, extensive environmental pollution in eastern Europe, and other instances of morally questionable conduct in our organisations.

Such observations lead to increasing realisation today that *organisational leaders need to be more sensitive to their moral obligations to larger society*, which includes all their stakeholders, i.e. consumers, employees, suppliers, government, local communities, etc.

As such there is an absolute need for moral leadership in organisations and in society, if we truly want to achieve the common good of human welfare at the personal, organisational and society levels.

THREE ASPECTS OF ORGANISATION ETHICS

The code of ethics can be important reminder that help individual employees engage in ethical practices.

An organisation's code of ethics establishes ethical principles that should govern the leader's decision and behaviours in order that the leader can fulfil the mission of uplifting the moral climate of the organisation. For this purpose *leader must develop morally as a person* and also *assist in the moral development of his followers*. This is possible, when corporate leaders focus their attention on three aspects of organisational ethics:

(i) The leader's development as a *moral person*, i.e. ethical qualities and no compromise on moral values.

(ii) The development of a *moral environment,* i.e. moral caliber of employees.

(iii) The promotion and encouragement of activities that serve *economic and ethical performance.* It is marriage between profit and social responsibility of business.

THREE DIMENSIONS OF ETHICAL LEADERSHIP

The ethical leadership manifests itself on three dimensions:

(i) Leader's intention/motive.

(ii) Leader's influence strategy.

(iii) Leader's character.

This will lead to development of both the leader and the followers which will strive to serve organisational and societal interests (for example: contribution to social welfare, community needs in areas of health, education, environmental pollution control, arts and culture and lobbying for public interest legislation).

The leader's moral development is an aspect of character formation through the practice of virtue in private as well as public life. This is facilitated by the leader through the use of morally appropriate influence strategies and tactics which are motivated and guided by moral intent.

Let us briefly discuss three dimensions of ethical leadership conceptualised by learned authors, i.e. M/s R.N. Kanungo and M. Mendonsa in their article.

1. Leader's Motives for Action

The overriding motive for ethical leadership is leader's altruistic intent as opposed to egotistic intent:

(a) Leaders are truly motivated by a concern for others (as against benefit to self), i.e. others are organisation members and society at large.

(b) Leaders have high need for affiliation motive. They regard warm and friendly relationships with their followers and are sensitive to their feelings and wishes. This suggests concern for others.

(c) The leader is not motivated by power motive to personal power (self-interest) but by power to serve the interest of the institution.

This institutional power need is derived by leader's identification with and commitment to organisation's objectives and interests.

(d) Achievement motive of leader brings satisfaction from achieving goals of the organisation and assuming high degree of responsibility for them.

Thus, leader's behaviours are guided by altruistic motivation (not egotistic) at operative level in-terms of afflictive interest, institutional power need, self-discipline or self-development and social achievement needs (and not personal power need and self-interest).

FIGURE

Ethical Leadership in Three Dimensions

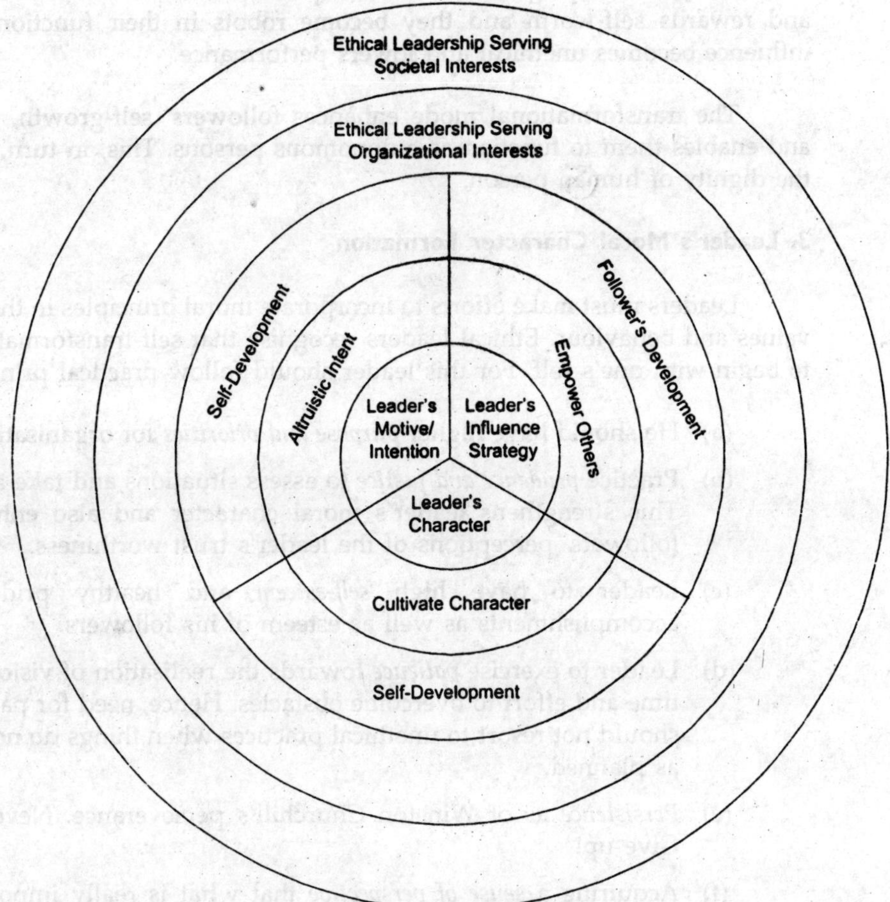

2. Leader's Influence Strategy (i.e. Transformational)

Under this, leader is to use empowerment (rather than control) strategies to bring about change in their followers' core beliefs and values as they move the organisation towards its future goals.

Leaders use their *personal expertise and good example* to transform their followers' beliefs and values that are consistent with the vision (not overt compliance behaviour).

The *empowerment strategy* achieves two objectives. First, followers internalise the beliefs and values. Second, empowerments changes followers' self-efficacy beliefs and they feel more competent to handle tasks required for realisation of the vision. Followers become more ethical and their effectiveness is high and enduring.

The above strategy of influence is in contrast to transactional mode where leaders use control to get followers' compliance. Further leader uses coercive and rewards self-worth and they become robots in their functioning. Here influence becomes unethical and lowers performance.

The transformational mode enhances followers' self-growth, self-worth and enables them to function as autonomous persons. This, in turn, promotes the dignity of human person.

3. Leader's Moral Character Formation

Leaders must make efforts to incorporate moral principles in their beliefs, values and behaviour. Ethical leaders recognise that self-transformation ought to begin with one's self. For this leader should follow practical principles:

(a) He should have higher *purpose and priorities* for organisation vision.

(b) Practice *prudence and justice* to assess situations and take a decision. This strengthens leader's moral character and also enhances the followers' perceptions of the leader's trust worthiness.

(c) Leader to have high *self-esteem* and healthy pride of his accomplishments as well as esteem of his followers.

(d) Leader to exercise *patience* towards the realisation of vision. It takes time and effort to overcome obstacles. Hence, need for patience. He should not resort to unethical practices when things do not proceed as planned.

(e) *Persistence* as of Winston Churchill's perseverance. Never! Never! Give up!

(f) Acquiring a *sense of perspective* that what is really important in a given situation through observing, inner silence that allow him to reflect on the higher purpose.

The above suggestions which leaders can adopt in their effort to develop their inner strength they need to function as ethical, moral persons.

A periodic examination of behaviour in the light of higher purpose can prevent one from, or at least alert one, that one might be treading the slippery slope of unethical behaviour.

To conclude, leader should set examples of personal commitment and loyalty and make efforts to maintain integrity of the organisation. Thus, leader's altruistic behaviour in three dimensions contribute to the development of both leader and the followers.

4. The Ethical Leader and Some Steps to Becoming an Ethical Leader

We reproduce here the views of Craig Thomas, Senator, USA (*Executive Excellence*, July 2001) regarding what he means by an ethical leader and also what are steps to becoming an ethical leader.

"What does it mean to be an Ethical Leader Today?

Being an ethical leader means living up to principles of conduct that you think govern yourself and your group. There are different views of what "being ethical" involves. But, to be an ethical leader, you need to adhere to a more universal standard of moral behaviour.

What Motivates a Leader to be Ethical?

The basic motivation comes from your decision to live a certain way; to conduct yourself in that way. It think you are motivated more when you're in public office or in a prominent leadership position. But, the decision is yours. Regardless of whether you're a leader or follower, you decide to conduct yourself in an ethical way.

So, you think it comes from within?

Yes, but then it radiates out. The people around you get a feel for what you think is the right thing to be doing—whether they accept it or not is another matter. But, if people opt to follow your leadership, they tend to follow that same conduct that you exhibit.

Who do you consider an Ethical Leader?

His beliefs carry through different posts and situations. I admire that, I believe most people are inclined to live and conduct themselves according to principles of authenticity and ethics. There are many heroes who do good things every day, in every community, because that's their belief, their role, and the conduct they believe is right—and they do it all the time. We often talk about high-profile people, but we should be grateful for the everyday heroes in every community.

What are some Steps to Becoming an Ethical Leader?

First, you have to establish some things that you believe in—based on your knowledge, education, experience, and background. To be consistent and strong, you have to be guided by your basic beliefs. Then you take your beliefs and mold them into a way of being effective, a style of leading, a way of showing that "here's what I believe in" and "here's why" and "here's how we can make progress by living this way." Then, I think that you need to work closely with the people around you, persuade them, lead them. That's what leaders are for—to have ideas and to sell those ideas, to listen, and to get people to move with you. So, first you have to believe, then you have to find a way to be effective, and then you have to work with people to cause them to join with you in doing what you're doing. I think what you do is lead by example. You have to do the right things. You live within the rules. You're open about what you're doing. You're willing to declare what you're doing.

5. Great People Leave Something Behind

Winners leave a legacy

Socrates taught Plato,
Plato taught Aristotle,
Aristotle taught Alexander the Great.

Knowledge, had it not been passed along, would have died.

Our greatest responsibility is to pass on a legacy that the coming generations can be proud of.

We gratefully acknowledge and reproduce an abstract of an article, "Ethical Leadership in Three Dimensions" by M/s R.N. Kanungo and M. Mendonca who are faculty members in the School of Management, McGill University, Canada, *Journal of Human Values*, 1998, Sage Publications, New Delhi/Thousand Oaks/London.

CHAPTER

23

VALUE-BASED MANAGERIAL LEADERSHIP

"Some say knowledge is power,
others say, the above is not true.
Character is power and wealth."

—*Satya Sai Baba*

Character is based on divine values.
Divine values are based on wisdom.

Management with proper combination of values and skills can assure harmony and progress of an organisation as well as society.

ETHICAL AND HUMAN VALUES

The most valuable human possessions are—health, harmony, happiness, wisdom, and above all character reflecting ethical and human values.

When these values are manifested in your thoughts, speech and actions, you are called a noble and enlightened person. As we think sincerely and constantly, so we become. Our actions and behaviour reflect our ideas and feelings.

We work (not only for name, fame, money, power and status) but for greater worth, for cultivating values for building up strong character, for wisdom so that our intrinsic value enhances.

WHAT ARE VALUES?

Values express wealth of *character* (divine nature) or Dharma (Indian ethos); and ideas of *integrity* (as in the west).

(1) Let us understand Integrity

Integrity is:

(i) Wholeness—meaning soundness, total perfection and completeness.

(ii) Goodness—covers values of honesty, morality, kindness, fairness, charity, truthfulness, generosity, etc. We need goodness in our thoughts, our speech and actions. Honesty is way of life.

(iii) Courage—telling the truth even in the face of danger/risk.

(iv) Self-discipline—self-control following norms/laws.

(v) Living by inner truth and inner mind—to remain yourself incorruptible, clean from kick backs, double dealings, etc. Let your mind be guided by conscience.

(vi) Steadfastness in all words, deeds and actions of the person.

(vii) A man of integrity is accepted, believed, trusted and befriended by all.

(2) Let us understand Dharma

Dharma is ways of life (law or right living) and conduct that shape character, which bring happiness to self and others. Dharma is almost synonymous with integrity, however, it has wider scope as it includes: (i) spiritualism (divine spirit to do right, do good, be good, (ii) righteousness (godliness—right action), (iii) fearlessness (due to 'his' protection to you).

Dharma alone accompanies the soul in its solitary journey after death. Dharma comprises those divine values of life, by living which, we shall be manifesting more and more of spiritual being in us.

SIGNIFICANCE OF VALUES

(a) Human values help in self-development.

(b) Human values help in good inter-personal relations.

(c) Human values help in reduced conflicts and disputes, improves process of improvement, customer, workers and citizen satisfaction.

(d) Human values enhance reputation, goodwill and image of the organisation.

Values	*Skills*
• To become ethical and human we need values.	• To 'do' we need skills.
• Values act as base to skills. Values are means of perfection.	• Skills must have sound values otherwise we manipulate skills, e.g. communication.
• Values are internal, dealing with internal development of a person, purify mind and heart. The person becomes good in thought, speech and in action, job or work.	• Skills only make a person proficient.
• Values bring excellence and universal good (software aspect) these are ends.	• Skills are mechanics of management (hardware). These are means.
• Values are enduring. Some principles and values are fundamental.	• Not enduring. Skills change with passage of time.

(e) It will be appropriate to understand differences between human *values* and *skills*/specialisations we possess.

VALUE DRIVEN MANAGEMENT

Effectiveness in performance of managers and employees is a function of values and skills together. A good manager has both.

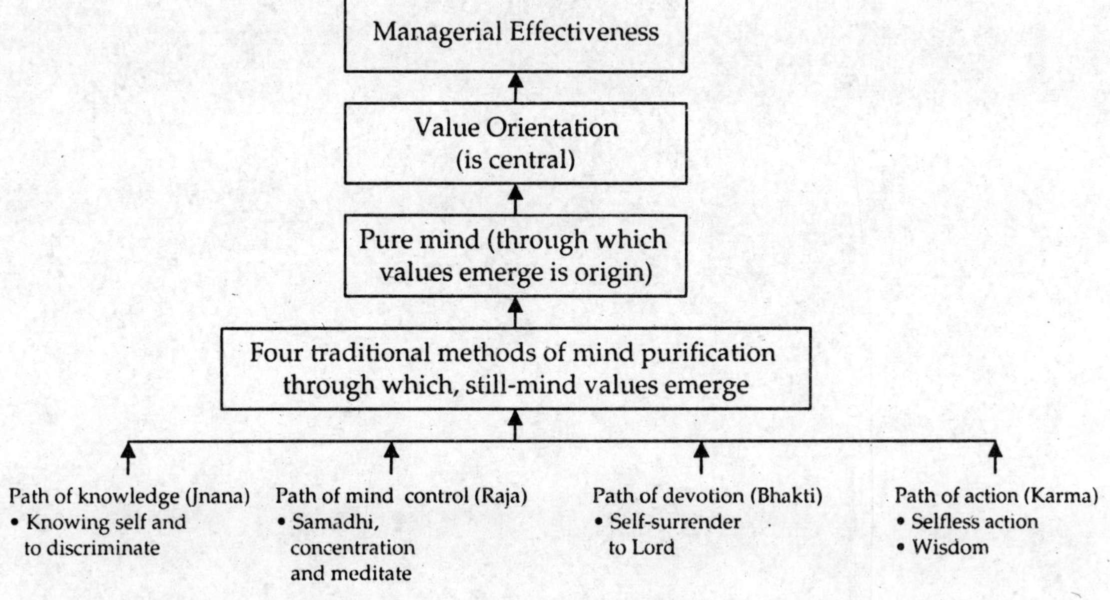

Every effort is to be made by top management to inculcate values. Values relate to internal domain of business, i.e. interactions with employees, customers, suppliers, creditors, public, etc. In the corporate vision, mission or creed we describe values, goals and objectives cherished by the organisation.

Success of Japan is based on values, using spiritual education and practices, e.g. concentration, meditation, mind stilling institution, etc. to neutralise evil effects of industrialisation and to synthesise the human values into management organisation. Japan has combined spiritualism and materialism and adopted value driven holistic approach in management and organisation.

CHAPTER

24

AN ETHICAL ORGANISATION: THE NEED OF THE DAY

We reproduce here the excerpts from speech of N.R. Narayana Murthy, Infosys Technologies conveying his views.

WHAT ARE ETHICS?

Ethics is not definable, is not implementable, because it is not conscious; it involves not only our thinking, but also our feeling said Valdemar W. Setzer.

Ethics is in origin the art of recommending to others the sacrifices required for cooperation with oneself—Bertrand Russell.

Ethical behaviour is doing what is best in enhancing the trust and confidence between two entities so that both the entities feel energised and enthused to work towards the betterment of the common good.

Dr. Stephen Covey who has a book on ethics in organisations says that interdependence is a higher value than independence. These entities that can potentially work together could be individuals, institutions, states or even nations. Generally, what is ethical in one society may be legal in another.

As a society becomes more developed, more and more norms of behaviour move from ethical to legal. For instance, before Sebi was established, insider trading norms were merely ethical issues in India while they were already legal issues in the US. Similarly, what I consider ethical now may become legal later on.

Thus, ethics go beyond the domain of legality It is about decent behaviour. It is about desirable behaviour. It is about putting the interest of the community ahead of oneself.

There are no policemen who can arrest us nor are there any courts that will try you for not being ethical. We will be judged only in the court of the Lord.

The need of the day is to remove poverty. This requires that we place the interest of the community above one's own. It is also about making sacrifices to ensure that the next-generation is better-off.

If India is what it is today, it because of the low ethical behaviour of our corporate leaders, politicians and bureaucrats. Unless we can change this, there is no hope.

ETHICAL BEHAVIOUR OF THE CORPORATION

Let me restrict my further discussions to ethical behaviour in corporations since I have a little bit of experience in this area.

The framework for ethical behaviour of a corporation is predicted on the ethical behaviour of its owners, managers, employees and directors towards its stakeholders—customers, investors, employees, vendor-partners, government of the land and the society.

To me, ethical behaviour is putting the interest of the company above that of one's own personal interest in all transactions.

- It is about fairness to all stakeholders.
- It is about transparency.
- It is about raising the trust and confidence of stakeholders in the way the company is run.
- It is about understanding and discharging societal responsibilities.
- It is about long-term thinking.
- It is about overcoming greed, insecurity and lack of self-confidence.
- It is about following every law of the land even when the law-enforcers may not be able to detect your violation.

The measure of a man's real character is what he would do if he knew he would never be found out, said Lord T.B. Macaulay.

While most people believe that Corporate Governance (CG) principles provide the legal and procedural framework for ensuring proper conduct of a corporation. I believe that it is an *issue of ethical behaviour* of the owner-managers of the corporation. Let me give you some examples of unethical behaviour.

Here are some examples of *unethical behaviour.*

The Chairman, CEO and CFO of a well known corporation sell shares with $ 150 million knowing that their corporation is shaky and then tell employees whose savings are in the company stock that all is well.

Nearer home, I have seen directors of several family-owned companies calling their homes, and stying in guesthouses, and booking all their expenses to the company.

There are sick companies but no sick industrialists!

A computer company ships a lower capacity machine to an uniformed customer and char ;es the price for a higher capacity machine.

A female sales employee of a company agrees to sleep with the prospective customer if he purchases her company's products.

A boss transfers his subordinate because she went over him to the senior level manager on an issue.

A senior manager tricks his boss into hiding information about his indiscretion.

HOW DO WE IMPROVE ETHICS IN A CORPORATION?

(a) The most powerful lessons about ethics and morality *come from family life* where people treat one another with respect, consideration and love.

Thus, I believe good behaviour is a result of your culture, your upbringing and the company you keep. It is a matter of the heart and not the mind. The solution is to develop such a culture.

(b) The behaviour of a corporation is generally shaped by the behaviour of its *CEO and other leaders.* This is particularly so in a feudal society like India.

Leadership is a potent combination of strategy and character. But if you must be without one, be without the strategy.

We need CEOs who are men and women of integrity—people who will walk the talk in demonstrating their commitment to a value system. As Nobel laureate Jane Addams has said: Action indeed is the sole medium of expression for ethics. Without this, no corporate governance will ever work. For example, at Infosys our value system can be summed up as: The softest pillow is a clear conscience.

The CEO should realise that the best index of success of a corporation is its longevity. The long-term success of a corporation is predicted on maintaining harmonious relations with employees, customers, vendor-partners, the government and the society. This is predicted on trust and confidence.

(c) I believe in *simple rules*. They are easy to understand, easy to follow, and easy to communicate. Above all, you cannot cheat with simple rules. CEOs should concentrate on simple business rules. If they want to implement complex rules, they should first understand them and translate them to a set of simple rules.

(d) Building *trust and confidence* requires an environment where there is premium on transparency, openness, lack of fear, fairness and justice. CEOs should encourage this. At Infosys, our philosophy is: When in doubt, How do we improve ethics in a corporation?

(e) We have to create a *climate of opinion* which says respect is more important than wealth. We can create this climate by instituting awards for good corporate behaviour and giving these awardees better exposure at international fora.

(f) Everybody in the company should accept meritocracy for, meritocracy forces ethical behaviour.

Respect for elders and God generally helps in practicing ethical behaviour.

Only morality in our actions can give beauty and dignity to life.—Albert Einstein.

Finally, pride is one-self, one's company, and one's nation is likely to inspire ethical behaviour.

Reference

N.R. Narayana Murthy, Chairman and chief mentor of Infosys Technologies. These are the excerpts from his presentation at the first Raman Kant Munjal Memorial Lecture in New Delhi).

PART V

PROFESSIONALS AND ETHICS

CHAPTER

25

Professional's Ethical Role

In today's deteriorating value system, ethics assume far greater importance in each dimension of life, as never before—be it private, professional or public life. The public life of a professional begins when he represents his fellow professionals on its governing body. In fact, *ethical values cast upon the members of a profession*, a duty to judiciously evaluate the candidates and cast their franchise in favour of a visionary, dedicated and committed contestant.

MEANING OF PROFESSION

Every profession has its own special knowledge and developing and recognizing that knowledge is key to any strategy for moving towards professionalism. In fact, a distinguishing characteristic of a professional is its *ability to combine ethical standards with performance of technical skills*. The Webster's New Collegiate Dictionary describes a professional as characterised by or conforming the technical or ethical standards of a profession. Ethics indeed are principles of conduct governing an individual or group. Therefore, in order to achieve the stature of a profession, it has to adhere to a set of ethical standards to guide individual or group decisions and actions.

The concept of *professionalism* itself provides an inspiration for service to *fulfil a social function*. The typical characteristic of a profession includes the primacy of service to the client over profit to the practitioner and the acquisition of special knowledge and skill beyond that ordinarily possessed by the non-professionals. These factors suggest the development of a code of conduct and a system of internal controls to enforce these professional standards, including requirements for admission to and maintenance in the profession.

SACHAR COMMITTEE OBSERVATIONS

The task of identifying a professional was undertaken, for the first time, by the High Powered Expert Committee on simplification of the Companies Act, 1956 and the MRTP Act, 1969. This Committee headed by Justice Rajendra Sachar and popularly known as Sachar Committee was appointed by the Government of India in June 1997 to focus on professionalisation of corporate management.

Looking to the wide gap between the control and ownership on one hand and the management and ownership on the other, the Committee expressed the view that professionalisation of management is not a mere concept but is, in fact, an inevitable necessity for the well-being of the company itself. In suggesting a definition of "Professional Manager", the Committee in its Report (Published in the year 1980) observed that—"A Professional Manager is an individual who:

(a) belongs to the profession of law, accountancy, medicine, engineering or architecture; or

(b) is a member of a recognized professional body or institution, exercising supervisory jurisdiction over its members; or

(c) is a holder of a degree or diploma in management from any recognized institute of management or from any recognized university; or

(d) is a holder of a post-graduate degree from any recognized university:

   (i) and possesses not less than five years' experience in an executive capacity in a company, corporation or a body corporate or in the Government, or

   (ii) possesses minimum of ten years' experience in an executive capacity in a company, corporation or a body corporate or in the Government."[5]

In suggesting a definition of a business manager, the Committee accorded equal weightage to qualification and experience.

CHARACTERISTICS OF A PROFESSIONAL

Let us find what is the characteristics of a professional as propounded by social historians, sociologists and affirmed by two epoch making judgments delivered by Scrutton L.J. (in the case of *Commissioners of Inland Revenué* v. *Maxse*) and Du. Pareq L.J. (in the case of *Carr* v. *Inland Revenue Commissioners*) in UK. Firstly, the nature of work done by a member of a profession must be *skilled and specialised* and a substantial part of the work to be undertaken is mental rather than manual. Secondly, every professional body prescribe a period of theoretical and practical *training* before an individual is admitted to become a member of that profession. Thirdly, an individual entering a profession is required to possess a strong *sense of social responsibility* and an exceptional commitment to safeguard and protect the interest of his clients in all possible ways, which transcends all other commitments. Fourthly, a professional is committed or expected to be committed to certain *moral principles* with a high degree of detachment and integrity, which go beyond the general duty of honesty. Fifthly, a professional is expected to provide a *high standard of service* all seeking his services without consideration of class, creed, caste, colour or religion. Sixthly, a professional must maintain total *confidentiality of the work* entrusted to him and more than anything have a wider duty of *ethical responsibility* which may on occasions transcend the duty to a particular client. Seventhly, every professional normally belong to an *organized professional body* or association constituted by a statue, royal charter or time tested rules and regulations and it has the power to admit an individual as a member and also the power to enforce an ethical code of conduct on such member while he is continuing as a member of that profession whether in employment or in practice.

THE PURPOSE OF ETHICS IN PROFESSIONALS

The purpose of ethics in profession is to direct the professionals to *abide by a code of conduct* that facilitates, if not encourages, public confidence in their services. Now the question is can ethics be taught and the answer is 'yes'. Infact at some point in life, ethics must be taught. People are not born with innate desires to be ethical or to be concerned with the welfare of others. The role of the family includes teaching children a code of ethical behaviour that includes respect for parents, siblings, and others. The family bears chief responsibility for ensuring that children will receive the necessary education and moral guidance to become productive members of society. The basic values such as honesty, self-control, concern for others, respect for legitimate authority, fidelity, and civility must be passed from one generation to the next, a fundamental process of the family.

Several managers belong to strong professions such as those of accountants, company secretaries and lawyers. There are others, which are fledgling to become true professionals like those of human resources, advertising, and marketing. These functions must recognize that a profession has an intimate connection with welfare, and is strongly based on aspects of ethics, and values. The standards, principles, codes and best practices evolved in these professions are founded on assumptions of human welfare. The professional is thus expected to owe an allegiance to his calling, which expects him to put his personal interests or that of the company behind those of the professional standards. A professional is expected to have five distinctive attributes:[1] [Dr. Y.R.K. Reddy, Strategic Approach to Human Resource

Management (1990)]:

(i) A commitment to a calling which has a set of normative and behavioural expectations.

(ii) A specialized education and training of substantial duration.

(iii) Membership of an association comprising of similarly trained and practicing individuals for the purpose of protecting and enhancing the interest of the calling.

(iv) A service orientation keeping in view the requirements of the client and the society.

(v) A relative degree of autonomy in the use of his/her knowledge and skills.

It is obvious that training and sensitization may not be insulation against fraud. Yet, an integration of ethics into corporate governance frame makes the proposition more robust, than a stultified view of corporate governance as a box-ticking process. Ethics as a professional compulsion will help progress on this integration. Despite the fact that there is no templates for such integration, Lacznaikk's ethical propositions could be of some help:[2] [Gene Lacznik, Business Ethics—Management Primer, Business (Jan.-March, 1983) in Ethics, Corporate Governance and State:]

1. Ethical conflicts and choices are inherent in business decision-making.
2. Proper ethical behaviour exists on a plane above the law. The law merely specifies the lowest common denominator of acceptable behaviour.
3. There is no single satisfactory standard of ethical action agreeable to everyone that a manager can use to make specific operational decisions.
4. Managers should be familiar with a wide variety of ethical standards.
5. The discussion of business cases or of situations having ethical implications can make managers more ethically sensitive.
6. There are diverse and sometimes conflicting determinants of ethical action. These stem primarily from the individual, from the organization, from professional norms, and from the values of the society.
7. Individual values are the final standard, although not necessarily the determining reason for ethical behaviour.

8. Consensus regarding what constitutes proper ethical behaviour in a decision-making situation diminishes as the level of analysis proceeds from abstract to specific.
9. The moral tone of an organization is set by top management.
10. The lower the organizational level of a manager, the greater the perceived pressure to act unethically.
11. Individual managers perceive themselves as more ethical than their colleagues.
12. Effective codes of ethics should contain meaningful and clearly stated provisions, along with enforced sanctions for non-compliance.
13. Employee must have a non-punitive, feel-safe mechanism for reporting ethical abuses in the organization.
14. Every organization should appoint a top-level manager or director to be responsible for acting as an ethical advocate in the organization.

CODE OF PROFESSIONAL CONDUCT AND ETHICS

A profession is formed on the basis of generally accepted body of knowledge; widely recognized standard of attainment, and an enforceable code of ethics. A code of ethics is a crucial element in forming a professional.

One of the universally accepted *characteristics of a profession is the observance of a strict code of conduct by the members* of the profession. The basic reason why code of conduct is strictly to be enforced in the case of professional is, that a professional is endowed with higher faculties conditioned by an elaborate preparatory education, rigorous instruction and valuable practical training, as to distinguish, above all, righteous act/conduct from those deviant and unedifying.

The services of a professional are personal to a client and the latter's affairs come into full knowledge of the professional when his services are engaged by a client. That a client would, therefore, expect the professional to be a person of character and integrity is given a firm assurance through the code of conduct evolved and effectively administered by the professional body concerned, of which the professional is a member. Code of conduct which also goes by the synonym 'Professional ethics' encompasses a professional's conduct towards his peers, the clients, the employer and the public at large.

The learned professions the world over have accorded highest priority to professional ethical standards in the dealings and relationship of professionals with their employers, employees, Government, fellow professionals and the public at large. The *fundamental principles* which should govern the conduct of a professional with others have been broadly identified as to encompass:

- Integrity;
- professional independence;
- professional competence;
- objectivity;
- ethical behaviour;
- conformance to technical standards, if any, prescribed; and
- confidentiality of information acquired in the course of professional work.

The history of human civilization bears ample testimony to the reverence and honour with which society looks upon persons who subjugate their personal gain to public good. Professionals, with their rigorous education and training belong to a class of people who have to uphold public good and serve wider public interest.

Theodore-Roosevelt, twenty-sixth President of the United States, said: "To educate a person in mind and not in morals is to educate a menace to society." The declining influence of social institutions has increased the role educators must play in shaping values and not leave to acquire them by chance.

The main reason for having ethical guidelines is not to provide a cookbook solution to every practice-related problem, but to aid in the decision-making process for situations that involve ethical questions. Business persons encounter novel situations in their jobs and need ethical guidelines to handle them effectively. Ethics codes are necessary to provide such guidance.

TO CONCLUDE

Most professions have today become very competitive, putting tremendous pressure, stress, strain and temptation to outdo others. This is high time to adhere to the highest professional and ethical standards as set out by the code of conduct and as accorded by the learned professions throughout the world in times of stress and strain.

In today's deteriorating value system, ethics assume far greater importance in each dimension of life, as never before—be it private, professional or public life. The public life of a professional begins when he represents his fellow professionals on its governing body. In fact, ethical values cast upon the members of a profession, a duty to judiciously evaluate the candidates and cast their franchise in favour of a visionary, dedicated and committed contestant. On the other hand, ethical values require a representative to work for betterment happiness and more fulfilled life of not only those whom he represents but the community as a whole. Therefore, the professionals in the Changing Pa[illegible] probably have a singular responsibility to integrate ethics into their conduct.

References

N.K. Jain, Professional Ethics, *Company Secretary*, November 2003.

S. Krishnamoorthy, Professional Ethics and Social Commitment, *Company Secretary*, November 2003.

Y.R.K. Reddy, Strategic Approach to Human Resource Management, 1990.

Gene Lacznic, Business Ethics—Management Primer, *Business* (Jan.-March 1983).

CHAPTER

26

PRINCIPLES OF PROFESSIONAL ETHICS

"The framework for ethical behaviour is more comprehensive and goes beyond just being legal. Acting ethically, thus involves making moral decision. Professionals have to set a procedure for developing a code of ethics for corporates with provision to scrutinize policies and practices by a process of self-evaluation."

ETHICS

Oxford Advanced Learner's Dictionary defines the word 'ethics' as "moral principle that govern or influence a person's behaviour." Ethics formulization is benchmarking of human behaviour. The conduct of mankind is influenced either by the emotions of life or the action people perform in specific situation. The coordination of action, emotion, religion and logic generate ethics and the man is bound to follow.

BASIC ETHICAL PRINCIPLES

The ethical process involves two steps. First, one *must know* what is right and what is wrong, and second, one must have the *personal discipline,* integrity and motivation to do what they know is right. Society puts in place punishments and penalties to protect the innocent and to motivate those with weak self-discipline, low personal integrity or poor judgment to act in accordance with accepted practices.

ETHICS AND VALUES

Values are strong held beliefs. Thus, values denote a sense of right or wrong, good or bad, and another judgemental criteria based on our strong sense of what the ideal ought to be. Values shape attitudes, perceptions, interests and finally personality.

Value is an acquired trust on certain philosophy, which activate human mind to determine the course of action a person is to render in his life. Value only leads the mental course and is nothing to directly with the performance of action. The business is not unethic. It is the individual action influences the business activities and the business in unethical situation.

Values at the individual level include faith, self-respect competitiveness, creativity, devotion towards work, tolerance sacrifice, courtesy, good just, civil sense, honesty, humility, simplicity reason, truth, forgiveness, fortitude, cleanliness, absence of egoism, detachment, poise, equanimity, etc. *Values that can be imparted to the members of organisation collectively* include harmony, resourcefulness, discipline, *dharma*, equity, brotherhood, unity, peace, social conscience, cooperation, live and let live, concern, care, mutual trust, love, team-spiritedness, efficiency, effectiveness, excellence, morale, productivity, responsibility, risk-bearing, accountability, sharing, sacrifice, etc.

ETHICAL CRISES

According to Dr. V. Balachandran and Dr. V. Chandrasekaran, "The thinking on ethical values in business was started in the decade of sixties but in India we started bothering about this since last one decade. It is not that the managers are not the believers of ethics in business but the fact is that the management thinkers and professionals gave very less attention over the ethics in business." In this situation the question is "Are we really having an ethical crises in corporate sector for which we should start bothering." The answer may vary from individual manager to individual thinker and the worker. Let us try to recognize the concept of ethical crises.

Ethical Crises = $i - p$

where, i stands for professional ideals (benchmarking) and p stands for professional practices (realities).

Thus, the *professional practices* that are not matching the *professional benchmarking* are deciding the volume of unethical crises in the corporations.

A study by Monappa in the Mid-seventies found that 72% of the executives surveyed tended to ignore ethics when they come to daily practice. Most Managers do believe in good ethics and they do consider the ethical implication on their decision; but various factors like unethical competition, company policy, and a plethora of rules and regulations often prevent them from putting their values into practice.

PRINCIPLES OF PROFESSIONAL ETHICS

Individuals acting in a professional capacity take on an additional burden of ethical responsibility. For example, professional associations have codes of ethics that prescribe required behaviour within the context of a professional practice such as medicine, law, accounting, or engineering. These written codes provide rules of conduct and standards of behaviour based on the principles of professional ethics, which include:

- Impartiality; objectivity,
- Openness; full disclosure,
- Confidentiality,
- Due diligence/duty of care,
- Fidelity to professional responsibilities, and
- Avoiding potential or apparent conflict of interest.

Even when not written into a code, principles of professional ethics are usually expected of people in business, employees, volunteers, elected representatives and so on.

FACTORS INFLUENCING ETHICAL ENVIRONMENT

People may claim several ways to manage the ethical crises in their organisation but the success is questionable in many cases. Following may be the factors influencing the ethical environment in an organisation:

- The ethical vision of the management which may need a review.
- The holistic human values the organisation has developed.
- The ethical code acquired within the organisation.
- The individual inspiration source.
- The managerial character and ethical dedication.
- The work place environment and compulsion to follow the ethical norms.

CORPORATE ETHICS

The framework for ethical behaviour is more comprehensive and goes beyond just being legal. The dictionary defines 'ethical behaviour' as behaviour conforming to accepted principles of right and wrong that govern the conduct of a profession. Thus, acting ethically involves making moral decisions, i.e., distinguishing between right and wrong, and not just being legal rather than illegal. Regulators rightfully monitor our behaviour, but individuals of integrity exhibit ethical behaviour for a much more important reason; because it is the right thing to do.

ETHICAL APPROACH IN CORPORATES

An ethical corporation is characterized by an ethical culture. This means that an ethical nature of the core business remains paramount and at the forefront of concerns embedded in the corporation's everyday activities. Furthermore, these ethical stances, by necessity, need to be explicit, accepted and openly acknowledged. In order to be considered 'ethical', then, first and foremost of all considerations, an ethical corporation will be characterized by *ethical awareness*. Secondly, with that corporation there need be an *acceptance by corporate personnel of responsibilities* for their actions, both individually and as a collective.

ETHICS AND ETHICAL STANDARDS

Ethics is a set of standards or a code, or value system, worked out from human reason and experience, by which free human actions are determined as ultimately right or wrong, good or evil. If an action agrees with these standards, it is ethical—if it does not agree, it is unethical. If we are to get back to the root source, or principle, of ethics, we must talk about human goals. Ethical standards are no different from any other kind of standards in this regard.

In organizational life, one faces several dilemmas for instance attending to his job, attending the work he likes, attending the work that satisfies the boss, appeasing a colleague, doing something for the sake of subordinates, helping out of way due to several reasons like corruption, favouritism and frustration. It is because the values create conviction, and will-power, for the rationale decision even in critical situations. A value of an individual is what a compass to a navigator both in personal and organisational life.

When ordinarily well behaved people behave unethically, they have usually talked themselves into a serene belief that they are doing nothing wrong. They have fallen for their own rationalisation. A rationalisation is a handy excuse. We use it to persuade ourselves that a rule which we know perfectly well, does not apply to our particular case. The most common rationalisation are that a rule doesn't "really" apply in this instance, or that you are "expected" to do something "slightly" unethical because it will help the company or that it is "safe" because no one will ever know what you did. Any of these excuses can be quite convincing to someone with a strong incentive to break the rule.

Many organizations develop a code of conduct for their employees. Such codes are often prescriptive and set out specific (but minimal) guidelines for their employees' conduct. There also exists another form of document called a code of ethics. These, unlike codes of conduct, are predominantly aspirational. They usually contain a smaller number of general or fundamental principles which will be of particular importance in instances where a code of conduct is silent or unclear. A code of conduct may help to make staff sensitive to their own behaviour and its ethical implications. Consequently, such a code may be a form of ethics education.

ETHICS EDUCATION

Ethics education is essential groundwork if employees are to develop into ethical decision-makers. Ethics education involves the imparting of knowledge, understanding and skills that will enable an employee to autonomously and authentically develop and maintain an ethical framework that is their own but is meshed in harmoniously with that of the corporation. Most significantly then, ethics education is directed towards developing moral autonomy.

CONCLUSION

Professionals have to balance their obligations to the undertaking which employ them, with the society at large, with other employees, suppliers, consumers and also of course with their own conscience. Their tasks at times are often invidious in that they are called upon to serve conflicting interests, which as a professional, they must attempt to reconcile. Indeed, the present changed environment has thrown open many challenging tasks and opportunities to the professionals. Today, professionals are required to maintain and enhance the quality of service by adopting a professional approach. Corporate Professionals can best contribute to an ethical corporate culture by 'leading by example'. This is best achieved in their relations with the other members of the corporate community. Such relationships should be characterized by respect, trust and consideration. Additionally, the corporate administer has a more formal leadership role. Among other things, they should encourage ethical discourse by encouraging the discussion of ethical questions by staff members. Professionals can set a procedure for developing a corporate-based code of ethics along the lines suggested above and should include the ethical scrutiny of corporate policies and practices within the regular processes of whole corporate self-evaluation.

REFERENCES

Bhatt, Rajesh J., *The Ethical Climate*, Commonwealth Publishers, New Delhi.

Kumar, A. Joshi, K.M., *Human Values: A Holistic Approach*.

Laurence M. Crane, NGIS.

Longstaff, S. 1994(a), 'What is ethics education and training?' in Preston, N. (Ed.), *Ethics for the Public Sector*, The Federation Press, Annandale.

Monappa, A., *Ethical Attitudes of Indian Managers*, AMA, New Delhi.

Soares, E., 'Values of Indian Managers, the Basis of Progress', *Indian Management*, Oct. 1981, p. 31.

'A New Corporate Ethics', *Business India*, 56-61, Nov. 18-Dec. 1, 1996.

V. Balachandran and V. Chandrasekaran, *Chartered Secretary*, November 2003.

CHAPTER

27

FOCUS IN PROFESSIONAL ETHICS

We present here views of experts emphasising the vital areas of professional ethics.

1. Professional Ethics involves making Moral Decisions—Dr. V. Balachandran and Dr. V. Chandrasekaran

Ethics is a set of standards or a code, or value system worked out from *human reason and experience*, by which free human actions are determined as ultimately right or wrong, good or evil. If an act *conforms with these standards*, it is ethical—if it does not agree, it is unethical The framework for ethical behaviour is more comprehensive and goes beyond just being legal. The dictionary defines 'ethical behaviour' as behaviour conforming to accepted principles of right and wrong that govern the conduct of a profession. Thus, acting ethically involves *making moral decisions*, i.e. distinguishing between right and wrong, and not just being legal rather than illegal. The business is not unethical. It is the individual action, which influences the business activities and places the business in an unethical situation. Regulations rightfully monitor our behaviour but individuals of integrity exhibit ethical behaviour for a much more important reason; because it is the right thing to do. Professionals can set a procedure for developing a corporate-based code of ethics and should include the ethical scrutiny of corporate policies and practices within the regular processes of whole corporate self-evaluation. Professional should have faith and commitment to the basic ethics of his calling.

2. Professional Ethics is to Serve Public Good—R. Ramachandran

The society respects and honours persons who subjugate their personal gains to public good. The professionals by their rigorous education and training are expected to safeguard and *serve public interest*. Such a professional is able to distinguish the righteous act/conduct from those of deviant and undesirable. Professionals to adopt a righteous path and uphold all that is good. They are to act right all that is in the interest of the society. The client, expects the professional to be a person of great character and integrity. This is assured by the administration of the code of conduct by the professional body on its members. Professional ethics covers the professional's conduct towards his peers, his clients, his employer, his fellow professionals and the various segments of the society.

3. Professional Ethics is Based on Code of Conduct and Law—P.T. Rangamani

A professional worth the name shall have faith and commitment to the basic ethics of his calling. Those who are members of an organised body with a statutory backing are *wedded to a code of conduct*, which emphasizes the imperatives of independence and integrity. The corporate professionals such as Chartered and Cost Accountants, Company Secretaries, besides Engineers, Architects, Doctors and Lawyers belong to this category. The government by enacting special laws gives them a pride of place in the society and expects them to perform their role with honesty and dignity. They are *the creatures of law* and owe their position to law. The legislature has placed faith in them to render reliable, quality service. The result of their service is reflected in their reports and certifications, which are relied upon by the various segments of the community and members of the public.

4. Professional Ethics is Based on Self-Regulation and Self-Discipline—Om Prakash Dani

In the liberalised regime, the accent is on *self-regulation* and *self-discipline* and the concept of management by exception is gaining wider acceptance. The profession is also becoming more and more competitive, which is putting much stress, strain and temptations to outdo others. At this juncture professionals have to continue to prove their integrity and excellence without resorting to unethical behaviour. They have to give the highest priority to the professional and ethical standards and due adherence to the code of conduct, as accorded by learned professions throughout the world in times of stress and strain.

5. Professional Ethics Represents Cultural and Spiritual Values of Social Commitment—S. Krishnamoorthy

'Ethics' is essentially a branch of spiritualism which is a banyan tree covering the entire gamut of human behaviour on righteous path for the well-being of human race. Ethics is relevant and useful to all individuals in a civil society but its importance and significance is much more for a professional because he is expected to play a more meaningful and useful role for the benefit of the society in discharging his social responsibility and accountability at a higher level compared to other sections of society. However, recent global events have conclusively proved that a quite number of people at the top level of corporate world who are all senior professionals do not attach much importance to ethical values and principles, compassion and true love towards other fellow beings because they are swayed by lavish life styles and material comforts in life. A professional should behave and play his role well drawing inspiration from the basic principles of our spiritualism, culture and rich heritage. This is all the more necessary because from all economic indicators our country is likely to emerge as a viable economic power with a strong professional cadre of people and we should be in the forefront to follow ethical principles and practices in letter and spirit.

6. Corporate Justice is based on Corporate Education—Satya Narain Agrawal

The concept of *Corporate Justice* emanates from the goal of justice, social, economic and political enshrined in the Preamble of the *Constitution of India*. In reality, *Corporate Justice is a pre-condition of good Corporate-Governance,* which cannot be achieved without realising the goal of Corporate Justice. There is a need for an integrated *Course of Corporate Education,* which should aim at corporate perfection through Corporate Justice. Corporate Education should provide an efficient Corporate Management Service and for the establishment of Corporate Accounting Service with cost analysis at national level for Corporate bodies to serve a variety of purposes. It would be necessary to *concentrate on the quality of Corporate Management and to dispense* with superfluous and superficial forms, rituals and ceremonies enjoined upon Corporate bodies under Corporate laws. The Government and the Professional Institutes should adopt the right approach to Corporate Education to cater to the requirements of the Corporate bodies, most of which are now reeling under a variety of pulls and pressures and many are nearing closure for want of right approach to the development of the Corporate sector. Corporate bodies should serve as instrumentalities of Corporate Justice.

7. Company Secretary has Special Role as Professional—D.K. Prahlada Rai

Company Secretary, renders a host of services to the corporate sector and other clients. The practising side of the Profession is fast expanding and the Company Secretary is being called upon to shoulder higher responsibilities. This calls for extensive training and an ability to distinguish between righteous conduct from those deviant and unedifying. The authorities and powers conferred on the Company Secretary by the Companies Act and other regulations are proof of confidence reposed in the Company Secretaries by the Central Government and other regulatory authorities like SEBI, Stock Exchanges and others. The Corporate Sector and other clientele also repose certain measure of confidence in the ability and capacity of Company Secretaries to perform the task entrusted to them in an objective manner. There is also a need to build clean image of the Company Secretary Profession.

Reference

Chartered Secretary, November 2003.

CHAPTER

28

SUCCESS, HAPPINESS AND ETHICS

I. SUCCESS

Life is a competition and we have to compete to face challenges of twenty-first century. The object is to succeed by achieving objectives or goals or attaining effectiveness or achieving excellence or surpassing the competitor's record or own self-record if that is highest. It is to bowl out the opposite. It is a passionate thread of enthusiasm and aggression. To be winner is doing exceptionally, superbly and fantastically well. To be winner is to put an effort or energy not hundred percent, even beyond oneself, which ultimately brings fulfilment through success. The only difference between successful person and unsuccessful person is that successful person surpasses his goal and unsuccessful falls short of his goal.

Ethics in Success

It is to succeed fairly, decently and by rules. Being a winner is a spirit. The winners keep success in perspective based on value system and applying some basic principles. For example, a racer may succeed by pushing the competitor and he may be declared successful. But is he the winner? No. To mention another example, recently in a Cricket World Cup 2003 match, a player was declared not out by both the empires, but he returned to the pavilion of his own, as he did not consider worth while. Is he winner? Yes. Most of us *associate success in life with the moral character* of a person. *Moral values* are such as telling the *truth,* obligation not to *harm others, justice, fairness, faithfulness* and *respect of an individual's dignity* are binding on every individual irrespective of his religion or place of living. Being morally true is inherently valueable, Plato said, 'human-beings would continue to follow morals'.

Keys to Success

There are certain basic individual traits or keys to success. These are:

- ❑ Ambition (dream).
- ❑ Commitment/fire to win/imagination/to be unstoppable.
- Responsibility (to take charge and to handle pressure).
- Hard effort (fortitude) stay tough and have a belief in it. Performance at the peak.
- Integrity (*dharma*).
- Positive mindset. If you think you can, you are right. Develop positive self-image.
- Persistence—never give up, hold your nerve and win mental toughness. Fighting back with amazing resilience.
- Sense of pride in excellence or achievements.
- Continuing to be a learner.
- A proper plan.
- Keep integrity high.

A successful person has self-belief, sustained enthusiasm, the courage to say no, innovative and looking for new opportunities, forgiveness, ability to face criticism, peace of mind, cheerfulness and ability to delegate and supervise.

If you can Dream, you can do it. Failure is Step towards Success

Success and happiness go hand in hand. Success is getting what you want and happiness is wanting what you get. Success is not measured by how high we go up in life, but rather by how many times we fall back, and then fight back that determines success. For illustrations—Thomas Edison failed numerous times before he could make light bulb. Beethoven was told he had no talent for music, but he struggled to give best music to the world. Thus, if you dream, think and you can do it. Men who win are those who think they can. Napoleon Hill stated, "Whatever the mind can conceive and believe, the mind can achieve." Only losers quit and give up. Aways try to struggle with your weakness. Nothing good comes in your life without struggle.

Attitude is Core of any Success

To some people success might mean wealth, to others it is recognition, position, to some it may be a good family, peace of mind, success means different things for different people. Success has three parts—attitude, skill and knowledge.

There are people with skills, knowledge and lot of talents but lack of attitude. "People know what they are but do not know what they can become." Success is not an accident. Success is *matter of attitude*. It is a result of what you think you are capable of. It is a matter of careful thinking and planning to be successful person. You must have a clear goal in your vision.

Some Obstacle to Success

- Ego
- Fear of failure
- No plan
- Lack of formalised goals
- Lack of commitment
- Lack of priorities
- Overcoming obstacles

People who have overcome obstacles are better than those who have never faced them. Problems sometime discourage and disappoint us, but winners don't get disheartened. We can not run away from our problems. Only losers quit and give up. Aways try to struggle with your weakness. Set clear cut goal in your life. Nothing good comes in your life without struggle.

Action Plan for Success

It is necessary to have an action plan to translate our aspirations and dreams. Such a plan must contain goals to achieve. We share some steps towards this process of success.

Step I: Dream a Vision and be Winner

Every one can succeed and be a winner. Success is a matter of choice and not chance or an accident. Our attitude determines a choice. All we need is self-improvement to gain a winning edge. Success is the progressive realisation of a worthy goal. Dream, ambition, inspiration are ingredients of success. Everyone can make a difference and the difference begins with dreaming. So visualise one's vision of one's future, we need to dream beyond what is possible within our ethical standards. We cannot succeed unless our primary concern is keeping hold on our integrity. Ethics can be an integral part of our ambition. There is no worthy success that is not ethically founded. Ethical ambition requires critical compassion and honesty towards ourselves and others.

Even one can re-cycle or transform one's personality. To be genius is to acquire ability to spark one's own fire. What one wants to be, it is his own choice. One has to choose an attitude which frees one from rut. The key to transformation and improvement is recognition of a need. To achieve this, it is important to redefine one's expectations from his side with determination one has to eradicate traps which are holding back self-development process.

Step II: Set Goals and Achieve

One great secret of success and achievement is creative visualisation of goals. Some say it is hard to acquire. On the contrary, it is quite easy. The first requisite is an open and receptive mind so that one is clear for further action. Goals are putting one's dream into practice. This is possible only when one changes one's beliefs and thought pattern. One has to dissolve one's self-made limitations. Positive and creative visualisation refers to accept the best and nothing short of it. There is second dimension to it, i.e. setting and pursuing goals for realisation. Another important factor is taking one's responsibility with a disciplined mind and inner energy. One has to plan one's goal which are challenging enough but realistic to achieve with due care and determination. Goals should be meaningful and consistent with our values. One must follow "SMART" rule while setting his goals:

S = Specific

M = Measurable

A = Achievable

R = Rational

T = Time-bound

Step III: Persistence and Perseverance is Vital

Success is an automatic result of hard work. Success is essentially a matter of concentration and perseverance. It's secret is a determination not to fail.

Nothing is impossible, problems and difficulties continue coming at all times. It is, therefore, essential to develop the right attitude towards them. Even failure enables one to a develop creative problem-solving approach for new possibilities. It strengthens one's resolve and confidence and drives one to face the future more optimistically. The right amount of effort in the right direction will surely produce that glorious thing called success. Success is result of consistent and regular work towards your goals.

Some setbacks and failures will strengthen one's resolve. Do not give up. The great failure is when one gives up trying, when he is just on the verge of success.

- Keep on—keep on—keep on.
- Never, never, never give up.
- Success comes to persistent person.

Step IV: Determination to Succeed

Success comes from within by control of one's mind. It is getting to think of ourselves as successful. Positive thinking is the key to success. One has to train one's mind for achievement of success. Develop a *passion* for success and achievement. Acquire the habit of being an optimist. Sincere efforts and performance pay in long-run. Excellence in performance brings feeling of achievement, pleasure and pride with humility in doing the best. Henry Thoreau has rightly said, "Men are born to succeed not to fail." Thus, faith in yourself and what you do is essential. For success, supreme secret is 'faith—"can do" attitude. Strengthening self-confidential is essential.

It is relevant to express this process as the ASAP model (See Figure below).

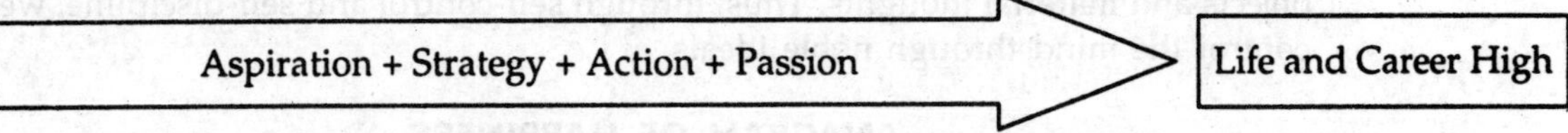

Step V: Have Faith in Actions and Results

May Lord's Grace help you, in thousand of ways, to attain success and prosperity in life. So have faith in Him and confidence in yourself. Think positive, talk positive, act positive. In fact, every thing depends on individual—to be successful and to be winner. Wish you good luck in your endeavours for meaningful career. Winner's mindset will bring you health, happiness and peace.

II. HAPPINESS

What is Happiness?

Is it?

- Riches and material comforts,
- Success in your endeavour,
- Love, affection, respect and reputation,
- More relationships and friends,
- Mental control, peace,
- Satisfaction, self-actualisation, self-fulfilment,
- Absence of sorrow, and
- Happiness wherever you get it, seek it.

According to Sabine Beecher, 'The key to happiness is in the way you think. One style of thinking leads to doubt and misery while another leads to self-acceptance and happiness." Happiness in not a commodity that can be bought from the market. It is not enjoyment in a pub or a pleasure trip to Singapore. These do give happiness, but are transitory. Happiness is rather a state of mind and a feeling of well-being. It is something that has to be earned.

Happiness is individual. It comes from within which is called internal upliftment or fulfilment. You are at peace-living. A life of peace and happiness is the goal of everyone.

Noble ideals and values are important for *peace of individual's mind.* Controlling of thoughts i.e. mind control brings peace and contentment. More we imbibe noble ideas and thoughts in our minds, we can purge out worldly objects and material thoughts. Thus, through self-control and self-discipline, we control the mind through noble ideals.

ANAGRAM OF HAPPINESS

H : Humanity, Health and Humour,

A : Appreciation and Acceptance,

P : Patience and Peace,

P : Persistence and Perseverance,

I : Initiative and Intuition,

N : Naturalness,

E : Empathy,

S : Simplicity and Satisfaction, and

S : Selflessness.

In order to get a complete understanding of the word Happiness, let us elaborate on each of the above words as explained by Z.V. Bhomisa.

Humanity, Health and Humour

Humanity means not only bestowing love on human beings but on everything that is created by God. Every small or big thing, like a bird, and insect or an animal is beautiful, having its own charm, intelligence, grace and uniqueness. Health is something that each and every individual desires to possess and maintain. Humour is another important factor which keeps a person bubbly and cheerful.

Appreciation and Acceptance

Majority of the people lack in this quality. They focus more on things which are not with them than those which are easily available like the abundance of sunlight and flowers. For example, parents with two daughters would strive to get a son rather than appreciate their two healthy and normal daughters. This leads to unhappiness for they are not contented with the things they have but are rather running after those they do not possess. People do not accept themselves the way they are. They constantly compare themselves with others and make themselves miserable. The way to happiness is to look constantly at the good about them.

Peace and Patience

These two words are extremely powerful in life. Very rarely do we find people who emanate peace and are patient. With industrialisation, people behave like machines working constantly and endlessly either to make ends meet or to make more dough than is needed. As a consequence they neither have peace of mind nor are they able to enjoy life. Why does one work hard? If the answer is to provide all the basic necessities for his loved ones, then the next question is 'where does it stop?' when the desire of a person is endless, he is stuck in a web where he has neither time for himself nor for his family which is needed for a happy and peaceful life.

Persistence and Perseverance

If happiness lies in achieving something in life, one should reach for it irrespective of the impediments or hardships put in one's way. One should be concerned with the end result, no matter what one undergoes. Few have fighting spirit within themselves. Many get disillusioned and leave the job halfway through. If one can develop the attitude to achieve one's target, one will feel happy and become strong and confident.

Initiative and Intuition

The belief that life is full of hardship depends on how one views life. It also depends on one's requirements. For some, it is easy going and happy while for others it may be tough and a constant struggle.

Naturalness

To be natural is not a simple thing. If one has to live in the society, one is to constantly put on false smile and try to please others in order to be in their good books. As a result, one loses one's own identity and tends to live an unauthentic life.

Empathy

Empathy is the power of entering into another personality and imaginatively experiencing his experience', it is one's willingness of putting oneself in the other person's shoes and understanding his problems just as he does. In other words, it is understanding the person you love which helps to build stronger relationships and greater appreciation for each other. This extremely important in maintaining a long-term and a happy relationship not only with your partner but also with all. If we are able to develop the quality of empathy within us, we are more likely to be satisfied and happy.

Simplicity and Satisfaction

There is an excellent phrase which is known to many of us. It is 'plain living and high thinking.' Most of us have forgotten its impact on life and have turned the entire phrase the other way round. Someone has mentioned a very brilliant phrase that states, "It is so simple to be happy but so difficult to be simple."

Selflessness

If out of every 100 people, even 10 people were to do selfless service like Mother Teresa, there would be more peace and happiness in the lives of our people.

To Conclude

Life is short, so live each day in a happy way and to the fullest, making use of each and every moment purposefully. It is very well mentioned, "Happiness lies in sowing and not in reaping."

Reference

Courtesy: The Mira, 23-12-2003). Z.V. Bhomisa, Better Life, Feb. 2004.

PART VI

ETHICAL VALUES

CHAPTER

29

VALUES

We will deal with the topic of values under following broad heads:

(i) Values, definition, characteristics, importance, types of values,

(ii) Personal values,

(iii) Formulation of values,

(iv) Managerial values,

(v) Corporate values,

(vi) Business values, and

(vii) Managing by values.

People at work have many opinions and preconceived notions in the form of values and attitudes. They often influence our behaviour. We have values about work, equality, authority, self-respect, freedom, honesty, obedience and other matters. These values provide the basic foundation for understanding a person's personality, perceptions and attitudes.

VALUES MEANING

Edward Spranger defines the values "as the constellation of likes, dislikes, viewpoints, inner inclinations, rational and irrational judgments, prejudices, and association patterns that determine a person's view of the world."

In other words, values represent basic convictions or enduring belief that "a specific mode of conduct or end-state of existence is personally or socially preferable to an opposite or converse mode of conduct or end-state of existence."

Values shape —> Beliefs —> Perceptions —> Attitudes —> Behaviour, Interests, Personality.

1. Features of Values

(i) Values are at the core of personality and are a *powerful force affecting behaviour.*

(ii) Values contain a *judgmental element* in that they carry an individual's ideas as to what is right, or desirable.

(iii) Values have both *content and intensity* attributes. The content attribute indicates that a mode of conduct or end-state of existence is important. The intensity attribute specifies how important it is.

(iv) Values are not fixed, but they *change over time.*

(v) Many values are relatively stable and enduring. This is because of the way in which they are originally learned.

(vi) All of us have a *hierarchy of values* that forms our value system. But everyone does not hold the same values.

2. Importance of Values

The study of values is fundamental to the understanding of managing and *organizational behaviour*. The value orientations of managers underlie managerial behaviour. Values are pervasive because they involve in the selection of missions, goals and objectives. The job of planning, organizing and controlling the behaviour of individuals should also be compatible with managers' values. Values lay the foundation for the understanding of attitudes, motivation and perceptions.

Fred E. Fiedler's theory of leadership effectiveness argues that managers cannot be expected to adopt a particular leadership style if it is contrary to their "need-structures" or value orientations. Moreover, managers' values are reflected in the evaluation of subordinates. Interpersonal activities of managers are based on different and contradictory values. Similarly, various managerial strategies and behavioural patterns are characterised by particular value orientations. Organisational conflicts can be solved by accommodating different values between managers and workers.

3. Types of Values

According to M. Rokeach (*The Nature of Human Values*, New York; Free Press, 1973) there are two types of values:

(i) *Instrumental values* are those values concerning the *way we approach* end states. These relate to *means* for achieving desired results. That is, do we believe in ambition, cleanliness, honesty or obedience, courage, etc. What factors guide our everyday behaviour?

(ii) *Terminal values* are those *end-state goals* that we praise such as comfortable life, a sense of accomplishment, equality among all people, self-respect, family security.

Both sets of values have significant influence on daily behaviour at work.

People are influenced by a wide variety of personal values. In fact, it has been argued that values represent a major influence on how we process information, how we feel about issues, and how we behave. Below are listed two sets of statements of personal values. The first list presents several instrumental values, while the second list presents several terminal values.

Instrumental Values

- Assertiveness; standing up for yourself
- Being helpful or caring toward others
- Dependability; being counted upon by others
- Education and intellectual pursuits
- Hard work and achievement
- Obedience; following the wishes of others
- Open-mindedness; receptivity to new ideas
- Self-sufficiency; independence
- Truthfulness; honesty
- Being well-mannered and courteous toward others

Terminal Values

- Happiness; satisfaction in life
- Knowledge and wisdom
- Peace and harmony in the world
- Pride in accomplishment
- Prosperity; wealth
- Lasting friendships
- Recognition from peers
- Salvation; finding eternal life
- Security; freedom from threat

According to Jones, E.E. and Gerard (1967) anything "for which the individual strives, or approaches, extols, embraces, voluntarily consumes, incurs expense to acquire is a positive value. Anything that the individual avoids, escapes from, deplores, rejects, or attacks is a negative value."

PERSONAL VALUES

Business leaders are surprised at the accusations of unethical behaviour of today's companies. Such as stock market manipulations, disregard of environmental hazards, bribes and kick-backs, adulteration. To understand this we must understand role of values and personal ethics.

Personal Values Serve Five Purposes in Organisations

1. Values Serve as Standards of Behaviour

Values serve as standards of behaviour for determining a correct course of action. Values place limits on our behaviour—ethical behaviour. Employees have to make decisions concerning what to them is right or wrong, proper or improper.

For example—Would you conceal information about a hazardous product made by your company, or would you feel obliged to tell someone? How would you respond to petty theft on the part of your supervisor? As individual, often determine for themselves what is proper and what is not, this is particularly true when people find themselves in "grey zone", where ethical standards are unclear. People have to determine their own standards of behaviour.

To some extent, ethical behaviour is influenced by societal values. Societal norms tell us it is wrong to engage in certain behaviour.

2. Guidelines for Decision-making and Conflict Resolution

Managers who value personal integrity are less likely to make decisions they know to be injurious to someone else. An interesting development in area of values and decision-making involves integrity or honesty tests.

3. Values Effect our Thoughts and Action

If the values are gracious, it consequently reflects in actions of the person—excellence brings forth excellent rewards. If values are not healthy, the quality of thoughts will be negative which only create sorrow and disaster.

4. Values Serve as an Influence on Employee Motivation and Influence Perceptions

Values affect employee motivation by determining what rewards are sought. Whether I prefer overtime work money or free time with family.

5. Values Generally Influence Attitude and Behaviour

For example, suppose you enter an organisation with view that allocating pay on the basis of performance is right, whereas allocating pay on the basis of seniority is wrong. How are you going to react if organisation rewards on seniority. You are likely to be disappointed and it can lead to job-dissatisfaction and you may not put high level effort. An employees performance and satisfaction are likely to be higher if his values fit well with organisation.

FORMULATION OF OUR VALUES

1. A significant portion is *genetically* determined say about 40 per cent.

2. *Environmental factors.* The rest is due to factors like culture, parental dictates, teachers, friends and similar environmental influences. In every culture certain values have developed over time such as in USA—achievement, equity and democracy, etc. as societal values. They change very slowly.

3. Values we hold are *established in our early years*—from parents, teachers and friends, etc.—on topics as education, sex and politics. For instance, we are taught that lying and stealing is always unacceptable. So values secure them firmly in our belief system.

As you grow old, *values may undergo change*. For example, in high school, if you join social club who believe that "every person should carry a gun", you change your values to align with club members. Even if it meant rejecting your parent's value that "only gang members carry guns and they are bad."

Figure on next page shows that a person's ethics are formulated through the operation of five key forces in the individual's environment: (i) family influences; (ii) peer influences; (iii) experiences; (iv) values and morals; and (v) situational factors (Griffin, 1990, pp. 809-10).

(i) Family Influences

The formulation of ethics begins when the individual is a small child. Thus, the family environment has significant influence in determining what the child learns about good and bad, right and wrong. Typically, when parents demonstrate high ethical standards, rewarding good behaviour and punishing bad behaviour, the child will adopt similar ethical standards.

(ii) Peer Influences

As the child develops contacts outside the home through school, play, and work, peers exert considerable influence on the individual's ethical beliefs. If the child makes friends that conduct themselves within high ethical standards, he

FIGURE

Determinants of Individual Ethics

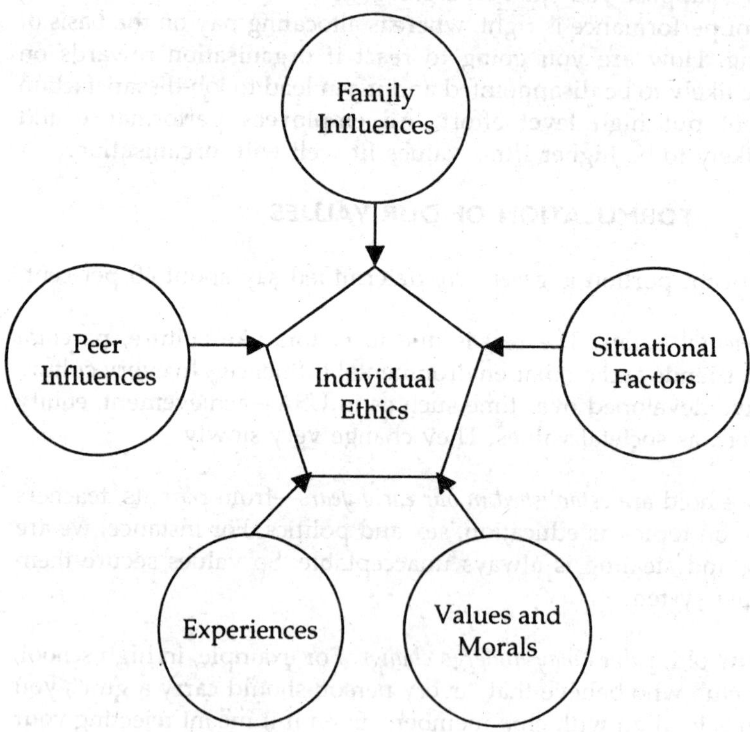

or she will come to adopt those same standards. On the other hand, if the child makes friends with peers who steal and use drugs, the child will probably accept those behaviours as being ethical.

(iii) Experiences

As a person matures and develops as a human being, he or she will be exposed to many critical experiences that will affect his or her ethical standards. If a person is punished or not appropriately rewarded for "good" behaviour, while others are seen as rewarded for "bad" behaviour, the person will probably alter both ethical standards and behavioural patterns.

(iv) Values and Morals

One's ethical standards are also greatly influenced by values and morals. People who place a high value on money and material possessions may not have strong ethical standards regarding behaviours that facilitate the accumulation of that wealth. People who value the quality of life enjoyed by all living creatures will probably have strong ethics with respect to the proper treatment of others.

(v) Situational Factors

People often change their ethics in response to unforeseen situational factors. An employee, who is threatened with losing a job that has been held for years, may commit unethical acts in order to save the job. A father with a sick child might use the threat of physical violence to secure treatment for the child at an understaffed clinic.

VALUES OF WORKFORCE

(a) Old Values of Work Life

Hard work, conservative, loyalty to the employer organisation.

(b) Present Values of Workforce

Job satisfaction, leisure time, loyalty to relationships, flexibility, success and achievement, ambition, loyalty to career.

They consider the ethical implications of their actions on others around them.

(c) Negative and Positive Personal Values

Personal values denote a sense of right or wrong, good or bad and other judgemental criteria based on our strong sense of what the ideal ought to be.

(i) Negative Values

- Anger
- Meanness
- Arrogance
- Crookedness
- Greed
- Lust

They generate negative thoughts.

(ii) Positive Values

- Integrity, honesty
- Truthfulness
- Kind heartedness, humility

- Friendliness
- Faith
- Self-respect
- Open mindedness
- Creativity
- Civil sense
- Simplicity
- Forgiveness
- Poise
- Detachment, etc.

They generate positive thoughts.

MANAGERIAL VALUES

1. *Managerial leadership values* are people's enduring beliefs regarding how they wish the leaders of their organisations *to conduct themselves ideally*. A core component of a managerial leadership philosophy consists of the values the organisation wishes its leaders at all levels to live out. Major organisations like Hewlett-Packard have defined clear codes of values that serve as a selection criteria and a foundation of the training and development. Their leaders receive, and provide guides to their behaviour.

2. *Preferred leadership values.* We share here the findings of a study regarding "Preferred Leadership Values" in a Wisconsin's (USA) organisation done in March, 2000. This study covered 518 respondents. The questionnaire contained 20 value statements for which rankings of values was to be given by executives from all functional areas of the organisation. A copy of questionnaire administered is attached which gives us idea of the managerial values.

The managerial values which emerged as most preferred are given in table below:

(a) Values that Emerged as Most Preferred

Ranking	*Value*	*Average*
1	Honest (trustworthy, truthful, reliable)	5.50
2	Competent (capable, qualified, skillful, effective)	5.41
3	Fair-minded (just, objective, unbiased)	4.70

4 Broad-minded (open, flexible, receptive)	4.67
5 Dependable (reliable, conscientious)	4.60
6 Supportive (helpful, championing, comforting)	4.42
7 Forward-looking (visionary, future-oriented)	4.37

(b) Do these Value Preferences go together? Yes.

Values	*Rank*	*Label*
Dependable + Honest	1	Good citizen
Fair-minded + Straight-forward	2	Open-minded
Supportive + Caring + Cooperative	3	Socially supportive
Broad-minded + Forward-looking + Imaginative + Inspiring	4	Visionary
Competent + Intelligent + Mature + Self-controlled	5	Emotionally stable
Ambitious + Dedicated	6	Career-minded

(c) The following, although all important, were rated as Least Preferred.

Ranking	*Values*	*Average*
20	Courageous (brave, bold, daring)	2.38
19	Independent (self-reliant, autonomous, original)	2.75
18	Ambitious (aspiring, eager, venturesome)	2.77
17	Mature (seasoned, experienced, wise)	3.22
16	Loyal (faithful, constant, steadfast)	3.51
15	Self-controlled (emotionally even, self-disciplined)	3.53
14	Imaginative (creative, innovative, inventive)	3.69

This study thus provide the managerial leadership values as general guides to appropriate leadership behaviour in dealing with their various stakeholders.

3. *Changing Managerial Values.* The organization must be a dynamic entity as it operates in changing environments. As the needs of its members change, managerial philosophies and values must change. Table below summarizes the major trends that are occurring in managerial values.

The Transition of Managerial Values

Away from . . .	*Towards . . .*
1. A view of people as essentially bad.	A view of people as basically good.
2. Avoidance or negative evolution of individuals.	Confirming individuals as human beings.
3. A view of individuals as fixed.	Seeing individuals as being in process.
4. Resisting and fearing individual differences.	Accepting and utilizing individual differences.
5. Utilizing an individual primarily with reference to the job description.	Viewing an individual as a whole person.
6. Walling off the expression of feelings.	Making possible both appropriate expression and effective use of feelings.
7. Maskmanship and game playing.	Authentic behaviour.
8. Use of status for maintaining power and personal prestige.	Use of status for organizationally relevant purposes.
9. Distrusting people.	Trusting people.
10. Avoiding facing others with relevant data.	Making appropriate confrontation.
11. Avoidance of risk taking.	Willingness to risk-taking.
12. A view of process work as being unproductive effort.	Seeing process work as essential to effective task accomplishment.
13. A primary emphasis on competition.	A much greater emphasis on collaboration.

CORPORATE VALUES

Many management theorists stress that companies must operate according to values that guide the thinking and behaviour of people in an organisation. But what should those values be? Rom Lebow, former director of marketing communications at Microsoft, and William L. Simon offer an important set of values for successful organisation.

People and Business Values

They introduce ten fundamental shared values. The ten shared values are:

Truth:	Treat others with uncompromising truth
Trust:	Lavish trust on your associates
Mentoring:	Mentor unselfishly
Openness:	Be receptive to new ideas
Giving Credit:	Give credit where it is due
Risk-taking:	Take personal risks for the good of the organisation
Honesty:	Be honest in all dealings, do not touch dishonest money
Caring:	Put the interests of others before your own Social conscience.

Responsibility and accountability

These are the people values that guide employee behaviour, specifically how they deal with each other. They represent the first step in creating a positive and productive work environment. In addition to adopting people values, a company must also develop its *business values*. These values guide what people do every day to be successful in the market place. Unlike people values, business values change from organisation to organisation. But they should all share certain characteristics. They should be aspirational, quantifiable, and controllable. They must affect everything in the organisation, not just part of it.

BUSINESS VALUES

Business in India is passing through turbulent times as there is lot of concern for business survival and growth due to various factors such as global and domestic competition of MNCs, ecological and environmental degradation, need for balancing multiple stakeholders' expectations, etc.

In view of the above circumstances, it is appropriate to mention the business values enunciated by a management thinker of international repute. Dr. M.B. Athreya, Advisor, Indian Industry and former professor at the London, Scotish Business School and IMM, Calcutta (article, "Business Values for the 21st Century"):

"(i) *Righteousness (Dharma)*: It is important for business to follow 'Dharma' in the creation and sharing of wealth; maintaining the highest standards of ethics and integrity in every action we take.

(ii) *Public Good (Loka Sangraha)*: Another important value is that individuals and organisations should work not just for private gain, but also for well-being of community/public good including external and internal stakeholders.

(iii) *Efficacy (Kauslam)*: It is critical that all businesses persue efficiency, productivity resource optimisation and conserve rsources so as to internalise the value of efficacy in the best interest of preserving mother earth for future generations.

(iv) *Innovation (Vivdata)*: Business has to be engine of innovation, constantly seeking more effective solutions to meet economic and social expectations.

(v) *Learning (Jigasa)*: Business will be the key instrument to solve the problems of growth, employment, eduction, consumption, information, entertainment and quality of life. Business will have to keep learning from the feedback. Loop from society and also through internal process of question, challenge, search, debates, sharing, training, monitoring, etc. The viability and health of nations and global society will depend on the skills of learning and utilisation of such learning by business. To put it in Senge's words the "Concept of Learning Organisation."

(vi) Learned Prof. M.B. Athreya adds other Business Values as "*respect for individual and human dignity*. These will increase creativity and team play."

(vii) *Dharmayudh*. We expect business to be aggressive, competitive, with lot of initiative, creating wealth, and, therefore, our philosophy talks about Dharmayudh. Yudh is necessary, but it has to be Dharmayudh. Translated into business that would mean that to the *marketing sales*. Your role is not lose your market share, but to increase market share. And for that whatever needs to be done you can do. But we can learn to be sure if that is not done ethically, in the long-run, it is going to erode business.

MANAGING BY VALUES

In a book that Ken Blanchard has co-authored with Michael O'Connor entitled, "Managing by Values", has highlighted that where there is alignment between core values and common practices, profitably will directly follow. We reproduce Ken Blanchard's "Three Precepts" (*Executive Excellence*, July 2001).

"To define, communicate, and align your values with your practices. Unless values are prioritized, you have nothing but situational ethics where anything goes."

(a) Identifying Core Values

Many companies claim that have a set of core values, but what they mean is a list of business beliefs that everyone would agree with, such as having integrity, making a profit, and responding to customers. Such values have meaning only when they are further defined in terms of how people actually behave and are rank-ordered to reveal priority.

For example, Disney's four core values are: safety, courtesy, the show (performing your particular role well), and efficiency. If these values aren't carefully ordered, people are left to their own devices. For example, a bottom line-oriented manager might overemphasize efficiency and thus jeopardize the three higher-ranking values.

Fortunate 500 companies first emphasize the beliefs, attitudes, and feelings that top management have about employees, customers, quality, ethics, integrity, social responsibility, growth, stability, innovation, and flexibility. Organizations today must know what they stand for and on what principles they operate. Value-based behaviour is a requisite for survival. Once you have a clear picture of your mission and values, you have a basis for evaluating your management practices and bringing them into alignment.

Ethics means doing the right thing by being honest, acting in a legally and socially responsible manner, being fair in our treatment of others, and acting in ways that result in feeling good about ourselves and our company.

(b) Communicating Core Values

Make sure that your values are evident to all stakeholders—employees, customers, suppliers, stock-holders, and the community. Involve employees in decisions that affect them—or better yet— whenever possible let them make the decisions.

(c) Aligning Values and Practices

Once your values have been broadly communicated, you need to assess how well these values are practiced. To be effective, values and strategies need to unite the energies of all people, especially those dealing with the company's various publics. Without some way of identifying gaps between values and behaviour, a set of core values is nothing more than a wish list.

In Fortunate 500 companies, the behaviour of the leaders is aligned with corporate values. Management "walks its talk." For example, if executives indicate that they value innovation and flexibility but then have an authoritarian-based bureaucracy, there is an alignment problem.

Or, if executives say that they value the full development of people's potential but then have a performance review system that forces managers to rate people on a normal distribution curve, again there is an alignment problem. Misalignment between values and practices creates an energy drain that sabotages productive behaviour. Alignment liberates energy and empowers people to act congruently. That makes for loyal customers and employees and a productive environment.

Closing the Values Gap

In using our values, we have to make some hard decisions that may not, in the short-run, enhance our bottom line. And yet, since ethics and relationships are our first two values, we would not be walking our talk if we acted as if we were only in business to make money.

ANNEXURE

QUESTIONNAIRE

Preferred Leadership Values

First, find the one value that you believe is most important and place its number under the column 7 below.

Next, find one value that you believe is least important and place its number under the column 1 below.

Proceed to column 6 and place in it the number of the two values that you believe are the next most important.

Go then to column 2 and select the two that you believe are the next least important.

Proceed in this fashion until you have accounted for all the 20 values.

1. Ambitious (aspiring, eager, venturous)
2. Broad-minded (open, flexible, receptive)
3. Caring (appreciative, compassionate, concerned)
4. Competent (capable, qualified, skillful, effective)
5. Cooperative (helping, hospitable, companionable)
6. Courageous (brave, bold, daring)
7. Dependable (reliable, conscientious)
8. Dedicated (devoted, resolute, persistent)
9. Fair-minded (just, objective, unbiased)
10. Forward-looking (visionary, future-oriented)
11. Honest (trustworthy, truthful, reliable)
12. Imaginative (creative, innovative, inventive)
13. Independent (self-reliant, autonomous, original)
14. Inspiring (enthusiastic, influential)
15. Intelligent (sharp, keen, acute, clever, ingenious)
16. Loyal (faithful, constant, steadfast)
17. Mature (seasoned, experienced, wise)
18. Self-controlled (emotionally even, self-disciplined)
19. Straight-forward (direct, candid, forthright)
20. Supportive (helpful, championing, comforting)

1 (least important)						7 (most important)

CHAPTER

30

Decline in Ethics— Should We Compromise with Our Ethics and Values?

Did a decline in Business Ethics set in sometime in the late 1970's? The issue is debatable. Nevertheless, a lot of people think so.

For decline in ethical standards, we should look to our *four stage model of values* for explanation.

Managers report that actions of their bosses are most important factor influencing ethical and unethical behaviour of their organisations. Given this fact, the values of those in middle and upper management should have a significant bearing on the entire ethical climate within an organisation.

Four Stages of Values

(i) Through mid-1970's, the managerial ranks dominated by protestant work ethic type (Stage I) whose loyalties were to their employer. When faced with dilemmas, their decisions were made what was best for the organisation.

(ii) In late 1970s, individuals with existential values (Stage II) begin to rise into upper levels of management.

(iii) They were soon followed by pragmatic types (Stage III). *By late 1980s*, a large portion of middle and top management positions in business organisations were held by people from Stages II and III.

The loyalty of existentials and pragmatic are to self and careers respectively. Their focus is inward and their primary concern is with "looking out for number 1." Such self-centred values would be consistent with a decline in ethical standards. This is the explanation.

(iv) The potential good news in this analysis is that recent entrants to the work force, and tomorrow's managers, appear to be *less self-centred*. Since their *loyalty is to relationships*, they are more likely to consider the ethical implications of their actions on others around them. Stage (IV) the result? We may look forward to an uplifting of ethical standards in business over the next decade or two merely as a result of changing values within the managerial ranks.

Well young managers, we trust, you will clear up the mess we have created. You are custodian of the country.

DOMINANT VALUES IN TODAY'S WORKFORCE

(Societal values in the period in which they grew-up can be a valuable aid in explaining and predicting behaviour)

Stage	*Period entered the workforce*	*Approximate current age*	*Dominant work values*
I. Pretestant work ethic	*Mid-1940s to late 1950s* during World War II, Berlin blockade	60-80 More conservative	Hard work, conservative, loyalty to organisation.
II. Hippie Ethics (Existential) Civil Rights Movement	*1960s to Mid-1970s* • Influenced by John Kennedy • Civil rights movements • Beatles • Vietnam War • Baby Boom.	45-60	More concerned by quality of their lives, non-conforming, seek autonomy, loyalty to self-rather than organisation.
III. Pragmatic (Conservatism)	*Mid-1970s to late 1980s* • Influenced by Regan conservatism, defence build-up, dual career, households.	35-45 Conservative	Ends can justify the means. Success. Achievement. Ambition. Hard work. Loyalty to career. Social recognition. (Rank high.)
IV. Generation X	*1990s to present* Lives shaped by globalisation, economic stagnation, fall of communism, aids, and computers	under 35	Value-flexibility Achievement of job satisfaction. Loyalty to family and relationships. Leisure time more important. Pleasure. Less willing to make personal sacrifices for sake of employer.

Should we Compromise with our Ethics and Values?

We all feel the erosion of our spirits: the degeneration of our values, a slow, but steady loss of character. While it seems that most individuals cannot even identify the cause, society as a whole already has—a lack of ethics.

There is an increased awareness about a lack of ethics. This word inspires talk about a certain kind of moral degradation. An increased lack of principles in our society. An almost non-existence of integrity in the corporate.

There is a *lack of integrity* in some managements these days. This could be because of the difference in the way things are and the way things we were taught were meant to be.

A general misconception is that character is evaluated only on the personal front. Cheating with your spouse, lying to your friends and family, duping them are the main parameters where a man's integrity is tested. What we fail to see or integrate into this mental mapping exercise is that character is tested on the professional front not just by refusing bribes or indulging in illegal activities but also by the decisions taken on any regular day. We may cover up our ethical dilemmas by diplomacy, thinking about what's best for the organisation or renaming retrenchment policies by calling it relocation of employees.

The fact is we do things that we personally do not like. The fact that we do it is a professional requirement. This is the conflict zone. However, an increasingly large number of corporate houses have now begun to realise the need to create a more relaxed, honest, fulfilling environment.

J. Patel observes that conflict is a part of life. The key lies in making the right choice. One lie gives birth to a hundred others. Doing things the right ensures mental peace and happiness in the longer-run.

The answer lies with us

In fact, the evidence suggests that the world at large is not full of crooks. It's just a little overcrowded with petty souls. We, too, have been such a character. Blame it on the system, but most of us survive by toeing the line. By doing the petty act that slowly steals away our soul. It's just that we've all collectively quit thinking about issues of integrity and honesty. We just don't seem to give it much thought. We continue to work in a human system that doesn't provide a support structure for a simpler, more honest existence. We continue to survive in organisations that passively or actively encourage us to compromise.

The ways of the World are being questioned. When the Dalai Lama won the Nobel Peace Prize, an exclusive dinner party was hosted in Newport Beach where a group of high-level American business leaders met Dalai Lama. The most often asked question that night by these true moguls of industry was, "How can we introduce more ethics and spirituality into our business and everyday lives?" The answer from His Holiness was gentle and interesting, "Do it from the heart, within your own culture."

The Quest—Look Inward

And the answer to this question has almost become a quest with many corporate leaders. There seems to be a new kind of enlightenment with managers all over the world. Various new management theories seem to be addressing a vast number of issues under the guise of Ethical Management, Dharmic Management. All designed to go beyond the regular concerns of task and structure. These seem to be addressing the more poignant questions relating to the human spirit. The world seems to be waking up, albeit slowly, to the fusion of spirit, character, human values and decency in the work place and in life.

The usual issues of productivity, organization, costs, profits and so forth will remain as critical as ever. Except, the concern about the humanness and health of the organisation including things such as culture, communication, relationships and morals are beginning to get equal importance.

R.K. Chakraborty states that we do not need to compromise. If we are right, no one can take advantage of us. The fear of doing something wrong results in making compromises with one's ethics and values.

Radhika Sachev states that an article carried in the January 2000 issue of *Harvard Business Review* in "The Making of Corporate Athlete" by Loehr and Schwarz, the two authors attempted to identify factors that make some managers flourish under pressure, while others wilt. Eventually, they concluded that the former have a strong spiritual fibre that enables them to move from the physical to the emotional and mental and finally the spiritual plane.

Spiritualism does not prohibit acquisition or enjoyment of material comforts of modern life but at the same time it puts a break on unhealthy, undesirable desires and wants. In simple terms it allows people to shape the life styles in conformity with our inherent value systems based on certain moral and ethical values and principles.

"Material life and spirituality are not two different things. They are not contradictory. In fact, they are two sides of the same coin. One air-conditions the outside world and the other air-conditions the inside world—mind: keeping it cool and balanced in all situations, whether they are easy or difficult, pleasant or painful. Spirituality teaches you how to live in this world."

References

It is an abstract of article titled, "Ethic Centricity" from *Training and Management*, Feb. 2002: 39. Gratefully acknowledged.

Radhica Sachdev, *HT Careers*, New Delhi, 26 September 2002.

CHAPTER

31

WORK ETHICS

MEANING OF WORK ETHICS

"Ethics" means a set of *moral principles*—A code of conduct. In any social set-up, the members of a group tend to adopt a set of *rules of behaviour for the establishment of good order*.

Such rules may be or may not be codified, but so long as they have the acceptance of the members of the group, they tend to be observed.

Work ethics refers to certain accepted *norms of behaviour* governing the conduct of a group of persons involved in work-situation to achieve certain desired objectives.

In some business organisations, such rules are codified and represent the "Do's and Don'ts", meant to be observed by the staff. For example:

Do's—Requiring members to do things that are morally good or right, e.g. punctuality, courtesy, efficiency, hard-work, sincerity, devotion to duty, regularity, discipline, promptness, enterprise, initiative, etc.

Don'ts—Seek to restrain the employees from doing things that are morally bad or wrong, e.g. insubordination, lethargy and indolence, corruption, dishonety, etc.

Work ethics is thus a part of moral philosophy.

DEFINITION OF WORK ETHICS

A work ethics can be defined at different levels:

(i) At the *basic level* it is about discipline, namely, coming to work on time, behaving with respect and dignity in relation to subordinates, colleagues and superiors, staying at work place during working hours, not wasting time by roaming and chattering, etc. There is strong *work orientation*.

(ii) At the *highest level*, work ethics is about commitment and *accountability*. Does manager feel responsible for the task assigned to him and does he complete in time and in satisfactory way.

(iii) *Another aspect* of work ethics is *protecting the interests* of the organisation by employees. Avoiding negative comments in public.

(iv) To *perform one's job* with devotion and perfection (Gita).

(v) Simply put, work ethics refers to the *strength of one's commitment and dedication to hard work*. It is employee's attitude. Americans work hard. Japanese work harder or too hard.

A professional manager describes work ethics as under:

"Work ethics embraces work responsibility, work conscience, ethical work conduct. If one has the satisfaction that he is *contributing* his very best to his organisation and is not just earning the bread, then this would be the true feeling of work ethics. Work ethics demands that one works for attaining organisational objectives in its fullest measure.

FOUR P's OF WORK ETHICS AND INDIVIDUAL ATTITUDE TO WORK

To explain it more explicitly, a person joining any work organisation does so under a "Contract"—that he will be entitled to receive or take from organisation, a package of compensation against what he gives to the organisation by way of physical and mental efforts leading to concrete tangible results.

Compliance with this *Contractual obligation* and *fulfilling this commitment* which he has made to his employer—organisation by entering into "work contract" is the crux of work ethics, that must honour.

In order to fulfil his obligations and commitment, he has to exhibit certain attitudes, apply certain skills to the desired levels of excellence. He has to translate certain desirable habits, such as, regularity, punctuality, discipline, promptness, initiative and so on. All these together, contribute an ethical value system, which every employee must follow.

However, organisational atmosphere presents a picture of anti-work ethics or absence of work ethics.

People seem to be obsessed with only 3 P's, viz. *Pay, Prospects,* and *Promotion* and forgetting the 4th viz. *Performance*—which is so fundamental to the concept of work ethics.

Thus, Central to Theme of Work Ethics is the Individual and his Attitude to Work

We give examples of poor work ethics. *Few Illustrations*: We are faced with numerous problems like—sub-standard performance, wasteful and restrictive practices by trade unions, apathy towards punctuality, quality of work, passing the buck, etc.

A Japanese visitor to India was impressed by widespread use of wrist watches by our people and remarked to his Indian friend that while every one here sported a watch, but no one is punctual and watch appears to be status symbol than useful instrument of punctuality.

We have aped western life style and habits. One common being calling our seniors by their first names. Fostering so intimate relationship with Boss has affected our work ethics adversely. Employees refuse to accomplish task and take advantage of intimacy. They show undisciplined behaviour, arrogance and irregular habits. All leading to bad work ethics. This does not happen in western culture calling first name is quite natural in their society.

IMPROVING WORK ETHICS

1. Solution to the problem of work ethics does not lie merely in spelling out in impressive codes of conduct. Let us not forget Swami Vivekananda's warning that man cannot be made moral by an act of parliament. The only way to change a man for the better character is through *imparting, man-making education*, i.e. education by which *character is formed, strength of mind is increased* and by which one can *stand on one's own feet* and not merely collect some degrees.

2. Other *Indian approaches* for improving work ethics are:

(a) Employer should love his employees. Loving does not mean refraining from punishing the guilty, inefficient and corrupt employees.

(b) To cultivate the attitude of sport or "Lila" towards work.

(c) Inculcating among employees shifting mindset from "taking" to "giving modes." We always look at what I am getting benefits from the organisation. We forget what we have to contribute. Change our attitude from "Begger's mode" to "Achiever's mode."

(d) "To work like a master and not like a slave." Swami Vivekananda further emphasises that 99% of us work like slave and this results in misery. It is all selfish work. We should work through freedom, work through love. To view work as an act of love and freedom, which can bring about a revolution in one's attitude towards work ethic. It is a case of tiger cubs believing themselves as to be lambs. How we can contribute as leader in work if we degenerate as slaves.

(e) Renunciation and service are twin ideals rest will take care of itself (Gita).

3. Organisations can *create strong work culture* through appropriate systems, as well as rewards and penalties. For example, in same building there are offices of private companies, government offices and public sector undertaking. Government work culture is highly undisciplined—people come to work at will, stay away from work. Productivity is poor. Parks around building are full with employees playing cards. On the other hand, if same person joins private employer, he puts in greater effort. It is ethos of government that is at fault. Number of holidays in government offices are numerous.

If work discipline in terms of *time and staying at work place* becomes mandatory and subject of penalties for non-compliance, we will quickly change culture. Top persons in organisations have to set examples.

4. Further, *commitment, accountability and taking responsibility* can be inculcated through various practices such as role clarity, performance evaluations to be objective, etc. for creating organisation discipline.

5. *Protecting the organisation from loose talk comes as a result of pride in the organisation.* This pride can be inculcated through good internal communications, such as to fully inform employees about company programmes. Work ethics can be created and nurtured among employees. Managerial action is required to achieve it.

6. *Involvement of employees* so that work is kept challenging, more satisfying and rewarding for individuals. It is productive.

7. *Developing an Attitude in Work.* It is relevant here to quote S.K. Chakraborty ("Human Values in Organisations—an Attitudinal Exploration of Values", in *Human Values for Managers,* Wheeler Publishing) that broadly, it is possible to *develop an attitude in work* situations on the following lines:

- I am blessed in this situation because, compared to millions of unemployed and underemployed, I have the *opportunity of working* in this position and enjoying relatively greater benefits and a better working environment.

- For whatever the organization has given me and done for me, I am grateful, and whatever *I do in return can never adequately compensate for them*.
- While it is my *duty to help my subordinates and peers* in enabling them to do their best for the overall welfare of the organization, it is not my business to sit in judgement over their actions, nor to take on the responsibility of reforming them to conform to what I think is right.
- The *Law of Karma* ensures a perfect balance between what I give to others and what I receive from them, no matter whether it is a mere thought/action/attitude, favourable or unfavourable, material or non-material. So, there is no reason for me either to feel depressed when PTE do not respond favourably to what I have done, or feel elated when my expectations come true.
- All those who work with me are essentially *different forms of my own true Self* and, therefore, I cannot injure others without in effect injuring my own Self, nor can I help them without in effect helping myself.
- If another person shows a negative attitude towards me, the real cause for that lies in myself and not in that person. It is infinitely more fruitful to *undergo introspection* to find and root out the negative attitude in my conduct.
- If I *discharge my duties properly, my rights will automatically be fulfilled*, sooner or later. It is the divine law. It is the law of Karma. It is the time-tested and confirmed theory of retribution and reward.

FUNCTIONS OF WORK, WHY IS WORK IMPORTANT TO INDIVIDUALS?

What Functions does Work Serve?

Some advantages from work are:

(i) First, work serves *economic function* in exchange for work we receive income to support self and family. It provides economic self-sufficiency.

(ii) Second, work serves several *social functions*. The work place provides opportunities for meeting new people and develop friends and source of social interchange.

(iii) Third, work provides a source of *social status* in community. One's occupation gives importance to an individual in society. It serves as a source of social differentiation and also a source of social integration.

(iv) Fourth, work is an important *source of identify and self-esteem* and it is a means for self-actualisation. It provides a *sense of purpose* and clarify their contribution to society. Work shows employees mastery or competence in their job. It also reassures that they are of value to others.

(v) *Without work*, individual's experience *meaninglessness and powerlessness.*

(vi) It will be relevant to quote Sorab Sadri (*Business Ethics*, McGraw Hill) what he calls as new work ethics:

- "Man is the *author* of his work.
- It is through work that man elect to *identify* and nurture his talents.
- Work can *neither* be goalless nor motiveless.
- It is the integrity and honesty with which a man *executes a role* that distinguishes him from others.
- In work, the mind of man should merge knowledge, faith, contemplation and action.
- Fundamentally, *work is the manifestation of man* himself.
- It is the nature of man to work, as it is the nature of the sun to radiate.
- To deny man of work unjustly, therefore, is *to deny him of the opportunity to manifest himself.*
- Ultimately, when work ethics are redefined, it is really man who is being redefined; for both work and ethics relate to man."

DIFFERENT VIEWS ON WORK

- Max-Weber's—Protestant ethics, i.e. hard work, conservative, loyalty to organisation.
- Argyris, McGregor and Brown feel that work is basically a pleasant activity—it is driving force which gives direction and meaning to one's life.
- Another view is that work is an escape from hunger, boredom and illness.
- Like the Greeks, the Hebrews too regard work as drudgery.
- According to Freud, "work is an unpleasant activity."
- Bhagwat Gita advocates an entirely new philosophy to work. While *Vedas* preached the ethics of desires.

The Upanishads advocated an ethics based on pure knowledge, but Gita based itself not only on the elements of "desires" and "knowledge" in human nature, but also on third element in it, "activity."

Here the call is to act, "Act in the living present"—*Karma Yoga. Karma* means action, duty or work done not with selfish motive, but with the object of serving humanity. A man's primary duty is to perform the job allocated to him with devotion and perfection. Only then he can hope to achieve salvation.

Thus, Gita gives new dignity to work. Work is not unpleasant activity or some sort of punishment, but a way of life ordained by the Lord.

Work is something inherent in the nature of people. McGregor says the same thing. The Gita preaches the *mantra* of *Karma Yogi.* It preaches devotion to duty, to one's calling regardless of it's consequences.

Work is not only necessary to keep the body and mind occupied, it is necessary for perfection.

No work is inferior. All men who work have to be treated with dignity. Work is an end in itself according to Gita. Work is worship.

Human relations is a passion with Gita. The Lord sets a unique example in human relations by acting as the charioteer of Arjuna. He wanted to emphasize that no job was low or high. Besides he wanted to establish that a leader has to serve the masses. A leader is not the master but the servant of the people.

CHAPTER

32

WORK CULTURE

BENEFITS OF GOOD WORK CULTURE

Good work culture enhances productivity and quality (in contrast to size of investment as in west).

Ensures utilisation of resources effectively.

Ensures proper work environment, worker development.

Essential for developing a country.

Definition

Culture is defined as values which get manifested in behaviour of employees at work place such as values of hard work, loyalty to organisation, quality of work life, success, achievement, job satisfaction, etc.

FACTORS HINDERING DEVELOPMENT OF WORK CULTURE

1. Lack of sense of discipline and minimum work ethos.
2. Lack of hard work and commitment.
3. Too many holidays, *bandhs*, processions, etc. Thus, resulting less work hours.
4. Wasting of resources—material, energy, etc.
5. Least concern for time and projects over-run/costs.
6. Too much control and regulations.

7. Unhealthy worker-management relations.
8. Poor working conditions.
9. Absence of spirit of nationalism.
10. Bureaucratisation and political interference.
11. Trade Union anti-work activities.
12. Poor quality of service.
13. Absenteeism.
14. Accidents/injuries.

APPROACHES TO DEVELOPING WORK CULTURE

1. Shared feeling and commitment of management and employees.
2. Mutual trust and confidence, maintaining trusting relationship and communication with employees. Avoid grape wine and develop shared vision.
3. Appreciation and perception of employees needs and aspirations and acceptance of management objectives by employees.
4. Ensuring employee involvement, worker's participation in management, recognition to avoid dissatisfaction syndrome.
5. Introducing decentralisation and functional autonomy.
6. Developmental role of trade unions, unions to accept challenge to make their organisation a highly productive and meet competition. Unions to concentrate in social, environmental and of life issues of employees.
7. Development of people (concern for QWL).
8. Making work more interesting and challenging and incorporating responsibility—through job enrichment, job rotation, job enlargement.
9. Quality control by worker themselves and not left to inspection.
10. Minimising supervision but encourage empowerment/delegation.
11. Conducive work environment:
    - Physical situation
    - Machinery
    - Colleagues
    - Style of supervision

- Human creativity.

12. Inculcating work discipline.
13. Equitable wage structure/human centred management.
14. Positive attitude to improving productivity:
    - Increased output with same input/less input.
    - Better utilisation of resources—men, machines, materials.
    - Organisation to unearth existing attitudes through diagnostic survey. Example—*Employees identified with company.*

      Co. A 19%

      Co. B 71%. It is at advantage to move towards productive culture.
15. Accepting responsibility for improving one-self.
16. Having a problem-finding attitude.
17. Individual's attitude of working and the reward will follow, constructive and cooperative attitude.
18. Thinking creatively and innovatively to find solutions to problems.
19. Grasping opportunities for business.
20. Training for workers to include:
    - Business and product awareness.
    - Customer service.
    - What employees can do to satisfy the market customers.
    - Explain concepts of production and productivity.
    - Develop job performance skills.

WORK CULTURE—UNION AND MANAGEMENT

Both management and union must come together to establish a most coordial atmosphere and each must accept their responsibility to make their own organisation highly efficient, customer friendly and profitable unit.

CHAPTER

33

Ethical Theories

EVOLUTION OF ETHICAL THEORIES

According to Jack Griffin in his article on "Development of Ethics and Ethical Theory" he has mentioned that "there are three periods in history of ethics such as Greek period (500 BC-AD 500), the medieval period (AD 500-AD 1500), and modern period (AD 1500 onwards).

1. Greek Ethics

In this period the man who performed his *duties* as a citizen was regarded as good man. When an individual realizes that his conscience shows to him the rightness of same action, which other people regard as wrong, his reflection is likely to lead him to the fundamental problem of ethics. What is in an action that makes it right or wrong or what standard or test by which we discriminate good or bad actions. According to Greeks, *"Man is the measure of all things."* He decides for himself what is right and what is wrong and there is no other standard.

Socrates, Plato and Aristotle emphasised the need and importance of understanding the nature of goodness. The Stoics emphasised that *goodness is natural to man*, for the laws of morality are the laws of nature, perfectly rational and so comprehensible to human reason.

2. Medieval Ethics

More attention was given to the *inner aspect of morality* because of the spread of Christianity in Europe. It had changed the previous view of Greeks that ethics is a part of politics, but on the other hand, it encouraged to increase inner aspect of morality. But middle age did not encourage moral speculation and consequent development of ethical theory. The standard of right and wrong was according to *God's law in the Bible* and it was against any doubts.

3. Modern Ethics

Individualism crept over priest's preaching and church's principle. Human freedom and human accomplishment were given more importance than Christian revelation. According to some thinkers, the difference between right and wrong was merely subjective, depending upon the *attitude of the individual* making moral judgement.

There are different ethical theories or ethical frameworks in this period with which to approach ethical decisions.

(i) Relativistic Ethics

This states that moral stand varies with different circumstances. According to Joseph H. Boyett and Jimmie T. Boyett (The Guru Guide to Knowledge Economy) "the proponents of relativism hold that we cannot decide on matters of right and wrong, or good and evil. Things are rarely black or white—there are so many shades of grey. Relativism proposes that ethics are *"relative" to the personal, social and cultural circumstances in which one finds oneself.* Relativists are torn by ethical dilemmas, since they do not believe that truth can be discovered by soul searching. Professor teach relativism so that students guard against it.

Relativism holds that *every person has his own standard that enables him to make choices.* No one can make a moral judgement about another person's behaviour. So many variables affect behaviour that an outsider cannot possibly be privy to all the elements that went into making a decision. For example, role relativism distinguishes between own private selves and our public roles. The public roles call for a 'special' morality, which we separate from individual making the choices. The president of a fishing company may personally dislike the incidental killing of dolphins in his company's tuna nets, but as an executive, he must not let his feelings interfere with the best interests of the company."

(ii) Absolute Ethics

According to this, there is one universal and eternal moral code, changing circumstances of different opinions make no difference.

(iii) Deontological Theory

This theory states that the rightness and wrongness of an action depends on the action itself and not on the consequences it produces. They maintain that fulfilling obligations, following proper procedure "Doing the Right Thing" and adhering to moral standards determine the ethical values of actions. It maintains that *actions are morally right independent of their consequences.* It also covers that an action is right, if it conforms to terms agreed upon (Social Contract Theory).

Managers who follow internal process model of management stress dutiful compliance with standards of efficiency and make decisions by the book regardless consequences.

4. Teleological Ethics Theories

This holds the view that *rightness and wrongness of an action depends on its consequences or results.* Pleasantness or unpleasantness it causes. They maintain that good ends and/or results determine the ethical values of actions. It can be ethical egoism, i.e. that an action is good if it produces results that maximise a particular person self-interest. It can be *utilitarism,* i.e. an action is good if it produces greatest amount of satisfaction for greatest number of affected by the action. *Example*—Manager prepares vacation schedule after obtaining preferences from all employees. He maximises the pleasure of employees.

Example—If manager enforces health and safety standards at work, he is ensuring natural components of happiness.

Rational goal theory managers support teleological ethics. "All is well that ends well", regardless of means used to produce results.

5. Virtue Ethics Theories

Virtue ethics theories maintain that habitual development of *sound character traits* determines the ethical values of persons.

Persons with strong character have cultivated intellectual, moral, emotional and social virtues to achieve the self-discipline to do the right thing. Character provides moral foundation for one's actions.

Virtue ethics maintains that sound, balanced character, motivation and intention is more important than actual conduct and its consequences.

Three major types of virtue ethics theories focus on individual, work and professional character:

(a) *Individual Character Ethics* maintains development of human traits of nobility—such as courage, moderation, justice, gratitude, sense of humour, self-discipline, reliability, benevolence, caring, sincerity, understanding and wisdom—determine value of human ethical interactions.

(b) *Work Character Ethics* maintains development of traits of work such as:

Competence, creativity, honesty, fairness, trust-worthiness, appreciation, task completion, loyalty, resourcefulness, shared work pride, level-headedness, dependability, empathy, cooperativeness, supportiveness, tolerance.

These determine ethical quality of work life. As more and more occupations, including management, undergo process of "professionalisation", standards of work character ethics increase.

(c) *Professional Character Ethics* maintains the credentialed expertise, licensed monopoly, self-regulation, trust, truthfulness, impartiality, independence of judgement and public service of individual in associated community. There is *loyalty to a professional code of ethics.*

Adhere to your conscience. The human relations theory of management stresses inter-personal development and team-building skills as the criteria of flexible work communities. Managers who endorse this approach demonstrate virtue ethics.

This approach emphasises supporting character, development, facilitating, participative decision-making, foster win-win dispute resolutions and recognising employees contributions. Such managers endorse the dictum "Character counts" and avoid pressurising people to use means or achieve ends that violate their conscience.

6. System Development Ethics Theories

System development ethics theories maintain that the nature of *supportive framework* for continuous improvement of ethical conduct determines the ethical value of actions. Managers implement ethics development systems that will sustain integrity building environments. Managers who do not implement recognition process for exemplary moral conduct by employees or refrain from taking swift action against wrongdoers at work are guilty of both moral and managerial malfeasance.

The *open system theory* of management stresses innovative adaptability and acquisition of external resources as the criteria of effectiveness. And managers who support this approach exhibit system development ethics. In concrete terms for managers, this approach emphasises creative change management, resourcefulness, respectful negotiation and collaborative networking with diverse global interests. Managers who adopt this perspective encourage organisational flexibility to make organisation moral progress and manage ethically.

Jack Griffin (article on *Development of Ethics and Ethical Theory*) has given summary of beliefs and problems in the five major ethical systems in tabular form. (Figure 1)

FIGURE 1

Summary of Beliefs and Problems in the Five Major Ethical Systems

	Nature of the Ethical Belief	*Problems in the Ethical System*
Eternal Law	Moral standards are given in an Eternal law, which is revealed in Scripture or apparent in nature and then interpreted by religious leaders or humanist philosophers; the belief is that everyone should act in accordance with the interpretation.	There are multiple interpretations of the Law, but no method to choose among them beyond human rationality needs an absolute principle or value at the basis for choice.
Utilitarian Theory	Moral standards are applied to the outcome of an action or decision; the principle is that everyone should act to generate the greatest benefits for the largest number of people.	Immoral acts can be justified if they provide substantial benefits of the majority, even at an unbearable cost or harm to the minority; an additional principle or value is needed or balance the benefit-cost equation.
Universalist Theory	Moral standards are applied to the intent of an action or decision; the principle is that everyone should act to ensure that similar decisions would be reached by others, given similar circumstances.	Immoral acts can be justified by persons who are prone to self-deception or self-importance, and there is no scale to judge between "wills", an additional principle or value is needed to refine the Categorical Imperative concept.
Distributive Justice	Moral standards are based upon the primacy of a single value, which is justice. Everyone should act to ensure a more equitable distribution of benefit, for this promotes individual self-respect, which is essential for social cooperation.	The primacy of the value of justice is dependent upon acceptance of the proposition that an equitable distribution of benefits ensures social co-operation.
Personal Liberty	Moral standards are based upon the primacy of a single value, which is liberty. Everyone should act to ensure greater freedom of choice, for this promotes market exchange, which is essential for social productivity.	The primacy of the value of liberty is dependent upon acceptance of the proposition that a market system of exchange ensures social productivity.

PART VII

INDIAN ETHOS IN MANAGEMENT

CHAPTER

34

Basic Principles of Indian Ethos for Management

(As Described in Upanishads and Gita)

Some basic principles of Indian Ethics for Management as contained in the Upanishads and the Gita are as under:

1. Each human being has immense *potential energy* and talents.

2. One (manager) must *develop one's third eye* (Janana Chakshu)—the type of wisdom, vision, insight and foresight. Wisdom worker has an integrated personality. Inner resources (divine virtues are much more powerful than outer resources, capital, materials and plant, etc.)

3. *Work is done as worship*. Karma Yoga (Selfless work). Do your duty without ego and without calculations of gain or loss. Pour your heart and soul in the performance of your assigned duty. Work offers double benefit, personal benefit (self-purification, salvation, personal growth) and social benefit (society). Work is a form of sacrifice (yogna), a spirit of renunciation, i.e. *tyag* and to serve others without self-interest.

4. Yoga means *excellence at work*. Seek to perform your assigned duty or work in an excellent manner. Perfection in work and quality of output. This leads to total quality management.

5. Indian ethos say that for human beings the royal road is *cooperation* as a powerful instrument for team work. The Gita says: "By cooperation and mutual help all shall achieve the highest human welfare."

6. Indian ethos give much greater *emphasis on values*—human and ethical.

Knowledge is not power. Character is the real power and wealth. Character is based on divine values. The divine values are based on wisdom. Manager with enriched quality of mind and heart can have effective management.

A management with proper combination of values and skills can assure harmony and progress of organisation as well as society. This is unique contribution of Indian ethos.

7. *Business is sacred.* We need not regard business as evil or unethical. It is a matter of attitude, approach and level of management consciousness. One can do business, make money, earn profit, it can be managed with due recognition to human and ethical values and respecting all persons in the organisation and in the society as human beings. It means *humanising the organisation* by:

(i) Creating best inter-personal relations based on equality, self-esteem, fraternal affection and promotion from within, effective communication and teamwork in an organisation.

(ii) Inner-management—mental and spiritual. Self-management, i.e. first learn to manage and control himself. So one should understand and know himself. Business management is a *sadhana* and manager must cultivate noble values.

8. *Self-introspection,* i.e. self-analysis and self-criticism helps to locate areas of friction and disharmony. We should prepare balance sheet of own strengths and weaknesses. Our mind and heart may indicate weak spots. Constant practice or *sadhana* helps us to discard unwanted traits and cultivate good values to purify our mind and heart. Master key is innermind or conscience which helps the entry of positive elements.

9. *Brain-Stilling* (Decision-making in meditative silence): Western management resorts to brain storming, i.e. loud thinking for decisions to solve management problems.

The Indian insights advocates a better alternative in the form of brain-stilling, i.e. silent mind is more effective medium to get sound solutions to management problems.

10. *Role of institution* in decision-making: Institution is the act of direct decision by inner mind through inspiration, instant awareness, past experience. Fully developed institution is effective for taking prompt and sound decisions.

Till 1990, management approach has in the belief on left brain style, i.e. logical, analytical style and deductive reasoning based on case studies and information. A new model is a combination of left brain (analysis and deduction) and right brain (contemplation, intuition and induction) and is now popular. It is blending of western and eastern management concepts. Managers with higher *intuitive ability* are creative, imaginative and are suitable for solving problems, e.g. personnel, advertising, public relations and crisis management, etc.

11. *Listen, Listen, Listen more:* Arjuna starts weakening. Arjuna starts mentally manufacturing cowardly thoughts of retreat from post of duty where destiny has called upon him to act. Fighting is Arjuna's *karma.*

Krishna listens to Arjuna and is silent as a statue. Arjuna becomes more appealing so as not to start the battle. Krishna listens. Krishna is silent. Arjuna goes on and on with his long-drawn limping arguments.

Let us draw an inspiration from this famous battle. In our day-to-day life at the office and at home, whenever we see difficulties ahead we come up with several mental scenes. We find excuses, Moods, Visions, Can'ts. We get into our cocoon, our shell, our box! The womb mentality!! Don't bully! Listen, Try, Act. You will be on the path of a Karmayogi. You will start thinking outside your box.

12. *Good Relationships* with people are more valuable than money, because you cannot buy good relationships. Networking is a higher form of *karma.* Do good to people, keep your visiting cards folder up-to-date. And don't keep a ledger—even a mental ledger—of debits and credits. Do it for the sake of giving, for the love of giving. You will become bigger than Ford, Billgates and Rockfeller, Tata and Ambani. Not in the eyes of the world around you may be—but in your own eyes. And that is good *karma.*

To sum up, as per Indian ethos, the *inner mind and inner aspects of man* are emphasised. Focus is on developing inner mind. Faith and sincerity are two needs of management philosophy. Work must be done in the right spirit and with right attitude and in perfect way. These are views of divine mother, Sri Aurobindo Ashram, Pondicherry.

CHAPTER

35

Indian Approaches for Management and Concepts of Human Resource Development

We shall cover in this chapter two aspects:

1. Indian Approaches for Management.

2. Concepts of Human Resource Development from Indian Ethos.

I. INDIAN APPROACHES FOR MANAGEMENT

We reproduce here some Indian approaches or concepts for management mentioned by learned Prof. S.A. Sherlekar in his book "Ethics in Management."

(i) Holistic Approach in Management

This is based on *spiritual* principle that entire humanity is one and there is respect for all human beings. Managers to follow whole man approach of combining values and physical aspects of life. Higher consciousness will adopt holistic attitude. It will bring out divine in man which will achieve perfection, and excellence in our work. It will achieve peace, harmony and prosperity within and without. Spiritual and worldly life are equally recognised. Thus, 'balance' or equilibrium is the keynote of Indian thought. There is close *relationship between spiritual and worldly life* and this is called whole man approach.

(ii) Each Person is a Potential Divine Human

The divine means perfection in knowledge, wisdom and power. Therefore, a human being has immense potential power or *energy for self-development.* Human being are more important than physical development and must be developed. Your boss gives you challenging work but may not be able to promote you. However he can make you "promotable" and if you are promotable, somebody will promote you, as the world is much bigger than your present organisation.

(iii) Selfless Work (Karma Yoga)

Work is worship. Do your duty without ego and without calculation of fruits of action. So pour your heart and soul in the performance of your work. Do your duty better and better. Work is important for *personal growth* and good of society (public benefit). Work brings inner joy of selfless service.

All work is worthy and honourable. The dignity of work is valuable means of purifying our mind and helps in gaining money, power, fame and name.

(iv) Indian Ethos give Greater Emphasis on Values

Human and Ethical Value-based management is essential to combine subjective (money materials, as well as human skills), objective phenomena (inner resources of human beings, i.e. wisdom and work ethics). So development of inner potential—vision, insight, values are important for wisdom and character.

(v) Cooperation and Team Work

Healthy competition is a powerful motivator for excellence and success in business success.

The Gita says: "By cooperation and mutual help all small achieve the highest human welfare." Cooperation is a powerful instrument for team work and success of any enterprise.

(vi) Excellence at Work

Excellence at work through self-motivation and self-development is the best means of total quality management.

To conclude, management with proper combination of *values* and skills can assure the harmony, progress of the organisation and society. Spiritual aspect is necessary to achieve worldly goals. This is the unique contribution of Indian ethos.

2. CONCEPTS OF HUMAN RESOURCE DEVELOPMENT FROM INDIAN ETHOS

Swami Tejomayananda quotes examples of Human Resource Development from epics like the Ramayana and Mahabharta as under:

(i) Awaken and Empower your People, the Way Master HRD Specialist Lord Krishna did

The role of HRD can be drawn with the striking example of Lord Krishna as a master HRD specialist. Look at him in the roles of a counselor, trainer, friend, philosopher, guide and motivator leading by example. He distinctly earmarked Arjun's role to achieve success. He even chose to become Arjuna's *sarathi* (driver) and impress upon him to pick up his bow and arrow to fulfil his duties and obligations. Lord Krishna gave Arjuna not only the sermon but also enthused him morally to fight his battle.

(ii) Love and Inspiration are Important to Develop Human Resources

The element of love in leaders enables them to collect and harness fortitudes of ardent and dedicated effort. nothing significant can be achieved by mere official authority, post or position. The Ramayana brings out this point beautifully.

Lord Rama and Ravana were both great, but with a vast difference in their greatness. Ravana tried to become big and great by making other people small. He thought that when others became small his own greatness would shine! On the other hand, Lord Rama's greatness was in that He made every small person also great and equal to Himself. He even elevated the restless monkeys to the status of divinity. He achieved "monkey resource development"! It is through the mobilization of the monkey forces that He gained victory over the invincible and well equipped Ravana. This is one of the most fascinating aspects of the Ramayana. The secret of Lord Rama's success was His pure love for all.

(iii) Respect the Authority of Others and do not Give Orders Directly

Another interesting aspect of Lord Rama's character was that He did not exercise any kind of authority over others. Sugreeva, the monkey king, offered his services along with his army to Lord Rama and awaited His orders. Rama however, declined to give orders and gave Sugreeva the freedom of planning the search for Sita Devi. You are aware of the problems of authority in Management. If the boss gives orders directly to the workers then the Departmental Head resents it and feels that his or her authority has been undermined or by-passed. Lord Rama understood this fact, and so He respected the authority of others.. Love and regard for others can do wonders.

Now look at the character of Ravana. He never listened to anybody's advice. He surrounded himself with sycophants and whoever opposed his views was thrown out, as the American saying goes "Do it my way or hit the highway"! He neither possessed a noble inspiration, nor sincere love or regard for others. It is no wonder that he destroyed himself and others as well. Thus, the study of the Ramayana has teaches us Human Resource Development.

(iv) Leader and Inspiration are Vital

The Mahabharata too contains many fine examples. We know that the Kauravas had a much larger army than the Pandavas, yet, the Pandavas won the war. Why? It was because of Lord Shri Krishna. He was their leader and inspiration. He mobilized them well. The Kauravas had no such inspiration on their side. Moreover, the Pandávas were convinced of their righteous cause and were totally devoted to Lord Krishna. This foo was lacking in the Kaurava.

(v) Surrender Individual for Higher Goals

Lord Krishna saw to it that a person must rise above individual importance f6r the sake of the totality. Without this sacrifice or higher goal great things cannot be achieved.

(vi) Right Job for Right Man

In this context it should be noted that the success of a project depends upon whether people are working for themselves or the project, and are they capable of doing their jobs efficiently or not. There is a view that people can do all kinds of work. However, experience does not back this theory.

The great Chanakya has said it well; a person should be engaged only in a job that he is capable of doing efficiently.

Yo yasmin karmani kushalash sa tasmin eva yoktavyah

Every person cannot do everything, but every person is capable of doing something. In this sense, all people are equal. As such, the leader will have to really find the capabilities of his workers and assign jobs to them accordingly.

(vii) Perform Your Work in Perfection

Lastly, keep the advice of your masters in mind; having discovered your potential and aptitudes, perform your work as your worship of the Lord. You will be free from all impurities of the mind. Such an act of worship will unfold your personality instead of making you self-centered. The Bhagawad Gita says that man attains perfection by worshipping the Lord by his own Karmas:

Swakarmana Tam Abhyarchya Sidhim Vindati Manavah.

Reference

S.A. Sherlekar, *Ethics in Management*, Himalaya Publishing House, Mumbai.

Swami Tejomayananda, Chinmaya Mission, *News Bulletin*, July 2001.

CHAPTER

36

ROLE OF GEETA IN MANAGEMENT

Shrimad Bhagawad Geeta is a marvellous book of guidance. Be you a seeker of spiritual enlightenment or a person facing a moral dilemma or a managing director of a multinational company working for success, the Geeta can guide people effectively in achieving your objectives. This article outlines the role of the Geeta in Management Science.

According to Swami Sharoopananda, Lord Krishna gives many useful suggestions for an executive on how to manage his company successfully. The executive must have the following qualifications:

1. Jnanam (Vision)

This means a *complete vision* of the entire organisation, its aims and objectives, its place in the country and also in relation to other nations. There may be many functional divisions in the organisation but the Head must see unity in all of them. The relationship between the parts and the whole must be understood very well.

2. Buddhi (Ability)

Discrimination and discretion. The chief should be capable of imparting his vision to all his workers at their own level of understanding and field of work. This *ability is Buddhi.* While translating this vision into reality there will arise many problems, difficulties and obstacles that may be objective or man-made as well. At such moments what is required is *Buddhi*—the *ability to understand the very cause of such problems* and to remove it effectively. *Buddhi* is required to manage two kinds of people: those who have difficulties and those who are difficult people! In order to do all this the Executive must have a good *knowledge of the human mind.*

3. Dhriti (Patience)

Dhriti means *patience and fortitude*. The ability to consistently hold on to your goal is called *Dhriti*. It is a well known fact that no goal is achieved easily and quickly. We meet with many obstacles which try our patience. Similar is the case when all workers are not able to see the vision and they act strangely enough as to frustrate even an effective leader. On all such occasions the leader must have *extreme patience to win them over and achieve the goal*. This ability is called *Dhriti*.

4. Right Person for Right Job

Another important point to be considered is that the success of a project depends on the *appointment of right persons for various jobs*. There will be diversity in jobs and functions but there should be unity in purpose and total dedication to it. The greater the goal and higher the inspiration, the more spectacular success will be. The way Lord Krishna managed the crisis at the time of war, teaching Arjuna and then leading the Pandavas to victory, is proof of this fact.

5. Theory of Karma (Result of Our Actions)

The law of *Karma* explains the entire phenomena of life. It is precise and comprehensive as the laws of science. Physics states that every action has an equal and opposite reaction. The theory of *Karma* postulates the universal accounting system in which each individual must experience the *appropriate result of his actions*. What is accumulated in the past life becomes the fate in the present life. So fate is the result of the past *Karma* and is of our own making. So we have to take the responsibility of the results of our actions. In the Bhagawad Geeta, Bhagwan Sri Krishna convinces Arjuna to shed weakness and act, take the responsibility and fight in the battlefield. The result of the action naturally will depend upon the quality of the action undertaken. (Swami Nikhilananda)

6. Meditation

6.1 Meditation is concentration. The flow of the same kind of thoughts, all related to the Supreme Truth, uninterrupted by contrary or different thoughts, is meditation.

When the mind becomes steady and concentrated, and the intellect is redeemed from its wasteful habits of wrong imaginations, then the equipment (body, mind, and intellect) is ready for higher flights through the path of meditation.

Meditation, consists in "withdrawing, by concentration, all the sense organs away from their respective sense objects into the mind, and then withdrawing the mind into the inner intelligence, and then contemplating upon the Highest." It is a continuous and unbroken thought-flow, like a stream of flowing oil. In order to pursue this path, naturally, the individual must have a dynamic head and heart—both minimally disturbed by their own subjective defects.

6.2 On What does One Meditate? The highest form of meditation consists of steady contemplation on the nature of the Self, the Atman. Other forms of meditation do exists in the vast variety of spiritual practices, such as meditating on a form, a sound, etc.

7. Choosing One's Career

One must choose in life a field of activity as per one's swadharma (one's own nature). To find success and satisfaction, it is important to be in the field of one s interest, a fact often overlooked in choosing a career.

8. Development of the Intellect

To control and direct one's action is important for success. This is possible through a strong intellect. The intellect acts on reason and judgment. Acting on one's likes and dislikes may give us an immediate sense of pleasure, but it ultimately leads to ruin.

Work Ethos

Choose a field of activity according to your own swadharma (own nature). It is important to be in the field of one's interest, a fact often overlooked while choosing a career.

9. Self-Control

Self-control is not self-denial. It is channelising our energies towards a purposeful end. Without disciplining the senses, no higher goals can be achieved in life.

The Bhagavad Gita is a companion for the journey of life. To relegate its study towards the ends of lie is to miss out on living meaningfully.

The above are basic requirements in successful management.

The Bhagawad Gita is the repository of the highest knowledge. This time-tested and renowned dialogue (in chapter X) holds answers to innumerable doubts that plague the human mind.

Bhagawd Gita is book of life in everyday living. The Bhagavad Gita is a technique for dynamic living and not a retirement plan, says Vedantin Swami Parthasarathy. Yet most people believe that the study of the Gita should be initiated after one's active life is over. Such a belief has deprived us of the benefits of this glorious message.

The message of the Gita is meant to be a preparation for life. It helps us be productive in life while keeping the mind at rest. The Gita rendered by Lord Krishna, who is an epitome of dynamism. It is given to Arjuna the greatest warrior of his times. The message is given in a battlefield where the two are fighting adharmic forces. The message pulls Arjuna out of a despondent state and enables him to gain victory and glory. How then can the message of Gita be directed towards inactivity and retirement?

References

Swami Swaroopananda, Chinmaya Mission, *News Bulletin*, November 2002.
Swami Nikhilananda, Chinmaya Mission, *News Bulletin*, November 2002.
Chinmaya Mission West, Piercy, California.
Alok Chopra, Mindtrack, *Hindustan Times*, 7-11-2003.

CHAPTER

37

KARMA YOGA

MEANING

Karma Yoga simply means, do your *duty without ego* and without calculation of gain or loss. Pour your heart and soul in the performance of your assigned duty. Work offers double benefit, personal benefit (Self-purification, salvation), personal growth and development and social benefits (that is to society). Work is a form of sacrifice, a selfless work. Focus on action, not fruit. The fruit is nothing but the proper culmination of one's actions. Focus on the job alone.

Yoga means *excellence* at work, seek to perform your assigned duty or work in an excellent manner. It is perfection in work and quality of output. This leads to Total Quality Management. Ethics is based on most important element of activity. In Geeta the call is to "Act in the living Present" that is Karma Yoga. Karma means action, duty or work done not with selfish motive but with the objective of serving humanity. A man's primary duty is to perform the job allocated to him with devotion and perfection, only then we can achieve salvation.

Thus, Geeta gives new dignity to work. Work is not unpleasant activity or some sort of punishment, but a way of life, ordained by the lord.

Work is something inherit in the nature of people. McGregor says the same thing that work is something inherent. Geeta practices the *mantra* of Karma Yoga. It preaches devotion to duty, regard less of its consequences. Work is not only necessary to keep the body and mind occupied, it is necessary for perfection.

FEATURES OF KARMA YOGA

(a) No living being can live without performing actions.

(b) Karma Yoga prescribes to place action above ego as against the usual ego—centric action. Egoness is the root cause of our problems and sufferings. But the moment the ego is detached from action, it becomes spiritual action in objective reality. The Geeta prescribes to *overlook the outcome of action*, but not the action.

(c) Karma Yoga is the path of right action and leads to harmony and solution to problems.

(d) The much talked doctrine of Karma Yoga is difficult to practise as it includes *controlling of senses* and overcoming desires.

(e) Karma Yoga is essentially wisdom in practice in daily life.

(f) The inner mind and inner aspect of man are important. Work must be done in right spirit and with right attitude and in perfect way. These are also the views of Divine Mother of Pondicherry.

(g) Action requires *determination*. Those who are of unstable mind and are attached to fruits of action are not determined. They cannot be good performers. Duty should be done without attachment and irrespective of consequences of action.

(h) Excellence can be achieved through Karma Yoga only. This would free you from anxiety and will attain you supreme bliss.

(i) Nishkama Karma Yoga (Self-Motivation) is the best route for self-development of all. Self-motivation can assure you self-development. In this process you grow and also other's grow. When everyone does duty towards others, everyone's rights are automatically assured. Work is performed without hatred, without arrogance and desire. Karma Yoga should also engage in welfare of the society.

(j) A person or society sensitive to its *obligations* is progressive and prosperous.

References

M.N. Kundu, *Hindustan Times*, New Delhi, 20.10.2003.

S.A. Sherlekar, *Ethics in Management*, Himalaya Publishing House, Mumbai.

CHAPTER

38

Personal Integrity is a Competitive Advantage

(I) IN DAILY PERFORMANCE WE APPLY A STANDARD OF INTEGRITY

- Finding the *right way in gray* areas.
- Creating an *environment* of integrity within our team and company.
- Building *trust among* those for whom we are responsible.

It is in fact near impossible for a person to have enduring success in business without a reputation of trust worthiness and integrity.

(II) THE NINE INTEGRITY CHARACTERISTICS

1. You know that little things count,
2. You find the white (when others see gray),
3. You create a culture of trust,
4. You keep your word,
5. You care about the greater good,
6. You are honest but modest,
7. You act like you are being watched,
8. You hire integrity, and
9. You stay consistent.

By integrating these steps into your everyday behaviour, you will gain the integrity advantage. These characteristics are explained in detail.

1. You Know that Little Things Count

To have the integrity advantage, you do not lie or cheat on the small things as a result, you are not corrupted by the larger temptations the lure of power, prestige or money. Just as importantly, if you have integrity, you stick to internal code of morality, even at the risk of losing your comfortable place in the world.

2. You Find the White (when others see gray)

To have integrity advantage, you do not make tough decisions alone. You ask questions, receive counsel, reflect, and take a long-term view. In short, you ensure that you never make a *decision that would violate* your internal code of integrity.

3. You Create a Culture of Trust

You help to create the right *work environment*, one that will not test the personal integrity of your employees or co-workers. You reinforce integrity through principles, controls and personal example. And you reward those in your employ who display personal integrity in their actions.

4. You keep your Word

Employees do not follow leaders they do not trust. Employers do not hire people or promote employees they do not trust. Clients do not buy from suppliers they do not trust. To have the integrity advantage, you act with integrity to gain trust.

5. You Care about the Greater Good

You are deeply committed to and take decisions that will benefit the entire organisation to which you belong. You care passionately about your company, products and services, and especially your teammates. Through your work, you gain sense of deeper purpose.

6. You are Honest but Modest

You do not proclaim your virtue or honesty. That is like boasting of your humility. You allow your actions to speak louder than your words.

7. You Act like you are being Watched

You assume your every move is being watched. You ensure that your integrity is passed along to future generations through your example.

8. You Hire Integrity

You hire and surround yourself straight people who have a strong sense of personal integrity. You promote those who demonstrate an ability to be trusted.

9. You Stay Consistent

You have ethical consistency and predictability. Your life demonstrates wholeness and harmony between your values and your actions.

(III) STEPS TO ENHANCE YOUR INTEGRITY

Step I

Assess your integrity using the nine characteristics of integrity rate yourself from 1 to 9 (9 being the highest).

Step II

Get a second feedback and a third. Write down names of few whom you trust and why. Contact these people and seek integrity feedback from them on 9 points about you. Ask them for complete honestly and this will not affect their relations. Information obtained is important. This is a step in the right direction.

Step III

Evaluate ethical health of the organisation in which you participate. The word trustworthy is central what we hope to achieve. Evaluate your organisation on nine characteristics of integrity. Look at little things. Do people you consider to be. Your friends cheat on their taxes and brag about it or steal from their employer. Integrity is as critical in these relationships as in your work organisation.

Step IV

Start an individual revolution. The truth can be achieved if we put some effort. Change requires momentum that momentum has to come from inside of you. For example, I won't use sick leave when I am not sick or I won't lie at work, etc. Focus on the behaviours, at a time, and you will be in your way to making the integrity advantage your advantage.

TO SUM UP

You can take integrity with you. A clergy man reminded a rich miser who was on his death bed that he could not take his riches with him. "Then I am not going", the man replied.

Integrity is one of the few things in life you can take with you, wherever you go, it becomes a part of you and sticks with you through economic downturns, just as it does in the good times. It is something no one can take away from you.

Integrity is truly a competitive advantage—in business and in life. Those people with integrity have one thing in common—they sleep well. Integrity often is its own reward. No one is happy with himself if he is not a good person.

CHAPTER

39

INDIAN WISDOM MANAGEMENT

(QUALITIES OF WISEMEN)

(1) Acquiring right intelligence/knowledge leads to wisdom.

(2) Wiseman keeps a perfect balance of body, mind and spiritual aspects.

(a) Body

Wiseman takes care of his body, keeping it fit and healthy and believes it must be kept clean and pure. He takes care of his material comforts (wealth and facilities, etc.). Self knowledge and care does not indulge in greed and wrong practices.

(b) Mind

Wiseman also is careful to keep his mind up to date of his environment and intellectual pursuits. He has positive thoughts and thinking which are the hallmarks of a wiseman. He influences his followers by love, compassion and high intelligence. He thinks positive in all circumstances and possess purity of thought.

No matter how lofty their station in life may be, wise men are *humble and eager* to learn. They accept correction and try to change when proven wrong. Having discovered the power and beauty of truth, they listen to good counsel. They seek out many advisers and toil in the process of finding information and knowledge. They invest their time, money, and labour in the quest of learning. They enrol in courses of study and *acquire libraries*. As they continually accumulate their knowledge, they both increase their ability to learn and increase the pleasure they get in acquiring it. Indeed, education and learning become a form of recreation for them.

(c) Spiritual

Spiritual man is oneIndian Wisdom ManagementIndian Wisdom Management who is in tune with and sensitive to natural impulses, rhythms and currents in life and acts intelligently in the light of this sensitivity. They do not harm others. There is moral purity. They have love for mankind.

Spiritual people respect *all* faiths and religious and have absolutely no difficulty in allowing every man to worship in his own way and in his own place, be it temple, mosque or church. The spiritual personality is not motivated by *Bhaya* (fear), the desire for *Sukha* (happiness) or the wish to escape *Dhuka* (pain or suffering)—the three major forces in life.

One of the oldest definitions of *spiritual living* is given in the Bhagawat Gita—to act without thought of the fruits of action. To act with complete detachment and selflessness because the action is right and necessary. To live selflessly in peace and inner joy/bliss, self-contended.

(3) Honesty

Wise persons are held to the highest standards of conduct which includes ethics, integrity, character, trustworthiness, truthfulness, morality, rightness. They show high consistency between word and deed.

(4) Vision

They have ability to "see into the future" and perceive an improved reality for the community. They have competence of leading through work, action and deed. They communicate their vision and provide direction to follow the vision. They encourage risk taking.

(5) Balance

They are integrated or well-balanced spiritually, mentally, emotionally and physically. This gives good vibrations to others, thereby elevating their spirits in addition to their confidence and passion for excellence.

(6) Self-Learning

They continuously learn of new knowledge and skills and develop cultural awareness and sensitivity, i.e. cultural flexibility.

(7) Self-Confidence

They have self-confidence in order to convince their followers of the rightness of goals and decisions.

(8) Patience

A wise man has patience; he controls his emotions. He quietly ignores an insult. He will not be provoked into a meaningless fight, choosing instead to hold back his anger and to use his intellect to seek peace and reconciliation.

(9) Wisemen Hate Evil

They have no appreciation for senselessness. They look with distaste upon things that are wasteful and destructive.

(10) Differentiate between Right and Wrong

The wise understand the true difference *between right and wrong*, good and evil. They know the real meaning of justice and fair play. They do not judge by appearances only, but they also see with depth. They have insight and foresight, enabling them to perceive both the underlying dynamics of things while accurately anticipating results and consequences. Therefore, they show good judgment and make correct decisions. Wise men are able to successfully perceive ahead because they have faith in the ultimate value of wisdom. And so the wise are law-abiding, heedful of both natural law and social law. They can see far enough ahead to know the benefits of right living.

(11) Self-control and Restrain in Speech

The wise are especially noted by their skill with words. First, they show self-control and restraint in their use of language. Realizing the power of words, they speak with great caution. When they do speak, what they say is true and relevant. Moreover, their words are both dignified and astute.

IN SUM UP

There is no strength like wisdom and there are no great men like the wise. In addition to their love of knowledge and their rejection of evil, wise men, everywhere demonstrate the following common characteristics. They are humble, behaving with cautious reserve and emotional control. Valuing knowledge they actively pursue it in order to live successfully. They eventually develop skill in learning and come to enjoy the process. Their use of words is likewise controlled, knowledgeable and effective.

A man of character expresses all ethical and human values. He is called a wiseman. He has wisdom and wisdom is born of contact with the divine. He has purity of mind/heart, higher consciousness is also called spiritual state of mind and combines in wisdom and values. We can bring about excellence in all work with the help of ethical devotion and spiritual values.

According to Prof. S.A. Sherlekar—"Western model of man and management" could not give rich dividends. It is inadequate in solving all the problems of modern society. Important concepts of Indian Wisdom and thought will enrich Western thought and provide a complete set of ideas for the management of organisations.

In Indian Wisdom, material and spiritual aspects of human existence or life are given equal emphasis and there is very close inter-relationship between worldly life and spiritual life. Both are manifestations or expressions of the divine or pure consciousness.

The holistic approach of Indian Wisdom is needed for modern management to integrate matter/spirit or skills/values or object/subject. Modern management must incorporate Indian ethos to perfect the truncated model of man (stressing only material progress at any cost) and recognise man as a *whole man* to assure wholesome human progress—spiritual as well as material progress—to satisfy the hunger of mind and soul as well as the hunger of physical and vital human being.

Values-based holistic approach to management will assure such all round wholesome human development and prosperity.

References

S.A. Sterlekar, *Ethics in Management*, Himalaya Publishing House, Mumbai.
Internet websites.

CHAPTER

40

A Person of Character

WHAT IS CHARACTER?

(i) Meaning

What is character? What are the hallmarks of fine character? A man of character strives to practise Truth, Non-violence, Non-Stealing, Fearlessness and such other vows. He is ready to give up his life, but not truth. He is prepared to die, but will not kill. He is willing to accept suffering, but not inflict it on others. He does not steal, nor takes bribes. He does not waste his time nor that of others, goes on doing his duty fearlessly.

It is in the hands of the students to make good the defects in their character for no one else can do this for them. We must first understand the aim of education. A student who desires to cultivate and build-up character, will learn how to do so from any good book on the subject.

The Lord of creation creates everything in this world as an admixture of good and evil. But a good man selects the good and rejects the evil.

(ii) Doing One's Duty

Performing one's duty is fundamental concept of work ethic.

It is observing certain discipline, namely, coming to work on time, behaving with respect and dignity with subordinate, colleagues and superiors, staying at work place. During working hours, not wasting time by roaming and chatting, etc. to have strong work orientation. To perform one's job with devotion with initiative and perfection.

One should fulfil one's commitment and be accountable for results. He should be dedicated to hard work. He should protect the interest of the organisation he works for. He should have satisfaction that he is contributing his very best to his organisation.

(iii) Develop Proper Values

Values provide that basic foundation for understanding a person's personality's perceptions and attitudes. Values represent basic convictions or what are right values and those are powerful force affecting attitude and behaviour. Values effect our thoughts, motivation, perceptions and actions. Values guide in our decision-making and resolving conflicts. Values bring *excellence* and perfection in our actions.

Values are internal, deal with internal development of a person, purify mind and heart. The person becomes good in thought, speech and in action, job or work. Thus, values help in *self-development*.

Human values enhance reputation and image of the person.

(iv) Man-making Education

Man-making education can make a man of character, i.e. by strengthening his mind and by which one stands on ones own feet and not swayed by others. Character is formed from the repeated choice of thoughts and action. Make the right choice—we shall have a firm and noble character.

(v) To Become Good Person

A person becomes good when he actually does good rather than not doing wrong. A good person *has qualities* such as fairness, compassion, courage, integrity, empathy, humility, loyalty and courtesy.

What makes these people good people? They are kind people, and are dependable, stand up for justice, help the needy, make life better for themselves and those around them. Benchmarks can be ethical or legal.

(vi) Building a Character Foundation for Society

Everyone has goals for society. To get society in high gear, every member of society needs to understand the role for societal wellness. Setting an example of morality, integrity and character is good place to start. Keep in mind that every person can make a difference.

IN SUM

Focus on character education by building on values of morality, integrity, putting good news at the front, building right attitude, etc.

Pay special attention to social issues such as, winning war on drugs and smoking, family break-ups, lead by example, etc.

Reference

Bhawan's Journal, March 2000.

CHAPTER

41

UNDERSTANDING SPIRITUALITY AND HUMANISM— BASIC PRINCIPLES AND VALUES

I. SPIRITUALITY

Spirituality is a refined or higher state of the mind. It is really one of the resources of consciousness. It is ability of human beings to view themselves and their own actions. It is ability of "self-consciousness." To be a spiritual person is not to have a particular belief in one or another God. It is the ability to transcend oneself, to see oneself.

We give here views of some personalities in spiritual field on the subject.

1. *Spirituality is about your mind* being happy, feeling free, sharing, and having enthusiasm for life. Spirituality is the essence of any culture or religion in any part of the world. It is self-realisation, self-contentment, love of humanity and mankind. It is establishing truth, justice, love and peace. It is keeping others interest before own. It is service all around welfare of humanity.

Meditation is a mind without agitation. It improves your perception, observation and expression in life. When you have a better perception of things, life becomes easier. You can accomplish things better.

When you meditate and are relaxed, then you can accomplish things better. Whatever you do with a relaxed state of mind becomes a success.

Each individual is unique. Our life-style, upbringing, etc. influence our growth, so we differ from each other in our capacity to understand. When you meditate, you tap different layers of this growth. Meditation polishes the mind to help imbibe the information available to a person from life itself.

When you meditate, you become eligible to receive. Meditation is a cleansing agent. Meditation is like a shower for the mind. Only right meditation technique and science of living can control minds and lead the man towards the path of enlightenment.

2. According to Swami Nikhilananda, spirituality becomes elusive for most people if it is not practical. For *practical spirituality* you have to lead a rational life. Spirituality does not require you to live differently or abnormally. People make a big mistake when they compartmentalise their lives. Most people think practical life has its own set of rules and regulations and spiritual life is not a part of that.

They are wrong, as worldly life or day-to-day life is the outer periphery of spiritual life itself. Everyone does not have to renounce the world to attain spirituality. Swamis and gurus renounce the world only because they want to focus on it more. They are just like scholars who withdraw from everything else to spend more time in research and study. Similarly, some people renounce the world to spend more time contemplating and thinking of God. But ordinary people need not separate spiritual life from worldly life.

You don't have to do something to become spiritual, but whatever you are doing should be done in a spiritual way. If you treat the people you meet as divine and show them the same respect you show a deity at a temple, saying *namaskar* to people. itself becomes as spiritual as visiting a temple. So, spirituality is divining each and every moment of your life in your relationships, work, behaviour, beliefs, etc.

BASIC PRINCIPLES AND VALUES OF SPIRITUALITY

(i) Avoid Selfishness

There are some *basic principles* and basic values about spirituality such as giving up selfishness. If you work in such a way that you do not think of yourself alone but also of the *welfare of others*, you become spiritual. Spirituality is thinking about and working for the welfare of everyone.

If you do business and think of your profit alone without worrying about the customer, then it's not spirituality. But if I think about the welfare of my customers, and give them proper care, you are spiritual.

Spirituality is about love, and love and selfishness cannot go together.

(ii) Prayer and Meditation

Being spiritual does not mean that you should be praying or meditating all the time. Leading a natural, value-based life is spiritual. Nature is spiritual.

Spirituality is regaining our natural balance and going back to nature. All of us are essentially spiritual. A newborn child is spiritual. Everyone wants to fulfil their desires, but spirituality is about fulfilling your desires without hurting anyone. You do your duty without hurting anyone.

(iii) Materialism and the Spirituality Go Together

Spirituality and materialism are not to be separated. Spirituality should have a touch of materialism and materialism should have a touch of spirituality. By materialism Swami Nikhilananda means practical things. At the Chinmaya Mission, we use computers and air-conditioners as we believe that spirituality does not mean you should be uncomfortable. Similarly, if a material person gives up his business and spends his time praying, it is wrong. A totally materialistic person can be spiritual and a totally spiritual person can be materialistic. Both extremes can go hand in hand.

The last *shloka* of the Bhagavad Gita says where there is Arjuna, there is Krishna. Krishna represents spirituality and Arjuna materialism, and when both go together, there is success and prosperity. So we should not separate worldliness and spirituality.

(iv) Knowledge

To define best conduct, knowledge is essential. Only when you know what to do and what not to do is important. Only when knowledge is applied to conduct, we have the true manifestation of spirituality.

(v) Self-Restraint

Interdependence means interaction. Interaction means the forming of equations. When you strike an equation with anybody there is need *to restrain* one's self-interest so much as to allow the other person's interest also to co-exist. When a balance is struck, it is called sustainable friendship, sustainable environment, sustainable development, etc. depending on the partnership.

(vi) Having Faith

Life has three aspects, the physical, mental and spiritual. Spirituality requires to have faith in the governing power you honour and obey and have personal faith. Spiritual wealth provides faith. It gives love. It brings and expands wisdom. Spiritual wealth leads to happiness because it guides us into loving relationships. Faith gives us security and comfort. Spirituality (faith) reinforces our stand for what is right. Spiritual wealth assures that there is a God who has interest in me, because he created me. Spiritual wealth gives me great peace of mind because my past has been forgiven. Greed, anger cause strife within a person and his dealings with others.

Besides having physical cravings, man also has spiritual aspirations. Man does not *aspire* for just economic and emotional (Artha and Kama) but (Dharma and Moksha) moral and spiritual.

(vii) Spirituality is Working for the Welfare of Everyone

You don't have to do something special to became spiritual, but whatever you are doing should be done in a spiritual way like treat the people you meet as divine and show them the same respect you show to a deity. Spirituality is divining each and every moment of your life: in your relationships, work, behaviour, beliefs, etc. Spirituality is *thinking* about and *working for the welfare* of everyone. If you give your customers, employees proper care, you are spiritual. Spirituality is about love, and love and selfishness cannot go together.

Leading a natural, value-based life and work in the present. Spirituality is about fulfilling your desires without hurting anyone. Only when knowledge is applied to conduct, we have the true manifestation of spirituality. It is necessary to treat every living entity with respect. Conduct is the gateway to self-realisation.

In bringing about a new synthesis of Science and Spirituality in the world of business and building a new universal empire of the spirit, the role of management education is of critical importance. Our management education needs to be inspired by a value system which prizes commitment to the simultaneous pursuit of excellence and social equity, celebration of pluralism and diversity, and acceptance of limits on space and desire in a world of finite resources.

We need entrepreneurs as trustees of society and who pursue the goal of creating more wealth, more as a social obligation to fulfil the national commitment for the removal of poverty, and not merely for the sake of personal enjoyment.

We need professional managers who are intellectually alert, operate on the frontiers of knowledge and are socially involved.

We need national consensus for social and economic regeneration. We should enable our people to lead a life of dignity and self-respect inspired by the humanistic values of civic morality. The task needs a powerful movement for moral regeneration and spiritual awakening of our people. We need human knowledge and education which would lead not merely to assertion of mind over life and matter but to the triumph of the spirit or soul over mind, body and life. India has to lead the world to realise that a bond of spiritual unity links the entire human kind.

Therefore, value-based, holistic and consciousness approach advocated by ancient Indian wisdom becomes essential.

(viii) Spiritually Prepares for Facing Hardships

Hardships are inevitable in life. They often come our way when we least expect them and at a time when we are not prepared to handle them. That is why they usually become stumbling blocks in our lives. But, if we learn to overcome them, they can actually become stepping stones.

Overcoming hardships in life can be likened to athletics, in which victory or defeat is determined by how well an athlete has practised. On the day of the event, the athlete can do nothing more than perform according to his/her existing ability.

Similarly, success or failure in dealing with an adversity depends on how strong we are spiritually when it comes our way. Be it a break-up in relationship, financial loss, disease, failure in getting what one wants or any other disappointment in life, all can be endured with spiritual strength. But lack of strength at the time of problems can break us in spite of all our efforts to overcome them.

Inner strength may not always solve at problem, but it does help us to carry on in life in the midst of hardships. For, it makes us accept the reality no matter how harsh,; and to take right decisions at the crucial time. Yet, some of us neglect the spiritual area of our lives and accept defeats.

Given that the spiritual health of our inner selves is of great importance, we need to integrate our spiritual activities with our other daily activities. Activities such as regular prayers to God; dwelling on spiritual truths such as God's love, universal values, and purpose in life; reading scriptures and so on must find a place in our 'busy' schedules. Such activities help us gain spiritual strength and make us conscious of God's presence. It also rejuvenates our trust in Him.

Only if we work out our inner selves in the absence of adversity, will we always be prepared to face and successfully overcome hardships in life.

—Visal Arora

(ix) Spirituality is Our Birthright, Make Sure You Seek it

Often, people are clueless about spiritual unfoldment. They often dismiss spiritual development by saying that it is not their cup of tea. They may think that spiritual life is meant for monks alone and may avoid seeking God altogether.

From time to time, God sends his emissaries to the world to make spirituality simpler and easier for us to understand. Through their teachings, these gurus make it absolutely clear that everyone is equally entitled to start on the path of spiritual discovery. It is their birthright and they must have it.

Guru Mantra

The aim of human life is to seek God. A person who has attained human life but chooses not to realise God is born in vain. As long as your heart is directed towards God, you cannot be lost in the ocean of worldliness.

Essentially each one of us is spiritual. But we are not conscious of our spiritual nature, because it is asleep deep inside us. It need to be awakened and brought to the surface.

We realise to get to know about spiritual awakening (God), when we realise that there is more to life than just material existence. Strive to awaken our dormant spirituality and keep the spiritual process on track. Seek guidance from a guru. Spirituality will give eternal peace and contentment.

HUMANISM

Humanism is a way of life which is democratic. It is concerned with dignity of man, i.e. right of the individual in relation to rights of others. It is personal liberty combined with social responsibility. Humanism is ethical. It is concerned with moral and social problems as mentioned below. It seeks and uses science creatively and not destructively.

(a) Humanism stands for two basic values: first and foremost, *love of fellow-beings* and solidarity and of mankind without distinction of race, caste, creed or nationality; and second, *intellectual integrity* and scientific spirit according to which all beliefs, however firmly held, are liable to modification or rejection in the light of further knowledge and experience.

(b) The consideration of moral and social problems in a scientific spirit.

(c) It is concerned with the preservation and furtherance of moral values in all relations and spheres of life, and with the building up of a better and happier human community.

(d) Humanism is not committed to any views about the existence or non-existence of God.

(e) Humanism regards the *basis of morality* to be a sense of values, which is inherent in human nature, and holds and morality requires no external sanction.

(f) Humanism seeks the *development of individuals* as persons and sees this as inseparable from their free and responsible participation in social relations.

(g) Humanism believes not only in the Understanding Spiritually—Basic Principles and valuesbeliefs between individuals and groups having different views but also in their active co-operation in the advancement of ideals which are common ground between them.

REFERENCES

Bhanumati Narasimham, *Hindustan Times*, New Delhi, 19.9.2003.

Swami Nikhila Nanda—Chinmaya Mission, *Hindustan Times*, New Delhi, September 5, 2003.

Tish Malhotra, *Hindustan Times*, 19.9.2003.

Parmarthi Raina, *Hindustan Times*, 29.9.2003.

Professor S.A. Sherlekar, *Ethics in Management*, Himalaya Publishing House, Mumbai.

Vishal Arora, *Hindustan Times*, New Delhi.

Humanism, Memorandum of Association, 1960, Indian Humanism Union.

PART VIII

CORPORATE GOVERNANCE AND PROFESSIONAL ETHICS

CHAPTER

42

Corporate Governance—Basic Ingredients

INTRODUCTION

Suddenly the entire corporate world is talking about a subject which was not in the vocabulary a few years ago—corporate governance.

Governance implies a degree of control to be exercised by key stakeholders' representatives. Governance is about governing. It is not merely about ownership. Even an owner has to learn to govern. Good governance implies that the institution is run for the optimal benefit of the stakeholders in it.

The recognition of issues relating to corporate governance is timely as it is appalling that we come across so many instances of well regarded corporates looting their shareholders for personal gains of managers or the owners.

The list of companies that usually indulge in unethical business practices perhaps exceeds the list of good companies. A few companies which have attained the dubious distinction of appearing in press are—NEPC Group, MS Shoes East Limited (arrest Pawan Sachdeva), Manu Chhabria Group, Orkay Mills, Harshad Mehta epic stock scam, Sterling Group, JVJ, recent UTI 64 Scam, and host of engaged in teak plantations.

Immediately after liberalisation of Indian economy in 1991-92 there were spate of public issues for capital (see Table 1) and hard earned money of small shareholder has been looted by the companies promoting public issues. Even their addresses are not available with the SEBI.

TABLE 1

Public Issues for Capital

Year	*No. of Issues*	*Money Raised (Rupees in Crores)*
1989-90	186	2522
1990-91	140	1450
1991-92	195	1400
1992-93	526	5651
1993-94	765	10824
1994-95	1343	13302
1995-96	1423	8882
1996-97	740	4671
1997-98	58	1132
1998-99	22	504
1999-2000	56	2975
2000-June	56	701
	5510	54024

These companies have betrayed the trust and confidence by not fulfilling tall promises made to investors at the time of public issues.

The current economic depression in Indian economy and stock market is not so much on account of international trends, but it is on account of fraud, cheating, and breach of trust by corporate sector.

MEANING OF CORPORATE GOVERNANCE

It is a *system by which companies are directed and controlled*. Thus, placing board of directors of a company in centre.

A corporate governance is "a conscious, deliberate and sustained efforts on the part of corporate entity to strike a *judicious balance between its own interest* and the interest of various constituents on the environment in which it is operating."

Adrian Cadbury in UK emphasises, "Corporate governance basically, has to do with power and accountability: who exercise power, on behalf of whom, and how the exercise of power is controlled."

It is Way of Life

Corporate governance is a way of life and not a set of rules. A way of life that necessitates taking into account the shareholders' interests in every business decision.

In practice, the term means to the role of the board of directors of the company and the auditors and their relationship with shareholders. The ethical duties of nominated directors to all shareholders (foreign/local) and beyond the sectional interests they may represent could also be covered.

The underlying philosophy in these efforts is to enhance the accountability of board members to shareholders. Good governance implies that institution is run for optimal benefit of stakeholders in it.

Even in a competitive environment, the expectations all around are of fair play and effort to excel by ethical means. Indeed ethical conduct promotes corporate success. It motivates the employees. Good corporate governance and ethical conduct is good policy for achieving success.

BASIC INGREDIENTS FOR GOOD GOVERNANCE

(a) Accountability of Board of Directors and their constituent responsibilities to the ultimate owners-shareholders.

(b) A key element of good governance is transparency and is perceived as such. It is shared way of corporate functioning and not a set of rules. Transparency in turn requires the right to information, timeliness and integrity of the information produced.

(c) System of checks and balances and greater simplicity in process of governance.

(d) Clarity of responsibility to enhance accountability.

(e) Adherence to the rules. Corporate action need to conform to letter and spirit to codes.

REASONS FOR RECENT INTEREST IN CORPORATE GOVERNANCE

Some reasons for recent awareness for corporate governance are:

(i) Directors must realise that their job is to represent the shareholders and other stakeholders, and not offer themselves as the rubber stamp of the managing director.

(ii) There is rise of institutional investors and safeguard their interest.

(iii) In the wake of globalisation, there are numerous takeover moves in corporate world.

(iv) Advent of investigating reporting in business journalism.

(v) Activism of regulatory bodies such as SEBI.

(vi) Corporate governance has to do with power and accountability.

Numerous companies have now laid elaborate systems, structures and processes as part of corporate governance. Companies are highlighting their practices of corporate governance in their annual reports. For better appreciation, an illustration of corporate governance in ITC Ltd. is given in Annexure I to this chapter. We have also included, as sample, corporate governance reports of two large companies, i.e. Telco and Reliance Industries Ltd. (see Annexure).

ROLE OF CODES

The norms of conduct for the members of Board of Directors are extensively dealt within the Indian Companies Act. It is now being realised that legislation alone cannot ensure ethical conduct; *self-regulation* is a more vital part in market systems. The spirit invoked by codes that are voluntarily administered is much more important than mere law. Thus, the Bajaj Committee of the CII (Confederation of Indian Industry) has a stricter norm in the codes than in the Companies Act and requires the director to resign if he does not attend at least 50% of the meetings. He cannot be a member of more than 10 boards, etc.

The most important happenings of the year 2001 from the corporate governance point of view are:

- SEBI asks all Group A companies to submit a corporate governance report along with their annual reports, starting April 1, 2001. This is one of the recommendations of the Kumar Mangalam Birla Committee Report on Governance.
- Tata Group Chairman Ratan Tata bags the Government of India award for corporate governance. It recognises the Tata Business Excellence Model (TBEM) that evaluates Tata companies on the basis of seven criteria—leadership, strategic planning, customer and market focus, information and analysis, process management, HR and business results.
- In a bid to comply with the corporate governance code, Dabur India inducts three independent directors, to its board, taking the total number of independent directors on its board to nine.
- ICRA announces its plan to rate companies based on corporate governance. The parameters, transparency, accountability, responsibility, and fairness.
- The Conference Board completes its report *Determining the Effectiveness of the Board of Directors*, which takes a critical look at some of the top 25 Indian companies.
- USAID agrees to fund Price Water House Coopers to train institutions like SEBI and UTI in areas of corporate governance and insider-trading.

To conclude, all knowledge shines more in practice than just theory. It is especially true of ethics. Gandhiji put this idea powerfully, when in response to a question on what his message to humanity was, he said: "My life is my message." He meant that people follow his attempt at ethical living, than read his speeches and writings, without any change in their lives.

Annexure

CORPORATE GOVERNANCE IN ITC LTD.

Corporate governance refers to their structure, systems and processes in a corporation, that are considered most appropriate to enhance its wealth generating capacity. Codes of corporate governance are necessary as business organisation has to match upto both societal expectations and stakeholders' aspirations.

In ITC, decision-making within company has been broadly divided among 3 levels:

(i) The *Board of Directors* at the apex, *as trustee of shareholders*. Board bears responsibility of strategic supervision of company apart from fulfilling statutory obligations. Board bears the principal responsibility of fashioning a governance code.

Board's composition is a balanced mix of executive and non-executive directors, with non-executive directors constituting a fair majority.

(ii) Major responsibilities of board are on recommendations of *various sub-committees*:

(a) Nominations committee,

(b) Audit, legal committee, and

(c) Senior management succession and appointment to board-related remuneration, compensation.

Membership of sub-committees is confined to non-executive directors as a measure of transparency.

(iii) *Strategic management is delegated to corporate management committee* (comprising of whole time directors and senior management) for reviewing strategic business plans.

Through this 3-tired inter-linked governance process, a balance has been created for need for executive freedom and need for supervision, control and checks and balances.

The formalised governance code prescribes the highest ethical standards in the conduct of company business. Chairman of ITC sets personal example so that governance code is internalised within the organisation and becomes part of its culture.

Source: Speech by Y.C. Deveshwar, Chairman, ITC Ltd. on 12.8.1998, *Economic Times*, 19th August 1998.

CHAPTER

43

COMPANY MANAGEMENT

In this chapter we shall briefly discuss the following aspects relating to managing companies:

(1) Government machinery for administration of The Companies Act, 1956.

(2) Functions of the board of directors.

(3) The Chairman of the board.

(4) The Committee's of the board.

(5) Duties of Directors.

(6) Role of Company Secretary.

(1) GOVERNMENT MACHINERY FOR ADMINISTRATION OF THE COMPANIES ACT, 1956

Central Government is to administer and enforce this Act through *Department of Company Affairs* under Ministry of Finance.

1.1 The Company Law Board

For day-to-day administration of the Act, the Company Law Board is set-up. Its powers have enlarged from 1991.

(i) It is a quasi-judicial body. It exercises powers of the court or hitherto with government.

(ii) Members of Company Law Board not to exceed 9 and are to be appointed by the Government and one of them to be the Chairman. Tenure of members is upto 3 years.

(iii) Members form separate benches and will enjoy powers of civil court to enforce inspection of documents/evidence.

(iv) Members have powers for execution of its orders.

(v) Appeal against the orders of the Company Law Board lies before High Court and is final.

1.2 Registrar of Companies (RoC)

He is for most of routine functions of Company Law Board, such as for filing documents and returns. RoC is basically a registry and an office of record. It has four regional offices at Mumbai, Kolkata, Madras and Kanpur.

Advisory Committee: It is to advise Company Law Board and the government as may be referred by either of them.

1.3 Jurisdiction of Courts

Respective High Courts have power for their jurisdiction. Central government may empower any district court to exercise powers of High Court except for:

(i) Investigation into company's affairs,

(ii) Power to sanction compromise with creditors, and

(iii) Sanction amalgamation.

Civil Courts under general law can exercise power for personal rights, i.e. matters such as breach of trust, compensation by company to shareholders.

(2) FUNCTIONS OF THE BOARD OF DIRECTORS

Good governance is the primary duty of the board. It is responsible for setting standards and ensurance that company achieves them. The Chairman will have a major impact. Board is considered as agent or trustees. They are liable for negligence, breach of trust under the Companies Law.

(a) Board is the representative of the shareholders to ensure the company has clear goals and to measure progress against these goals.

(b) The board will agree the strategy and resources needed to achieve it.

(c) The chief executive is appointed by the board who monitors his performance.

(d) Board must annually review succession and management development plans.

(e) Board will set and monitor the operating climate in the company through statement of values (policies, etc.).

(f) Limiting senior executive's compensation.

(g) Environmental protection.

(h) Avoidance of fraud within company.

(i) Hiring and firing key executives.

(j) Caring for employee's interest.

(k) Ensuring active participation in local community welfare schemes.

(l) Acquisition and disposal of assets of the company or its subsidiaries.

(m) Investments, capital projects, authority levels, treasury (banking policies and risk management policies).

(n) Director to act in good faith and act honestly.

(3) THE CHAIRMAN OF THE BOARD

It is proper to separate role of Chairman from Chief Executive in the interest or providing checks and balances.

- Chairman is leader of the Board.
- Chairman must set standards for Board of Directors.
- Chairman is a link between Board and shareholders.
- Chairman must be satisfied with corporate reporting to shareholders such as interim and annual results, annual general meeting, etc.

(4) THE COMMITTEE'S OF THE BOARD

There are three major committees of the Board. Their role is explained:

(i) Audit Committee

(a) Most important committee for providing checks and balances and for internal control.

(b) Review the interim and final accounts.

(c) Keep board informed of financial reporting and areas of disagreements with the auditors.

(d) To decide impartially disputes between management and external auditors.

(e) Audit fee is appropriate and auditor work plan is adequate.

(f) Meet atleast twice a year.

(g) It comprises of minimum three directors who are non-executives.

(ii) Remuneration Committee

(a) To keep lid on executive remuneration.

(b) To have a reward policy that can attract, retain and motivate director's to achieve goals of the company.

(c) Acts independently with access to its own external advice.

(d) Performance packages decided are linked with shareholder interest.

(e) Annual Report presents clear view of policies of the company.

(iii) Nomination Committee

It is chaired by the Chairman and non-ex-Director's are brought in for selection.

(5) DUTIES OF DIRECTORS

1. To attend board meetings and devote attention and care to the affairs of the company.
2. Not allow other Directors to commit liable acts.
3. Not to exceed his powers.
4. Act in best interests of company and stakeholders and customers, also creditor (not to defraud them).
5. Maintain confidentiality.
6. Not to make secret profits.
7. Not to misapply company assets.
8. Not to compete in business with the company.

Directors to "act in good faith and genuinually otherwise liable in the court under Secs. 201 and 633 of the Companies Act, 1956. Court to be satisfied that director had acted honestly and reasonably.

(6) ROLE OF COMPANY SECRETARY

The Company Secretary finds his or her rightful place as a professional by virtue of being a member of a recognized professional body, which exercises supervisory jurisdiction over its members. The Institute of the Company Secretaries of India highlights that in every corporate, there is a strong backbone—the company secretary. By virtue of integrated knowledge of multiple disciplines of law, management, finance and corporate goverance, a Company Secretary is the vital link between the company, its board of directors, shareholders, government and other agencies.

The Compant Secretary is:

- An expert in corporate laws, securities laws and capital market and corporate governance.
- Chief advisor to the board of directors on best practices in corporate governance.
- Responsible for all regulatory compliances of company.
- Corporate planner and strategic manager.
- Continuing professional development.
- Pre-membership Training (16 Months).
- Final Examination (9 Papers).
- Intermediate Examination (8 Papers).
- Foundation Examination (5 Papers).

CS Course: Eligibility

- For Intermediate Course: Graduation.
- For Foundation Course: 10+2.
- Students of any discipline in Arts, Commerce and Science excluding Fine Arts can pursue this course.

Under the Company Secretaries Act, 1980

When the ICSI became a statutory body under the Company Secretaries Act, 1980, the code of conduct envisioned in the First and the Second Schedules to the Act became a statutory prescription. These schedules describe certain items of conduct, which are prohibited and they are considered as "Professional Misconduct." The Company Secretaries are required not to indulge in such practices. The professional misconducts are broadly described in the said schedules as under:

First Schedule

Part I: Professional misconduct applicable to the members of the Institute in *Practice*—(12 Clauses).

Part II: Professional misconduct in relation to the members of the Institute in *Service*—(3 Clauses).

Part III: Professional misconduct in relation to members of the Institute *generally*—(4 Clauses).

Second Schedule

Part I: Professional misconduct in relation to the members of the Institute in *Practice* requiring action by a High Court—(10 Clauses).

Part II: Professional misconduct in relation to the members of the Institute *generally* requiring action by a High Court—(2 Clauses).

With the Companies (Amendment) Act of 1988, the practising side of the Company Secretaries Profession came into being. This aspect has been growing very fast during the last few years, as can be seen from the certification works mentioned below:

(a) With the increase in the threshold limit to Rs. 2 crores, for appointment of whole-time secretary, secretarial compliance report has been introduced in the case of companies having a paid up share capital of ten lakhs of rupees or more, as to whether the company has complied with all the provisions of the Companies Act, 1956 and such a Certificate of Compliance issued by a Secretary in whole-time practice should be attached to the Board's report.

(b) Certification of Annual Return by a Secretary in whole time practice in the case of listed companies.

(c) Certification of certain forms and returns filed with the ROC.

(d) Secretarial Audit Report introduced by SEBI regarding reconciliation of total admitted capital with both the depositories and the total issued and listed capital.

(e) Certification of Compliance of Corporate Governance.

(f) Various recognitions and certification work secured by the Institute.

The Companies (Amendment) Bill, 2003 proposes to enlarge further the scope of practice by a Company Secretary, as under:

(i) The Central Government may at any time, direct Secretarial Compliance audit of a Company, if that Government is of the opinion that the affairs of the Company are not being conducted in accordance with the provisions of the Companies Act, 1956 and such an audit should be conducted by a Company Secretary—Section 383B of the Bill.

(ii) All documents, returns, and forms required to be filed with the Registrar or any statutory authority should be pre-certified by a Company Secretary in whole-time practice [Section 383C of the Bill].

Need for Evolving New Norms of Professional Ethics and Etiquette

What the Company Secretaries Act, 1980 describes as professional misconduct are minimum expectations. There is no limit for maximising and enhancing these values and norms.

Any effective system of code of conduct or misconduct cannot be legislated to meet all situations. There is a limit to legislative effort. At the same time, any code of conduct, however pervasive it may be, cannot remain static, as the value system keeps changing from time to time.

The professional misconducts described in the Company Secretaries Act are prohibitive in nature, as they are worded negatively. However, the professional ethics and etiquette must make positive assertions of uncompromising honesty, integrity, professional competence, high quality of service, maintenance of confidentiality of clients' information and a high degree of ethical behaviour and morality. These are sterling qualities of head and heart and needs to be cultivated consciously.

Observance of Code of Conduct and Professional Ethics

It is clear from the above that the Company Secretary, be it in employment or practice renders a host of services to the corporate sector and other clients. The practising side of the Profession is fast expanding and the Company Secretary is being called upon to shoulder higher responsibilities. This calls for extensive training and an ability to distinguish between righteous conduct from those deviant and unedifying.

P.T. Rangamani states that Professionals are key figures in corporate management. They are change agents with the capability to clean up the organisation and put in place proper legal and ethical strategies as part of the day-to-day management. A professional worth the name should have faith and commitment to the basic ethics of his calling.

References

S. Krishnamoorthy, Professional Ethics and Social Commitment, *Chartered Secretary*, November 2003.

D.K. Prahlada Rao, Code of Conduct and Professional Ethics, *Chartered Secretary*, November 2003.

Code of Conduct for Company Secretaries, issued by ICSI.

P.T. Rangamani, Ethics, Business and Professions, *Chartered Secretary*, November 2003.

www.icsi.edu

CHAPTER

44

CORPORATE GOVERNANCE (CG) FACTORS FOR ORGANISATION SUCCESS

I. C.G. SUBJECT NOT IN VOCABULARY A DECADE AGO

C.G. has an important role to play as an instrument of *investor's protection*. It is a tool to judge and evaluate the standards and ethics of corporate management.

C.G. Code *is a guide* to govern the operations and affairs of the company in a manner which will *enhance the long-term* value of thé company for all those who are associated with it, viz. shareholders, creditors, customers, government, employees and society at large.

The importance of C.G. lies in its contribution both to *business prosperity* and to accountability to shareholders. C.G. has its origin in U.K. Issues involving C.G. are taking a high profile and have *come to the fore* recently *in India.*

Awareness of C.G. in India is timely as it is appalling that we come across many instances of *corporates looting their shareholders* for personal gains of owners.

IMF study shows that after liberalisation between *1992 to 1998* large number of *public issues* for capital collected large amounts:

- IMF study states Indians deposited hundred billion dollars in *foreign banks.*

Period	No. of Issues	Money Raised (Rs. in crores)
1991-92	195	1400
1992-98	4855	44462
1998-99	22	504

- USA research study during 1994 and 1995, showed India's capital *flight to USA* was to tune of four to eleven billion dollars.

To mention some scams in India—Harshad Mehta, Ketan Parekh, UTI, RIL, etc. Corporate accounting scandals have created a crises of investor's confidence.

USA also facing scams—Worldcom, ENRON, TYCO, VIVEDI, MARCONI, QUEST, MERC, XEROX, etc. in 2001. Greed and dishonesty has lead to dismal ethical standards in business. USA is passing through trying time.

Pressures of competition have raised *fresh concern about legal, ethical and moral* dimensions of enterprise, such as invoking codes of conduct and benchmark best system and practices as a part of good corporate responsibility.

II. MEANING AND BASIC INGREDIENTS OF GOOD GOVERNANCE

Meaning

In practice, C.G. means *role of the board of directors* of the company, and *its auditors,* towards protecting the shareholders (in fact all stakeholders) interest in every business decisions. The board of directors have *to set proper* organisation structure, systems, norms and processes for *direction, supervision* and *accountability* of their corporation.

Basic ingredients of CG are:

(i) *Accountability* of board of directors to ultimate owners - shareholders and their satisfaction programme. Promoting a social and economic order.

(ii) *Transparency in timely disclosures* of right information with integrity.

(iii) *Clarity in responsibilities* of directors, chairman and managing director through empowerment to enhance accountability.

(iv) *Quality and competence of directors* and their track record. Popular participation in decision-making, implementation and responsiveness.

(v) *Checks and balances* in governance. Conforming to, laws, rules and spirit of codes.

- Thus good C.G. is adaptation of *best practices* by ensuring higher level of *transparency* and *accountability, fairness* in operations, *full disclosure,* and *integrity* and compliance to laws.

III. CORPORATE GOVERNANCE FOLLOWED BY COMPANIES

Now companies are explaining in their annual reports about the compliance of C.G. I.T.C. Ltd. highlighted C.G. (in August 1998) compliance set-up in their corporation.

Every year the prestigious "Golden Peacock award for excellence in Corporate Governance and Corporate Social Responsibility" is given. Last year it was won by TISCO.

IV. FACTORS FOR SUCCESS OF CG

1. Structural-Dimension

Norms of conduct for board of directors are laid in *Indian Companies Act.* Activism of *regulatory bodies (SEBI)* is essential. Lot more tightening of regulations is needed.

Legislation alone cannot ensure ethical conduct. The spirit invoked by *voluntary codes* is also important. *Chairman has to set* personal example so that governance code is internalised within the organisation. Emphasis on this is a positive trend, but still more to go.

2. Cultural-Dimension

Society—their values, morals and awakening, their *responses to corrupt practices* are crucial to be highlighted by investigative business journalism. Role of internal "*whistle blowers*" is vital to bring to light wrong practices.

In final analysis, success of corporation depends on the professional ethics of managers/directors and they should not offer themselves as rubber stamp of M.D./owner. They have to create a *value-based* organisation culture by following ethical standards. The chairman has to set personal example to interalise code of corporate governance.

3. Corporations have to recognise the importance of *commitment to values and servicing the interest of the stakeholders,* which alone can ensure survival and growth in the long-run. Good C.G. can be created *consciously adhering* to entrepreneurship and pursuit of excellence. Corporation to ensure that highest *standards of ethics* and responsible conduct *are met* throughout the organisation.

It is now established that a high sense of professional morality must comprise one of the core-values of corporate governance, for long-term as well as short-term success of the industry. Ethical values are now a days not looked upon, any more, as costs imposed on the industry, or a check on efficiency and profit maximization, but are considered imperatives for sustainable corporate growth. Prof. Armartya Sen asserts that ethics can be good economics and, thus a valid pursuit of corporate governance.

A high-developed sense of integrity and ethics enables corporate governance to build a trusting, long-term relationship with customers and consumers. Ethics, thus surely makes a lot of economic sense.

V. FACTORS INFLUENCING QUALITY OF GOVERNANCE

Quality of governance is influenced by integrity of the management, ability of the board, adequacy of the processes, commitment level of individual board members, and quality of corporate reporting and participation of stakeholders in the management. [Sanjiv Agarwall]

Quality of governance depends on the following factors:

(i) *Integrity of Management*: A Board of directors with a low level of integrity is tempted to misuse the trust reposed by shareholders and other stakeholders to take decisions that benefit a few at the cost of others.

(ii) *Ability of the Board*: The collective ability, in terms of knowledge and skill, determines the effectiveness of the Board.

(iii) *Adequacy of the process*: Board of Directors cannot effectively supervise the executive management if the process fails to provide sufficient and timely information to the Board, necessary for reviewing plans and the performance of the enterprise.

(iv) *Commitment level of individual board members*: The quality of a board depends on the commitment of individual members to tasks, which they are expected to perform as board members.

(v) *Financial Reporting*: Accuracy and transparency in financial statements and disclosure, internal controls and independence of auditors.

(vi) *Participation of stakeholders in the management*: The level of participation of stakeholders determines the number of new ideas being generated in optimum utilization of resources and for improving the administrative strûcture and the process.

(vii) *Quality of Corporate Reporting*: The quality of corporate reporting depends on the transparency and timeliness of corporate communication with shareholders. This helps the shareholders in making economic decisions and in correctly evaluating the management in its stewardship.

Best practices of corporate governance will broadly include—a definition of practices that define good governance; a code of best practices covering the constitution of the board, its various Committees, defining their goals and responsibilities, exploring preferred internal systems and disclosure requirements. Qualitative improvement in the corporate governance in our country based on a code of good corporate practices and meaningful disclosure of information to shareholders hold the key to corporate success.

This is necessary in the context of changing profile of corporate ownership, with the increasing flow of foreign investment, preferential allotment of shares to the promoters of companies and the new role being given to mutual funds. This means better governance and management of corporate bodies, prompt compliance of legal and financial obligations and adherence to ecological and environmental standards. The benefit of such governance must accrue to the investors, customers, and lenders of finance and to the society at large.

Objective of Good Governance

It is felt that objective of corporate governance, i.e. the overall objective of wealth generation and competitiveness for the benefit of all can best be achieved through the twin components of:

- An "inclusive approach to *director's duties* which requires directors to have regard to all the relationship on which the company depends and to the long, as well as the short-term implications of their actions, with a view to achieving company success for the benefit of shareholders as a whole; and
- Wider *public accountability*: this is to be achieved principally through improved company reporting.

VI. TO CONCLUDE

Corporate governance is a *process or a set of systems and processes* to ensure that company is managed to suit the best interest of all stakeholders. The stakeholders may be internal (promoters, members, workmen and executives) and external (shareholders, customers, lenders, dealers, vendors, bankers, community, government and regulators etc.). It is interplay between company's, shareholders creditors, capital markets, financial sectors, institutions and law. Corporate governance is concerned with the *establishment of a system* whereby the directors are entrusted with responsibilities and duties in relation to the directions of corporate affairs. Maximization of shareholder's wealth is the cornerstone of good governance.

The concept of corporate governance hinges on total transparency, integrity and accountability of the management, which includes non-executive directors. The importance of corporate governance lies in its contribution both to business prosperity and to accountability.

CG has attained international importance. More than profits, it is the quality of governance which will ensure corporate survival and growth and reinforce the faith of different stakeholders in a company. This will help in retaining customer's loyalty in the knowledge millinnium. Leadership's ethical values can infuse new work culture throughout the organisation.

References

Sanjiv Agarwall, Corporate Excellence—A Product of Good Corporate Governance, Vistar, New Delhi.

CHAPTER

45

Codes of Corporate Governance and Audit Committee

In view of many scandals and frauds in accounting, it is felt that corporate governance should extend beyond corporate law. There should be greater *transparency* and maximising *shareholder's value*, so there should be good corporate code containing corporate practices.

Many developed countries have documented corporate codes to meet the need.

I. WORK ON CORPORATE GOVERNANCE IN INDIA

India has formulated codes of corporate governance through various committees, more important ones being:

(i) CII (Rahul Bajaj) Committee, 1996 Recommendations

On Board of Directors

(i) Simple structure of Board and should meet 6 times a year and 1/2 days' discussion.

(ii) Listed companies in excess of Rs. 200 crores and above to have non-executive directors atleast 30%. They were to pay an important role in the interest of shareholders.

(iii) Director not to be on the board of 10 companies.

(iv) Director who does not attend 50% or more meetings not to be considered for re-appointment.

(v) Audit committee to be appointed to assist the Board.

(vi) All key information to be placed before the Board of Directors.

Rules for Governance of Companies

(i) Members of the Board to have clearly defined responsibilities.

(ii) Board should not be bull dozed by the nominees of the management.

(iii) Financial institutions to divest their stake if less than 10% stake in company.

(iv) Company should not accept further deposits, if they have defaulted on fixed deposits.

(v) Key information e.g., annual operating plans and budgets, quarterly results, internal audit reports to be reported to the Board.

(ii) Kumar Mangalam Birla Committee on Corporate Governance (2000) Recommended that:

- Board to set-up qualified and independent audit committee to enhance the credibility of financial disclosures and to promote transparency.
- Companies to provide consolidated statements in respect of all its subsidiaries in which they hold 51% or more of the share capital.
- Shareholders to show greater degree of interest and involvement in the appointment of directors and auditors.
- SEBI norms to be laid.

(iii) Naresh Chandra Committee on Corporate Audit and Governance (2002) Recommended that:

- Audit firm's rotation is not required.
- Every five years, audit partner should rotate.
- Audit committee to be set-up of all independent directors.
- Companies to have atleast 50 percent independent directors.
- Certain professional assignments should not be undertaken by auditors.

(iv) Recommendations of Narayana Murthy Committee

SEBI constituted a Committee on Corporate Governance with the Chairmanship of Shri N.R. Narayana Murthy. The Committee included representatives from the stock exchanges, chambers, commerce and industry, investor associations and professionals, and debated on key issues and made recommendations as under. Some mandatory recommendations of the Committee are:

(a) Audit Committees of Publicly Listed Companies should required to review the following information mandatorily

(i) Financial statements and draft audit report including quarterly, half yearly financial information.

(ii) Management discussion and analysis of financial condition results of operations.

(iii) Reports relating to compliance with laws.

(iv) Management letter/letters of internal control weaknesses issues by statutory/internal auditors.

(v) Records of related party transactions.

(b) Disclosure of Accounting Treatment

In case a company has followed a treatment different from the prescribed in an accounting standard, companies should be give reasonable period of time within which to cure the qualifications SEBI/Stock Exchanges. Mere explanations from companies is not be sufficient.

(c) Risk Management—Board Disclosure

Procedures should be in place to inform Board members about the risk assessment and minimization procedures.

(d) Training of Board Members

Companies should be encouraged to train their Board members on the business model of the company as well as the risk profile of the business parameters of the company, their responsibilities as directors and the best ways to discharge them.

(e) Written Code of Conduct for Executive Management

It should be obligatory for the Board of a company to lay down the code of conduct for all Board members and senior management of a company. The code of conduct shall be posted on the website of the company.

All Board members and senior management personnel shall affirm compliance with the code on an annual basis. The annual report of be company shall contain a declaration to this effect signed-off by the CEO and COO.

(f) Nominee Directors—Exclusion of Nominee Directors from the Definition of Independent Directors

The committee recommends that there shall be no nominee directors where an institution wishes to appoint a director on the board, such appointment should be made by the shareholders. An institutional director so appointed shall be subject to the same abilities as any other director. Similarly, nominee of the Government on public sector companies shall be similarly elected and shall be subject to the same responsibilities and liabilities as other directors.

(g) Non-executive Directors' Compensation—Limits on Compensation paid to Independent Directors

All compensation paid non-executive directors may be fixed by the Board of Directors and should be approved by the shareholders in general meetings. Limits should be set for the maximum number of stock options that can be granted to non-executive directors in any financial year and in aggregate. The stock options granted to the non-executive directors shall vest after a period of at least one year from the date such non-executive directors have retired from the Board of the company.

(h) Internal Policy on Access to Audit Committees

Personnel who observe an unethical or improper practice (not necessarily a violation of law) should be able to approach the audit committee without necessarily informing their supervisors. Companies should take measures to ensure that this right of access is communicated to all employees through means of internal circulars, etc.

(i) Whistle Blower Policy

Companies should annually affirm that they have not denied any personnel access to the audit committee of the company and that they have provided protection to 'whistle blower' from unfair termination and other unfair or prejudicial employment practices.

The appointment, removal and terms of remunerations of the chief internal auditor must be subject to review by the audit committee. Such affirmation shall form part of the Board's Report on corporate governance that is required to be prepared and submitted together with the annual report.

2. COMMITTEES ON CORPORATE GOVERNANCE: GLOBAL PERSPECTIVE

A number of Committees were set-up to look into the various aspects of corporate governance. These include:

(i) Sir Adrian Cadbury Committee on Financial Aspects of Corporate Governance (1992).

(ii) Mervyn E. King's Committee on Corporate Governance (1994).

(iii) Greenbury Committee on directors' remuneration (1995).

(iv) Calpers global corporate governance principles (1996).

(v) Business Round Table (BRT) Statement on Corporate Governance (1997).

(vi) Hampel Committee on Corporate Governance (1998).

(vii) Blue Ribbon Committee on Improving the Effectiveness of Corporate Audit Committees (1999).

(viii) Combined Code of best practices (LSE), 1998.

(ix) OECD Principles of Corporate Governance (1999).

(x) CACG principles for Corporate Governance in Commonwealth (1999).

These committees/codes recommended the following in relation to accounts, reporting audit.

(i) Cadbury Committee on Financial Aspects of Corporate Governance (1992)

- Audit committee to have minimum three members, written terms of reference and authority to investigate.
- Listed companies to publish full financial statements annually and half yearly reports interim.

Code of Best Practice to Incorporate

(i) Board to present assessment of company's position.

(ii) Directors to report on effectiveness of internal control systems.

(iii) Aspects to be included by audit committee.

(ii) King's Committee on Corporate Governance (1994)

- Effective internal Audit function.
- Establishment of Audit Committee.
- Observance of highest level of business and professional ethics.
- Accounting standards in line with international standards.

(iii) Blue Ribbon Committee on improving the Effectiveness of Corporate Audit Committees (1999)

- Members of Audit Committee to be independent.
- Audit Committee to consist of independent directors only.
- Audit Committee to have minimum of three directors—each to be financially literate.

- Audit committee to have formal written charter, approved by the full board, specifying.
    - o responsibilities, and
    - o structure, process and membership.
- Charter to specify outside auditor's responsibility towards board and Committee.
- Companies to attach with Annual Report a letter from Audit Committee as to whether or not:
    - o management reviewed the audited financial statements with the committee;
    - o outside auditors discussed with the committee, their judgements; and
    - o committee believes that company's financial statements are fairly presented in conformity with generally accepted accounting practices (GAAP).

(iv) CACG Guidelines—Principles for Corporate Governance in the Commonwealth (1999)

- ensure that the corporation complies with all relevant laws, regulations and codes of best business practice;
- ensure that the corporation communicates with shareholders and other stakeholders effectively;
- serve the legitimate interests of the shareholders of the corporation and account to them fully;
- Regularly review processes and procedures to ensure the effectiveness of its internal systems and control, so that the decision-making capability and the accuracy of its reporting and financial results are maintained at a high level at times; and
- Ensure annually that the corporation will continue as a going concern for its next fiscal year.

(v) Hampel Committee on Audit and Accountability

Companies and auditors should apply the following principles:

- *Financial reporting*—The Board should present a balanced and understandable assessment of the company's position and prospects.
- *Internal control*—The Board should maintain a sound system of internal control to safeguard shareholder's investments and repay assets.

- *Relationship with auditors*—The Board should establish forms and transparent arrangements for maintaining and appropriate relationships with the company's auditors. Audit committee should be established and be responsible to board. It should review the scope and result of the audit, its cost effectiveness and the independence and objectivity of auditors.
- *External Auditors*—The external auditors should independently report to shareholder in accordance with statutory and professional requirements and independently assure the board on the discharge of its responsibilities (financial reporting, internal control) in accordance with professional guidance.
- *The auditors have dual responsibility*—The public report to shareholders on the statutory financial statements and on other matters and additional private reporting to directors on operational matters.

Ronnie Hampel's final findings are as follows:

- Each company should establish an audit committee of at least three non-executive directors, at least two of them independent. It does not favour a general relaxation for smaller companies, but recommend shareholder to show flexibility in considering cases of difficulty on their merits.
- It does not recommend any additional requirements on auditors to report on governance issues, nor the removal of any existing prescribed requirements.
- It suggests that the bodies concerned should consider reducing from 10 percent the limit on the proportion of total income which an audit firm may earn from one audit client.
- It suggests that the audit committee should keep under review the overall financial relationship between the company and its auditors to ensure a balance between the maintenance of objectivity and value for money.
- It recommends that the directors should report on the company's system of internal control. It also recommends that the auditors should report on internal control privately to the directors, which allows for an effective dialogue to take place and for best practice to evolve.
- Directors should maintain and review controls relating to all relevant control objectives, and not merely financial controls.
- Companies which do not already have a separate internal audit function should from time to time review the need for one.

- The requirement on directors to include a "going concern" statement in annual report should be retained.
- Auditors are inhibited from going beyond their present functions by concerns about the law on liability. Account should be taken of these concerns by those responsible for professional standards and in taking decisions on changes in the law.

Similar principles have been incorporated by combined code of good corporate governance and code of best practices as adopted by London Stock Exchange.

3. NEED FOR AUDIT COMMITTEES

(a) The corporate accounting malaise is spreading world over. The reasons for accounting failures could be varied, but are certainly worrisome. The examples of Enron Corporation's financial scandal, Worldcom's accounting absurdity and myriad of complex financial interrelationships between widely dispersed subsidiaries, Xerox's overstating revenues, Merck, Quest Communications, etc. These suggest the clue that audit committee function can come to rescue to solve this problem. In India too, there are reasons that demand necessity for strengthening of accounting and audit function—siphoning of funds, capital erosion, non-repayment of deposits and debentures, etc.—all have something to do with financial reporting. It is now seen everywhere that it is the *accounting issues that are becoming major issues of corporate governance.*

(b) An effective audit committee should not function as a policing agent, to assess risk or to guess or judge audit performance. A good *audit committee should satisfy themselves* that auditors are to watch the interests of stakeholders if something foul and fishy is observed. Audit committee should instill confidence and trust amongst readers and uses of financial statements. Infact, more valuable than the qualified report one gets from the auditors, might be an assurance from the audit committee that the figures and reporting ought to be correct and reliable.

(c) Corporate scandals are the good reasons for having effective audit committee.

(d) Recently, KPMG in UK has launched a UK Audit Committee Institute (ACI) to help members of audit committee meet their increasing governance demands placed upon them.

(e) Audit Committee as a Committee of Board

The Audit committee should ideally comprise of at least 3-4 non-executive directors (wholetime directors to be invitees). The Audit Committee is established to give additional assurance regarding the quality and reliability of the financial information used by the board and financial information issued by the company. Its activities would normally include reviewing financial statements and inspection reports, ensuring the sound functioning and compliance with various relevant statutes; monitoring: (a) control of corporate risks, (b) establishment of an appropriate internal control framework, (c) activities of the internal audit department; and liaison with external auditors. The Audit committee should ensure that adequate mechanism for prevention and detection of frauds, is in place. The Audit Committee should confirm to the board once a year that the internal controls of the company are adequate. The Committee should meet at least four times a year.

(f) Audit Function under Sarbanes—Oxley Act

The Sarbanes—Oxley Act, 2002, a recent enactment in US which deals with corporate governance and corporate social responsibilities has also emphasized on the audit function and financial disclosures. It strengthens the power, importance and *independence of audit committee.* It provides for constitution of Public Company Accounting Oversight Board to oversee the audit of public companies that are subject to securities laws, establish audit report standards and rules and inspect, investigate and enforce compliance on the part of registered public accounting firms, their associates and accountants. It also lays emphasis on audit independence and prohibits an auditor from performing specified non-audit services alongwith an audit. Audit firms will be appointed by and will report directly to the audit committee and subjected to rotation of partner and firm.

In India, the office of Comptroller and Audition General (CAG) functions as an oversight audit body for audit of public sector companies.

(g) Audit Committee: Statutory Provisions in India

Section 292A of the Companies Act, 1956 (inserted w.e.f. 13.12.2000) contains a provision relating to establishment of audit committee by every public company having paid up capital of Rs. five crores or more.

Clause 49 of the uniform listing agreement prescribed by the Securities and Exchange Board of India is applicable to all listed companies. Clause 49 of listing agreement deals with corporate governance and prescribes for setting up of a qualified and independent audit committee.

(h) As per section 292A of Companies Act, 1956, audit committee should have discussions with the auditors periodically about internal control systems, scope of audit including the observations of auditors and review of the half yearly and annual financial statements before submission to the board and also ensure compliance of internal control systems. It shall have authority to investigate into any matter in relation to such matters and shall have full access to information contained in records of the company.

(i) As per clause 49 of the listing agreement, audit committee is empowered to investigate any activity within terms of reference, seek information from any employee and recommend appointment and removal of external auditor, fixation of audit fees, approval for payment for other services, review with the management the annual financial statements before submission to board, review adequacy of internal control system, oversight of company's financial reporting process and disclosure of its financial information to ensure that financial statements are correct, sufficient and credible, reviewing adequacy of internal audit function, reviewing company's financial and risk management policies, etc.

4. RECOMMENDATIONS OF NARESH CHANDRA COMMITTEE

Naresh Chandra Committee on corporate audit and governance has suggested that the audit committees should consist entirely of independent directors. An audit committee charter would have to be prepared which would lay down the role and functions of the audit committee. It has suggested that audit committee of listed companies and unlisted public company with paid up share capital and free reserves of Rs. 10 crore or more or turnover of Rs. 50 crore or more should be made up entirely of independent directors.

Naresh Chandra Committee on Corporate audit and governance which submitted its report in last week of December 2002, has also not recommended statutory rotation of audit firms but favoured compulsory audit partner rotation on the lines of recently enacted US Sarbanes Oxley Act. Going by global practices and the fact that there is no conclusive proof of the gains before deciding the audit firm rotation, it has observed that rotation of audit firms would not result in any better governance. Rotation of auditors is likely to cause a major dislocation when a new auditor firm is appointed. It takes time to understand the complexities of a business and more mistakes tend to happen in the first two years.

It has suggested that the partners and atleast fifty percent of the engagement team (excluding article clerks and trainees) responsible for the audit of either a listed company or companies whose paid up capital and free reserves exceed Rs. 10 crore or companies whose turnover exceed Rs. 50 crore should be rotated every five years. It has also held that persons who are compulsority rotated could, need be, allowed to return after a break of three years, as prevail in European Union and IFAC. It has, however, recommended setting up of Corporate Serious Fraud Office/Quality Review Boards for punishing erring professionals.

REFERENCE

Sanjiv Agarwal, Corporate Governance and Audit Committee, *Chartered Secretary*, October 2003.

CHAPTER

46

TOWARDS BETTER CORPORATE GOVERNANCE— SOME CRITICAL AREAS

1. INTRODUCTION

The bedrock of good corporate governance is conducting the affairs of a Company in such a way as to ensure fairness to customers, employees, investors, vendors, the government and society at large. It requires quality of leadership, values, transparent management, vision and goals, respect for law, and sense of social responsibility for which there are no rigid standards. One crucial aspect of governance is investor-friendliness. Companies will have to focus on understanding the expectations of diverse groups of investors and constantly communicate with them. We reproduce here extracts from an article by B.D. Pande.

2. THE INDIAN EXPERIENCE

By virtue of being family owned and managed, in most Indian Companies, in 1920s and 1930s, the executives and directors were either the promoters themselves or their kith and kin—people they trusted.

During pre-independence period, Jamsetji Tata, G.D. Birla and Kasturibhai Lalbhai business empire more out of a spirit of entrepreneurship than any motive of accumulation of personal wealth, they set their own standards of good corporate governance. There is no better standard of corporate governance than the philosophy that owners are "trustees."

Jayaprakash Narayan wrote about the Tata Trusts—"The concept of trusteeship fostered by Mahatma Gandhi received a much-needed fillip in Tata enterprises. After all, what is this concept of trusteeship? Under it, all wealth is a social trust and every individual—the employer, the engineer or even the ordinary mistry—is a trustee entitled to its proper utilization for the common good. True to the ideals of its founder, the House of Tata has always promoted this concept of trusteeship and today, more than 85% of its profits go to trust."

The House of Tata had progressive and nationalistic outlook right from the very beginning. Jamsetji Tata, the Founder of House of Tata.

While the House of Tata has maintained its track record of good corporate governance, companies like Infosys, HLL, AVB group, Wipro, Bajaj Auto, Satyam Infoway, Dr. Reddy's Lab, Maruti Udyog, ICICI, L&T, ONGC, HDFC, Amul and Ranbaxy are some of the companies well known for good corporate governance.

The House of Tata has instituted THE JRD QUALITY VALUE AWARD for corporate excellence incorporating the highest standards of corporate governance for the group companies to compete and achieve. Tata Steel was the first company in the group to achieve this prestigious award as a milestone in their efforts towards greater excellence in 2000 after tremendous efforts put in over several years. *The Economic Times* award for CORPORATE EXCELLENCE was achieved by Tata Steel in 2001.

Critical Area for Good Governance

1. The Board of Directors

The Board of Directors of a company have to overview the performance, vouch for the accuracy of company's disclosure and disgorge personal profits from corporate wrongdoings. When Enron Corporation collapsed, board of directors of the company were rightly singled out. The board has to keep a watchful eye on management and the shareholders should watch the board. Every board should conduct an extensive self-evaluation, involving a review of board policies and an anonymous appraisal of individual directors. The findings should be made public and every three years, the board members with the lowest ratings should resign. The board should contribute substantially in the performance and growth of the company.

The external directors in the board should be selected purely on the basis of their experience and expertise. Companies should work on making their boards more independent. This can be achieved by creating a *Nomination Committee* consisting of only external directors, which will decide on the composition of board in terms of choosing external directors as well as the employees who deserve to be promoted to the board. Only shareholders or the Nomination Committee should have the powers to remove external directors. Another important committee is the *Audit Committee.* This committee should consist of only external directors with the authority to appoint external and internal auditors. Yet another important committee is *Compensation Committee* which determines the compensation-package for the members of the company's board. This committee should also consists of only external directors.

The nominee directors, in most cases, play a limited role to the extent that they ensure that the companies meet their obligations to the financial institutions represented by them. They seldom play an active role in discussing matters like corporate strategy, annual plans, capital, budgets, future business plans, human resource development and succession, etc.

The chairman and CEO must set the tone and take the lead being the custodian of corporate ethics and must set example on issues of morality and business principles. As the old axiom goes, "The bottleneck is at the head of the bottle."

The code of governance has now become mandatory in the case of listed companies. As such, the chairman and CEOs ensure that independent directors make an effective contribution in an increasingly competitive environment.

2. Executive Pay

Management Guru Peter F. Drucker has long warned that the growing pay gap between CEOs and workers could threaten the very credibility of leadership. He argued in the mid-1980s that no CEO should earn more than 20 times the company's lowest paid employee. He said that if a CEO took too large a share of the rewards, it would make a mockery of the contributions of all the other employees in a successful organization. Stock-option was once viewed as a symbol of enlightened governance. But it has resulted into CEOs commanding a vast wealth through the use of this (Stock option) financial instrument. There is a fundamental difference between investors who have put their own money at risk in the share market and option-holders, who do not. But companies have gone even further to shield top executives from losses in a falling stock market. Worse still, the system does not provide an incentive for outstanding performance. Employees feel betrayed by bosses who grow rich on stock options, huge salaries and other benefits.

3. Accounting

Corporate accounting is very important. The spate of recent accounting scandals reveal involvement of all the players. The board fingers management, management blames the auditor and the auditor blames the rules. They all pass the buck on others making it difficult to fix up accountability. As a matter of fact, the audit panel should review all non-audit engagements to ensure that they don't jeopardize the audit. The auditors should rotate after certain years to ensure a fresh look by an audit firm. An expanded auditor statement in the annual report should be there instead of just asserting that the financial statement meet generally accepted accounting principles. The auditors are placed in a unique position to judge how dependent the financial statements are on assumptions that could prove faulty.

4. Analysts

Analysts are often rewarded for their ability to attract and maintain investment business. They are generally under pressure from the companies they analyse to maintain a positive ratings. These are conflicts that may never be resolved. But there are some steps that could alleviate the pressures that prevent analysts from telling the truth.

First, the investors should be imparted information about their investment. They should realise that the free research which they get is often just a marketing tool. Secondly, it should be mandatory that reports prominently disclose a firm's specific investment-banking-relationship with the company that has been covered. Thirdly, normally most ratings sound like variations on "we think, this is a decent stock that you should own." In ratings, terms such as "accumulate", "hold" and "sale" are part of an elaborate web of euphemism in which "neutral" means "dump this loser and run for your life." It would make sense if all analysts used the same terms. Analysts should present real position of a company. They should not play with words and figures and misguide investors. The searching eye of the research analysts has been a material factor in making corporate managements more alive to their responsibilities.

5. The Regulator

The Security and Exchange Board of India (SEBI) was first set-up as an administrative entity in 1988. In January 1992, it was granted statutory powers. However, the regulator still lacks the teeth to police the market effectively. The SEBI took two years to complete its investigation of Harshad Mehta's 1998 rigging of share prices of Videocon, Sterlite and BPL. It is true that SEBI does not have enough powers. Justice Dhanuka report, which recommended strengthening of SEBI in November 1998, is still pending with the Ministry of Finance. In addition to more powers, SEBI needs expert services of professionals, not bureaucrats, to make it independent and market-savvy. And instead of its decisions being reviewed by appellate tribunals, they should go to the High Courts directly. Nowhere in the world, quasi-judicial decisions by market regulators are reviewed by an arm of the executives. SEBI should be given greater freedom which will create confidence amongst domestic as well as FIIs that India is a well-regulated market.

6. The Stock Markets

The early 1980s witnessed the equity cult gaining ground. In April 1988, the SEBI was constituted. Over the Counter Exchange of India (OTCEI) was formed in 1992 to encourage small companies list their securities. The creation of the National Stock Exchange (NSE) by leading financial institutions in 1992 triggered the move to screen-based trading for equities, debt instruments, and hybrids. Globalisation had opened up the Indian Capital markets to Foreign Institutional Investors (FII) in 1992. Foreign custodians and brokerage firms have brought their best global practices to Indian markets. Equity research gained prominence. Dematerialise (Demat) form of settlement was introduced in 1996. Derivatives trading began in June 2000.

However, the globalisation of markets has made the Indian financial markets more vulnerable to external events, as a result of which, any movement in the global markets have a corresponding ripple-effect in India. In our home grounds also, we had a spate of stock-scams. Mundhra scandal in 1957, the Securities scam in 1992, the M.S. Shoe scam in 1994, the CRB scam in 1997, the Mehta's second scam in 1998, Vanishing Companies scam in 1998, Plantation Companies scam in 1999, Ketan Mehta scam in 2001, and Nagpur District Co-operative Bank and other Co-operative Bank scams in 2002 had rocked our stock-markets. These scams reveal cracks in the foundation of Indian stock markets, and call for higher corporate governance standards.

With the globalisation, companies merely find themselves short of capital. One way to address this shortage could be sourcing of global capital by way of ADRs, GDRs, FDI, and financing by way of debt. To do this, there is no alternative except to subscribe to the highest standards of corporate governance, and create confidence in FIIs that their fund will remain safe and provide good return on their investment.

CONCLUSIONS AND SUGGESTIONS

- Several corporate executives have committed breach of trust by cooking the books, shading the truth, and enriching themselves with huge stock-options while shareholders suffered breath-taking losses. Demise of Enron corporation reveals corporate excess and wrong doings by a renowned company. Such incidents erode the goodwill giving way to widespread suspicion and mistrust.
- It is the primary goal of a corporation to maximize shareholder's value in a legal and ethical way. Shareholders invest their money in a corporation and trust the management to the extent that their money will be utilized properly and they will receive a decent return on their investment. The corporation has to sell its products and services and optimize return on the investment.
- If investors lose faith in corporations, they could choke-off access to capital. The loss of trust threatens the ability to create new jobs and reignite the economy. It also leaves a taint on the executives who act with integrity

- Directors who fail to direct and CEOs who fail at moral leadership pose the most serious challenge for the corporate world today. The case of Enron corporation and their dealing with Arthur Andersen is nothing but a perfect storm where greed, lax oversight, and outright fraud had taken place.
- If the governance of the modern corporations is not transparent, it will create a severe crisis of confidence. Corporations having high degree of professionalism, sound system and procedure, and transparency in reporting are considered investor-friendly and enjoy high valuation on the stock-exchanges.
- The SEBI should follow International accounting standards. It should work closely with the London-based International Accounting Standards Board to create one global accounting framework. It should be improved in terms of accounting for off-balancesheet entities, stock-options, intangible assets, and much more.
- The SEBI should also establish national standards relating to the qualifications and responsibilities of board of directors by refining the definition of what constitutes an independent director and specifying the duties of the Audit Committee and Compensation Committee.
- Corporate governance has to take care of social responsibility of business. The gap between the haves and the have-nots has to be reduced by finding out ways to involve the have-nots in the business-process. A company can not thrive if it standsout as a pillar of prosperity in a sea of poverty
- The shareholders should be involved in all major decisions. All special resolutions need to be approved by them, and the company should send them not only the annual report, but also the quarterly financial report. Issues related to ownership and control in family-managed companies need to be sorted out.
- The Chairman/CEOs of corporations should make projection about future financial performance of their company which is being done by companies like Infosys, Tisco, Satyam Computer, Wipro, etc.
- There should be a consensus on the ideal governing structure for public sector companies where the board,—thanks to a large number of controlling authorities,—have been rendered irrelevant. These boards have little autonomy and have to function strictly within the policies laid down by their respective government departments. The chairman and CEO of these corporations are transferred frequently. They are either ex-bureaucrats or Senior Secretaries whose tenure seldom exceeds 3 years. Such boards remain largely ineffective which reflects in the poor performance of majority of public sector

undertakings.

- The shareholders are the true owners of a corporation. They trust the corporation enough to invest time, effort, and money in it. The market share will hold managements accountable, and will punish those in whom their trust has been misplaced.
- Organisation of tomorrow will need to be more fleet-footed, flexible, and seekout opportunities to grow rapidly as never before.
- The concept of accountability should be broadened as found in Germany to include not only the management, but all individuals or institutions involved in the decision-making process.
- To ensure independence of non-executive directors, the professional bodies may develop panel consisting of people of great acumen and honour in their own right as the financial institutions do, and also to assist them in developing their skills which will help evoke positive response from the investors.
- All efforts should be made to enhance the value adding capability of auditors in general and to make the internal audit effective in particular on priority.
- A good corporate governance makes the corporation assume the role of trusteeship with all the attendant checks and balances to create a high performing company.
- Matters like corruption and political activities of a company should be brought in the knowledge of all concerned and such activities should be watched with a view to take corrective action in time.
- Corporate consolidation through mergers and acquisitions is the buzz word in today's corporate world to face competition and challenges of change for survival. It provides the economy of scale. Mergers and acquisitions are widely accepted as a good way to grow and acquire competitive advantage. Corporate governance, however, is necessary for take-over methods, disclosure of bids and creeping acquisitions, etc.
- A stable government with enough goodwill in world-community is also essential for corporate governance. FIIs park their money in those countries where a stable government exists with a liberal and progressive economic policy and continuous reform-process. India has been facing very tough competition from Asian Countries such as Singapore and Thailand in FIIs investment.

Reference

Courtesy: B.D. Pande, National Institute of Personnel Management, *Personnel Today*, June 2002.

CHAPTER

47

CORPORATE EXCELLENCE—A PRODUCT OF GOOD CORPORATE GOVERNANCE

CORPORATE GOVERNANCE AND EXCELLENCE

Achieving corporate and professional excellence is what we all aim at in our life. This is what will make us different from others and this is what we can achieve as ultimate. Business must be lead by example. That example is set by good governance practices.

I. Corporate Governance is a Means to Corporate Excellence

"Corporate Governance" is a more important concept of lasting value. It is an important concept and a means to an end—that of achieving corporate excellence. The Corporate Excellence can be achieved only by proper tapping and nurturing good corporate governance practices.

1.1 *Corporate Governance is the most appropriate tool for achieving Corporate Excellence.* Companies should identify, assess and establish core values, core capability and core purpose to achieve Corporate Excellence.

It is imperative that all corporates be innovative, creative and responsible citizens to bring excellence in their vision, mission and action. Good Corporate Governance is a source of competitive advantage and *a critical input* for achieving excellence in all productive, economic and social pursuits.

1.2 Excellence and Good Governance are so intertwined that achieving one without the other or at the cost of other is simply unimaginable.

Corporate governance brings about *equilibrium between the expectations* of owners, employees, customers and other stakeholders to achieve corporate excellence. A recent survey by McKinsey and the World Bank has found that institutional investors are willing to pay 20 percent more on average with a good governance record.

1.3 A company's most valuable asset is goodwill it enjoys with its stakeholders, which can only be earned by actions, not demanded.

1.4 Good governance is a necessary condition for achieving excellence, not a sufficient one. Good governance is a source of competitive advantage and critical to economic progress. The essence of Corporate Governance is transparency, accountability, investor protections, better compliance with statutory laws and regulations, value creation for shareholders (as also for other stakeholders) and societal value.

1.5 It is being increasingly recognized that being a responsible corporate citizen is important in ensuring long-term success of a company India's corporate sector has a new tryst with destiny. To face the formidable challenges of the future, the corporate sector has to be empowered with a new vision, dynamic mission and a new mandate to follow best practices of governance.

1.6 Corporate governance is the one and *only route to achieve corporate excellence.* Every corporate has become alive to the reality of having to stay lean and fit in order to deliver its best strictly in consonance with the principles of corporate governance. Any attempt on the part of corporates to circumvent this reality and resort to shortcuts to achieve excellence will only result in short-circuiting their ill-conceived efforts.

2. Intrapreneurship is a key element incorporate culture and growth, and is an important tool for achieving corporate excellence. Intrapreneurrs are an asset to any organization; they lead to geometric growth of an organization and help achieve Corporate Excellence.

3. What does corporate excellence or success really mean would depend on one's vision. Excellence has been defined in many different ways. Some commonly accepted measures of excellence in the modern economic model of the firm include:

- Profitability.
- Satisfied stakeholders, such as, customers, employees and shareholders.
- Revenue and profit growth.
- Growth in market share.
- Growth in market value (Stock Market Capitalisation).

If these are the measures of excellence, what are the pre-requisites of achieving this? Peter and Waterman in one of his works, "In Search of Excellence" has studied 10 large American corporations with demonstrated variables which that can explain corporate excellence. These are:

(1) A bias for action.

(2) Closeness to the consumer.

(3) Autonomy and entrepreneurship.

(4) Productivity through people.

(5) Hands on, value driven.

(6) Sticking to the knitting.

(7) Simple form, lean staff.

(8) Simultaneous loose-tight properties.

4. One can see importance being given "to Corporate Governance" issues, as we understand them today. Look at the importance being given to satisfied stakeholders, closeness to customers productivity through people and value driven organizations.

Corporate Excellence and Governance an closely connected concepts and it is felt that in the long-run, it is difficult to achieve excellence without good governance.

5. As we move towards the knowledge society and witness center of power shifting away from owners/shareholder and towards the consumers and the knowledge worker, we will see the process of democratization of enterprises. Thus, links between excellence and governance are likely to be much stronger in the future.

6. Peter and Waterman gave a new view of excellence in organisation. They highlighted seven 'S' approach that is, structure, strategy, system, style, staff, skills and super-ordinate goals. According to them when seven variables are aligned, we have an organised excellent company. Further companies which operate with super-ordinate goals and strong cultures, they found that people at all levels know, what they are supposed to do in most situations *as guiding values* are clear. Seven factors will be driving force for excellence in organisation.

7. As rightly observed by Martin Luther King, Jr., "We shall have to repent in this generation, not so much for the evil deeds of the wicked people but for the appalling silence of the good people." The message is loud and clear. The corporates can ill-afford to be silent, overlooking and laid-back. Doing nothing is not an option. They have to proactively formulate a code and stick to it to survive as well as to excel.

8. *Corporate Governance according to Indian ethos*: For Corporate Governance to lead to Corporate Excellence, it must be structured according to the principles of the Vedas, aligned with natural law.

In the Indian context, corporate governance can be drawn from the following *age-old 'mulyas'* (*values*):

(a) public good which means greatest possible good of all;

(b) *Dhanam*, creation of wealth through competence (*kaushalam*) and productivity (*utpadakta*);

(c) *Swatantrata*, autonomy and independence, in business decisions;

(d) *Vishwastata*, trusteeship, implying that management is a trustee of stakeholder;

(e) *Dharmyudh*, fair battle, providing a level playing field to all and ensuring fair competition.

(f) *Vividhata*, variety or innovation ensuring flexibility in approach.

It is important to be genuine in purpose, straight forward in execution and not to repeat mistakes.

Corporate governance means being true to own belief and it constantly teaches the value of understanding the stakeholders.

It builds enduring bonds with shareholders, employees, investors, depositors, borrowers, suppliers, customers and business constituents.

We have shared age-old *mulyas* (values) practiced in ancient India, derived by the principles of the Vedas. It may be stressed that corporate governance is not merely about enacting legislation. It is about establishing a climate of trust and confidence. Ethical business behaviour and fairness cannot be legislated. Strengthening Corporate Governance is basically a political, social and cultural process in which government and the private sector have to synergise. Corporate Governance is about how a company fulfils its obligations to investors and other stakeholders. It is about *commitment to values and ethical business conduct and a high degree of transparency*.

REFERENCES

Sanjiv Agarwal, "Corporate Excellence—A Product of Good Corporate Governance, Vistar.

S.K. Bhatia, Management of Change and Organisation Development, Deep & Deep Publications Pvt. Ltd., New Delhi.

CHAPTER

48

EVALUATION FOR IMPROVED CORPORATE GOVERNANCE AND ROLE OF THE CHAIRMAN

Evaluation is a process of judging performance and efficiency of boards. Whether boards are executing its role and responsibility effectively.

It is like *introspection* and a part of board planning process. It helps in continuous feedback as termed by Zandera.

Feedback Cycle in a Board

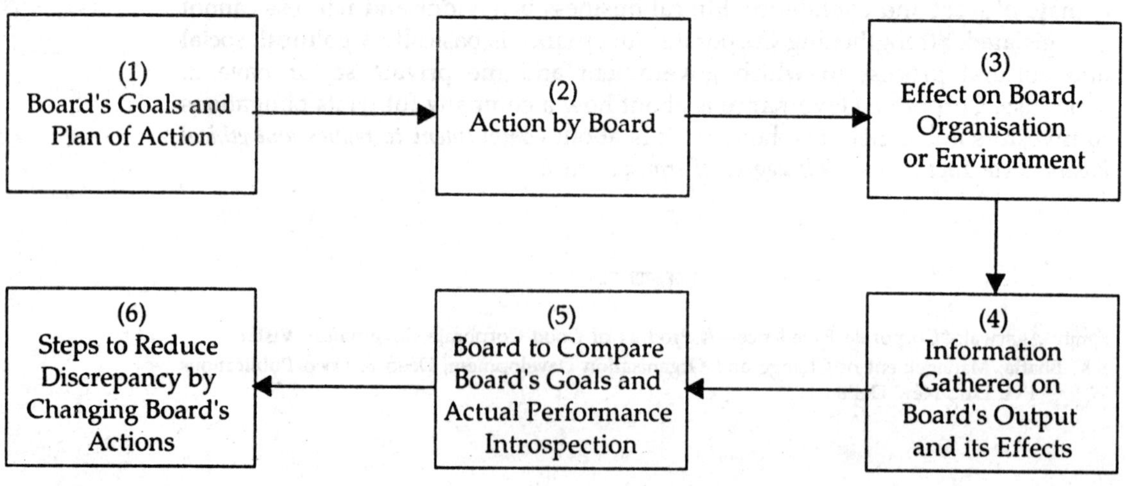

CONDUCTING BOARD'S PERFORMANCE EVALUATION

Demb and Neubauer has suggested evaluation as under:

(a) The Directors Themselves

Their *intent* e.g. of CEO/Chairman; loyalty to company and stakeholders, choosing directors with skill, balance, their numbers, identify departures.

(b) The Role of Board

Agreeing on board's mission; allocation of responsibilities (fortfolio); setting priorities, decide delegations to management to avoid undue power compliance of legal requirements; level of board's involvement.

(c) Board's Working Style

Setting committees; enough meetings for monitoring; ensuring adequate information to board for decision.

(d) Assessing Individual Directors by the Chairman

Directors preparedness for meetings, whether they do their home work, ask probing questions, exhibits ideas and enthusiasm, make suggestions on innovations and planning. Board to adopt rule of retirement age or director's term, etc.

(e) The Chairman

Board as a whole to decide appraisal of the chairman. Directors may air dissatisfaction on various areas.

(f) The CEO

He has service contract. Comparing performance against set task standards, e.g. financial ratios, comparing with other similar companies. Conduct evaluation of CEO in his absence and other executive directors.

With increasing responsibilities and accountability being placed on the board of directors, performance evaluation may emerge as an essential tool for in-house introspection and continuous improvement.

ROLE OF THE CHAIRMAN OF THE BOARD

We present here extracts from the book titled "Chairman of the Board" by Brian Lechem, John Wiley & Sons, appeared in *Hindustan Times*, New Delhi.

Chairman of the Board provides practical guidance on this critical role. The title Chairman of the Board conveys a number of meanings. The word 'Chairman' is said to be gender neutral as a person chosen to preside over a meeting of a corporate body. The terms he, she, his or her—are frequently used in this context to signify that both men and women can occupy this position.

With globalisation, the role of the Chairman has assumed greater significance. In fact, today the Chairman should ensure that the company's Board comprises efficient team members who can pave the way for strategic and successful leadership.

The role of the Chairman is subject to change with time. The person occupying the position is responsible for ensuring that the board fulfils its obligations and commitments. S/he should see that the board is committed to work towards its goals.

The following lines suggest *some of the duties* that a Chairman must fulfil order to ensure smooth functioning of the company:

- The Chairman must provide a style. While autocracy or consensus styles are tolerated, democratic views are more welcomed by the Board members.
- The Chairman must also structuring the agenda. This does not mean imposing one's will upon the Board.
- The Chairman must maintain a balance while discussing matters. Spontaneous participation tends to militate against constructive and pragmatic dialogue.
- The Chairman must ensure prompt implementation of all action plans taken during Board meetings.
- Efforts should be made by the Chairman to ensure that the Board meetings are properly conducted.
- Many corporate commentators have suggested that the corporate failure in the recent times had efficient boards. And that it was quality of decision-making that deteriorated leading to the collapse of the company.

Leadership

The Chairman must *show leadership capabilities* apart from maintaing relationship with the top management. Traditionally, the Chairman acts as the spokesperson of the company To fulfil this role, s/he must be briefed well. The Chairman must also cultivate appropriate temperament, personality and public speaking skills.

Selecting the Chairman

Often the Chairman's selection does not occur as prescribed in books. In theory shareholders elect the Directors at the AGM. In private and closely held companies, this theory may be followed to an extent. In theory, however, the Directors are supposed to be elected in the annual meetings. But in reality, the company owners select them and rest is a formality. Shareholder's participation is rarely witnessed. However, larger companies form nominating committees that operate independently though recent surveys suggest that personal acquaintance is disproportionately important in the selection process of a Director.

Training

A growing need has been felt for training the Directors before they assume responsibilities. Induction and orientation are two different components of a Director-training programme. Many companies have initiated the process of providing newly appointed Directors with a briefing kit comprising past board minutes, current and previous financial statements, organisation charts, and the key decisions taken by the company

Balance of Roles

Usually the Chairman is often considered as the CEO of the company. It's therefore extremely crucial to maintain the balance between the two roles. Clearly, the CEO holds a great deal of power. S/he controls the agenda and the flow of information to the Board, has massive knowledge of the affairs of the company makes recommendations regarding senior appointments, handles capitals spending initiatives, etc.

A Board must maintain the checks and balances on management. The crucial point is that the role of the Chairman is essentially different from that of the CEO. Not every one who makes a good CEO is a successful Chairman. The following are few of the touch-stones that should be remembered while executing the roles of both the Chairman as well as the CEO:

- There should be a clearly accepted division between the Heads of a company to ensure a balance of power and authority.
- The Board should include non-executive Directors of sufficient calibre to carry significant weight in the Board's decision.
- The Board should have a schedule of matter specifically reserved to ensure that the decision and control of the company is firmly in its hands.

Succession Plan

The most important role of the Board is to safeguard the succession of the CEO. The first thing that the Board should do in evaluating the CEO performance is to detect a period of relative mediocrity as early as possible rather than being complacent and wait until the situation demands more urgent action.

Board in Action

The purpose of the Board meeting is to deal with an agenda. In other words, the meeting must be planned and not left to informal unstructured discussion.

Collective Responsibillty

The term 'principle of collective responsibility' is very powerful. Even if the Director votes against or abstains from the motion s/he is bound by the decision of the majority and, by law, is equally liable for the implications of the decision.

Developing Corporate Strategy

Until recently the Board used to be the only approving-body in the process of strategy development. The management took care of the complete process. The fundamental in developing a corporate strategy consists of determination of precise objectives according to a specified time frame. It gives a clear idea of what we are trying to achieve and how long should it take us to get there. Strategy development consists of SWOT analysis that helps in identifying the strengths, weaknesses, opportunities; and threats to the organisation. Strategy development involves preparation of a set of clear-cut objectives that shows the changes necessary in marketing, production and use capital, management, human resources.

Legal Liabilities—Interpretation of the Situation

Many Directors have expressed concern that in this age of technological change, it is impossible, or perhaps not practical to know everything that's going on in the company or the extent of potential legal liability. Unfortunately, the law does not easily distinguish between the different types of Directors. They are all considered equal and are equally exposed legally. If the Directors individually or collectively make discerning inquiries or independent judgements, then they will perhaps have a better chance to prove that they've acted diligently.

Reference

Extracted from 'Chairman of the Board' by Brian Lechem (John Wiley & Sons). (*Courtesy*: K.B.S. Kumar, Trainee Analyst, ICFAI Press), *Hindustan Times*, New Delhi, gratefully acknowledged.

CHAPTER

49

Corporate Governance— Some Views of Learned Professionals

Here we present some views of expert professionals particularly Company Secretaries, suggesting direction and trends in corporate governance:

(i) Corporate Board Members are Governors of the Company and should be Dedicated to Ethics and Morality—Justice Ashok A. Desai

Now members of the Board are rated as governors of the company. They have to raise themselves above the personal urge and aptitude. When the corporate governance, by their governors attains impersonal character, accountability and transparency would obviously persist as most natural and perennial feature. That interest also comprehends corporate ethics and morality. This could be accomplished with singular dedication and determination of the governors to the ideals of corporate governance.

(ii) Managers should not Reduce themselves to Figurehead or Abuse their Authority—N.J. Jhaveri

Corporate governance has to be designed to oversee manager's decision-making without impairing managerial effectiveness.

Board members, in addition to relevant skills, ought to respect basic organizational discipline and demonstrate high quality professionalism.

(iii) The Work of Professionals to be Subject to Reivew by Independent Quality Review Board as Recommended by Naresh Chandra Committee—D.K. Prahlada Rao

The success stories of a few companies like Infosys, Wipro, Reliance and a host of others, including efforts of some of them in raising capital in the international markets through ADR/GDR issues brought home the vantages in strictly following the new norms of governance. The corporate sector also reacted in a positive and pro-active manner to the new norms of governance.

(iv) Corporate Governance to be Implemented in Real Spirit and not merely to Confining to Legal Compliance—Amit K. Vyas

Corporate governance has been a much debated buzzword since the year 1998 with a large number of seminars, workshops, conventions and programmes devoted to it. It has been the most favourite topic for the able writers, learned speakers and business luminaries during the last 5 years. In practical realm we see examples of sheer hypocrisy with even some top corporate names shying away from the implementation of CG in its real spirit and merely confining its application to the four walls of the laid down law.

(v) Confidence in Corporate Governance of a Company is Dependent on Role of Professional(s) Associated with it—(a) Dr. K. Dileep Kumar, and (b) B.S. Bhaskar

(a) In order to bring about 'real' change and improvement in corporate governance practices, it becomes necessary, firstly, to stop deterioration of good practices, then to cognize new responsibilities of those at the helm of affairs, reform them and strengthen their skills, adopting sound governance principles. Professionals like company secretaries, accountants and auditors shall have to work together more closely in the years to come so as to help restore confidence and trust in the companies they work for.

(b) The directors are supposed to safeguard the investment of shareholders and are duty bound to aggrandize their net worth. If anything illegal or unethical is observed, the concerned professional should be bold enough to prevent such happening. Great responsibility is fastened on the shoulders of professionals such as company secretaries, chartered accountants and lawyers to safeguard and protect the deteriorating ethics and values.

(vi) Governance Value Creation Code (GVCC) should Help Create Shareholder's Value—S. Ramanathan

Unless performance is measurable it has no value. This is an accepted principle of business enterprises world over. So the attempt to rate a company based on the right governance practices adopted and creating a shareholder's value over a period of time is the right move to measure the performance of the corporate *vis-a-vis* its counterparts as far as shareholder's stake is concerned.

(vii) The Ultimate Result of Corporate Governance: Value Management—Ranjan Mukherjee

Corporate governance is not meant for only bringing transparency in management and board functioning. Ultimately, the Board has to deliver best possible financial results so that the expectation of the stakeholders could be satisfied. The corporate governance models should not restrict itself to graphical presentation in the annual report, or in prize distribution on corporate governance. How best value could be created by a corporate on continuous basis should be the prime objective of any Board of Directors. Corporate governance is to be practised in such a manner so that all stakeholders attached to the company can derive benefit out of it.

(viii) Corporate Advisory Board: An Emerging Trend—Vivek Sadhale

Advisory boards can play a useful function for attaining the goals of the company. Competence and motivation of the CEO to have an effective advisory board is the prime criteria for its success or failure. It is important to maintain a good balance in terms of size and competence on the advisory board.

(ix) Corporate Professionals are to be Technology Savvy in Digital Era—Nandan M. Nilkani

Corporate pr fessionals such as company secretaries have a responsibility to ensure that corporations possess the necessary skills and capacities to engage in electronic and Internet-based transactions, and to adapt its strategies and business practices to the new digital paradigm. Corporate professionals need to be aware of, and be updated on, the implications of the newly introduced cyber laws to their companies. They also need to ensure that corporations work in full compliance with all legal requirements with respect to these types of transactions. This job becomes all the more onerous, considering that such transactions are increasingly becoming mainstream.

Infosys is a role *model of corporate governance*; perhaps, the only company in the world to publish financial statements in accordance with the accounting standards of eight countries (Australia, Britain, Canada, France, Germany, India, Japan, and the U.S.). The company's annual report discloses compensation details for directors and very many top executives as well.

(x) Governing the Corporation (Views Abroad)

There is plenty of evidence to show that a weak and ineffectual board—especially one dominated by a powerful CEO—will sooner or later commit strategic errors that will seriously damage the company's performance and in some cases may bring to the brink of ruin.

There are several causes for these weaknesses:

(i) Boards have not been in a position to really govern the business as they are busy in routine rituals and CEO only has effective power.

(ii) Combining the offices of CEO and Chairman reduces effectiveness.

(iii) Sometime boards are simply the big.

(iv) Independent directors are not qualified to the job properly.

(v) Most external directors lack the motivation and/or the time to do the job properly.

(vi) Lack of relevant information about the company and its problems.

Board need to focus its attention on key activities:

(i) Focusing on core activities.

(ii) Adding value and reducing cost.

(iii) Providing a business culture that embraces change.

(iv) Moving with the market.

(v) Leading the business.

(vi) Integrating e-Business activities, aligning and optimising resources.

(vii) Managing risk.

(viii) Establishing and maintaining good corporate governance.

These activities can be grouped into three main areas:

(a) How best to set the strategy and direction, i.e. more focusing on cost-cutting or on the core business. How the enterprise will create value and improve.

(b) Managing financial performance.

(c) Ensuring operational effectiveness.

In short, the board must drive the company, and not the other way around.

(xi) Call for Governance—Academy

Infosys Technologies chairman and chief mentor NR Narayana Murthy has urged the industry to set-up an academy to train independent directors to bring stringent corporate governance practices. "India requires at least 4,000 independent directors with more training in corporate governance."

"The academy can offer basic training in accounting practices, corporate governance, management analysis and foreign bourses' norms.

(xii) Find Governance Rating Index

The Securities and Exchange Board of India's (SEBI) plan to put in place a corporate governance index has hit a road-block as rating agencies are finding it difficult to come up with a rating model which would effectively capture two attributes, creation of wealth and corporate governance.

(xiii) (i) "The Cadbury Committee was of the view that good corporate governance serves not only the company interest but also the society in which it operates.

(ii) The key to good corporate governance is the realisation on the part of corporate managers that they are accountable for their performance.

(iii) There is also a general feeling that there must be much more value-addition from members of the Board, particularly the non-executive directors.

(iv) Boards should draw up a code of ethics and statement of business practices and not only publish them, internally and externally, but also set a role model by living up to these practices.

(v) The failure of Indian corporates have made it clear that good corporate governance can only be brought about effectively by *greater self-regulation* and pressure of public opinion generated by large investor groups. The regulatory mechanism of government and legal agencies has failed in ensuring even the minimum standards of proper corporate governance . . . ."

(vi) Corporate governance is basically a system of making *directors accountable* to the shareholder for effective management of the companies and also with adequate *concern for ethics and values.*

(vii) "Transparency and accountability are generally resisted by corporate managers, including family entrepreneurs who are not enlightened enough to see the change in their role. Left to itself, the process of change in corporate governance would be very slow. Hence, the need for a regulatory framework which will ensure effective monitoring for good corporate governance."

To Conclude

Professionals like company secretaries, accountants and auditors shall have to work together more closely in the years to come to help restore confidence and trust in the companies they work. There has to be more proactive participation in the process of planning and setting up of corporate governance strategies, implementation and devising built-in safeguards against downfall.

The key to the secret of corporate governance practice is a goal for attaining highest standard of good governance meticulously.

References

Editorial summaries of Articles, *Chartered Secretary*, August 2003.

Indian Management, October 1998.

CHAPTER

50

Corporate Governance Essential for Market Capitalism: Few Lessons for the USA

We reproduce here interesting and analytical suggestions from Prahlad K. Basu for tightening corporate governance in India.

From Adam Smith to Alfred Marshall, the underlying thrust in the working of markets had been that whatever deficiencies surface on the demand and supply side of the market, they would be cleared through *competitive price mechanism*. Although Marx raised his voice of dissent—which centered round the markets of the factors of production, notably capital—the economic history of the growth of capitalism proved him to be wrong.

Today, the voices of concern are once again being raised. Not only about 'market failures' but also failures, *sometimes deliberate*, of those who manage corporate empires and the auditors who are supposed to be independent and on whom the shareholders ultimately depend. To ensure smooth functioning, *corporate governance needs both checks and balances.*

In India, the 'market failure' syndrome after the country's Independence was tackled through the mixed economy 'models' of Nehruvian socialism—by creating public enterprises in power, steel, fertilisers, chemicals, mines and other sectors of the economy—who could provide the 'supplies' in the market instead of importing them at prohibitive price. In terms of *value added*, India's private enterprises continue to have a dominant share of the market.

Following the practices adopted in the developed countries, we also set up the Company Law Board, the Monopolies and Restrictive Trade Practices Commission, the Securities and Exchange Board of India, the Institute of Chartered Accountants, the Institute of Costs Accountants, the Institute of Company Secretaries, etc. It is time we look into these institutions so that they can be suitably restructured before they *prove to be helpless and redundant*.

The initiative taken by the government to introduce a bill on setting up the National Competition Commission is timely and welcome, provided it is efficient not only in *contro'ling monopolies* but also in providing effective competition in the market. In this context, it is necessary to provide a word of caution about the disinvestment initiative taken by the present government. Hopefully it will not 'undo' these proposed reforms by creating new monopolies and oligopolies.

What are the new initiatives needed to provide checks and balances in India's market capitalism? The answer to this question should be sought not only to check the 'scams' of Harshad Mehta, Ketan Parekh and UTI, and a whole host of *non-performance* companies protected behind BIFR's fig leaf, who are responsible for the 'loot' of the non-performing assets of the Indian banking system. We also have to check the new 'scams' of the kind the US and UK markets are facing today with WorldCom, Enron, Tyco, Vivedi, Marconi, Quest, Merc, Xerox, etc.

For someone like me who teaches 'management' to young minds and sees the working of companies as non-executive director on the boards—India's 'preparedness' in this direction has so far been inadequate. It is common knowledge that any *company can 'fudge'* their accounts in a number of ways.

Getting the *revenue figures* right is the first step in assuring fair and accurate financial reporting. Fictitious figures of amounts receivable, capitalised revenue expenses, provision for deferred tax, special purpose vehicle loans outside the balance sheet are common methods whereby accountants and auditors can hoodwink any company's shareholders. Thus, *auditing* the auditors is an extremely important area of reform—on which India has yet to take even the first step. The system of dual audit for the much maligned Indian public enterprises has its internal checks and balances which does not apply to private companies.

The US initiative in enacting a comprehensive legislation which was passed by the US Congress in the last week of July under the leadership of Paul Sarbanes, the Democrat Senator, and Senator Oxley, should be studied in India so that we can also take similar steps taken by the US government in this direction. Indian companies with US 'listing' should be deeply concerned about the possible consequences of this legislation in the days to come.

There are four foundations of the recent US legislation.

- A strong, *independent public oversight board* will set professional standards for the accountants and auditors to make sure that they adhere to their standards. Such a board with investigative authority to oversee the Institute of Chartered Accountants in India would be a step in the right direction.
- The US act would *safeguard the independence of US auditors* by prohibiting accounting firms from non-audit management consulting services, which, in a company like Anderson, compromised the integrity of the audit for Enron. Anderson earned more in consulting fees than it did in performing audit. Price Waterhouse Coopers and KPMG in India should be encouraged to *divest their management consultancy wings*—as already done by Ernst and Young and Deloite groups.
- New standards introduced under the US act for corporate accountability *requiring executive certification* of financial statement, expanding rules governing conflicts of interest and instituting severe punishment for corporate fraud and other wrong doing should also be instituted in India.
- Finally, new act will give the *oversight bodies* the resources they need. Both the new Oversight Board and the Federal Accounting Standards Board in the US would be independently funded by public companies.

The aim of the US reforms is that with *tougher accounting rules* and corporate bodies can get back to serving customers, investors and employees. In India, our reform must also ensure that the corporate bodies must serve the government by paying taxes on their profits—to remove the blot from India's scandal sheet of less than 10 per cent of GDP currently raised in tax revenue by the central government compared to between 40 and 50 per cent by the governments in eastern and western Europe and north America.

In India, we should also aim at a new model of public-private competition—following the example of China—to achieve the desired results of an efficient market economy. The *entire disinvestment strategy* should be remodelled accordingly with an eye on both 'efficiency' and 'welfare'.

The Sarbanes Oxley Act, 2002, in the US, compliments the Al Gore initiative taken to enact the Government Performances and Results Act (GIPRA), 1994, whereby every functionary in the US government has to deliver performance through targets and results which is an essential feature of any modern state-of-art bureaucracy. The urgency for enacting the GIPRA for India can hardly be overstated.

The Indian bureaucracy will be modernised when every member of the bureaucracy—from top to bottom—will be under tremendous pressure to set *measurable performance targets* and fulfil them, as they are in the US under GIPRA. This would also provide an effective remedy to the Indian malady of corruption in the bureaucracy.

It will be of interest to mention that Former Enron chief executive Jeffrey Skilling turned himself into the FBI Thursday and was shown on national television being led in handcuffs to face reported fraud charges. Skilling, who wore a white shirt, dark suit and no tie, was escorted into a car with his hands cuffed behind his back for a trip to court in Houston, Texas, major net-works showed.

The 50-year-old Harvard graduate, who resigned from Enron four months before its December 2001 implosion in a welter of accounting scandals, defiantly denied wrong-doing to Congress two years ago.

Now, prosecutors are ready to indict him for fraud and conspiracy, similar to the case they made against former chief accounting officer Richard Causey last month, several US newspapers reported. Enron's former chief financial officer Andrew Fastow, who pleaded guilty to conspiracy last month, is reportedly helping prosecutors.

Fastow was the architect of complex financial transactions that Enron used to disguise the true state of its accounts until it filed for a bankruptcy that was unprecedented in scale. Another senior company official, David Delainey, who admitted insider trading in October, also was cooperating, the press said. The probe into Enron, once the seventh-largest US company, led to criminal charges against at least 20 people and put Enron's former accounting firm, Arthur Andersen LLP, out of business.

The Enron bankruptcy—the biggest at the time but later eclipsed by the failure of telecoms group WorldCom—left approximately 20,000 creditors owed about 67 billion dollars. Skilling would be the highest-ranking Enron official to be charged in the scandal.

Former Enron chairman Ken Lay is reportedly under investigation. Skilling's lawyer Bruce Hiler last week issued a statement saying his client had acted on advice from dozens of lawyers, accountants, and subordinates who approved Enron's businss deals and accounting maneuvers.

The Justice Department's Enron Task and regulators at the Securities and Exchange Commission focused on Skilling's statement to Congress that Enron was financially sound when he quit, the *Washington Post* said.

References

Prahlad K. Basu is Professor of Management, Nottingham Business School, UK, and a former Secretary, Government of India, *Hindustan Times*, September 23, 2002.

Agence France Presse, Houston, 19.2.2004, *Hindustan Times*, New Delhi.

PART IX

CULTURE

CHAPTER

51

Culture— An Introduction

In an earlier Chapter 14, we had discussed how organisation culture promotes ethical corporate behaviour. We have devoted more chapters for explaining the various facets of organisation culture particularly in building and maintaining value-based culture.

IRCON International Ltd., a leading public sector company—Indian Railway Project Construction Corporation adopts a policy of appointing top personnel from India and other staff from host country in case of foreign assignments. Why is it so? Anil Jain, a senior executive gives the reason as—greater understanding of the country by the local personnel. This understanding relates to the understanding of the people, their customs, norms and systems of the country. But here comes one more problem—the top management personnel from the home country have to supervise the host country staff. This is a major problem because the living and working patterns of both the countries are different. The only solution to this problem according to Anil Jain is making the Indian personnel at the top aware of the culture of the host country. This is because of it that is the culture of the country has bearing on the conduct of business in every functional area.

Internationalisation of businesses has posed new challenges for the organisations. The major challenge that is faced by any global business house today is that of handling diversity in the cultures as explained in the example above. At the root of this diversity are the cultural aspects of the nations. To begin with, we shall understand:

(1) Meaning of culture;

(2) Components of culture;

(3) Characteristics of culture;

(4) Precursors of culture; and

(5) Effects of culture on individuals and organisations.

MEANING OF CULTURE

Culture, today, is being defined as an intellectual or moral discipline and training, a state of intellectual and artistic development or a historically transmitted pattern of meanings. Culture has also been described as a set of rules, values and beliefs—good or bad—which community adopts as its norm.

CULTURE: CHARACTERISTICS

Components of Culture

1. Communication

Some cultures are polite and gracious, others are demanding. Japanese are more non-verbal and we have to understand their total communication.

2. Language

Language can become a confusion or convey clear meaning.

3. Dress and Appearance

Dress and appearance identify culture. Arabs wear particular type of dress.

4. Food Habits

Food habits typify a culture, for example, Pizza is cherished in Italy, Dosa in India.

5. Time

Time consciousness from punctuality of Japanese or Americans to flexible attitude towards time of Arabs and Indians.

6. Rewards and Recognition

Rewards and recognition differ from country to country, for example, giving 15% of fare tip to taxi driver in USA is customary, in India it is optional.

7. Values and Norms

Values and norms, e.g. attitude towards corruption vary in Germany and Italy.

Characteristics of Culture

The culture is associated with following characteristics:

1. Culture is Learnt

Culture is acquired through experience and learning. People learn culture of a group when they become members. Children are born into a family and are taught the values and norms of that family and society.

2. Culture is Shared

People who are members of particular groups, organisations, and societies share a particular culture; it is not specific to a single individual. These groups include family groups, occupational groups, regional groups and national groups.

3. Culture is Transgenerational

Culture is passed on in the cumulative process from one generation to the next, from parents to children, from teachers to pupils and similarly in organisations. This process is called socialisation.

4. Culture is Symbolic

Culture depends upon individual's capacity to symbolize or to use one thing to represent another.

5. Culture is Patterned

Culture processes structure and is integrated. Change in one aspect of culture causes changes in another.

6. Culture is Adaptive

Culture depends on human capacity to adapt to change.

7. Culture is Descriptive

Culture defines the boundaries of different groups. These boundaries act as demarcations for characterising those groups.

8. Culture has Historical Dimension

A particular nation's *culture develops over-time* due to history, economic development, etc. A warm climate, for example, limits inhabitants to a completely different life style than a cold climate. The *societal norms* that develop over-time lead to the development of institutions such as family patterns, religious, political and legal systems which reflect these shared ways of acting and thinking. For example, social inequality is more generally accepted in France than in Netherland.

9. Finally, Culture has Different Layers

Hofstede (1991) mentions four levels of culture:

(a) First level consist of *symbols*, e.g. words, gestures and objects that carry a particular meaning for the members of a society such as country's flag, its national anthem.

(b) *Heroes* constitute the *second level* of culture. This refers to persons that are highly prized in society and who may serve as role models.

(c) *The third level* of culture consists of *rituals*. These are social norms that need to be followed. For example, how we greet friends, etc. which may differ from one nation to other nation.

(d) *The deepest level* of culture distinguished by Hofstede consists of *shared values* which represent collective beliefs and feelings what is good, rational and valuable. We normally take values for granted. We become aware of own values when we meet people from other cultures with different set of values. We normally consider our values as most appropriate. In international collaboration such a belief increases the potential for conflict.

Precursors of Culture

The constituents or rather the precursors of culture are the interrelated concepts of beliefs, values, attitudes and behaviour.

Here, one factor leads to another in sequence but the feedback loop is multifaceted, indicating that consequences of a given behaviour will have implications for each of the precursors, which in turn define culture. Each of these factors can be understood as under:

1. Beliefs

One's beliefs are the result of direct observations as well as from inferences that are drawn from previously learnt relationships. One's belief system is the cognitive representation of one's relevant environment, complete with right-or-wrong, good-or-bad, and cause-and-effect relationships. The Principle of Belief Congruence holds that we tend to value a given belief or a belief system in direct proportion to the degree of congruence with our own belief system, and we tend to value individuals with respect to the degree to which they exhibit beliefs and belief systems congruent with our own.

2. Values

A value is "an enduring belief that a specific mode of conduct or end-state of existence is personally or socially preferable to an opposite or converse mode of conduct or end-state of existence." A value system is "an enduring organisation of beliefs concerning preferable modes of conduct or end-states of existence along a continuum of relative importance." Thus, a value is comprised of one or more *centrally-important* and *enduring beliefs*.

Values have a considerable influence on the *identity and role* of individual rights and duties as opposed to collective ones. For example, in most Western European countries and North America children are raised to be self-sufficient as adults. Children are taught to take their own decisions and solve their own problems. This *reflects individualism*. In contrast, in other societies children are taught that they belong to extended family and they owe their loyalty. Similarly, property in western society belongs to individuals while in others it is shared with other members of the group.

3. Attitudes

An attitude is "a learned predisposition to respond in a consistently favourable or unfavourable manner with respect to a given object." Attitudes are based on central belief and value systems.

4. Behaviour

Beliefs lead to values that, in turn, are predispositions to behave in a certain prescribed manners. Therefore, belief and value systems are maintained by the consistency of behaviour that is predisposed by the person's strongest values. If the behaviour results in positive consequences, that feedback will reinforce and strengthen the person's related beliefs, values, and attitudes; and the person will acquire even greater predisposition to behave in that manner again. If, however, the behaviour results in negative consequences, the person's related beliefs, values and attitudes will be weakened; and the person will be less disposed to behave in that manner again.

Hence, the combined relationship between beliefs, values, attitudes and behaviour may be seen as components of culture.

CULTURE: ITS EFFECTS ON ORGANISATIONS

The culture of the society comprises the shared values, understanding, assumptions, and goals that are learned from earlier generations, imposed by present members of the society, and passed on to succeeding generations. This shared outlook results, in the large part, in common attitudes, codes of conduct, and expectations that sub-consciously guide and control certain norms of behaviour. One is born into a given culture and then gradually internalizes its subtle effects through the socialisation process. Culture results in the basis for living grounded in shared communication, standards, codes of conduct, and expectations. These differences result from societal, or socio-cultural variables of culture, such as religion and language, in addition to prevailing national variables, such as economic, legal, and political factors.

CULTURAL DIVERSITY AND THE WORK ORGANISATION

Initially, national culture shapes the organisation through values, attitudes which leaders bring into the organisation. They will shape organisation according to dominant preferences, norms and values of that environment. For example, a society characterised by distinct inequalities of the son-parent, pupil-teacher, it is anticipated the work organisations will also reflect this tendency. In most Asian countries, it is common to accept the authority of one's elders. So superior-subordinate relationship in the organisation are also characterised by a larger power distance and by centralisation of authority.

In a second way, national culture shapes the organisation through institutions in that country. For example, participative legislation which grants employees a say in organisational decision-making may be reflection of shaping of power and influence in that country.

REFERENCES

Helen Deresky, International Management: Managing Across Borders.
Manab Thakur, Concepts of International Management.

CHAPTER

52

Organisation Culture— Building and Maintaining

Organisation culture is a *common perception* held by the organisation's members. Organisation culture is the shared understandings of norms, values, attitudes and beliefs—of an organisation, which can foster or impede change.

It is a system of shared meaning. An understanding to employees of "the way things are done here." Organisation culture conveys the ways in which "people work and think."

Organisation culture may be referred to pattern of beliefs, values and learned ways of coping within an organisation. These are visible in structures and processes of the organisation and the ways its employees behave.

"An organisation's culture consists of the shared values and common assumptions held by the people within the organisation." In dynamic organisations, these values and assumptions drive behaviours that create value for the organisation's major stakeholders, be it customers, employees or other groups such as suppliers, etc. As opposed to developing individuals' resources, building a 'Cultural Identity' for the organisation is what Cultural Competency is all about. People are crucial for gaining organisational advantage. The environment and cuture will stimulate individuals to perform in the desired manner.

The strong, widely recognised corporate culture is frequently cited as a reason for the success of such companies as IBM and Procter and Gamble. A company's predominant culture may change quite rapidly or be forced by competition into change. Vijay Sathe has shown that culture's durability and efficiency represent both an asset and a liability for an organisation, and a smart manager must learn when to stop perpetuating a culture that is unresponsive to the needs of business. In such circumstances Chief Executive may institute a change in overall organisational culture, which involves not merely structural and technological change, but also change in shared symbols, rituals and beliefs.

In this chapter, we have attempted to share some vital aspects of the organisation culture:

1. Importance of organisation culture as a technique in OD.
2. Characteristics of organisation culture.
3. Elements of organisation culture transmitted to employees.
4. How organisation culture starts in an organisation.
5. Socialisation process—familiarisation with organisation culture.
6. Maintaining organisation's culture.
7. Can organisation culture be altered or realigned?
8. Is corporate culture now in crisis?
9. Steps for rebuilding organisation culture in highly turbulent competitive environment.

IMPORTANCE OF ORGANISATION CULTURE AS A TECHNIQUE IN OD

1. Background

In USA, during 1980s, CEOs were successful in taking over a firm that had problems, by cutting the work force and rebuild organisation to be effective. However, during 1990s, much different approach has followed for survival a growth of an organisation:

(a) Create pride and enthusiasm in *the firm;*

(b) CEOs worked as *role models* to direct and work long hours to attain goals;

(c) Encouraging *positive way* how things can be done efficiently and differently;

(d) CEOs *shared* in meeting with managers to turn out best programme; and

(e) To *look after the best people* and place them best suited jobs, so as to encourage team work and creative ideas, etc.

Thus, various aspects which influenced culture were initiatve, trust, support and innovation. *One culture is usually typified* by quality of excellence, high quality, openness in communication, participation in decision-making, high standard of safety, good corporate citizen, emphasis on new technology, modern management trends.

The other extreme type culture can be devoid of initiative and flexibility, lack of discipline, *chalta hai* mentality, mere conformity to rules rather than ends.

Thus, it came to realised that corporate culture is important to corporate growth, success, excellence and survival. It has motivating effect on employees. Culture influences an organisation's competitiveness over time. It can make organisation more effective. If developed to be a strategy for organisation effectiveness, which OD aims at. It has various advantages for the organisation such as:

(i) Organisation culture is necessary to adapt for changes arising due to competition.

(ii) Values and beliefs provide a sense to common direction, energy and guidelines for day-to-day behaviour. Common bond promotes emotional and social cohesion and establishes sense of identity. Values provide a spirit and drive for achievement. Values also provide guidelines for employees for taking decisions.

(iii) It influences every one's perceptions of business and accepted ways of behaving.

(iv) Strong and positive culture give many benefits to companies. It leads to high morale, sense of commitment and organisation pride. Strong cultures are core values (shared by majority) are intensely held and widely shared.

(v) Variations in cultural values has significant impact on employee turnover and job performance.

Any organisation that wants a lead over its competitors, therefore, needs to have a clearly defined, *commonly shared set of values* which guide the stakeholders in all their actions and decisions. If these are not in place, the decentralised organisation may well become the disintegrated organisation.

2. Characteristics of Organisation Culture

Stephen P. Robbins has stated that the following seven primary characteristics, capture the essence of an organisation culture:

(i) The degree to which employees are encouraged to be *innovative and risk-taking.*

(ii) Degree of expected *precision and attention to detail.*

(iii) Degree to which management focuses on *result orientation* rather than techniques and processes.

(iv) Degree to which management has *people orientation*—its decisions effect of outcomes on employees.

(v) Degree to which activities are organised on *team work* rather than individuals.

(vi) Degree to which people are *competitive and aggressive* rather than people are easy going.

(vii) Degree to which organisation activities emphasise *on stability* (maintaining *status quo*) in contrast to growth.

These characteristics exists on a continuum from low to high. How things are done in organisation and the way members are supposed to behave.

How organisation culture effects the performance and satisfaction of employees? We have observed that seven characteristics highlighted by Stephen P. Robbins (Organisation Behaviour) are the essence of organisation culture. These characteristics exists on a continuum from low to high. If those characteristics are appraised as high by the employees then they perceive the organisation's culture as favourable. Their common perceptions then affect employee's performance and satisfaction as high. This is depicted in Figure 52.1.

FIGURE 52.1

How Organisation Culture Effects Performance and Satisfaction

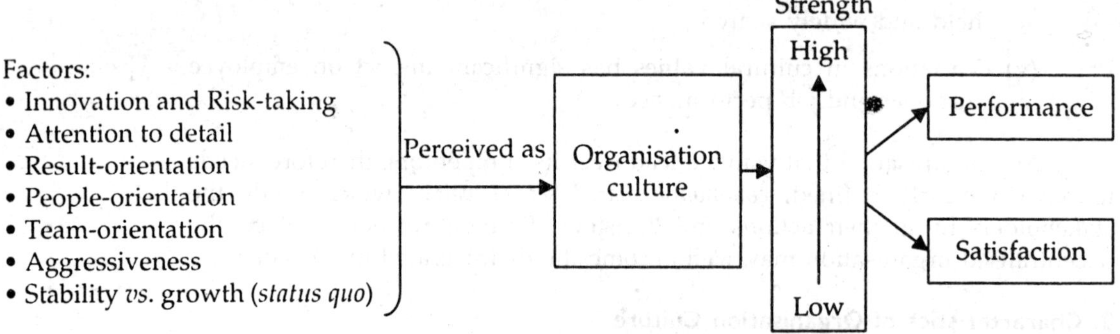

3. Elements of Organisation Culture Transmitted to Employees

Employees learn organisation culture in number of forms, the most potent being values, rites and rituals, stories, heroes, etc.

(a) Values

Values are core of the culture. Both values and beliefs provide guidelines for employees to follow in their work. Values provide sense of direction and shape behaviour. They indicate what matters are to be attended carefully.

Few examples of Credo's in organisations are: Cater Pillar (USA) committed to customers "in 24 hours parts service anywhere in the world." Larson and Tubro (India)—"People are prime movers." Bill Gates (USA)—"Computer on every desk and every house." TERI (India)—"Faith in youth and tap the youth."

(b) Heroes

Heroes personify these values. Manager's provide as role-models for employees. They set the standards of performance and dress norms as formal codes of behaviour.

(c) Rites and Rituals

If culture and values are to thrive (and not die) these must be ritualised and celebrated repeatedly. These rituals may be of different types such as social rituals, work rituals, management rituals, recognition rituals, etc. For example, some companies celebrate their annual day function on regular basis and publically recognise outstanding performers at these functions which serves as motivator.

(d) Setting-up of Cultural Network for Communication

These are story tellers, priests, gossips. This network reinforces the values of the organisation. Some jargon and jokes are only understood by insiders. These elements are manifestations of organisation culture and new people have to learn them. When employees interpret the meanings of these, their beliefs, perceptions, experiences constitute culture. During the days of Henry Ford II when he was Chairman of the Ford Motors Company, it was famous story reminding his executives. When one got too arrogant with the chairman, he would point that "It is my name that is on the building." The message was clear: Henry Ford ran the company!

4. How Organisation Culture Starts in an Organisation

Some steps commonly adopted by organisations in starting and maintaining their culture are indicated in Figure 52.2.

These steps are elaborated as under:

(i) Schein has emphasised the role of the founder in creating organisation value (culture) in his book *Organisation Dynamics*, 1983. Founder has an idea for new enterprise. Leadership behaviour sets the culture tone. *They formulate a statement of organisational philosophy* and communicate to employees. A particularly deep intervention is

FIGURE 52.2

Starting, Formation and Maintaining of Organisation Culture

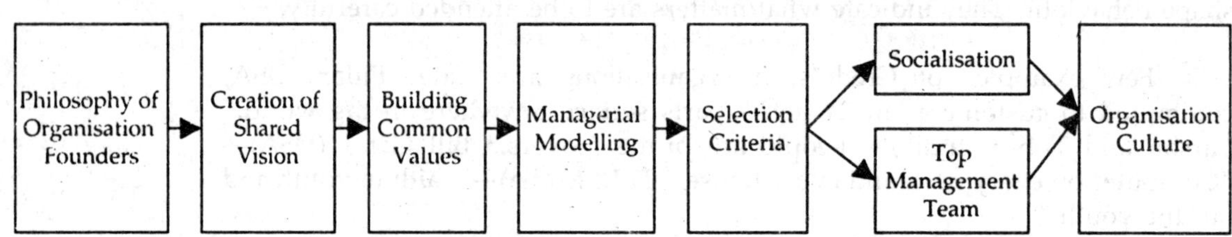

E.H. Schein's *"cultural analysis."* It probes deeply into the organisation:

(a) Artifacts (such as symbols, modes of dress, office layout),

(b) Values behind artifacts, and

(c) Cultural assumptions in group meetings.

Some contemporary examples of founders who had an immeasurable impact on their organisational culture would include Bill Gates at Microsoft, Akio Moritra at Sony, David Packard at Hewlett Packard, Naraina Murty at Infosys and Azim Premji at WIPRO.

(ii) *Creation of a Vision*: Transformation leadership *creates a vision.* He provides *mission* and *mobilises commitment* and support.

(iii) Takes key people and creates a core group that *share a common vision*, mission, values, goals and strategies so that it is institutionalised and become reality.

(iv) Founding group *acts in concert* to create an organisation culture. They *adhere* faithfully to the values.

(v) Involving of others' employees and common values begin to be *built and solidify*. Organisation's values are in various areas such as—relationships to customers, social responsibility, managerial style are focused.

(vi) *Managerial modelling behaviour* strongly influences the employees.

5. Socialisation Process—Familiarisation with Organisation Culture

New employees are unfamiliar with the organisation culture. The new employees are thus potential who may disturb the beliefs and customs of a new place. The organisations, therefore, want to help new employees to *adapt to its culture*. This adaptation process is called *socialisation*.

The most critical socialisation stage is at the time of entry into the organisation. This is when organisation seeks to mold the outsider into an employee, i.e. its standards and norms. Socialisation can be conceptualised as a process made of 3 stages—*pre-arrival, encounter, metamorphosis.* (Maanen and Schein) (See Figure 52.3).

FIGURE 52.3

A Socialisation Model

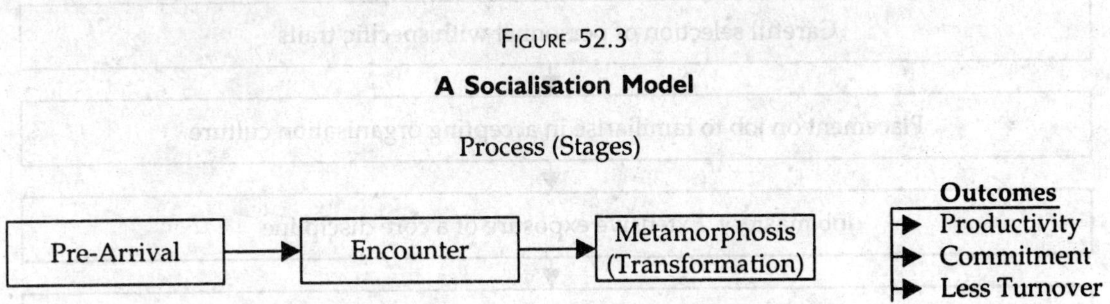

(i) Pre-Arrival Stage

It is process that occurs before new employee joins the organisation. The success depends on the degree *new candidate* has correctly *anticipated* the expectations and desires of selection members. Those type of people should be selected, who will fit into organisation culture.

One major purpose of a business school is to socialise business students to the attitudes and behaviours that business firms want. Management students should value the will to work, loyalty, desire to achieve and willingness to accept directions from superiors, then firms can hire executive from business schools, who have been pre-moulded in this pattern.

(ii) Encounter Stage

This is a stage in socialisation process in which new employee sees what the organisation is really like and *detatch his previous assumptions* and replace them with another set that the organisation deems desirable.

(iii) Metamorphosis Stage

This is a process in which a new employee *adjusts* to his work group values and norms. He has become comfortable with the organisation and his job. He is now committed to the organisation and productivity increase.

6. Maintaining Organisation's Culture

Once organisation culture is build, various steps of socialisation are given below. These steps are also explained in Figure 52.3.

(a) *Selection Criteria*: *Selection of entry-level personnel,* Using standardised procedures and seeking specific traits that lead to effective performance and candidate will fit into the organisation's team-oriented culture.

FIGURE 52.4

Steps in Socialisation of Organisation Culture

Careful selection of personnel with specific traits

↓

Placement on job to familiarise in accepting organisation culture

↓

Job mastery. Extensive exposure of a core discipline

↓

Reward individual performance and control systems to reinforce desirable behaviour.

↓

Adherence to important values enables the reconciliation of personal views

↓

Reinforcing the organisation stories

↓

Recognition and promotion of role models

(b) *Socialisation—the process that adatps employees to the organisation's culture: Placement on the Job itself.* Exposure to different experiences whose purpose is to cause them to question the organization's norms and values and to decide whether or not they can accept them.

(c) *Job Mastery*: Once the initial "cultural shock" is over, the next step is mastery of one's job. This is done via extensive and carefully reinforced field experience.

(d) Measuring and rewarding indvidual performance and matching employee's values to those of the organisation. The actions of top management have a major impact on the organisation culture as to what actions will pay-off in terms of pay raises, promotions and other rewards.

7. Can Organisation Culture be Altered or Realigned?

Organisation culture can be altered. It can be managed and realigned to the strategic direction an organisation wishes to take. Bate (1995) argues that, within organisations, culture is a dynamic, continuously developing phenomenon. If managers can manage organisations' cultures they can change culture and also prevent its change as well as abandon or destroy it (Ogbonna, 1993). We explore possible frameworks for managing both gradual or developmental change and more radical or transformational change to a new culture.

Frameworks for Managing the Change

Lewis (1996) reviews a range of frameworks for managing cultural change. One of the most widely quoted of these is Lewin's (1952) three steps of unfreezing, moving and refreezing. Lewin's framework emphasises that before an organisation can be transformed to a completely new culture, the embedded culture must be unfrozen and made more susceptible to change. Subsequent to the change his framework highlights the importance of stabilising and institutionalising the new culture, in Lewin's words refreezing.

Cultural change can occur from and within an existing organisational culture and be influenced by wider societal and national cultures. Strategies for cultural change can be either top-down or bottom-up approach. Change in organisation culture may take a form explained in Figure 52.5.

FIGURE 52.5

The New and Old Organisational Cultures (developed from Hastings, 1993)

Old Culture	New Culture
• Hierarchies • Boundaries • Internal focus	• Teams • Connections • External focus
• Paternalistic • Second guessing • Controlling	• Empowerment • Trusting • Supportive
• Analysis • Risk aversion	• Action • Calculated risk-taking or innovation

8. Is Corporate Culture now in Crisis?

Even in the beginning of new millennium the "corporate culture" had become widely accepted term in business.

Commonly shared values and assumptions are important, but are of no use, if they are just a set of phrases and sayings that are written down, but not actually practised, by each and every person in the organisation. In fact, when an organisation pays only lip service to its values, the management of organisation loses credibility and faith not only within, but also outside the organisation.

Terrence E. Deal and Alian A. Kennedy have now focussed that the *corporate culture landscape has shifted*. In some corporations traditional cultural pattern have seriously eroded, e.g. GM, GE, Kodak, IBM, Woolworth. It is not easy to maintain a cohesive culture in the face of external flux and economic ups and downs. It is *difficult to balance* the conflicting demands of customers, shareholders and employees. So managers are bereft of ideas for where to turn.

Factors Causing Crisis in Corporate Culture

According to them the corporate cultures are in crisis—due to following factors:

(i) *Shareholder's value* movement and the impact it has had on corporate decision-making.

(ii) Focus on *downsizing*, which has cut the soul of many corporations.

(iii) *Outsourcing* has emerged as new tool of cost-cutting when conventional cost-reduction approaches have begun to run out of steam.

(iv) How *corporate merger-mania* has forced the most—unlikely combinations on the work-forces which are still dealing from waves of cost-cutting of early 1990s.

(v) How *computerisation* (potentially a tool for relieving employees from drudgery), has instead violated employees from one another and made them *servants to machines*.

(vi) How *narrowing boundaries* of the world have thrown peoples together in *global work place*.

Combination of these factors have thrown traditional corporate cultures, replacing joy, commitment and loyalty with fear, alienation and self-interest.

Need for Building New Corporate Culture

So they have stressed the need for rebuilding new corporate culture. So task is to rebuild cohesive cultures:

(i) *Importance of leadership*. In an effort to rebuild the cultural cohesion of buisness leadership role is vital. They can add momentum to a culture re-building.

(ii) It is essential to rebuild the *social context of work*, if *people are to be motivated* to give their best efforts to their employers. This is the challenge of decade.

- Manager can begin the process of *redefining the work place* as a meaningful *human environment* with high potential for top productivity.

- They can help to make work an attractive place to be.
- Managers can recapture the spirit of employees and channel this energy into furthering the goals of the business. But they can do so only if they recognise the *mutual dependencies* of employees and employers and need to create a cultural milieu that benefits all. Managers who accept this challenge will become the business leaders of tomorrow.

9. Steps for Rebuilding Organisation Culture in Highly Turbulent Competitive Environment

Terrence and Kennedy have suggested following steps:

(i) Making people *want to go to work,* by providing good *favourable compensation* and remove pay as demotivating factor.

(ii) Reasonable level of *job security*. Employers have created the problem of rampant job insecurity by their own actions. Although the promise of a job security for two years is hardly enough to allow workers to feel secure, even such a limited guarantee can make a much difference. All it takes on the part an employer is a little foresight and a willingness to be *fair to employees.*

(iii) Focus on *job content and job satisfacton*. Decentralisation of work can help in this aspect.

(iv) A *socially rewarding environment*:

- the first crucial element is *respect* for employee and feeling that *he is valued,*
- building *happy and productive* employees through fun and adventure (full of challenge) at work, and
- *fellowship at work*. Teamwork with similar values.

(v) Physically comfortable work environment:

- cleanliness, and
- *informal place for interaction* and socially friendly working environment.

(vi) Preparing to *live in globalised world,* such as *cross cultural differences* and preparing to learn from others:

- Develop potential synergies to be gained from *understanding and using other's values, knowledge and experience.*
- Not to undermine foreign cultures and team members to work together.

(vii) Building a *learning environment at work*, e.g.:

- ❑ creating a knowledge-based environment,
- ❑ steps for individual learning and organisation learning, and
- ❑ knowledge people as the basis of future business.

Terrence and Kennedy have concluded with the observations that *business inevitably moves in cycles*. Americans are optimistic enough to balance and shake-off some of the recent excesses. The rebalance of business interests is needed to help restore some semblance of sanity to the work place. The ability to judiciously manage and balance the competing interests (of the stakeholders) is of vital importance. The need of any one particular stakeholder is best met by serving the needs of all the stakeholders. A study spanning 172 companies in 19 industries, conducted over 11 years by Kotter and Heskett shows that multi-stakeholder culture companies are far more successful than those with a narrow focus. For sustaining the culture, it is imperative that the movement is oriented to a higher good.

Long-term higher goals, by their very nature are unselfish. They focus on the good of many rather than advantage to a few. If we take a look at Japanese companies which have been storming the world with high quality, low price products, we will find that these organisations never have selfish or limited motives such as mere generation of profits as their long-term higher goal.

An example of such a company would be Sony. Co-founded by Akio Morita, the company was able to produce high quality products only because of the desire to provide good products to the people. It could have as well, made a quick buck by producing cheap products, but the higher goal guided it towards an unselfish, and in the long-run, a phenomenally successfully objective.

CHAPTER

53

MANAGING CULTURAL DIVERSITY IN ORGANISATIONS

There have been considerable changes, in almost all societies, brought about by technological advances, social alterations, economic influences and political and environmental pressures. The existing and future trends will throw new challenges in managing cultural diversity in organisations.

(a) Some major forces for change currently happening are:

(i) Technological

- ❑ Artificial organs and transplants
- ❑ The space shuttle
- ❑ IT and internet revolutions
- ❑ Biotechnological revolution

(ii) Social

- ❑ Women's movement
- ❑ Human rights movement
- ❑ Growth in higher education
- ❑ Stress and tensions

(iii) Economic

- ❑ Rise in living standards

- Rapid expansion of the checkless society (i.e., credit cards)
- Fluctuating interest rates and inflation rate
- Global competition
- Tax rates

(iv) Political

- Religious "terrorism"
- Medicare for the aged
- "Star Wars" space defence system

(v) Environment

- Pollution, wild-life protection
- Customers and employee protection

(b) Further societal trends will vitally influence peoples' cultural norms and values. Some trends and practices are seen in organisations are:

- *Creation of bio-modal workforce of the future*: With distribution in two large groups with very different earnings and professional backgrounds. The tensions between two groups, i.e. workforce and professionals will grow. There is need for more employee participation and non-financial rewards by the organisations.
- *Management's move to make their organisations 'lean and mean'*: Employees are getting less secure in their jobs. There will be "corporate divorce" in the decades to come, when they early retire their employees to improve productivity and at the same time out-sourcing young employees.
- *Dual career couples* as the one-bread-winner household is rapidly disappearing. This will decrease employees mobility and focus will be on the local job markets. To attract and retain female employees, the organisations will provide more day care services. Work-related health problems, especially back strain, eye strain may have to be reduced by having ergonomically designed furniture in offices.
- *Working at home* by IT savvy workforce: More people will be employed in this manner and through part-time service.
- Though there will be fewer people unionised, the rift between unions and management will continue.

The environment in which managers work today is more dynamic than in the past. The individuals with whom they work in future will be diverse in intents, abilities, values and motivations. Thus, there will be challenges in managing its people and culture diversity in organisations.

In the remaining part of this chapter we shall attempt to summarise our thinking on managing cultural diversity under following headings:

(i) Meaning of cultural diversity.

(ii) Importance of cultural diversity.

(iii) Two aspects of cultural diversity:

  (a) global business operations, and

  (b) work place diversity in organisation.

(iv) Managing cultural diversity.

(v) Advantages of managing cultural diversity.

(vi) To conclude.

(I) MEANING OF CULTURAL DIVERSITY

Culture is "software of the mind", the way people think, act and perceive others and it is shared by societies. Three primary components of culture, relevant to international business are language, religion and attitudes.

Cultural diversity (CD) indicates the characteristics that may make an individual culturally different from another. These differences may be:

(a) Cultural differences involving patterns of life styles, values, beliefs, ideals, practices.

(b) Differences may include race, national origin, language, religion, age, etc.

(c) Differences in views held about the world, codes of social behaviour, communication styles.

(II) IMPORTANCE OF CULTURAL DIVERSITY

1. Cultural diversity is one of the major challenges facing global business organisations, as it is important for success and vitality of the organisation.

2. Management process is increasingly becoming cross-cultural with opening of Indian economy and globalisation. It becomes necessary to have an understanding of various cultures, and the ways to manage the cultural diversity for achieving competitive advantage. This brings one of the major challenges for the MNCs, exporters, tourists, sportsmen, entrepreneurs, artists, diplomats of foreign service, financial experts, researchers, etc. who operate in diverse cultures.

3. It has importance in all activities of life and more so in international business operations, such as:
   - cross-cultural differences in communication can be source of problem due to different meaning and tone of words to different people. So awareness of certain characteristics of other culture reduces misinterpretation and thus in improving communication in business introductions, telephonic conversations and meetings is important.
4. It has implications in all fields of management, such as:
   - in international marketing practices
   - in international advertising
   - in international business negotiations
   - in international human resource management
   - in international practices in industrial relations
   - in international management functions (PODCC)
   - in international developing strategies in global
   - in international organisation structure
   - in international manager's role (MNCs) in global market.

(III) TWO ASPECTS OF CULTURAL DIVERSITY

(a) First Aspect Relates to Global Cultural Diversity

People of one country have common characteristics that differentiate them from people of other countries. This is called international diversity.

Understanding of common characteristics within a particular country is important if we are going to successfully manage in an international business environment.

For example:

- Manager with awareness of national differences knows that British protect their privacy, so Indians would avoid asking British personal questions. In contrast, asking personal questions in India is acceptable. It is sign of showing interest.
- Communication is often difficult with Japanese, Americans value directness. Japanese are more subtle and view directness as not proper.
- Further, Japanese believe in group consensus in decision-making

which does not fit well with Americans who are used to making fast decisions.

- ❑ In greetings Americans are smiling, firm handshake and eye contact, while Japanese bowing, exchange business cards.
- ❑ In U.S.A. women in business have equal rights, opportunities and treated seriously, while in Japan women are not considered for higher management positions. In middle-east women stand to disadvantage.

So MNCs have to develop global strategies to take advantage world- wide by properly managing cultural diversity. This calls for the need to design country specific management practices for each country in which the organisation wants to operate.

(b) Second Aspect Refers to Workforce Diversity in an Organisation

- ❑ This aspect looks at differences between people inside the work organisation. The composition of employees is changing to show heterogeneity of whole population. Thus, employee mix is undergoing change and no exclusive population in organisation.
- ❑ Workforce is now multi-lingual, multi-racial which have different life-styles, values, beliefs, ideals and practices.
- ❑ Even, language, religion, codes of social behaviour, custom, festivals are diverse.
- ❑ Workforce includes more women now, older persons. Women require protection against gender discrimination, flexible work schedules, and child care programmes.
- ❑ In addition, there are minority workers and disabled individuals.
- ❑ Diverse workforce is more educated.
- ❑ So the aim is not to remove the differences in cultures, but managers to respond to individual expectations and valuing differences to learn the details of different cultural norms which will help employees to bring out best in them.

(IV) MANAGING CULTURAL DIVERSITY

1. Thus, there is need for preparing managers for foreign assignments through cross-cultural training such as in history, culture, religions, values, political, legal, economy of that country to overcome cultural shock.
2. To develop international business negotiations strategies such as positive overtures, dealing problems and not personalities, emphasis on win-win solutions, create an open and trusting climate, build

lasting relationships.

3. To develop second generation organisation structures which (in addition to strategy and structure) take two other aspects:
   (i) Strategic flexibility, and
   (ii) Management process.
4. Train transnational managers with competencies in understanding of:
   (a) Global perspective of world market business environment.
   (b) Knowledge for cultural responsiveness.
   (c) Cross-cultural interaction skills with foreign clients.
   (d) Global strategist to identify unique business opportunities, technologies, etc.
5. Avoiding discrimination in policies, to make a harmonious work place so that all employees benefit from wider range of experiences and ideas. Discrimination can be identified in practices of the organisation, such as racial discrimination in recruitment, employee training and career development opportunities. For example, wearing of turban by Sikhs in U.K. was discriminated. Differences in job prospects among England's ethnic minorities are now almost as big as differences between them and the majority. White community, according to a Cabinet Office strategy unit study published in March 2003. The Report emphasises that employers still discriminate on basis of ethnicity.
6. To develop policies on sexual harassment, grievance systems and for equal opportunities.
7. Barrier in this change is *mind-set*. It has to be recognised that such as prejudice against other cultural and racial groups, unknown fear of their dominance, avoidance of contact, lack of integration, etc. to be eliminated.
8. In managing diversity, ethics programmes are useful in acknowledging different values and perspectives.
9. To develop organisation culture for valuing differences.
10. HR management systems to be (bias free).
11. Some other steps such as: Involvement of women, cultural differences knowledge to be imparted and accepting for higher career assignments.
12. Education of employees for mind-set about diversity.

(V) ADVANTAGES OF MANAGING CULTURAL DIVERSITY ARE THAT IT CAN IMPROVE ORGANISATIONAL PERFORMANCE

- Groups of people from diverse backgrounds can be more creative and better at problem-solving.
- Companies which manage cultural diversity can develop favourable reputation of good prospective employers of minorities such as Tata, HLL and many more.
- Cultural diversity can get better customers which has a variety of people.
- Organisations which handle multiculturalism well, create cost advantages over those who do not.
- Ability to manage cultural diversity increases the adaptability and flexibility of management to react to environment changes.
- Belief that people of many different backgrounds can work together and lead to coexistence is now university accepted. In nut shell managers must take positive steps to manage issues of cultural diversity.

Infact, successfully managing cultural diversity can lead to global business advantages. Indian IT sector, which have successful in their global operations, have to be careful in developing cultural sensitivity and preemptive in understanding political and economic environment of the host country.

(VI) TO CONCLUDE

1. Organisations are increasingly becoming multicultural and it is one of its major challenge to have competitive global advantage.
2. Managements have to understand different cultures where they do business and respect each other.
3. Organisations not only to adapt to local culture but also to design practices to suit the culture of each country.
4. Take positive steps:
   - Prepare transnational managers for foreign assignments.
   - Develop HR policies and practices (bias free).
   - Avoid discrimination and provide equal opportunities.
   - Educate employees to change mind-set and prejudice.
   - Develop organisation culture for valuing differences. Open culture develops tolerance for cultures of their employees.
   - To foster mutual adaptation is the only approach works in

managing diversity. To make harmonious work place people and employees try to keep "their identity" while on the other hand they are being "homogenised."

- Top management to support the company's multi-cultural events and encourage employees to attend.
- Managements must recognise that a heterogenous group will produce better ideas and strategies than homogenous group.
- A "world culture is a dream." We have to be more realist in taking above steps.

Reference

S.K. Bhatia and Poonam Chaudhary, Managing Cultural Diversity in Globalisation, Deep & Deep Publications Pvt. Ltd., New Delhi.

CHAPTER

54

Indian Culture—Characteristics

INDIA: A MULTI-CULTURE NATION

India is said to be country of multi-cultures. It is because of long history of thousands of years. At different times different rulers ruled over the country. Further, at the same time there had been different rulers in different parts of India. The different rulers had different systems of governance and social practices. All these factors left a deep imprint on culture. As in olden days means of transport and communication were very poor; large number of languages, systems, habits, values developed which continue even today. These facts of history made India a multi-culture nation but as will be evident from later discussion the core values are same throughout the country. Thus, *there is unity in diversity*. But the diversity gave birth to ever increasing number of states. At present, there are 29 states and six union territories, each having its own culture and in some states there are more than one sub-culture.

In this chapter we have attempted to share some characteristics and traditions of Indian culture. It has both positive aspects and non-work elements. We have covered this under following headings:

(1) Values of Indian culture.

(2) Norms of behaviour in Indian culture.

(3) Factors influencing development of different cultures in India.

(4) Common core values in Indian culture.

(5) Cultural integration in India.

(6) Differences between Indian culture and western culture.

(7) Functionality and dysfunctionality of some characteristics of Indian culture.

(1) VALUES OF INDIAN CULTURE

Indians believe in *freedom of thoughts*, beliefs and experiences which has given birth to democracy, freedom of press, free communication, independent judiciary, freedom of choice of products as per one's preferences and freedom to enterprise to develop products, new technologies but not to exploit consumers who have been given freedom to complaint for deficiency in product or service. Indians believe in *spiritualism, faith and luck*.

(2) NORMS OF BEHAVIOUR IN INDIAN CULTURE

The norms of public behaviour is another important aspect of culture which relates to *public appearance*. For instance, in the west there is full freedom of dress specially at beaches, swimming pools, hotels, but too much exposure in India in dress is considered obscene and nudity in public or even in private is not permissible. In India, there is *respect for elders*. Disrespect of elderly persons is considered bad behaviour in India. Children specially sons are expected to look after their parents in old-age.

Another norm is *respect to women* in Indian culture and religion. No Pooja is complete without wife. But they enjoy lesser freedom of jobs and movement. But now gradually in urban areas women are taking to jobs making them more independent economically.

(3) FACTORS INFLUENCING DIFFERENT CULTURES IN INDIA

The various factors influencing different cultures are:

(i) Geographical Factors in Indian Sub-continent

India, being a country of many states and union territories, exhibits diverse cultures. Each state and in some cases different regions in single state have different culture. For instance, in U.P. even after division of the state there are different cultures in Bundelkhand, Ruhelkhand, East U.P. and West U.P. In Madhya Pradesh, Vidharbha has lot of cultural differences compared to rest of M.P. Rajasthan is one state but culture of Jaipur, Jodhpur, Udaipur, Bikaner, Jaisalmer, etc. have different distinct features. Culture of Assam, Bengal, Gujarat, Goa, Karnataka, Kashmir, Punjab, Haryana, Pondicherry, Mizoram, Nagaland, etc. differs widely from each other. Therefore, consumer preferences also differ and same policy cannot succeed every where.

(ii) Language

India is a multi-language country. There are 18 languages officially recognised in the constitution which are spoken or used in different parts of the country.

Besides 18 languages, English is official language in most private offices and for interstate correspondence, teaching of technical courses. There are also wide variations of languages from district to district in spoken language and if they are used by marketer in communication in person, and on radio they have greater impact on consumers and population at large.

(iii) Religion

Religion has great impact on culture and buying behaviour of consumers. In India, there are following major religions as per 2000 census. Religions: Hindus, Muslims, Sikhs, Christians, Jains, Buddhas. Every religion has its own values, faith, beliefs and greatly affect consumer behaviour.

(iv) Races and Ethnic Groups

India has large number of races like Dravidians, Aryans, Mangols and through immigration many ethnic groups have settled in India during British Rule; Anglo-Indian communities are found largely in Kolkata. There are Chinese who have settled in shoe business in Kolkata. Within Hindus there are large number of ethnic groups like Jats, Rajputs, Gujjars, Tyagi, Brahmins, Yadavs and so on. In Jains there are Agarwals, Oswals, etc. These groups have more affinities with the group and culturally they are near to each other and there are certain distinct features in their behaviour and customs. Then there are tribes and each tribe has its own customs and preferences. Customs of Sindhis are different than that of Parsis or others and each one of them has to be approached differently.

(v) Education

The level of education has great impact on the extent of development, knowledge, level of income. It also affects values, faiths and beliefs. A poor educated country has greater faith in superstitions and traditions and greater belief in luck, fate and god.

(4) COMMON CORE VALUES IN INDIA

Though there are wide variations in various cultural variables in the country, there are some core values which are common to all the cultures of India. These widely held beliefs, interests, feelings, relationships has brought similarity in diversity (variations) and unified the country. These core values should be properly understood for business.

(a) Tolerance

Tolerence is very fabric of all Indian cultures and our society is based on this principle. The co-existence of various religions, cultures, languages has been possible due to tolerance.

(b) Liberty and Equality

The principle of equality of sex, castes, religions, voting right and employment have been provided in various articles of the Indian constitution.

(c) Respect to Religious Leaders

The religious leaders are given great respect by followers of their religion. They are respected by every one irrespective of his economic and/or political powers. Many wealthy persons build places of worship, education and charitable institutions on their advise and interaction. All the big industrialists and politicians seek blessings of religious leaders and *sadhus*.

(d) Importance of Cross Culture

Indian society whether urban or rural feel that foreign goods, goods made by MNCs or with their collaboration by and large are better than other Indian product, hence, there is big market for smuggled products and services, they often have premium over Indian goods and are sought after. For the same reasons foreign brand names like Gillete, Surf, Palmolive, Colgate, Tide, Honda, Sony, LG, etc. are preferred.

(e) Faith in Superstitions

Indians by and large irrespective of level of education and income have great faith in superstitions. People normally do not buy goods made of iron on Tuesdays and Saturdays. They would prefer to make any big investment in Navratras and would not purchase during Pitra Paksha which is considered unauspicious. No new clothes, consumer durables, house and so on will be bought during this period. Therefore, for fifteen days sales come down and so the price of certain products. There are many symbols and numbers which are considered lucky or unlucky.

(f) Care of Tomorrow

Indians think more for tomorrow, they save good percentage of their income for future (around 22% in 2000-01) for their children education, marriage and life insurance, providend funds, bank deposits and like. Because of sense of insecurity people do not enjoy life and care more for their children than for themselves.

(g) Value of Time

In America, UK, Japan, etc. people are punctual and activities are held on schedule. But in India and many other countries it is a fashion to be late in social functions and marriages but Americans are irritated if one misses appointment or arrives late; the same applies to delivery. In USA or Japan the delivery must be strictly as per schedule otherwise food or service will not be accepted because it disturbs all their planning, same is the culture in many other countries. But there are many African and Asian countries for whom time is less valuable and they do not keep to the time.

(h) Persistance in Efforts

Effort is rewarded, competition is encouraged and achievement is paramount. Entrepreneurship is result of these values. They have optimism much more than in some other countries and spirit of competition much more than in east and in the socialist countries, but in some countries it is not every thing, someone will win and some one will loose. This spirit encourages to continue to make efforts and achieve one's mission.

In conclusion, it may be stated that basic core values are narrowing down in various countries through cultural interaction which has been made easy by revolution in transport, communication and information technology but still there are lot of cultural differences for which markets will have to be segregated.

(5) CULTURAL INTEGRATION IN INDIA

In a country like India, there are large *number of sub-cultures* like Bengal culture, Punjabi culture, Marathi culture, Gujarati culture, Malyali culture, Bihari culture and so on. These sub-cultures are due to various factors explained earlier, among which language, race, history, religion, region are some of the most important factors. But the greater interaction of people of various cultures, long period of stay in metros atleast children learn local languages, they develop taste for local food, dress and participate in festivals of the region though they continue to have affection with people of their culture. *English language* in India has influenced many sub-cultures and have brought them nearer to each other. When students of different sub-cultures study in same *school*, they learn other cultures and gradually two or more sub-cultures merge into each other.

The *art of communication* has also helped to bring various sub-cultures nearer to each other. In this respect Hindi films have played a very significant role which are viewed in all parts of the country. They have helped people of South India, Bengal, Gujarat or Assam, etc. to understand culture of North and it has helped to propagate Hindi language in all parts of the country and so the culture of North. However, with the settlement of people from Southern region in North, East and West and travel of people from these regions to South has made Bada, Dosha and Idli popular in all parts of India from Srinagar to Kolkata, Mumbai and even Assam. Similarly, *lassi* of Punjab or sweets of Bengal have become popular in other parts of the country. Chinese food shops have been established in vast numbers and people of various regions have developed taste for them. Chinese food has become delicacy. Italian pizzas and French fries have also become popular.

Print media, TV, internet and other such devices have also helped to bring various sub-cultures closer to each other and sub-cultural differences are narrowing down, but social and religious differences are keeping various cultures and sub-cultures away from each other whether it is India, USA, Arabs,

European or Africans. Everyone feels himself to be superior and right because of which even now there are disputes and long political or military struggles. In India, more states have been divided on culture factors and demand is still going on for more states. Ethnic differences are quite strong in India.

(6) DIFFERENCES BETWEEN INDIAN CULTURE AND WESTERN CULTURE

Basis	*Indian Culture*	*Western Culture*
❑ Belief in faith and luck	Strong believers.	Do not believe in faith and luck. Rather believe that everything is possible through hard work and efforts.
❑ Belief in spiritualism	Indians believe in spiritualism.	Westerners believe in materialism.
❑ Public appearance	Exposure of body in dress strongly objected to and considered obscene.	Fashionable clothes even exposing they may be are 'in thing' in west.
❑ Care of old people	Sons are expected to take care of their parents.	Old parents are not cared for. They have to look for old persons' homes.
❑ Respect for women	No religious ceremony is complete without wife. Woman is given respect in traditional sense.	Women are looked as an object of pleasure.
❑ Freedom to women	Lesser freedom of doing jobs and movement.	Women are very free in every aspect.

(7) FUNCTIONALITY AND DYSFUNCTIONALITY OF SOME CHARACTERISTICS OF INDIAN CULTURE

India has old cultures, which have functional (pro-democratic or pro-equity or positive aspects) as well as dysfunctional (non-work, non-equity) characteristics. We here quote learned Prof. Udai Pareek about the elements of Indian culture. He has stressed that "culture of an organisation can give it competitive advantage, provided it is rooted in the functional aspects of the country's culture. This should be accompanied by the development of new functional values to keep the organisation pro-active, as well as to empower individuals and teams to achieve results."

TABLE 1

Functionality and Dysfunctionality of Some Characteristics of Indian Culture

Aspects of Culture	*Functionality (Positive aspects)*	*Dysfunctionality (Non-work aspects)*
1. Fatalism	(i) High realism. (ii) Awareness of constraints.	(i) Individuals and groups become passive, reactive and tolerant of dysfunctionalities. (ii) High level of superstition. (iii) Lower self-confidence. (iv) Low urge for change.
2. Ambiguity tolerance	(i) Development of role flexibility.	(i) Low respect for structure and time.
3. Contextuation	(i) Better insight into social complexities. (ii) Empathy for deviation/deviants. (iii) Sensitivity to others (including groups). (iv) Quicker understanding of contexts.	(i) Delay in developing common norms and procedures. (ii) Confusion in interpretation of some facts.
4. Present-orientation	(i) High involvement in current activity. (ii) 'Here and now' focuses on current problems.	(i) Lower long-term perspective. (ii) Poor in long-term planning. (iii) Low commitment to future goals.
5. Collectivism	(i) Maintenance of good relations. (ii) High potential for collaboration. (iii) More frequent consensus. (iv) Shared work and reward. (v) Strong sense of belonging.	(i) Lack of initiative by individuals. (ii) Slow development of identity.
6. Particularism	(i) High identification with group.	(i) Low objectivity. (ii) Favouritism (iii) Clique formation

Source: Udai Pareek, Cultures as Competitive Advantage.

References

http://www.globalsources.com

Peer J. Dowling, Denice E. Welch and Randal S. Schuler, "International Human Resource Management", South Western College Publishing, Cincinanati.

Udai Pareek, "Cultures as Competitive Advantage", in *Designing and Deveoloping Organisation for Tomorrow,* edited by Anup R. Singh, Rajan K. Gupta and Abad Ahmad, Response Books, New Delhi.

PART X

CORPORATE SOCIAL RESPONSIBILITY

CHAPTER

55

Social Responsibility of Business

INTRODUCTION

Business depends on society for the *needed inputs* like money, men and skills,

Business also depends on society for *market* where products may be sold,

Thus, business depends on society for *existence, sustenance* and *encouragement*, and

Being so much dependent, business has definite responsibility towards society.

MEANING

Social responsibility of business means the obligation of business enterprises to make decision and follow lines of action which are desirable in terms of the objectives and values of society. Decisions may affect environment, consumers and the community.

Social responsibility is thus an *obligation of decision-makers to take actions* which *protect and improve the welfare of society* as a whole along with *their own interests.*

Every decision the businessman takes have social implications. Be it, opening new branch, closure of existing branch; replacement of men by machines, laying-off employees, sub-contracting. Society is affected in one way or the other.

Social responsibility is not new to our country. In olden days, whenever famine, floods, etc., leading business of area would provide food and other assistance to needy. Examples of Tatas.

CHANGING VIEWS OF MANAGEMENT'S RESPONSIBILITY

There have been changes in attitudes of managements in taking social responsibility in the past century. Let us examine these:

Phase I. **Profit maximising management**: This derives strength from Adam Smith's "Wealth of Nations", entrepreneurs produce what people want and they want profit. They produce more for self-interest to earn more profit and benefit all. Thus, competition will bring down prices. "What is good for business, is good for country."

The classical economic doctrine of maximising profit was against corporate social responsibility.

Phase II. **Trusteeship management:** It began with diffusion of corporate ownership as shareholders. So managers are not only to maximise profits, but also serve as trustees of employees, stockholders, suppliers, customers and public at large. They emphasised concern for the interest of others as well as one's own. The change in society's attitudes and expectations is reflected in the socio-economic model of business. This model views business as a sub-system of society.

Phase III. **Quality-of-Life Management (QOL)**: The values of QOL management contrast with both the profit maximiser and the trustee manager. Now the essential equation becomes "what is good for society is good for our company." While accepting profit as essential, the QOL management would neither produce nor sell unsafe or shoddy goods.

It also considers government as a partner in a joint effort to solve society's problems.

Modern View

A case for social responsibility—modern view. Peter Drucker argued that management should assume social responsibility. It is thus important for management to consider the impact of every business policy and action upon society. It has to consider the actions are likely to promote the public good, to advance the basic beliefs of society, and to contribute to its stability, strength and harmony.

Drucker observed that managements to consider demands made by the society on the enterprise. It is for management to convert these demands from threats into opportunities with least damage to the enterprise. Here focus is on "quality of product and customer service."

Now feeling (Sandra Holmes in her study of 540 Top Executives) is, in addition to making profit, business should help solve social problems whether or not business create these problems.

THE SOCIAL RESPONSIBILITY OF BUSINESS INVOLVES ETHICS

The social responsibility of business *involves ethics* which must be reflected in the philosophy of business organisation. To be effective, a sound ethics must be recognised by top management and reflected in the policies of the firm. Members should voluntarily accept it.

Right leadership, integrity, proficiency, commitment to social values of a manager can change the expected behaviour of individuals.

Top management commitment, leadership, examples are crucial to corporate ethics/culture. This commitment is communicated in many ways such as—speeches, directives, company publications, policy statements and most important, actions. Top management should establish clear policies that encourages ethical behaviour.

Management must assume *responsibility for disciplining* wrong doers.

Companies should *provide mechanism for 'whistle blowing'* as a matter of policy. Any employee becomes aware of unethical behaviour should be encouraged to report incident to his superior.

Managements should *give training/orientation programmes* explaining their organisation's code of ethics. By offering course in business ethics in MBA programmes helps in creating conscientious managers with a morally responsible approach to business.

CHAPTER

56

ARGUMENTS FOR SOCIAL RESPONSIBILITY

Some relations for business to discharge social responsibility are as under:

1. *Public Expectations from Business has changed.* It is argued that business exists because it satisfies the needs of society. If business at any time fails to live up to society's expectations, it may extinct.

If business wishes to remain viable in the long-run, it must respond to society's needs and give society what is wants. Business has debts which it owes to society as duty—of gratitude.

2. *Society creates better environment for business.* A firm which is more responsive to improvement of community quality of life will get better community in which to conduct business. Getting manpower will be easy, crime will be less.

3. *Public image is improved* if firm supports social goals. It may gain more customers, better employees.

4. Before government stretches its long arms, business should *discharge its obligations to society.* Otherwise society will force government to make laws/ regulations.

5. *Balance of responsibility with power.* Business has vast social power and it affects economy and social problems. So equal amount of social responsibility is required.

6. Business has *vast pool of resources* (men, talents, money, functional and professional expertise, etc.) and is in better position to work for social goals.

7. Other *institutions have failed* to handle social problems, *so society is turning to business.*

8. *Prevention is better than cure.* If business delays dealing with social problems, it may have to deal with more serious social breakdowns, therefore, business has moral responsibility.

9. *Citizenship argument.* Corporations are citizens and citizens have civic duties and responsibilities, corporations must discharge these voluntarily.

SOCIAL RESPONSIBILITIES STRATEGIES

Business responses to social responsibility tend to fall within four degrees/categories.

(i) *Social opposition.* This view is taken by the business which feel they have no obligation to society in which they operate. When they are caught for any offence, they cover it up by denying it. For example: M.S. Shoes for price rigging of shares.

(ii) *Social obligation.* Companies have firm believe that they have obligation to obey the laws, e.g. install safety equipment required by the law.

(iii) *Social response position* is taken by some companies that meet their social obligation as laid by law, and they will go beyond the legal requirement, if benefits out-weigh the costs.

(iv) *Social contribution* is the position taken by companies which believe that they have deep obligation to serve society. They are responsible citizens and are eager to contribute to the improvement of society.

The approaches to social responsibilities are explained in the figure below.

FIGURE

Approaches to Social Responsibility

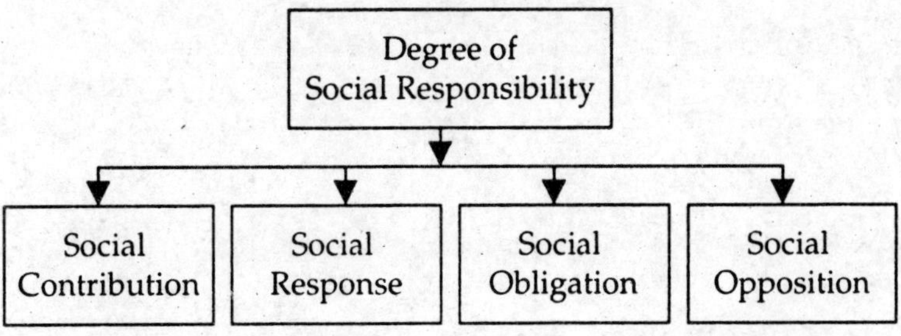

Source: Gene Burton and Manab Thakur, *Management Today*, p. 570.

ACKERMAN'S MODEL OF SOCIAL RESPONSIBILITY

Kobert Ackerman suggests that *responsiveness should be the goal of corporate endeavour*. He described *three stages* through which companies pass in developing response to social issues.

Phase I. *Awareness Stage*: Corporation's top managers learn of a existing social problem. CEO merely acknowledges the problem.

Phase II. *Planning Action Stage*: Hires specialist or consultant to prepare plan for dealing it.

Phase III. *Implementation Stage*: While resolving the problem, there is integration of policy into ongoing operations. Managements commit resources and organisational commitment is obtained at all levels.

Example: It has been suggested that women who use computer stand higher chances of having problem pregnancies. Management responsive to this problem may well be the only responsible for taking course of action.

CHAPTER

57

BUSINESS AS RESPONSIBLE PERSON

Business plays a very significant role in economic, social, political and technological affairs. So business owes responsibilities to all segments of society.

Wealth of a country is to a great extent controlled by business. This gives business and its executives "enormous power" to affect the lives of employees, consumers, shareholders, etc.

Business is a part of the total environment in which we live, being influenced by it, while being a force in influencing it. The relationship between business and its environment is one of mutual benefit—as explained in Figure 57.1. Both take from and give to various segments. Only through such a relationship can a business survive and prosper.

FIGURE 57.1

Modern business has acquired a sense of social responsibility to society in general and to its different segments in particular. *The objective of business is to balance the conflicting claims of 'stakeholders'.* Business is not to confine to productive or commercial activities as its social concern, but, it has to take into account social problems which arise due to its activity. Social and ethical considerations must equally concern the business.

WHY BUSINESS SHOULD ASSUME SOCIAL RESPONSIBILITY?

There are five broad reasons:

1. *Responding to demands of society*: As business gets larger, the public takes more interest in it, as it has greater impact on the community. Managers respond to public opinion so as to maintain public image of their company.

If an organisation does not respond, the society will either force it to do so through laws or society may no longer permit it to survive, e.g. safety of products, etc. The original purpose of corporations was to serve the public good.

2. *Longer-run self-interest of business*: For example, (a) Concern for employees can harmonise with company's best interests, (b) Responsibilities to shareholders for attracting investment, and (c) Avoiding environmental pollutions.

3. *Moral justification*: Business now tends to participate in the development of better world.

4. *Ethical behaviour and generation of profits* for shareholders is *not incompatible.*

5. *All stakeholders have a "stake"* in companies because they can be harmed, if a company behaves unethically.

Government has enacted number of laws to check these practices and to bring in an element of ethics into business. Government will continue to intervene by enacting legislation and impose penalties for unethical practices.

WHATEVER IS LEGAL IS ETHICAL?

This is to judge the business activities exclusively from the point of view of law. No this is inadequate view. For example, though maximisation of profit is one primary goal of an organisation, but charging unfair prices or exploitation of workers are considered as unethical practices.

Some unethical practices in business are:

- Piracy of products and copy rights,
- Deceptive advertising,
- Bribery, payment of kickbacks, corruption, scandles,
- Employee theft,
- Sexual harassment,
- Discriminatory personnel policies, favouritism in promotions, compensation, etc.,
- Black-marketing,
- Production of unsafe products,
- Exploitation of environment by manufacturers,
- Giving confidential information/secrets to competitor by employees, and
- Under invoicing.

Such acts, which indirectly create moral stress and impair the ability of competent managers to act with total integrity. Improved managerial ethical decision-making and moral performance can lead to both increased profitability and desirable organisational order.

CHAPTER

58

SOCIAL RESPONSIBILITIES OF BUSINESS TOWARDS DIFFERENT GROUPS

In this chapter we have attempted to present social responsibilities of business for various interest groups. These can be divided under two broad categories:

1. Internal interest groups.
2. External interest groups.

Various interest groups which have stake in the business are explained in the Figure 58.1 (see next page):

INTERNAL INTEREST GROUPS

1. Responsibilities towards Owners

It is to be ensured that owners, share-holders, partners get fair dividend or a fair return on the capital invested. Fair return has to be more than bank rate and it should be reasonable.

Further share-holders expect security of investment and share in capital appreciation as bonus shares.

2. Responsibility towards Employees

The traditional concept of "master-servant relationship" has to change to the concept of "partnership" between labour and management.

FIGURE 58.1

Business and its Interest Groups

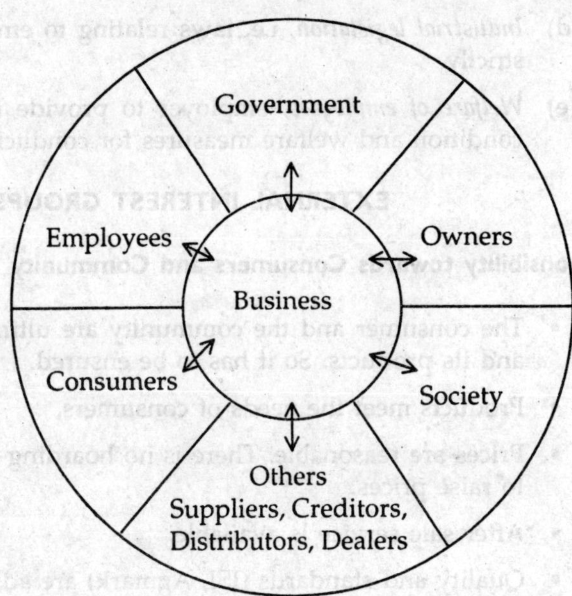

The major areas of relationship are:

(a) *Wages*—These should be need-based and productivity-related.

(b) *Salaries for managerial personnel* are to be linked to responsibilities. Ceiling on managerial remuneration by government to be adhered to.

Besides it is to be seen there are not much disparities between wages of employees and salaries of managerial personnel.

(c) *Relationship between employers and employees.* There are various *lapses on the part of employers* which include:

- Unsympathetic treatment to employees by supervisors.
- Favouritism in promotions, etc.
- Lack of communication between management and workers.
- Lack of *appreciation of meritorious achievements* and no condemnation of neglect and lethargy.
- Delay in settling *grievances/disputes* with employees.
- Lapses on part of employees, i.e. indiscipline in carrying out orders.

- Lack of desire by employees to improve efficiency.
- Role of politically inspired trade unions frequent strikes, *gheraos*, etc.

(d) *Industrial legislation*, i.e. laws relating to employees to be followed strictly.

(e) *Welfare of employees*, employer to provide health, safety, working condition and welfare measures for conducive work environment.

EXTERNAL INTEREST GROUPS

1. Responsibility towards Consumers and Community

- The consumer and the community are ultimate judges of business and its products. So it has to be ensured.
- Products meet the needs of consumers.
- Prices are reasonable. There is no hoarding—cornering of products to raise prices.
- After sale service is available.
- Quality and standards (ISI, Agmark) are adhered.
- Consumer associations are to be vigilant and to report falling of standards.

2. Businessmen's Responsibilities towards Government

- Employer has to be law abiding, follow laws relating to trade, factories and labour.
- To pay his dues and taxes fully and honestly.
- Not to purchase political support by unfair means.
- Not to corrupt public servants.
- Avoid adulteration.
- To maintain fair trade practices and avoid hoarding and cornering.

INDIAN SCENE—BUSINESS AS A RESPONSIBLE PERSON

Indian socio-economic environment have lent an added significance to the concept of business as a "responsible person."

(i) Indian government has been committed to socialistic pattern of society, in which private interest is to be subordinated to national considerations.

(ii) The Constitution of India provides for economic and social justice for all, welfare state, laws have been enacted for social justice.

(iii) State financial institutions contribute to a great part of the financial needs of business.

(iv) Emergence and development of professional management is wedded to the fulfilment of socio-economic objectives.

(v) There is growing public awareness and consciousness about the role of business in maintaining environmental protection and cleanliness.

(vi) Growth of trade unions for protection of employee's interests.

(vii) Emergence of consumer protection agencies/forums.

These factors contribute towards corporate social responsibility.

Many large enterprises in India have emphasised their social responsibility in their annual reports, e.g. TISCO, ITC, SAIL, BHEL, ONGC, etc. have developed neighbourhood projects. The Sachar Committee (1978) appreciated that some enlightened business houses are contributing to solve problems of rural development, environment protection, control of pollution and provision of clean water. They are recognising social responsibility as development of corporate ethics.

To conclude, by being more socially responsive, business may avoid further regulations which limit the freedom of business.

It has to be realised that the future of business depends on its *ability and willingness to respond to the changing expectations of society*. Corporations must present themselves as being committed to social causes. A global company has to develop global sensitivity.

The corporations are now doing *'social audit'*, i.e. presenting additional objectives and comprehensive information about organisation's social performance which reflect social responsibilities. Some areas covered in social audit are i.e.:

(a) Social benefits to the staff—various facilities, etc.

(b) Social benefits to the community—local taxes paid to panchayat, municipality, environmental improvements, generation of job potential.

(c) Social benefits to the public—taxes paid and follow the duties toward government.

CHAPTER

59

Business Ethics' Core Responsibilities of Entrepreneurial Performance

According to Peter Pratley (The Essence of Business Ethics), "it is important to define core moral responsibilities at a minimal level. By accepting an outspoken commitment to these responsibilities, TQM can gain a lot. The core moral responsibilities are three-fold.

First of all, the corporation is committed to its original and basic moral core responsibility: that is, *producing goods and services that are functional and safe for the individual consumer*. On top of this perennial cornerstone of business, other core activities now have to be added.

The second moral commitment therefore concerns the larger *environment: environmental core and reduction of resource depletion.*

Finally, the third accepted responsibility refers to *the quality of the corporation itself as a moral community*. At a minimum level this implies the absence of certain abuses.

These three core moral responsibilities for business organisations aim at guaranteeing a minimum of moral excellence. They are linked with an idea of normative entrepreneurial performance and encapsulate what the public may at least expect from an entrepreneur committed to quality management.

These three entrepreneurial responsibilities also imply a redefinition of corporate objectives. It pushes the meaning of the famous separatist expression 'mind your own business' in a quite opposite direction. Corporate mission statements that include these moral responsibilities enlarge the matters for which the public may hold business accountable for by insisting on safe and reliable customer relationships, environmental care and humane working conditions.

The entrepreneur should gain this broader perspective as the corporation commits itself to wider human objectives, especially in relation to our common future. Although industry will go through even more stringent reductions of employee numbers in the future, certain minimum standards of working conditions should be agreed upon by all those committed to quality goods. This statement is a moral appeal for legal means and voluntary covenants to enforce respect for minimum labour rights.

To summarise our discussion:

1. The corporation producing quality products and services accepts specific moral responsibilities. At a minimum level, there are three such corporate responsibilities:
   (a) consumer care, expressed by satisfying demands for ease of use and product safety;
   (b) environmental care; and
   (c) care for minimum working conditions.
2. Corporations should not remain mute about their moral performances and commitments. A balanced presentation of one's corporate response in face of specific moral concerns can create a basis of understanding with one's own employees as well as with the concerned public. Communicate the priorities you have in your commitment to quality management by a sophisticated use of moral talk."

Source: Peter Pratley, The Essence of Business Ethics.

CHAPTER

60

PROMOTING VALUE-BASED GOVERNANCE IN ORGANISATIONS

When one tries to analyse the current value system that Indians hold, one notices that most of our cultural values are gradually degenerating. Our character has been devalued faster than our rupees. The worse that has happened is that we have started rationalizing and justifying our degraded value system on one or the other pretext. Therefore, there is an indispensable and urgent need for introspection to revive our value system to old glory.

PRESENT SCENARIO OF VALUES SYSTEM IN INDIAN BUSINESS ORGANIZATIONS

In this present turbulent times, a breakdown in values is noticeable in almost every sphere of life ranging from family, religion, administration, public life and management of corporate sector. This decline is more obvious in business, industries, public institutions, government departments, voluntary organizations and professional institutions. Owing to the process of privatization, liberalization and globalization intense competition has evolved as basic guidelines for business survival. It is simply a mad-race where each person wants to win over the other, irrespective of the consequences, which leads to erosion of value system.

Our whole attitude has become negative, indifferent, fatalistic, escapist, cynical, rigid and argumentive thus what is needed in this hour is not only fulfilling short-term objectives, but also fulfilment of long-term objectives incorporated with ethical and moral responsibilities by corporate houses, to survive intense completion. Management should develop human values by setting examples so that they are perceived as role models—the winning combination should include.

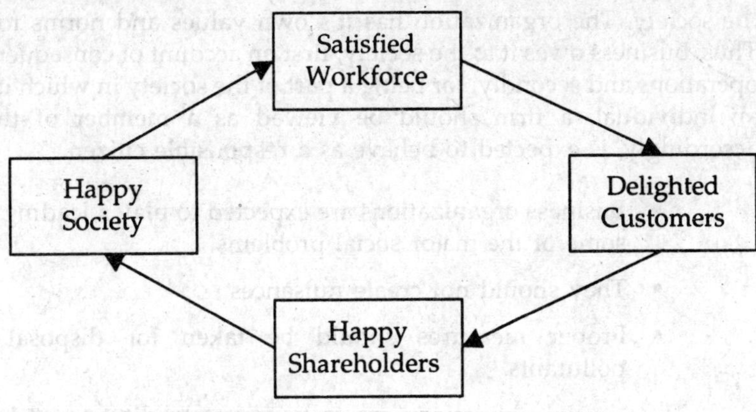

GUIDE FOR VALUE

Following are some guidelines on how to promote value-based governance through value creation for workforce, customers, investors/shareholders and society.

1. Value Creation for Workforce

An organisation culture should create a sense of commitment in the workforce. They must love their job and should be a dedicated lot and this must be reinforced by the management.

2. Value Creation for Customers

The survival of the organization depends upon the necessary expertise and capability to satisfy global markets. Customers are awakening individually and collectively day-by-day regarding their rights. Growing awareness of needs and rights is changing their behaviour. Customers are becoming increasingly assertive in demanding high quality products and services and they are no more passive onlookers, as they used to be.

3. Value Creation for Investors and Shareholders

Shareholders, investors are the company owners, they have the legitimate right to expect proper return on their investment. So, fair and ethical treatment should be provided to them in the following manner:

- The money invested by them should be judiciously used.
- No personal expenditure should form part of the investor's money.

4. Value Creation for Society

Organisation exists within a society and their members are drawn from the society. The organization has it's own values and norms towards society. Thus, business owes it to the society, first on account of consequences of it's own operations and secondly, for being a part of the society in which it operates. Like an individual, a firm should be viewed as a member of the society and accordingly, is expected to behave as a responsible citizen.

- Business organizations are expected to play a leading role in solving some of the major social problems.
- They should not create nuisances.
- Proper measures should be taken for disposal of industrial pollutants.

Thus, social obligations are to be properly discharged by the business organizations.

5. Leadership Values

Values get transferred from one generation to the other through family, teachers and other members of society. Taking this path of transmission, an individual in an organization perceives his/her superior to be the repository of ethical values. Managers should act as role models for their co-workers. The value-oriented managers have to lead their workers with adequate, (i) interpersonal communication and feedback, (ii) teamwork, collaboration and participation for company goals, (iii) share knowledge, (iv) leadership towards the collective success of the whole team, and (v) make employees at ease with receptive and open to suggestions.

So the leadership should try to assess the spirituality quotient (SQ) of the employees, as well as of themselves, in addition to intelligence quotient (IQ) and emotional quotient (EQ) and follow balancing style:

- Positive attitude
- Self-confidence
- Faith
- Strong will-power
- Sense of responsibility
- Empathy.

TO CONCLUDE

Organisations of tomorrow will crave for self-ordered, self-controlled, self-disciplined and self-motivated employees to survive amidst a dynamic, competitive and changing global economic environment. Employees with commensurate human values to that of organizational values can meet such exacting demands. Such value system can create and sustain perennial satisfaction level and can develop human resources. We have to transform our personality and that of our organization, by improving following value systems in our organization:

- Gaining knowledge
- Hard work
- Entrepreneurship
- Regular self-introspection
- Spirit of service
- High goals of integrity

These are the key to organizational excellence.

Source: Amulya Khurana and Bijaya Mishra, Deptt. of Humanities and Social Sciences, IIIT, New Delhi, NIPM, July 2001.

PART XI

PROTECTION OF STAKEHOLDERS

CHAPTER

61

BUSINESS AND ENVIRONMENTAL ETHICS

Protection of environment is the major issue that confronts business decision-makers.

Problems such as—pollution due to—disposal of toxic waste, eroding of the earth's ozone layer—acid rain and others are serious ecological problems. Causes of these and other threats to environment have their *source in industrial production*. As such the theme of business and environmental ethics has become an essential issue in the field of business ethics.

Some examples of environmental pollution are:

(i) Bhopal Gas Leakage Tragedy

Shortly after midnight on December 3, 1984 outside Bhopal, India, a cloud of deadly methyl isocyanate gas leaked from a pesticide plant owned by the Indian subsidiary of Union Carbide. The choking gas covered the town, quickly killing hundreds—including many children, who were less resistant to the gas than adults—and forcing Bhopal's 6,70,000 inhabitants to flee in panic. By the end of the week more than 2,000 people had died from inhaling the gas, and 1,50,000 more had to be hospitalized for respiratory and eye damage, making Bhopal's 'night of death' the worst industrial disaster in history. Images of stunned families burying or burning their dead and blaming Union Carbide for their agony were boradcast worldwide.

There were immediate repercussions for Union Carbide and for the chemical industy as well. The Indian government accused the plant management of failing to take adequate safety precautions and indicated that it held the parent company ultimately responsible. Lawsuits brought by American lawyers on behalf of the victims asked for billions of dollars in compensatory and punitive damages and threatened to send the company into bankruptcy. Union Carbide's stock price plumetered; it halted production of methyl isocyanate at the one West Virginia plant that produced the chemical in the United States.

Officials in the United States and India called for increased regulation and inspection of chemical processing plants. Many U.S. localities considered passing "right-to-know" laws that would require chemical companies to provide detailed information about hazardous materials to the employees who make them and to residents living near the plants. Several companies countered with voluntary right-to-know programmes to head off public sentiment for government regulation. In the wake of protests against Union Carbide in other parts of the world, some multinational corporations claimed that the Bhopal disaster had chilled the international climate for U.S. business.

Union Carbide, which had earned an above-average record on industrial safety over the decade preceding the disaster, appeared paralyzed by the magnitude of Bhopal's suffering. Corporate Chairman Warren Anderson rushed to India to inspect the site and was briefly arrested by Indian authorities. Union Carbide's one hundred thousand employees observed a moment of silence for the dead and injured; many donated money for disaster relief. Top management spent sleepless nights grappling with the company's crushing problems and its uncertain future. Morale at the company was low; production at many plants temporarily dropped. However, while expressing profound sympathy for the Bhopal victims and promising to make a fair restitution, Union Carbide maintained its essential innocence. "There's no criminal responsibility here", said Anderson.

(ii) Storage Tank Leakage of Pennwalt Corporation

Mr. High, a plant manager at Pennwalt Corporation was at home on vacation, when he got a call on 2.1.1985 that there had been accident at the plant. Mr. High rushed there and found that a storage tank containing sodium chlorate had collapsed and flowed into nearby canal. In less than two hours, his lawyers say, Mr. High surveyed the damage and informed US Coast Guard and Washington State Department of ecology of spill which he estimated at 20,000 gallons of sodium chlorate. But in May 1988, more than 3 years later, Mr. High and Pennwalt Corporation were indicted on charges of negligence. They were also accused of coverning up the full extent of spill, which was later found

Sources: This case was based on material from the following articles: "India's Night of Death", *Times*, December 17, 1984, pp. 22-31; Judith Dobrzynski, William Glaberson, Rosa Kig, William Powell, Jr., and Leslie Helm, "Union Carbide Fights for its Life", *Business Week*, December 24, 1984, pp. 52-56; and Maria Recio and Vicky Cahon, "Bhopal has Americans Demanding the 'Right to Know'", *Business Week*, February 18, 1985, pp. 36-37.

75,000 gallons. Pennwalt Corporation was fined $ 8 million, while Mr. High was fined $ 650,000 and sent to jail for 9 years.

(iii) Disaster of Super-Tanker Exxon

Another example worth quoting is of environmental disaster of Super Tanker "Exxon" and here crude oil flowed in sea in Alaska, North America. Marine mammals, fish and other wildlife were killed. Exxon cleaned up operations and spent $ 1.28 billion in its efforts. Exxon proclaimed their clean up a "success", but government of USA was not satisfied and one of the greatest marine disaster in history became an ethical issue for America's largest corporation. Environmentalists continue their attacks on industry.

There are numerous examples of environmental pollutions. So there are many recent cases where corporate organisations and individual managers were prosecuted for environmental crimes. In USA between 1982-89, there were 486 cases. The lawyers say criminal charges should be filed only in instances of deliberate misconduct, not in accidental situations such as Pennwalt Corporation.

Many companies are not aware that all major environmental laws contain criminal enforcement provisions.

The problems of environment have come to the fore in India only during recent years. These have gripped the attention of enlightened people, organised groups, governments, judiciary in India also.

WHAT IS AN ENVIRONMENT?

The environment is defined as the totality of man's surroundings. Today's environment may be said to consist of elements each of which is resource. The resources may be grouped into two categories:

(i) *Natural resources*: Land, water, air, fauna and flora, energy and fuels and raw materials, i.e. minerals, and

(ii) *Man-made resources*: The socio-economic structure, cultural heritage, the people.

It is widely recognised now that the quality of environment is fast deteriorating through: Industrial Pollutions—i.e. toxic chemicals, oil spills in the ocean, deforestation.

Air pollution largely caused by automobile exhausts, and other measures, i.e. carbon monoxide, lead, carbon dioxide, sulpher oxide, asbestos.

Water pollution through sewage discharges and drainage from mines, waste composts, chemicals which are toxic for human life, fishes and birds, etc.

Ecology is study of plants, animals, people and institutions in relation to environment. Ecology refers to the inter-relationships between people and fauna (birds and animals).

The flora (plants and trees) and their physical surroundings.

Ecosystem is the totally of-living and non-living elements in the ecological community interacting with one another and the environment.

Partly, the environmental problems may be attributed to negative effects of process of industrialisation and economic development; partly it is also due to poverty and underdevelopment.

Business has, therefore to be concerned with public health, safety, environmental protection.

ENVIRONMENTAL PROTECTION IN INDIA

Various steps have been taken such as enactment of laws, establishment of regulatory bodies, semi-judicial authorities. These are as under:

(i) *Legal*. The directive principles of state policy in the Constitution of India lay emphasis on protection of environment. Some laws enacted are as under:

1. The Air (Prevention and Control of Pollution) Act, 1981, amended in 1988.
2. The Environment (Protection) Act, 1986.
3. The Water (Prevention and Control of Pollution) Act, 1974 amended in 1974 and 1988.
4. The Hazardous Wastes Act, 1989.
5. The Wildlife Protection Act, 1972.
6. The Forests (Conservation) Act, 1980 amended in 1988.

(ii) *Regulation*. Administrative orders/policy guidelines have been laid by government. A separate Department of Environment, Government of India was created in 1980.

(iii) Certain regulatory bodies or quasi-judicial authorities have been established such as:

- National Afforestation and Eco-development Board, and
- National Wastelands Development Board.

(iv) Manufacturing units have been closed in cities. High Court of Delhi ordered shifting of manufacturing units out of Delhi and closing them. Similarly, Courts have ordered for removal of foundaries from Agra city, and shifting of manufacturing factories from Kanpur.

(v) Various industrial pollution control projects have been started, e.g. Clean Ganga Action Plan, Pushkar Lake Valley, Auroville (T.N.), Tumkar (Karnataka), Gopeshwar in UP, Shivalik Foothills (Punjab).

(vi) Various programmes on environment education, seminars creating awareness and resource management have started.

(vii) Government has also laid (EAP) Environment Action Plan.

All these legal and other steps taken by the Government, central and states have not achieved desired results. The main problem is that there is laxity in the enforcement of the legal provisions. There is lack of coordination between centre and state governments.

NEW FOCUS

(i) Now *more importance to environmental protection* is being given. Social groups, judges are taking initiative. Government is trying to involve NGOs as eyes and ears in terms of grass-root monitoring of environment quality. Government response to environmental concerns is increasing.

(ii) The industry is not only to *obey current environmental laws,* but also to *go beyond them.* To work on solutions to various ecological problems so as to demonstrate, it holds environmental values. Environment laws now a subject for study in courses, research, and to improve equipment, innovate new projects.

(iii) Many companies are not aware that nearly all major laws on pollution control contain criminal enforcement provisions. This *awareness* is making industries to follow statutory provisions seriously.

(iv) Initially, business has been resisting to their role in protection of environment. But now business is *looking for remedial measures* as professionals in industry realise it. This type of resistance was there in consumer protection also in the beginning in the USA.

(iv) Government, business, politicians admit that environment is to be protected gradually, so that industry does not die.

(v) Trust for Environment Education and Community Action, New Delhi (WildwondersIndia@rediffmail.com) is actively involved in conservation movement.

The mission of TEECA is to provide meaningful platform to individuals, students, community groups for interacting and getting real insight into the immediate environment around so that they can have the capacity to know all about the problems and can find solutions to these problems on their own.

CHAPTER

62

UNETHICAL PRACTICES IN INDIA

Lot of concern is expressed about unethical practices being followed in India. Corrupt practices are probably maximum in India. Chairman of Prevention of Corruption Committee reported that 25% of plan expenditure has been lost because of corruption.

Each state government is having scams, scandals, as well as in the central government. Number far exceed 4000 scandals.

India is rated as corrupt nation in the world according to some surveys carried out by reputed agencies.

Most common unethical practices being followed include:

1. Relating to Consumers

(a) Adulteration of:

- Food items causing health problems.
- Deceptive weights and measures.
- Poor quality of products.

(b) Spurious products in the market such as:

- Life saving medicines
- Life saving injections

(c) Duplicates of:

- Soft drinks

- Popular brands, e.g. jams, detergents, etc.
- Variations in the packs.

(d) Supply of Injurious products for commercial gains though they are health hazards.

(e) Deceptive advertisements are made so that people are tempted to buy foods, etc. There are "Sales" offering-gifts and prices and rebates.

(f) Promotional contests.

(g) Higher prices.

2. Unethical Practices against Government and Community

(a) Tax evasion and consequent black money.

(b) Pollution of air, water and noise. Pollutions continue unabated by industries, automobiles.

(c) Bribes have become a style today of business operations to get any normal thing done otherwise nothing moves. Poor quality construction is cleared by officials. There are certain set percentages paid to officials, through touts/agents/advocates, and their role is unbecoming.

3. Relating to Employees

(a) Low salaries.

(b) Poor working conditions, inadequate light, ventilation, bare welfare facilities or safety measures.

(c) Exploitation of:

- Bonded labour still exists in India.
- Getting receipts for salaries more than what is actually is paid.

4. National Economy

(a) Scandals, scams in banks, government.

(b) Government expenditures on rise due to corrupt bureaucracy.

(c) Political degradations.

CHAPTER

63

CONSUMER PROTECTION

IMPORTANCE

Consumerism is an indispensable part of day-to-day affairs of all of us. Attitude of business to the consumers has been very indifferent, particularly operating in seller's market.

It has been recognised in recent years, all over the world that business owes responsibilities to all segments of society, e.g. shareholders, workers, suppliers, consumers, local community and the state. The survival and growth of business will depend upon its relations with all these interest groups. So concept of "business as a responsible person" has emerged. Business has certain rights and obligations, viz. achieving social purpose.

Now it is stressed that essence of all business activity should be "consumer protection and satisfaction." Business has to identify and anticipate consumer demands, produce and distribute authentic quality, goods and provide services of right quality and reasonable price.

REASONS FOR BUSINESS TO CHANGE ATTITUDE TOWARDS CONSUMERISM

Business has to change attitude towards consumerism as:

(i) Consumers are now more sensitive to social and environmental needs;

(ii) Consumers are discontent and complain now as compared in the past when they ignored;

(iii) Consumers have now choice as there is competition and variety of products are available;

(iv) As business leaders, they cannot ignore customers;

(v) Further rise of higher education of consumers has created awareness of their rights; and

(vi) Finally, legislation leading to consumer protection has created awareness among consumers about their rights and remedies available to them.

APPROACHES TO CONSUMER PROTECTION

We give below four approaches for protection of consumer interests:

(i) *Business self-regulation and self-discipline.* Now numerous trade associations are to check the malpractices.

(ii) *State role is becoming more aggressive,* i.e. legislature, executive and judiciary into enforcement of laws. These laws serve as potent tool to improve status of consumers.

(iii) *Consumer's associations have been given status* in many laws and they are playing active role.

(iv) *Consumer has to be alert.* When consumer is cheated he should not say "forget about it." 'Self-help is the best help'. As such consumers have to assert their rights and perform their duties.

In this connection, it may be relevant to quote Patrica Hayes Andrews and Richard Therschel (Organisation Communication, AITBS Publishers and Distributors, for protection of consumer interest as under:

(i) An exemplary organization widely recognised for its strong ethical character and keen sense of social responsibility is Johnson & Johnson. In 1982, seven people died after ingesting one of the firm's products, Tylenol capsules, that had been laced with cyanide. Even though the poisoning had occurred outside Johnson & Johnson's premises and was limited to the Chicago area, the company withdrew all Tylenol capsules from the U.S. market, at an estimated cost of $ 100 million. At the same time, the company initiated a comprehensive communication effort, involving 2,500 employees throughout the organization, aimed at the medical and pharmaceutical communities. The company's handling of the tampering crisis (its second such crisis) promoted the President Ronald Reagan to applaud Johnson & Johnson's leadership in a speech to the Business Council in Washington, D.C. Noting its commitment to socially responsible behaviour, Reagan said, "Let me congratulate one of your members, someone who in recent days has lived up to the highest ideal of corporate responsibility and grace under pressure. Jim Burke of Johnson & Johnson, you have our deepest admiration" (Benson, 1988, p. 62). *The Washington Post* wrote of the incident, "Johnson & Johnson has succeeded in portraying itself to the public as a company willing to do what's right, regardless of cost" (quoted in Aguilar, 1994, p. 164).

In the aftermath of the Tylenol tamperings, James Burke noted, "I think the Tylenol story is the most powerful thing that has occurred in American business to underline the value of a moral statement" (Aguilar, 1994, p. 68). Focus on presents Johnson & Johnson's current Credo.

(ii) Although it might seem that large corporations have the greatest opportunities and resources to *demonstrate a social conscience*, those who run smaller organisations have been known to make impressive contributions as well. One woman who runs a private communicational consulting firm in Washington, D.C., for instance, became deeply concerned about the plight of single mothers wh were trying to gain employment after the birth of a child but either could not find or could not afford child care. This woman bought and renovated a large house, identified five needy single mothers, and rented the house to them for $ 100 a month each. Then she found five elderly people who had no families but who were in relatively good health and loved young children. They, too, were brought to the house to live—and they cared for the children while the mothers went to work. Besides the initial cost of the house (over $ 250,000), this businesswoman spent an additional $ 5,000 each year, just to keep the house running and in good condition. Thus, through her effort and generosity, she helped meet the needs of single mothers, several young children, and the elderly—on a small scale, but in a truly significant and enduring way."

CONSUMER PROTECTION

Legislation can serve as a potent tool to improve the status of consumers. There are various laws which protect consumer against different forms of deceit, injury and exploitation. Some laws for protection of consumers are as under:

1. The Agricultural Product (Grading and Marketing) Act, 1937, e.g. get Agmark quality items and businessmen advised to obtain certificates for winning consumers' goodwill.
2. The Bureau of Indian Standards Act, 1986. Certification from BIS for standardisation of quality consumers to look for ISI mark products.
3. The Cigarettes (Regulation, Production, Supply and Distribution) Act, 1975. It requires informing the public about health hazard. For example, "Cigarette smoking is injurious to health" is written on the packets.
4. The Drugs and Cosmetics Act, 1940, to ensure these items are of standard quality, purity and strength and packed in containers giving necessary information about contents of drug.

5. The Drugs and Magic Remedies (Objectionable Advertisements) Act, 1954. The act provides for controlling advertisements of drugs relating to vineral diseases, sexual stimulants, etc. and also to avoid self-medication.
6. The Essential Commodities Act, 1955. This act empowers government to regulate and control of prices, supply, transport, etc. of essential commodities, e.g. coal, drugs, edible oils, petroleum products, milk.
7. The Hire Purchase Act, 1972. It provides essential requirement of hire contract which will then culminate into sale.
8. The Indian Penal Code, 1840. Certain provisions check fraudulent use of false weights or measures, adulteration of drugs, etc.
9. The Prevention of Black Marketing and Maintenance of Supplies of Essential Commodities Act, 1980 to ensure supply to consumers.
10. Prevention of Food Adulteration Act, 1954 to provide for penalties against offences affecting public health (IPC). For example, mixing milk with water, and arrangement for analysis of food articles.
11. The Standards of Weights and Measures Act, 1976:
    - Prohibits non-standards weights and measures;
    - Controller of weights has to exercise checks that weights conform to standards; and
    - Manufacturer has to mention date of package, quantity in package, etc.
12. The Trade and Merchandise Marks Act, 1958:
    - To provide for trade-marks—Bata, Fiat, Birla-Yamaha for generators, Onida for TV.
    - To prevent fraudulent trade-marks of deceptively producing similar products resembling the original items.
13. The Water (Prevention and Control of Pollution) Act, 1974 to prohibit on use of stream or well for disposal of pollution and to check samples.
14. Some recent steps are:

    (i) The Consumer Protection Act, 1986. It lays a three-tier forums for redressal of grievances of consumers:

    —District forums—for loss below 1 lakh.

    —State Commission—for loss 1-10 lakhs.

    —National Commission.

It is quasi-judicial machinery to provide speedy and simple redress to consumers. A complaint can be in letter form only is adequate, e.g. complaint of Housing Society *v.* MTNL. Consumer Protection Council can suggest amendments to the Act.

(ii) Concept of Lok Adalats introduced for speedy and economic redressal of consumer grievances, e.g. MTNL, DESU, Dak and Pension Adalat, etc. They also provide free legal aid.

(iii) Instituting a National Youth Award for Rs. 20,000 on consumer protection.

IMPACT OF LAWS

Management of Laws. There are large number of laws/orders/rules which teach the spirit of consumerism. But it has become a wonder land of lawyer's paradise and hardly few cases succeed in court. There is not proper implementation of enforcement of laws even in some cases implementation left to municipalities.

As such the role of these laws to protect consumers has not been satisfactory. Besides consumers are also ignorant. There is poor business response and weak consumer movement. As such consumer associations have to become active.

To conclude, self-help is the best help. Let us hope Indian consumer awakes from his slumber! Let us also hope Indian business responds to keep alive.

CHAPTER

64

PROTECTION OF EMPLOYEES

SCENARIO OF EXPLOITATION

The scenario has been of exploitation of employees inspite of various laws on labour such as:

- Malpractices of short payment and irregular payments. There are arbitrary deductions from wages.
- Payment of low wages and rising prices.
- Unsafe work place and bad working conditions, long working hours.
- Employment of women and child labour, for long hours.
- Unfair practices in recruitment—casual and contract labour.
- Employment terms are not laid by employer. Hire and fire without following any procedure and arbitrarily.
- Unfair labour practices, retrenchment and closing of factories without following of proper procedure in the laws.
- There has been no security against old-age.
- Denying compensation for accident inquiries and death at works.
- Hardly any redressal of grievances.

ALIENATION OF EMPLOYEES AND PROBLEMS

The exploitation of workers has led to alienation of workers and some problems are:

- Absenteeism.
- High labour turnover.
- Numerous industrial disputes pending in courts.
- Loss of production.
- Neglect of welfare of workers.
- Indebtedness of industrial workers.
- Automation and consequent problems.
- Illiteracy.
- Low productivity.
- Bad quality of workmanship.

The exploitation of employees led to both the birth of trade unions and an era of government regulation and control.

International labour organisation established in 1919 influenced in the protection of labour provided in its various conventions.

Advent of independence quickened the pace of growth of trade unions due to changed outlook towards labour and awakening in the country.

Various provisions on labour are made in the Constitution of India and labour laws enacted after independence.

CONSTITUTIONAL FRAMEWORK OF LABOUR LEGISLATION

(i) The *Fundamental Rights* laid in the Constitution of India provides certain guarantees for labour:

(a) Equality before law or equal protection of laws.

(b) Right to form associations or unions.

(c) Freedom of speech and assembly.

(d) No discrimination on grounds of caste, sex, religion.

(e) Protection against exploitation.

(f) No child below 14 years shall be employed in factory/mine on hazardous employment.

These fundamental rights are enforceable in the court.

(ii) Matters relating to labour are provided in the *concurrent list* of the Constitution of India, and both central and state governments can enact laws on labour.

(iii) *Directive principles of state policy* in the constitution lays guidelines for state policies. Some provisions are:

(a) Equal pay for equal work for men and women.

(b) Children are protected against exploitation.

(c) Just and humane conditions of work and maternity relief for women employees.

(d) Aspiration for living wage.

(e) Participation of workers in the management.

LABOUR LAWS

Labour laws refers to body of enactments by the central and state legislatures to protect and promote interests of working class. These laws are to ensure good working and living conditions for workers and to maintain industrial peace and cordial relations between employers and workers. These laws ensure:

(a) Social justice;

(b) Social equality;

(c) International uniformity through International Labour Organisation (ILO); and

(d) Industrial peace for growth of national economy.

A few labour laws for protection of employees, women and children are classified for reference:

1. *Laws on Wages/Compensation*

(a) The Payment of Wages Act, 1936.

(b) The Minimum Wages Act, 1948.

(c) The Payment of Bonus Act, 1965.

(d) The Equal Remuneration Act, 1976.

2. *Laws on Working Conditions*

(a) The Factories Act, 1948.

(b) The Shops and Establishments Act, 1951.

(c) The Mines Act, 1952.

(d) The Plantation Labour Act, 1951.

(e) The Contract Labour (Regulation and Abolition) Act, 1970.

3. *Laws on Industrial Relations*
   (a) The Industrial Disputes Act, 1947.
   (b) The Trade Unions Act, 1926.
   (c) The Industrial Employment (Standing Orders) Act, 1946.
4. *Laws on Social Security*
   (a) The Workmen's Compensation Act, 1923.
   (b) The Employees' State Insurance Act, 1948.
   (c) The Employees' Provident Fund Act, 1952.
   (d) The Payment Gratuity Act, 1972.
   (e) The Maternity Benefit Act, 1961.

It may be mentioned that we have over 140 laws relating to labour matters in India and even we cannot name them. Of late, many of these labour laws have become out-dated in the context of changes in the economy and its failure to maintain peaceful industrial relations. With the result militancy and strikes still continue unabated. Reasons for this state of affairs are:

(a) Labour laws are *complicated* and difficult to understand by industrial relations managers. It has become lawyers' paradise.

(b) There is *inadequate enforcement* of labour laws by labour departments.

(c) Besides, there is *ineffective implementation* of labour laws.

EMERGING RELATIONSHIP BETWEEN EMPLOYER AND EMPLOYEES

However, there is growing awareness to bring about change in labour relations. Some signs are:

(i) There is change from *master-servant relationship to contractual* (reciprocal and mutual partnership).

(ii) From *conflict to collaborative* relationship.

(iii) It is realised by employers that *unions are now part of industry*. They are taking steps to live with unions.

(iv) New focus is to *settle differences through negotiations*, collective bargaining.

(v) *Several schemes* and innovative practices such as—'participation of employees in management' and setting of 'quality circles' are improving commitment of employees at work place.

(vi) The workers are *losing interest in trade unions* as the role is only confined as a protest institution and trade unions do not look to interest of the organisation.

(vii) Instead *trade unions have to adopt a new role* of developmental. Due to global competition trade unions have to avoid restrictive practices and coercive measures.

(viii) Managements are encouraging linking of incentives with productivity of workers and several innovative schemes are now in operation.

(ix) Technology has brought a shift from *blue collar to white collar workers.* As a result, militancy is on the decrease.

(x) The new thrust is on *produce more and distribute more.* It has to be realised that most of the employment conditions would be now determined by the market forces rather than by the political and/or member strength of trade unions.

CHAPTER

65

Building Corporate Image

IMPORTANCE OF CORPORATE IMAGE

Nothing matters more to a company than its corporate image. The Tatas, Infosys, Wipro, Reliance . . . more and more companies are realising the *virtues of brand*, positioning and building up corporate images.

The *role of CEOs* is vital. Some CEOs have become *brands for their companies*. We have numerous examples:

- Microsoft flashes image of Bill Gates.
- GE flashes image of Jack Welch.
- Infosys flashes image of Narayana Murty.
- Wipro flashes image of Azim Premji.
- Tata's flashes image of Ratan Tata.

Their companies have made them household names through their personal charisma and drive.

Companies dynamic image is dynamic actualisation of the CEO's vision, mission and strategic plans. Their approach fuses corporate reputation, social responsibility, governance, code of ethics and reflects ethics in society at large. Leaderships are *brands* driving corporate image and business values, which make impact on the *performance* of a firm.

Importance of CEO's reputation is more significant than ever before. A brand name CEO can make a company stand out in a crowd. The picture we see is of personal values of Murty, institutionalised to create this unique position.

New generation business leaders, (A.V. Birla Group, Ratan Tata, Murty, AT&T, Disney) have realised the *value of CEO brands* and are leveraging these to gain a unique edge for their business. They have recognised the values of environment and social responsibilities, they represent for their business and bring in the minds of multiple stakeholders.

SOME STEPS IN BUILDING CORPORATE IMAGE

There are numerous initiatives required to build corporate image. Amitabh Baxi has summed up that corporate should *express interests of stakeholders*. Some steps are:

(i) Win Customers

Prime responsibility is reaching across the *customer's mind and heart*, fulfil social responsibility and help in governance of the country.

(ii) Distinct Organisation Culture is Critical Element

Intrinsic values within a company and expressed by in every action reflects its culture, culture is made up of the vision, mission, corporate strategy, inherent values, ethical business practices, financial openness, human resource practices, sensitivity and responsibility to community and environment. *Values* based on true integrity of the performance of a corporate counts.

(iii) Fair Business Strategy

Business strategy that is fair, open, transparent based on truth keeps a balance between internal and external stakeholder of the company, customer's satisfaction, are basic for building a strong image.

(iv) Building and Sustaining Trust and Confidence of Shareholders

This is pre-requisite for good corporate image. While it takes years to build good relationship, the confidence can be lost overnight. Company to address key issues and *communicate* in transparent manager to shareholder.

For creditability and trust in relationship some degree of hype and manipulations created through *advertisements* to promote the use of its products, is also crucial for success. Image is made more creditable *through actions* that deliver across all stakeholders.

Corporate positive image should be based on *integrity*, equality and feelings that people want to have. To cite example of multinational power giant Enron, corruption personal or corporate when discovered, becomes the identity and ruins the reputation. Same is the case of Arther Anderson. Infact, image has to be presented truthfully.

(v) Employees are Most Critical Stakeholders of a Company

What employees do and say about the company they work for, influences the perceptions of multiple points of contact, i.e. vendors, customers, social acquaintances and even media, enhances a credible image or destroys it.

Just think of what 'six sigma' has done for GE—driving internal excellence and sustaining a corporate image as a world's most admired corporation.

(vi) Relationships with Stakeholders

An organisation has to *create successful* relationships based on trust and creditability with its employees, media, regulators, analysts, investors and associates. This is done by identifying the needs of business, their current and future marketing battle fields and being sensitive to needs of the society. Fundamental perceptions will play critical role whether to do business or not.

(vii) Corporations Engaged in Genuine Community Activities Exude a Positive Image

Further consumers have greater respect for companies that involve and care for environment and social responsibilities. Socially responsible corporate behaviour has a positive impact on business economic performance and adds to shareholder values. Now corporate social responsibility has increasingly become an integral part of corporate strategic planning and operational performance. How company understands social needs, its progress and thus investing in the infrastructure, health and education, family planning, drinking water, technical guidance to youth, etc., are viewed positively.

Tatas derive a large part of their corporate image from community programmes in Jamshedpur, that started with basic quality of life for its employees. Hindustan Lever Ltd. has worked with village communities near Etah (UP) to improve standard of living. Thus, *social vision* of leadership is critical to help the community.

(viii) Ethics in Global Economy

People have taken two extreme positions concerning how managers should behave when conducting business in a country other than their own. Some argue that local customs and practices should always be followed even if they would be considered unethical or even illegal in one's home country. Others argue that the ethical and legal standards of the most developed country should always be applied. However, authors of the "Guru Guide to the Knowledge Economy" say, neither extreme position is entirely correct.

According to Trompenaars, International and transnational structures allow us to *synthesis the advantages of all cultures while avoiding their excesses.* Families are quite capable of nurturing independence and encouraging achievement. Managing across cultures gives you more possible pathways to your goal.

To conclude, in the words of A. Baxi (*Economics Times,* 17.3.2002), "corporate image management will continue to play an increasingly important role in today's increasingly information-driven and competitive markets. It could well be the ultimate tool for winning and maintaining customer relationships."

CHAPTER

66

BUSINESS ETHICS IN KNOWLEDGE ECONOMY

FOCUS ON TRIPPLE BOTTOM LINE

Successful knowledge economy takes more than technology. It takes cultural change and changes in the reward structures that drive behaviour in most companies. The business today must pay attention to a triple bottom line:

(i) Economic prosperity,

(ii) Environmental prosperity, and

(iii) Social justice.

In this connection, seven revolutions are driving business to focus on the triple bottom line:

1. *Changing markets* have given companies greater freedom of action but has also brought greater scrutiny from financial markets and customers.

2. *Changing values.* Soft values such as concern for future generations are becoming as important as "hard" values such as financial performance.

3. *Increased transparency*. Stakeholders have access to much more information about the behaviour of companies. Companies now live in gold fish bowl.

4. A demand that *companies manage the product/service life cycle*. Companies are being held accountable for the life cycle performance of their products and services.

5. Companies to *be partner* for triple-bottom-line performance. Companies are being forced with each other and with non-governmental organisations such as the environmental groups to find ways to improve the life-cycle performance of their products and services.

6. *Time and Long View*. Companies are being forced to manage for the long-term.

7. *Revolution in the Board Room*. Social and environmental activities are increasingly demanding to be heard by the board of directors of companies.

Source: Joseph H. Boyett and Jimmie T. Boyett, "The Guru Guide to the Knowledge Economy", 2001.

CHAPTER

67

Knowledge Workers and Knowledge Management

MEANING

"Knowledge is the only *meaningful* resource today" asserts management guru Peter Drucker. What the assembly line was to 20th century manufacturing, knowledge is proving to be just that the 21st century business. Knowledge people (professionals) are representatives of new global economy.

I. Some Feature of Knowledge People

(a) Knowledge is Superior Resource

Human being is self-conscious. He is aware of himself, and aware of others. He has a mind and a heart. He wants to know. He has power to think. He can have creative and innovative mind. He can be self-motivated to manage himself also. All these make knowledge people *more superior than any other resource* (such as technology, capital, information, etc. which are available to all companies). Knowledge people generate ideas which are now valued. Knowledge is actually a combination of know-what, know-why and know-how which is possessed by human beings who have great potential.

(b) Knowledge can Provide Competitive Edge

A company can attain edge over its rivals in a global market due to knowledge workers. These knowledge employees provide three abilities:

(i) Innovation in the market,

(ii) Originality of service, and

(iii) Deep understanding of customer needs which market surveys yield.

Increasingly, the real value addition is knowledge. Knowledge is core competence for coping with change. The importance of knowledge workers is also due to their scarcity.

(c) Knowledge People are Necessary for every Operation in a Company

Due to their creativity and innovation, such as for product design, excellence in product to service, team work, total quality, global competition as environment is fast changing. Inspiring, and motivation of potential energy of knowledge workers is critical. So individual knowledge is the starting point of organisational knowledge. Only knowledge people can spread/share knowledge across the company. So management must create favourable climate in the organisation. Organisation needs knowledge to leverage all organisational capabilities. Knowledge people can be the most important asset of the organisation. We are in the era of brain-power industries such as—computer, software, telecommunication, semi-conductor chips, internet, knowledge people are core-workers.

(d) Learning is an Ongoing Process of Acquiring Knowledge by Individuals

Innovative patterns of learning individually or collectively lead to success in global market. The new people management philosophy, i.e. learning organisation can be created by:

- Keep the company in a state of *constant change,* from vertical (hierarchical) to one that will operate horizontally and collaboratively across organisational borders.
- Practicing to unlearn old and obsolete knowledge and acquiring knowledge by sharing or creating network world-wide for interaction.
- *Innovative culture,* i.e. recognition of ideas, values or emotions for conceptualisation.
- *Creating conditions* under which individuals, teams and organisations learn. Peter Senge calls it systems learning ("The Fifth Discipline") or generative learning.
- To anticipate and learn from change through experimentation and feedback. This means to *practice proactive approach* to problems by the management.
- To *institutionalise knowledge* and values so that these are transferred when individual leaves.
- Fostering *positive mental mindset* among employees for their ability to meeting all future solutions.

- *Learning from mistakes* and taking calculated risks in business for increasing opportunities.
- Employees must learn *system thinking* (Holistic approach) which means to understand the forces, inter-connections and inter-relationships that shapes the behaviour of systems. This calls for coordination, integration and synthesis of all components for having harmony in the working of the organisation.
- Learning organisation constitute the future environment. Learning organisation brings the people closer to the problem, who have knowledge and ideas. It is an age of knowledge capital. The owners of knowledge and wisdom, i.e. people are real assets of the company in 21st century.

2. Background

We are in knowledge era. Alvin and H. Toffler, the grand masters of future thinking, had predicted long ago in terms of transformational change, a few true turning points in history, each associated with the emergence of different systems of wealth creation.

First Wave: The invention of agriculture provided the human race with a new way to convert the earth's resources into wealth, and almost everywhere launched a 'First Wave' of change in civilization that gave rise to *peasant-centered* economies as means of human subsistence.

Second Wave: Similarly, the *Industrial Revolution* triggered a 'Second Wave' of change that gave us a factory-based system for wealth creation. In turn, this led to mass production, the drive for larger and larger markets, and the need for bigger, ever more bureaucratic business organizations. Until very recently, most of what was taught in management texts and in schools of business reflected 'Second Wave' thinking.

Third Wave: Today's *knowledge revolution*, having launched a gigantic 'Third Wave' of economic, technical and social change, is forcing businesses to operate in radically new, continually shifting ways that stand 'Second Wave' notions on their head. The industrial faith in such things as vertical integration, synergy, economies of scale and hierarchical, command-and-control organization is giving way to a fresh appreciation of outsourcing, minimization of scale, profit centers, networks and other diverse forms of organization. Every shred of industrial-era thinking is now being rescrutinized and brilliantly reformulated.

In knowlege era, the primary factor of production is knowledge, for wealth creation. Knowledge is a dynamic and ongoing process that involves our human capabilities to see existing patterns and at the same time envision new patterns. We expect to tap the fuller potential of both our people and computer-based systems. So now there is much need for synergy of technological and human capabilities. An increasing amount of work is being done by consulting firms on questions of knowledge management—the assessment of knowledge assets. New approaches to organisational and in individual learning, attempt to create a metric for dealing with knowledge.

3. What is Knowledge Management?

Knowledge Management (KM) is the process through which organizations *generate-value* from their intellectual and knowledge-based assets. Most often, generating value from such assets *involves sharing* them among employees, departments and even with other companies in an effort to devise best practices. It's important to note that the definition says nothing about technology; while KM is often facilitated by IT, technology by itself is not KM. The key to KM is *achieving better business results*, which could come from improved organisational learning. So, KM is *about learning*, learning is the process by which we get knowledge. It helps us to apply knowledge. From the business point, learning is important.

4. What Constitutes Intellectual or Knowledge-Based Assets

Not all information is valuable. Therefore, it's up to individual companies to determine what information qualifies as intellectual and knowledge-based assets. In general, however, intellectual and knowledge-based assets fall into one of two categories: *explicit or tacit*. Included among the former, i.e. *explicit* are assets such as patents, trademarks, business plans, marketing research and customer lists. As a general rule of thumb, *explicit knowledge* consists of anything that can be documented, archived and codified, often with the help of IT. Much harder to grasp is the concept of *tacit knowledge*, or the know-how contained in people's heads. The challenge inherent with *tacit knowledge* is figuring out how to recognize, generate, share and manage it. While IT in the form of e-mail, groupware, instant messaging and related technologies can help facilitate the dissemination of tacit knowledge; *identifying tacit knowledge* in the first place is a major hurdle for most organizations.

5. K.M. has now made any Information Accessible at a Click

When L&T's engineering and construction (E&C) business division executed turnkey projects in various corners of the country, problems at the site would mean a flurry of phone calls to locate experts within the company who might be able to solve it. In the process, time, a crucial element in completing projects, would be at a premium. Obviously, communication costs mounted. Not surprising, therefore, that the E&C business division was the first in L&T to embrace knowledge management with its portal KnowNet in late 2000.

Currently, KnowNet helps L&T to not just solve niggling problems at project sites, but also to identify alternative cost-effective solutions on the use of raw materials. Example: While executing a project for a public sector refinery in South India, L&T's engineers felt that the specified material of construction was of a higher grade than required. The result would be higher cost and a longer lead time because the material was more difficult to source. By delving into the learnings of KnowNet, L&T engineers discovered that in three similar projects in the past, a more cost-effective grade of material had been used without any problem. This was double-checked with other contractors who had executed similar projects. As a result of its KnowNet learnings, L&T was able to save nearly Rs. 1 crore on the project. Says K. Venkataramanan, president (operations) of L&T: "KM goes beyond storing information. We are trying to leverage tacit knowledge, which lies in the skill of our people, to deliver results."

Just as L&T uses KM to roll out real-world construction projects at lower cost, infotech major Infosys Technologies, which executes software projects both onshore and offshore, is another pioneer in the use of KM in India. Reason: projects heads and staff tend to be mobile in software. Unless the *learnings from* one project are captured and templated permanently, the speed and quality of execution may suffer. This is simply unaffordable in an era where software vendors are being squeezed on margins by cost-conscious customers.

6. Driving Forces for KM

There are actually two drivers behind the new-found enthusiasm. One is competition, and the other is IT. At a fundamental level, companies know that in a *super competitive marketplace* the right knowledge at the right time makes all the difference to performance. With products and services getting commoditised, it is speed and customer and market knowledge, among other things, that gives the edge. It is not enough to have this information in your database somewhere; you need this at the point—and at the instant—when your customer makes a call to the call centre to make a complaint. Companies that can bring deep customer knowledge out of the can and into the heart of day to-day decision-making cannot do so without adopting KM.

The second *driver for KM is IT push*. Today there is not a single major international software vendor without a KM-related offering: IBM, Microsoft, Oracle, Siebel, SAP, the works. Not to speak of a whole range of smaller software companies focusing on niche KM areas. From "brainstorming" and collaborative tools to content and document management, from data mining to expert and decision-support systems, from indexing and search engine tools to intelligent agents, every segment in the knowledge management chain has vendor selling solutions or prices of it.

To be sure, KM is not about IT. It is about *creating, recognising, accumulating, sharing and using knowledge to add value to organisations*. When it comes to adding value to corporates, it is organisational knowledge—and not individual knowledge—that matters. This has led to a more formal approach towards managing knowledge, by not just pre-serving information but analysing it and presenting it in a access-friendly format on company intranets.

7. Companies are Encouraging their Employees to Share Knowledge

Many recent entrants are devising ways and means of encouraging their employees to share knowledge. Because employees will only visit the knowledge portal if the information they are looking for is available. In the case of ad agency Lowe, it offers K-Points to employees who contribute to the portal. To encourage usage of the portal, employees who access the information also get points.

8. How to Build Human Networking into Enterprise?

Some steps are as under for sharing KM:

- Working together in *virtual task-focusing teams,* i.e. human networking enterprises.
- Developing *visionary capabilities about the challenges* in our enterprises, through networking or knowledge. Developing data integration strategy and also grow the knowledge base.
- *Encountering blockades* in transition process by listening and learning from one another.
- Extend virtual task-focusing teams which can *include* suppliers, partners, distributors and customers.
- To practise of *continual learning* and work more in parallel.
- We can share learning to enhance our capabilities in an ongoing process approach advanced by Petersenge. He has suggested five human values of learning organisations:
  (i) Personal mastery (competencies and skills);
  (ii) Spiritual growth—mental models of values and principles;
  (iii) Shared vision;
  (iv) Team learning and unlearning; and
  (v) Systems thinking.

Thus, we can use the new source of "wealth-creation."

9. Process of Implementing Knowledge Management

Knowledge management is as much *an activity* ("something you do") as it is a *type of system* or technology. That's why it's worthwhile to explore what's involved in implementing KM, or to put it more formally, in *capturing* existing knowledge within an organization, and then *adapting* that knowledge while capturing new knowledge going forward. Once such knowledge is captured, KM professionals can apply *the processes* of analysis, organization, assigning relationships and priority rankings between questions and answers.

(a) Document knowledge

Analyze all possible sources of organizational knowledge to build a taxonomy-of-knowledge-types, and to decide what attributes and values should be associated with each type (let's call an instance of some knowledge type—a specific item of knowledge—a knowledge element). Next, examine all possible sources to uncover existing knowledge elements, and make it possible to discover new knowledge elements.

(b) Share Knowledge

Start by recording all known knowledge elements from documents, communications, and subject matter expert interviews. At each step along the way, include input forms to elicit feedback from KM system users about knowledge elements, element organization, element search and retrieval, and element relevancy.

(c) Apply Knowledge

This is where *customers and support staff interact with* the knowledge base to locate and use relevant knowledge. At this stage it is essential to refine the contents of knowledge elements and to adapt the structure of the knowledge base in response to such interaction. The ability to make and suggest useful relationships between problems and solutions is powerful enough to enlist a strong buy-in from support staff and knowledge management professionals when they see that a dynamic system can improve search results, agent productivity and customer satisfaction. In general, and within the context of customer service systems based on customer contact centers, KM encompasses the broad range of capabilities needed to logically capture, organize, share and use knowledge elements in order to recognize problems and suggest possible solutions to customer service queries.

10. Benefits of an effective KM Programme should help a company do one or more of the following:

- *Foster innovation* by encouraging the free flow of ideas.
- *Improve customer service* by streamlining response time.
- *Boost revenues* by getting products and services to market faster.
- Enhance *employee retention* rates by recognizing the value of employees' knowledge and rewarding them for it.
- *Streamline operations* and reduce costs by eliminating redundant or unnecessary processes.

These are the most examples of strategic benefits. A creative approach to KM can result in improved efficiency, higher productivity and increased revenues in practically any business function. KM to deliver business results.

11. Must have a Specific Business Goal

A KM programme should not be divorced from a business goal. While sharing best practices is a commendable idea, there must be an underlying business reason to do so. Without a solid business case, KM is a futile exercise.

12. KM is not Static

As with many physical assets, the value of knowledge can erode over time. Since knowledge can get stale fast, the content in a KM programme should be constantly updated, amended and deleted. What's more, the relevance of knowledge at any given time changes, as do the skills of employees. Therefore, there is no endpoint to a KM.

To Conclude: Think!

"What is greater than knowledge?" asked the mind.

"A heart that can see and care", whispered the soul.

References

1. Thirumoothy Paramasivan, "Knowledge Management Your Key to Develop Competitive Advantage", Jims 8M, Oct.-Dec. 2003.
2. Prasad Sangrameshwaran, "Knowledge Management Initiatives", *Indian Management*, May 2003.
3. Bhatia, S.K., "Knowledge Organisation", *Management of Change and Organisation Development*, Deep & Deep Publications Pvt. Ltd., New Delhi.

CHAPTER 68

Origin of Corruption is Human Mindset

To understand origin of corruption, let us examine its various aspects, i.e. definition, causes, consequences and basis. Even though many definitions are given for corruption and corrupt, there exists an unanimous view that corruption is both harmful and wrong. It is not only at petty level but is at grand scale in bureaucratic, political and industrial circles. We quote here views of G. Suresh, CWC.

1. Corruption—Definitions

One of the definitions given to corruption is "giving something to someone with power so that he will abuse his power and act favouring the giver."

Another definition given is "the offering, giving, soliciting or acceptance of an inducement or reward, which may influence the action of any person."

2. Corruption—The Causes

Among the several causes of corruption, the important ones are greediness, circumstances, opportunities, misconception, petty excuses, special temptations, etc. A little more elaboration with illustrations is given below (Prevention Fraud and Corruption—Denis Osbome, U.K., 1999):

Greediness. People want an unfair advantage over others. For example, to pay less tax, to get appointment or promotion, to win a contract, to get something done quickly or to avoid fine, etc.

Circumstances. Particular circumstances provoke further demands.

Opportunities. People get opportunities for taking bribes.

Misconception. People pay bribes because they think they have to, they think that officials will not do their job or take decisions which they ought to take unless they are paid a bribe.

Petty Excuses. Many people make excuses for their being corrupt—they say, 'it is common and everybody does it' or 'it is only something small and nobody is harmed'.

There are certain special temptations, which are peculiar and are different for different groups of people like:

- Politicians seek contributions to party funds, or money to use for patronage.
- Politicians and officials who fear loss of office seek corrupt benefits as insurance.
- Officials need extra money to maintain their standards of living if salaries have not been raised to match inflation, to meet commitments for housing, car, school fees, etc.
- Employees feel resentment over bad management or pay levels they think unfair.
- Employees who refuse to participate in a corruption 'racket' may be suspected and under threat from their colleagues or superiors.

Some seek status, not only for having more riches than their colleagues but because corrupt officials may be admired by friends and family for their skills on outwitting authority.

Other groups of people have special motives or opportunities for corrupt gains.

3. Corruption—Its Consequences

It is obvious that the loss to society is often far greater than the value of the bribe involved.

(i) Preventive Vigilance

G. Suresh, CWC, states that one of the reasons why more emphasis is being given to preventive vigilance is that it is cost-effective. Prevention is much more cost-effective in reducing corruption than investigation and prosecution, etc. Not only that, by preventing corruption the worst seen consequences could be avoided. The consequences with some of their illustrations are as follows (Preventing Fraud and Corruption, Denis Osborne, U.K., 1999):

Corruption threatens people and their governments.

(ii) It makes Societies Unfair—It Hurts People

- It denies the poor their share—particularly when they have no money to pay bribes.
- It increases poverty—this happens when the resources allocated for poverty relief get diverted to the rich.

(iii) It makes Societies Uneconomic—It Slows Development

- It reduces revenue (tax, customs)—government lose more than corrupt officials gain.
- It increases cost of contracts—by more than the value of the bribes.
- It reduces quality of work (value-for-money)—supervision ineffective, can be dangerous.
- It distorts policies—decisions based more on expected individual gain than by society's needs.
- It subverts companies and NGOs if companies pay bribes employees are more likely to take bribes.
- It leads to shortages and delays because officials use these to seek bigger bribes.

(iv) It leads to poor administration if officials are appointed because of family or ethnic links, or corrupt payments—who will not be the most competent and they will not be motivated to work well-expecting promotion by the same means.

(v) It makes Societies Unsafe—It puts People's Lives at Risk. It makes Regulations Ineffective

- It increases criminality, when police or judges are bribed that creates havens for drug dealing, arms smuggling.
- It escalates! Those enriched by bribes want more and expect to "earn" it by same means.
- It breeds revolution through people's discontent and anger.

4. Corruption—Its Link with Investment

As per the World Bank Report, 1997-98, a country's ratio of Gross Investment/GDP is reduced by:

- Thirty-two per cent of corruption is perceived as high.
- Twenty-five per cent more, if uncertainty is also high, i.e. bribes may not produce the intended result, and have a low probability of doing this.

5. Categories of People

Having seen all these about corruption, four broad categories of people are involved in order to accommodate everyone. They are people:

- who are not at all corrupt under any circumstances (almost hypothetical),
- who are guilty of corruption,
- who benefit from corruption, and
- who are potentially corrupt.

So far we have seen various facets of corruption and with this insight let us try to stretch out and see where exactly lies the origin of corruption. Would it be proper to term 'corruption', a 'phenomenon'?

6. People say that it is a Universal Phenomenon

The next question comes to the mind is whether it was a result of the natural phenomena or a man-made one. Why not, then, look at the meaning of corruption *vis-a-vis* corrupt.

Due to poor mindset, thoughts and values. Corrupt are those who are morally depraved, suspect, unreliable,. influenced by illegal means, etc. These are the qualities, which are the results of the *poor mindset, putrid quality of thinking* and *lack of ideology* and so on. In any case, there is nothing physical about them. They are all the products of the metamorphic or catalytic reactions taking place in the mind.

A microscopic viewing of these meanings of 'corrupt' in their real sense would suggest that the phenomenon of corruption is psychological and, all psychological processes are supported to be natural, may be under the influence of various parameters.

It, therefore, goes without saying that corruption is a natural phenomenon, which has its own and the only origin, i.e., *the human mind*, which is the seat of all vanities.

It is a crisis of *intellectual, moral* and *spiritual* dimensions. Whether, wherever and in whichever forms the corruption existed and existing, it is so just because of the *unbalanced metabolism of the human mind.*

India High up on Graft Graph

A globally recognised annual survey, 2002 (Berlin-based NGO Transparency International) of corruption has put India at No. 71 in the list of 102 countries, where No. 1 is least corrupt and No. 102 the most corrupt nation.

Dirt Report

The Cleanest Three	*Rank*
Finland	1
Denmark	2
New Zealand	3
Bottom of the Pile	
Nigeria	101
Bangladesh	102
Where we stand	
India	**71**
Pakistan	77

7. Serious Cure Called for

In a nutshell, it is a disease rather an infection developed in the human mind and diffuses all over dangerously and therefore, what it requires is a serene *psychiatric cure* at the first place and then comes the Law, Rules and Regulations for removing it.

Thus, we have concluded that the origin of corruption is the human mind, let us not just be optimistic alone and wait for the moment of it reaching its own end, as this will not take place of its own. We, being responsible for bringing it to this spot from its origin, take the responsibility for pushing it to its coffin too. Sooner or later it has to happen, being a Universal concept. It depends entirely on us. Why not make it sooner and save over-sleeves?

Values and ethics are important for all human beings. They are especially important for businessmen, industrialists, bureaucrats, politicians as they are custodians of immense economic power vested by the society, major role of managements is to harmonise the interests of organisation.This is made possible only with the development of values among individuals in the organisation.

8. Attack Three Unexamined Axioms that are Barriers to Implementation of Curtailing Corruption

Ronald Berenbiem, who is Director of Working Group on Global Business Ethics Principles in his paper on Anti-Corruption (*Executive Excellence*, July 2001) has stressed that most resistance to anti-corruption efforts is based on three flawed axioms: tolerance, compliance, and whistle blowing. We reproduce his views:

"Proponents of Ethics often encounter resistance in promoting anti-corruption initiatives. But in recent years, business ethics has gained wide acceptance. Still, we need to sustain our efforts to persuade business leaders that corruption is costly to their companies. In particular, we need to attack three unexamined axioms that can be barriers to implementing changes needed to cut-off corruption's supply side.

(i) Tolerance: When Operating in Different Cultures' Business Practitioners Need to be Tolerant of Local Customers and Practices

Today, most companies, regardless of their products or services, compete in global markets. Respect for different ways of doing things is a critical element in business success. Still, the need for tolerance does not justify crime. All countries, regardless of customs or culture, prohibit bribery. The tolerance for culture argument is most often invoked in customary practice that some cultures have of giving lavish gifts. Admittedly, there can be some tough calls, but you ought to know bribery when you see it.

(ii) Compliance: Since Many Companies Regularly use Middlemen to get around Federal Corrupt Practices Acts, Governmental Anti-corruption Mandates and the Compliance Systems that Follow in their Wake are Wasted Efforts

But few of these concerned companies have an active anti-corruption effort that includes a detailed anti-corruption statement, discussion and training programmes, requirements that local managers certify code compliance, and reports of irregular incidents. One critical step is including a statement in the code that adherence to the company's anti-corruption policies may result in lost revenues. Without a strong compliance component, a company does not have an anti-corruption programme worthy of the name.

(iii) Whistle Blowing

Whistle blowing systems can help to achieve open communications when ordinary channels fail. But rarely are these systems fully utilized. Some companies and countries have a strong cultural disposition against reporting other people—however inappropriate their behaviour may be.

Whistle blowing or hotline systems play a key role in any anti-corruption effort. Still, many workers are unwilling to report questionable practices or to seek advice in making difficult decisions.

The success of our anti-corruption efforts will determine our progress in cutting-off corruption's supply side."

Sources: (i) Article by G. Suresh, Central Vigilance Commission, *Indian Management*, March 2000, New Delhi.

(ii) *Executive Excellence*, July 2001.

(iii) *Hindustan Times*, 28.8.2003.

CHAPTER

69

Guarding against Sexual Harassment in the Work Place (SH)

MEANING

Legally, sexual harassment is defined as unwelcome advances, requests for sexual favours and other verbal or physical conduct of a sexual nature.

Most studies confirm that the concept of power is central to sexual harassment. It comes from a superior, a colleague or a subordinate.

In August 1997 judgement of the Supreme Court of India on sexual harassment of working women in the case of *Vishaka* vs. *The State of Rajasthan* has identified sexual harassment as a separate category of legally prohibitive behaviour. The court has laid down guidelines in accordance with international standards to deal with the issue at work place.

In another case the Supreme Court of India has ruled that sexual harassment at the work place is a violation of fundamental rights.

DEFINITION OF SEXUAL HARASSMENT

According to the orders of the Supreme Court of India sexual harassment is any unwelcome:

(i) Physical contact and advances,

(ii) Demand or request for sexual favours,

(iii) Sexually coloured remarks,

(iv) Display coloured remarks,

(v) Showing pornography, and

(vi) Any other unwelcome physical, verbal or non-verbal conduct of a sexual nature.

Supreme Court has further laid down that:

Actual assault or touch is not required. In such cases, the courts are required to examine the broad possibilities of the case and not get swayed by insignificant discrepancies or narrow technicalities or the dictionary meaning of the expression 'molestation'.

RESPONSIBILITIES OF EMPLOYERS TO IMPLEMENT, MONITOR THE GUIDELINES TO TACKLE SEXUAL HARASSMENT

The Supreme Court guidelines lay down certain responsibilities on employers/management to implement, monitor the procedure in their organisations, public as well as private.

1. Procedure for Complaints by Women

The guidelines direct employer's to set-up procedure through which women can make their complaints heard.

A *complaints committee* headed by a woman, and/or of which half the members are women should be deputed to look into complaints of sexual harassment. To prevent undue pressure from within the organisation, the committee should include a third-party representative from an NGO.

All complaints should be handled in confidential manner within a time-bound framework. Annual report should be submitted to the concerned government department.

2. Preventive Steps to be taken like by Employers

(a) An express prohibition of sexual harassment should be notified, published and circulated.

(b) Amendment of conduct and service rules to include sexual harassment as an offence and provision of appropriate discipline against the offender.

(c) Management also include in S.O. (Standing Orders), personnel manual of their organisation.

(d) Providing such working conditions to ensure there is no hostile environment.

3. Awareness of Guidelines

(i) Employees to be allowed to raise sexual harassment issues at workers' meetings.

(ii) Sexual harassment issue to be discussed in employer-employee meetings.

(iii) Rights of women workers to be notified.

(iv) Where such act is offence under IPC, employer to initiate action and complaint.

(v) Complainants or witnesses not to be victimised while dealing cases.

(vi) Employer to assist the employee if sexual harassment takes place by an outsider.

IMPLEMENTATION PROBLEMS

Several public and private sector organisations have constituted committees and cells to comply with the Supreme Court guidelines. Experience of implementing guidelines has highlighted some issues:

- It is important that the top management takes serious interest on this issue.
- It is noticed that in many cases recommendations of the committee are ignored and thus denial of justice.
- The usual defence that the harasser puts up is of "inefficiency of complainant or it is conspiracy against him."
- In many cases 'caste factor' is brought in.
- Witnesses do not come forward due to job/careers at stake.
- Too much legalities of evidence, proof from witnesses is asked by the committees.
- If harasser holds a very superior position then it becomes difficult for committee members to secure justice to victim.
- The seat of power becomes tool of misuse, and it could be cloaked as a lure for promotion or increment. Most of the times, divorced, separated or submissive women are the victims.

HOW TO MEET HARASSMENT DILEMMA

It will be relevant to mention views of Nan Demars (You Want To Do

What, Which, Where and How To Draw The Line, Simon and Schuster, USA).

"If we remain silent and tolerate harassment, it will continue. I urge you to confront you harassers, document every suspect incident and follow-up conversation. Let it be known that you are taking their inappropriate and unprofessional behaviour seriously. Then, as soon as, you can, try to stop the objectionable behaviour through the use of informal, one to one discussions and incrementally stiffer consequences. When all else fails, resort to formal avenues of protest inside and outside your company."

SEXUAL HARASSMENT AND THE LAWS IN INDIA

(i) There are several provisions in IPC (The Indian Penal Code) and include:

(a) S. 354—Assault or criminal force against a woman with the intent to outrage her modesty.

(b) S. 509—Words, gesture or act intended to insult the modesty of a woman.

(c) S. 209—Deals with obscene acts and songs.

(ii) Case can be filed under Rule 5, Schedule 5 of the Industrial Disputes Act, if an employee suffers unfair dismissal or denial of employment benefits as a consequence of her rejection for sexual harassment.

(iii) A civil suit can also be filed for damages under tort laws. The Indecent Representation of Women (Prohibition) Act, 1987 has also potential to be used for such cases.

(iv) In case of a senior IAS officer Rupan Bajaj and KPS Gill in July 1988. Gill was fined by Supreme Court of Rs. 2.5 lakhs in lieu of 3 months' rigorous imprisonment for offences under S. 294 and S. 509 of IPC.

(v) Sexual harassment has been included as misconduct in:

(a) CCS (Conduct) Rules, 1964, and

(b) Industrial Employment (Standing Orders) Act, 1946.

Who can Face Sexual Harassment?

- An individual at the work place.
- A staffer—from a sweeper to a CEO.
- A non-staffer in any capacity—student, housekeeper, volunteer, on honorarium, maid or consultant.
- Dressed in a sari or suit.
- Working in public or private sector units or non-government

organisations.

- Working in the unorganised sector—large or small.
- A person who believes it only happens to others.
- And it could be either gender, male or female.

The Employer's Responsibilities

- Recognise sexual harassment as a serious offence and include it in the rules and regulations.
- Prevent and punish sexual harassment at the work place.
- Conduct anti-sexual harassment awareness training for regular and contractual employees as well as for new inductees.
- Formulate an anti-sexual harassment policy, which should:
    - o clearly state the employer's commitment to a safe work environment,
    - o define Sexual Harassment with examples and explicitly term it an offence,
    - o constitute a Complaints Committee as per Supreme Court guidelines,
    - o be aware of the fact that the complainant may delay in lodging a complaint,
    - o ensure confidentiality of the complainant and witnesses,
    - o not punish or harass or transfer the complainant and witnesses for complaining, rather should give the complainant the option to seek transfer of the perpetrator or their own,
    - o make the enquiry procedure time bound,
    - o provide for maintenance of accurate records of the enquiry procedure, with a copy of it given to both parties,
    - o ensure that the Complaints Committee makes recommendations in their enquiry report, the duty of the employer being implementation of the recommendations, and
    - o ensure that a copy of the enquiry report along with the recommendations is given to both parties.
- Ensure that the equity be conducted as per the law of natural justice.
- Display/distribute the policy/information about the redressal mechanism.
- Prominently display the addresses/contact number of the

Complaints Committee members.

- Ensure that third parties or service users such as hotel guests, airline passengers, are aware of the Policy.
- Take prompt action on the complaint even if the complainant does not have eyewitnesses.

Effects of Sexual Harassment on the Individual

- Physical, emotional and psychological trauma.
- Loss of self-esteem.
- Isolation and ostracism.
- Absenteeism and lowered productivity.
- Loss of job, promotion or job-related activities such as training.
- Suicide and spillover effects into family life.

Now the Effect these will have on the Organisation

- Decreased productivity.
- Lowered profitability.
- Valued employees quitting or losing jobs.
- Poor public image.
- Costly court litigation.
- Expensive compensation payouts.
- Unhealthy work atmosphere.
- Strain and mistrust in interpersonal relations.

Employee's Responsibilities

- Don't blame yourself.
- Don't ignore sexual harassment—it will not go way by itself.
- Recognise the nature of harassment.
- Talk to the perpetrator.
- Talk to others at the work place or in your family about the harassment and talk with the union, if any.
- Maintain a detailed chronological account of sexual harassment.
- Try and have a witness to the incident.

- Write a letter and/or send your organisation's anti-sexual harassment policy to the harasser by registered post.
- Always retain a copy of the documents/letters sent in connection with your complaint.
- Ensure that the employer formulates an anti-sexual harassment policy and has a redressal mechanism.
- Ask for regular awareness programmes and training to be conducted.
- Approach a women's organisation or call the local helpline or both.
- Lodge a formal complaint without delay.
- Seek counselling.

How an act amounts as sexual harassment or not depends between consenting co-worker? In sexual harassment or in ethics, it is the thought that counts. Gifts are given every where.

CHAPTER

70

QUALITY OF WORK LIFE (QWL)

QWL seeks to create a work commitment in organisations and society at large so as to ensure higher productivity and greater job satisfaction of the employees. It is a process by which an organisation attempts to unleash the creative potential of its personnel by involving them in decisions affecting their work lives. "QWL is a process of work organisations which enables its members at all levels to participate actively and efficiently in shaping the organisation's environment, methods and outcomes. It is a value-based process, which is aimed towards meeting the twin goals of enhanced effectiveness of the organisation and improved quality of life at work for the employees."

Quality of Working Life is the degree to which members of a work organisation are able to satisfy their personal needs through their experience in the organisation. Its focus is on the problem of creating a human work environment where employees work cooperatively and contribute to organisation objectives. The major indicators of QWL are job involvement, job satisfaction and productivity.

AREAS OF QUALITY OF WORKING LIFE

(a) Compensation

The reward for work should be above a minimum standard for life and should also be equitable.

(b) Health and Safety

The working environment should reduce the adverse effects of pollution that can adversely affect the physical, mental and emotional state of employees.

(c) Job Security

Employees should not have to work under a constant concern for their future stability of work and income.

(d) Job Design

The design of jobs should be capable of meeting the needs of the organisation for production and the individual for satisfying and interesting work.

(e) Social Integration

The elimination of anything that could lead to individuals not identifying with the groups to which they belong. This includes the elimination of discrimination and individualism, whilst encouraging teams and social groups to form.

(f) Protection of Individual Rights

The introduction of specific procedures aimed at guaranteeing the rights of employees at work.

(g) Social Relevance of Work

Initiatives to increase the understanding among employees of the objectives of the organisation and the importance of their part in them.

(h) Respect for Non-work Activities

Respect for the activities that people engage in outside the work place. The impact of work activities on private life should also be recognised.

METHODS TO IMPROVE QWL

In order to improve the quality of working life, the following steps may be followed:

(a) Job Enrichment and Job Enlargement

These attempts to provide a person with exciting, interesting, stimulating and challenging work. In other words, it improves the quality of the jobs. These motivate the employees with higher level needs and overcome problems of monotony in the jobs.

(b) Autonomous Workgroup

Under this, each group of workers is given freedom of decision-making on production methods, distribution of tasks, selection of team members and leaders, work schedules and so on.

(c) Flexibility in Work Schedules

Employees demand more freedom at the work place, especially in scheduling their work. Among the alternative work schedules capable of enhancing the quality of working life for some employees are:

- *Flexitime.* A system of flexible working hours.
- *Staggered hours.* Different groups of employees begin and end work at different intervals.
- *Compressed work-week.* It involves more hours of work per day for fewer days per week, e.g., five days a week.

(d) Job Redesign

Job redesign based on participative system helps in better job satisfaction.

(e) Opportunity for Growth

Opportunity for growth is important for achievement-oriented employees. If the employees are provided opportunities for their advancement and growth and to develop their personality, they will feel highly motivated. Their commitment to the organisation will also increase.

(f) Employees' Participation

People in organisations have a need for participation in matters affecting their lives. So they want participation in the decision-making process. Employees' participation in the form of suggestion system, management by objectives (MBO), workers' participation in management, etc. provides psychological satisfaction to the employees.

INDIA ON THE SUPER POWER HIGHWAY TO IMPROVE QUALITY OF LIFE

It is heartening to learn that India's economy is in the same league as that of the US, China and Japan. For the second time, it has been ranked the world's fourth-biggest economy by the World Bank's purchasing power parity (PPP) index. The PPP of a currency is the number of units required to purchase the same basket of goods and services as a dollar would buy in the US. The PPP thus allows a comparison of real price levels between countries and the actual cost of goods in any country when calculated in accordance with US prices. India's Gross National Income (the GDP plus net receipts of primary income from foreign sources) of $ 477.4 billion thus translates into $ 2,913 billion — higher than the GNI of Germany, Canada and Russia. While India's GNI has grown from $ 2,530 billion to $ 2,913 billion during 2001-02, China's has shrunk from $ 5,415 billion to $ 5,027 billion in the same period.

Being the fourth largest economy indicates that India, like China, is a huge market and an attractive destination for foreign investment. How did India achieve this status? Because of a steady GDP growth, moderate inflation and higher net receipts from foreign sources each year, India has increased the access of goods and services available to its population over time. Yet, this ranking shouldn't give rise to complacency as there are still many gaps to fill in the delivery of public goods to citizens.

Guaranteeing basic education and health to all and better access to safe drinking water and clean air pose a monumental task before the government. With 260 million people surviving on less than a dollar a day, there are also huge economic disparities between the rich and the poor. There is need for more jobs and higher public expenditure in urban low cost housing and civic amenities like sanitation. Once the *quality of life* improves, India can indeed be an economic superpower.

(*Hindustan Times*, New Delhi, 15-4-2003.)

CHAPTER

71

STRATEGIES FOR WORK-LIFE BALANCE

Training and job challenges are viewed by employees as the biggest motivations for joining organisations. These factors are also considered by employer's for attracting and retaining employees. However, due to ever changing work environment, employees have to face new challenges—problems, wide-ranging responsibilities, greater productivity and competitiveness at work place. These tend to stress and pressure, bringing imbalance in lives of employees.

We shall discuss this topic under following headings:

1. Concept of work-life balance.
2. Its importance.
3. Major factors of change that push emphasis on work life balance.
4. Corporate strategies to cope work-life balance.
5. Outcomes.

I. CONCEPT OF WORK LIFE BALANCE

Inspite of landmark improvements in information technology, internet, telecom, travel, scientific research, stress and monotony at work place continues. Management experts call it as a syndrome of improper work-life balance.

According to Raja Achanta, life is known to be set of pursuits. The list includes: *family, health, wealth, career, social obligations, intellectual* and *spirituality*. A perfectly balanced life for an employee needs a careful adjustment of these quests.

The first two pursuits, i.e. family and health need special attention as these aspects, like glass panes cannot be mended on development of any crack. But the remaining aspects are flexible and provide scope for fixing them. This continuous juggling pulls the employees into a grind and leaves them stressed and stretched. Thus, managing work-life balance is one of the major challenges of new generation of 21st century, as the work place schedules take its toll on employee's health, relationships and well-being.

2. ITS IMPORTANCE

Importance of work-life balance is being realised both by corporates and employees. With changing times, more and more *employers* are facing the need to adopt the rule, i.e. it is the *productivity* that matters most, *rather than hours spent* by the employees in the office. Employers are making efforts *to be flexible* and trying to face the operational challenges.

Similarly employees today want to have freedom and live lives their way. They value balance between work and life than ever before.

3. MAJOR FACTORS OF CHANGE THAT PUSH EMPHASIS ON WORK-LIFE BALANCE

These reasons are as under:

(i) Employees in 21st century place *personal life on a higher pedestal* than work-life. The work place schedules take it toll on employee's health, family relationship and well-being. There are rising divorce rates, spouse relationship problems relating to children and household affairs. Employees expect more life outside work.

(ii) Corporates today function on the principle of empowering employees—which means based on flexibility and freedom for employees to take decisions. So employees want from their employer flexi timings, focus on results and overall avoidance of long work hour culture.

(iii) In global organisations the working is becoming *round-the-clock customer service*. This has lead to work-life balance of employees more essential. At the same time technology has added to *the speed* of operation to fight competition and also to meet tougher *deadlines.* Today's world does not go to sleep due to across the globe operations.

(iv) Another factor is rise *in dual* earning couples. Particularly working mothers are major populations (80%) who adversely get affected in balancing jobs performance and family life.

4. CORPORATES STRATEGIES TO COPE WORK-LIFE BALANCE

Corporates have recognised the importance of work-life balance. Some methods adopted by them are to overcome the ill-effects on the overall company performance and individual life.

(i) *Flexi-time* to enjoy flexible hours, this is formulated, by having a core time when the employee presence at work is mandatory, but after these hours, employees can manage their own time accordingly. The scheme works to build trust among employees while also meeting the business needs. This helps in creative work, reducing stress and improving productivity. It helps to balance both personal life and work-life.

(ii) Other flexible arrangements, such as:

- Providing freedom of part-time working, home teleworking, unpaid breaks, job-sharing, parental leave, compressed working week.
- Providing with facilities and services.
- Membership of sport and social clubs and health clubs.
- Leave for career development.
- Employees to develop their own attendance schedules—self-rostering.
- Working long and short days and by accumulating hours of non-working time to use it in future when necessary.
- "Well-being" centers in offices for employees to go and relax.
- Creating employee health management group to prevent and manage work place stress.

(iii) *New Initiatives by Companies*: These cover yoga, group meditation and exercise, gyms are all taken to energise employees through their natural energy systems and bring fun in their work. Companies are sponsoring sessions like "art of living" for its employees.

Employees are now more conscious that life has four corner stones—family, work, leisure and friends. When planning changes to the structure of one, one has to careful not to make any changes to another area. They learn to relax mind, keep themselves physically, mentally and spiritually fit as possible. They are aware not to hide their feelings as frustration is a major cause of stress. They limit their exposure to stress by cutting back certain commitments and work load.

5. OUTCOMES

All these steps create an atmosphere of trust and communication between management and employees.

Thus, balance between work and life is now more critical factor for job satisfaction and motivation. Organisations are interested in rejuvenated and more productive employees. It is involving the hearts and minds of the employees thus enable them find overall fulfilment and full potential. Thus, employees to feel better and perform better.

References

Raja Achanta, "The Work-life Balance", *HRM Review*, March 2004. Gratefully Acknowledged.

S.K. Bhatia, Boost Your Professional Career, Deep & Deep Publications Pvt. Ltd., New Delhi.

CHAPTER

72

A TRIBUTE

J.R.D. TATA— AN EPITOME OF ACHIEVEMENT OF BUSINESS ETHICS IN INDIAN INDUSTRY

J.R.D. TATA

India has several outstanding entrepreneurs but there had been one towering personality whose outstanding achievement was his regard for ethical standards—a staunch supporter of business ethics and social audit in business.

Within organisation, values are imparted by the founder-entrepreneur or a dominant chief executive and they remain in some form, a long time after that person is not there. J.R.D. Tata, the previous Chairman of the Tata group, when asked to define the House of Tatas and what links the different Tata companies together said: "I would call it a group of individually managed companies united by two factors. First, a feeling that they are part of a larger group which carrers the name and prestige of Tatas, and *public recognition of honesty and reliability—trustworthiness*. The other reason is more metaphysical. There is an innate loyalty, a sharing of certain beliefs. We all feel a certain pride that we are somewhat different from others" (Lala, 1981).

In the year, 2001, Tata Group present Chairman Ratan Tata bagged the Government of India award for Corporate Governance. Here is a brief profile of this towering personality J.R.D. Tata: J.R.D. Tata became the Chairman of Tata Sons on the eve of World War II. There was a lesser known shade to his personality that few knew about his deep passion for flying. He piloted a flight from Karachi to Bombay at the age of 24 and repeated the feat in his 'eighties. As a business strategist, he diversified Tata's interests in chemicals in 1938-39 into Tata Engineering and Locomotives in collaboration with Mercedez-Benz and went on to become the leading manufacturer of Tata Trucks. He went on to purchase tea plantations from James Finally and set-up Tata Airways, which later came to be known as Air India. In J.R.D. Tata's time, Air India was ranked as a leading international carrier and remained so till 1977-78. The Taj chain of hotels was also enlarged during JRD's time both in India and abroad. However, what is still regarded as one of his most outstanding achievement was his regard for *ethical standards*—a staunch supporter of business ethics, social audit and population control. Till his end, he rendered the high leadership and entrepreneurial dynamism wedded to high quality standards, research and development as he went on to set-up Tata Administrative Services in pursuit of global excellence. He formulated the Bombay Plan in 1944-45 to double India's GDP with seven other industrialists and won many international awards. In my opinion, he was uncompromising in the ideals he held and lived quite modestly.

Role of a Citizen

JRD Tata took the *role of a citizen* very seriously and never failed to be of service to the nation. His nation-building activity began soon after he was appointed a trustee of the Sir Dorabji Tata Trust in 1932. The concept of establishing Asia's first *cancer hospital* in Bombay was implemented under his guidance in 1941. Citizen Tata's greatest gift to the scientific establishment came in 1945 when he gave the founding grant to Homi Bhabha to set up the *Tata Institute of Fundamental Research*. This institute has proved to be, in Bhabha's words, "the cradle of our *atomic energy programme.*"

JRD Tata was among the first Indians to be drawn to the cause of *population in control* when he realised the drag unchecked population growth could have on the country's developmental efforts. In 1951, when he came across statistics revealing that India had crossed the 350-million population mark, JRD sounded out .Jawaharlal Nehru (the country's first prime minister) on the issue. Nehru ignored the issue. But JRD didn't wait for the government to act. He part-funded Avabai Wadia's efforts to start the Family Planning Association of India.

JRD firmly believed in *employee welfare* and espoused the principles of an eight-hour working day, free medical aid, workers' provident fund scheme, workmen's accident·compensation schemes, which were later adopted as statutory requirements in the country.

These measures were introduced at Tata Steel, Jamshedpur, and many more were added during JRD Tata's regime. In 1956, he initiated a programme of closer "employee association with management" to give workers a stronger voice in the affairs of the company. He also introduced a scheme of 'ex-gratia payment for road accident while coming to or returning from duty'.

In 1970, he started the *Family Planning Foundation* jointly with the Ford

Foundation, and was instrumental in conditioning the thinking of an entire generation, treating the issue as one of essential transformation of society. For his crusading endeavours in the field, JRD Tata was bestowed with the United Nations Population Award in 1992.

For these endeavours, JRD Tata was awarded the country's highest civilian honour, the Bharat Ratna, in 1992—one of the rare instances when the award was granted during a person's lifetime.

Other awards won by him include commander of the Legion of Honour by France, Knight Commander of the order of St. Gregory of the Great, Knight Commander's cross of the order of merit of the Federal Republic of Germany, Hon. Air Vice Marshal of the Indian Air Force and has been named international Management Man.

He passed away on November 29, 1993. On his death, the Indian Parliament was adjourned in his memory—an honour not usually given to private citizens. His home state of Maharashtra too declared three days of mourning. Though Mr. J.R.D. Tata is no more, the *values, traditions and business ethics* which he lived by will continue to be the driving force of the Group. Mr Tata made his mark on India during his lifetime, and his legend lives on after him.

Egon Zehnder (A Global Consultant's Company) has selected Mr. Ratan Tata on the corporate governance board. Reasons given by them are: We needed somebody who is truly an international personality and I think Mr. Tata fits into that mould. Secondly, we needed to raise the level of debate on corporate governance in India. And at least one company that is doing something about corporate governance here are the Tatas.

References

P.N. Agarwala, A noted author, htc carrers @ hindustan times.com

Azhar Kazmi, Chairman, Deptt. of Business Administration, Aligarh Muslim University.

ANNEXURE I

CORPORATE GOVERNANCE REPORT, 2002-03 (TELCO)

Company's Philosophy on Corporate Governance

As part of the Tata group, Tata Engineering's philosophy on Corporate Governance is founded upon a rich legacy of fair and transparent governance practices, many of which were in place before they were mandated. The Corporate Governance philosophy has been further strengthened with the adoption, a few years ago, by the Company of the Tata Business Excellence Model, the Tata Code of Conduct and the adoption of the requirements of Corporate Governance under Clause 49 of the Listing Agreement with the stock exchanges. In its endeavour to safeguard the interests of the investors, during the year, the Company adopted the Tata Code of Conduct for Prevention of Insider Trading as also the Code of Corporate Disclosure Practices in pursuance of the Securities and Exchange Board of India (Prohibition of Insider Trading) Regulations. The Company is in full compliance with the requirements under Clause 49 of the Listing Agreement with the Stock Exchanges.

Board of Directors

During the year under review, 8 Board Meetings were held on June 5, 2002, June 6, 2002, July 25, 2002, September 23, 2002, October 30, 2002, December 20, 2002, January 22, 2003 and March 27, 2003. The composition of the Board, attendance at Board Meetings (BM) held during the financial year under review and at the last Annual General Meeting (AGM), number of Directorships and memberships/chairmanships in public companies (including the Company) are given below:—

Name of the Director	*Category*	*FY 2002-03* *Attendance at*			*As on date* *Committee positions*	
		BM	*Last AGM*	*No. of Directorships* @	*Member* ♦	*Chairman*
Ratan N Tata	Non-Executive, Chairman, Promoter	7	Yes	13	6	—
N.A. Soonawala	Non-Executive, Promoter	8	Yes	13	7	3
J.J. Irani ◎	Non-Executive, Promoter	8	Yes	15	8	1
J.K. Setna	Non-Executive, Promoter	8	Yes	10	6	1
V.R. Mehta ❖	Non-Executive, Independent	7	Yes	11	7	3

R. Gopalakrishnan	Non-Executive, Promoter	8	Yes	14	9	1
N.N. Wadia	Non-Executive, Independent	5	Yes	11	3	1
Helmut Petri ⅄	Non-Executive, Independent	0	No	2	—	—
S.A. Naik	Non-Executive, Independent	8	Yes	2	2	1
Ravi Kant	Executive Director	8	Yes	5	1	—
Praveen P. Kadle	Executive Director	8	Yes	9	6	1
V. Sumantran	Executive Director	8	Yes	2	—	—
Peter K.M. Fietzek *Alternate Director to H. Petri*	Non-Executive, Independent	2	No	1	—	—

@ excludes Directorships in foreign companies.
♦ Member does not include Chairman.
◉ Tata Steel Representative.
⁘ Institutional Representative of UTI as an investor.
⅄ Daimler Chrysler AG Representative.

As may be seen from the above, the Non-Executive Directors constitute more than half of the total number of Directors. The Company has a Non-Executive Chairman and one-third of the total strength of the Board comprises of independent Directors. The day-to-day operations of the Company are being overseen by Mr. Ratan N. Tata as a member of the Committee of Directors, comprising himself and Mr. R. Gopalakrishnan. The required information as enumerated in Annexure I to Clause 49 of the Listing Agreement is made available to the Board of Directors.

Messrs. N.A. Soonawala, J.K. Setna and Helmut Petri are liable to retire by rotation and being eligible, offer themselves for re-appointment. Information as required under Clause 49 (VI) of the Listing Agreement is annexed to the Notice of the AGM.

Audit Committee

The Audit Committee of Directors comprises of Messrs. V.R. Mehta, Chairman, S.A. Naik and J.K. Setna. The scope of the Committee includes:

(a) Overseeing the Company's financial reporting process and the disclosure of its financial information, to ensure that the financial statement is correct, sufficient and credible;

(b) Recommending the appointment/removal of external auditors, fixing audit fees and approving payments for any other services;

(c) Approving fees for non-audit consulting/services provided by the firms of Statutory Auditors;

(d) Reviewing with management the periodic financial statements before submission to the board, focusing primarily on

- Any changes in accounting policies and practices;

- Major accounting entries based on exercise of judgement by management;
- Qualifications in draft audit report;
- Significant adjustments arising out of audit;
- The going concern assumption;
- Compliance with accounting standards;
- Compliance with stock exchange and legal requirements concerning financial statements;
- Any related party transactions, i.e. transactions of the Company of material nature, with promoters or the management, their subsidiaries or relatives, etc. that may have a potential conflict with the interests of the Company at large;

(e) Reviewing with the management, external and internal auditors, the adequacy of internal control systems and recommending improvements to the management;

(f) Reviewing the adequacy of internal audit function, including the structure of the internal audit department, staffing and seniority of the official heading the department, reporting structure, coverage and frequency of internal audit;

(g) Discussing with internal auditor any significant findings and follow-up thereon;

(h) Reviewing the findings of any internal investigations by the internal auditor into matters where there is a suspected fraud or irregularity or a failure of internal control systems of a material nature and reporting the matter to the Board;

(i) Discussing with external auditors before the audit commences, the nature and scope of audit as well as conduct post-audit discussions to ascertain any area of concern;

(j) Reviewing the Company's financial and risk management policies; and

(k) Initiating investigations into the reasons for substantial defaults in the payments to the depositors, debenture-holders, share-holders (in case of non-payment of declared dividends) and creditors.

During the period under review, 7 Audit Committee meetings were held on May 24, 2002, June 5, 2002, July 25, 2002, September 24, 2002, October 29, 2002, January 21, 2003 and March 19, 2003. All the Members of the Audit Committee were present at all the meetings. In these meetings, *inter alia,* the Committee considered 114 audit reports covering operational, financial and other business risk-related areas. The Audit Committee meetings are held at

Corporate Headquarters or at the Company's plants and usually attended by the Executive Director(s), the Finance head, the Chief Internal Auditor, the Statutory Auditors and the Cost Auditor. The Operation heads are invited to the meetings, as required. The Company Secretary acts as the Secretary of the Audit Committee. The Chairman of the Audit Committee was also present at the last AGM of the Company.

Managerial Remuneration

(a) Remuneration Committee

The Remuneration Committee of the Company is empowered to review the remuneration of whole-time directors, retirement benefits to be paid to them and dealing with matters pertaining to Employees' Stock Option Scheme. The Company has not issued any stock options to its directors/employees. The Remuneration Committee comprises of 3 Independent and 2 Non-Executive Directors, viz. Messrs. N.N. Wadia, Chairman, Ratan N. Tata, N.A. Soonawala, V.R. Mehta and S.A. Naik.

During the year under review, one Remuneration Committee meeting was held on June 5, 2002 wherein all the Members of the Remuneration Committee were present. Besides, the Committee also passed a resolution by circulation. The Chairman of the Remuneration Committee was present at the last AGM.

(b) Remuneration Policy

The remuneration of the whole-time director(s)/appointee(s) is decided by the Remuneration Committee based on criteria such as industry benchmarks, the Company's performance *vis-a-vis* the industry, performance/track record of the whole-time director(s)/appointee(s), Macro-Economic Review on remuneration packages of Heads of Organisations and is reported to the Board of Directors. The Company pays remuneration by way of salary, perquisites and allowances (fixed component), incentive remuneration and commission (variable components) to its whole-time directors. Annual increments are decided by the Remuneration Committee within the salary scale approved by the Members and are effective from 1 April annually. The Remuneration Committee decides on the Commission payable to the whole-time directors on determination of profits for the financial year, within the ceilings on net profits prescribed under Sections 198 and 309 of the Companies Act, 1956 (the Act) as also the incentive remuneration. The Members had, at the Extra-ordinary General Meeting held on March 27, 2002, approved of revised terms of appointment of Mr. Ravi Kant and the appointment of Mr. Praveen P. Kadle and Dr. V. Sumantran as Executive Directors. The remuneration of Rs. 18,29,365 pertaining to previous years was paid to Mr. Ravi Kant during the year on receipt of the Central Government's approval.

The remuneration by way of commission to the non-whole-time directors is decided by the Board of Directors and distributed to them based on their attendance and contribution at meetings. The Members had at the ACM held on July 25, 2000 approved the payment of remuneration by way of commission to the non-whole-time directors of the Company, of a sum not exceeding .1% per annum of the net profits of the Company, calculated in accordance with the provisions of the Act, subject to a ceiling of Rs. 15 lakhs per annum for a further period of five years commencing October 1, 2000. The commission for the financial year 2002-03 will be distributed amongst all or some of the said directors in accordance with the directives given by the Board. The attention of the Members is invited to the Notice wherein it is proposed to pay remuneration to the non-whole-time directors, as per the limits set under the Act.

A sitting fee of Rs. 5,000 per meeting of the Board, Audit Committee, Remuneration Committee, Investors' Grievance Committee, Committee of Board, Ethics and Compliance Committee and Finance Committee is paid for attendance at the meetings of the said Board/Committees to its Members (excluding Executive Directors). The sitting fees paid/payable to the non-whole-time directors is excluded whilst calculating the above limits in accordance with Section 198 of the Act.

(c) Remuneration to Directors

In respect of the financial year 2002-03, the following remuneration and sitting fees were paid to the Directors:

Non-Wholetime Directors:

(in Rupees)

Name	*Commission for FY 2002-03*	*Sitting Fees paid during FY 2002-03*
Ratan N. Tata	3,60,000	70,000
N.A. Soonawala	1,50,000	75,000
J.J. Irani	95,000	50,000
J.K. Setna	1,25,000	1,15,000
V.R. Mehta	2,20,000	1,05,000
R. Gopalakrishnan	2,45,000	1,15,000
N.N. Wadia	1,30,000	30,000
Helmut Petri	—	—
S.A. Naik	1,55,000	1,35,000
Peter K.M. Fietzek	20,000	10,000

Executive Directors:

Name	*Salary*	*Perquisites and Allowances*	*Commission*	*Incentive Remuneration*	*Stock Options*
Ravi Kant	1680	1553	4000	Nil	Nil
Praveen P. Kadle	1560	1212	3500	Nil	Nil
V. Sumantran	1740	1046	3500	Nil	Nil

Salient features of the agreements executed by the Company with the Executive Directors:

Period of Appointment	*5 years effective from:*	*Ravi Kant*	*—July 12, 2000*
		Praveen P. Kadle	*—October 31, 2001*
		V. Sumantran	*—November 12, 2001*

Remuneration	
Salary Scale	Rs. 70,000 - Rs. 2,00,000
Incentive Remuneration	Upto 200% of salary to be paid at the discretion of the Board annually
Commission	At the discretion of the Board annually within the stipulated limits under the Act
Perquisites and allowances (excluding Company's contribution to provident, superannuation and gratuity fund and leave encashment	Upto 125% of salary
Minimum remuneration in case of inadequacy of profits during any financial year	Salary, incentive remuneration, perquisites and allowances as mentioned above but excluding commission
Notice period on either side	Six months
Severance fees payable by the Company	Six months' salary

Investors' Grievance Committee

The Investors' Grievance Committee of the Board is empowered to oversee the redressal of investors' complaints pertaining to share/debenture transfers, non-receipt of annual reports, interest/dividend payments, issue of duplicate certificates, transmission (with and without legal representation) of shares and debentures and other miscellaneous complaints. Its scope also includes delegation of powers to the executives of the Company/share transfer agents to process share transfers and other investor allied matters. During the year under review, 3 Investors' Grievance Committee meetings were held on June 3, 2002, November 26, 2002 and February 18, 2003.

The composition of the Investors' Grievance Committee and attendance at its meetings is given hereunder:

Composition	S.A. Naik (Chairman) Independent Director	R. Gopalakrishnan Non-Executive Director	Ravi Kant Executive Director	Praveen P. Kadle Executive Director
Number of meetings attended	3	3	2	3

Dissemination of Information

H.K. Sethna, Company Secretary, who is the Compliance Officer can be contacted at:

Bombay House,
24, Homi Mody Street,
Mumbai - 400 001
Tel: 5665 8282, 5665 7824
Fax: 5665 7799
Email : inv_rel@telco.co.in

16601 Members' complaints/queries were received during the period under review. 13 complaints/queries, 47 transfer requests and 111 demats were pending as on March 31, 2003 (these were lodged in the last two weeks of March 2003 and were subsequently processed).

Shareholders' Satisfaction Survey

On the recommendations of the Investors' Grievance Committee, a survey on shareholders' satisfaction was conducted in November/December 2002. 5976 (2.49% of shareholder base) questionnaires were received from the shareholders, which when analysed reflected an overall satisfaction level as Excellent/Very Good on various service parameters at 66%.

Placed alongside are the graphs depicting satisfaction levels on various parameters of service/quality related to the Investor interface with the Company. A detailed presentation of the Survey conducted is given in the Investor Section on the Company's website-www.telcoindia.com

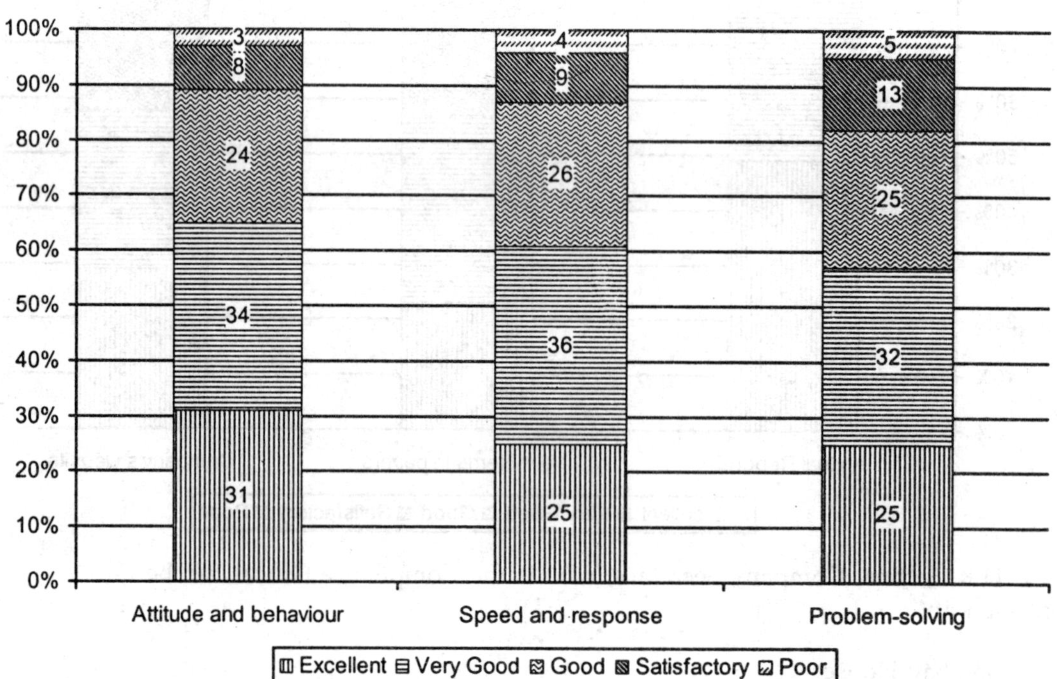

Action required regarding non-receipt of dividend, proceeds of matured deposits, redeemed debentures and interest thereon

In case of non-receipt/non-encashment of the dividend warrants, Members are requested to write/get in touch with the Company's Registrars/ the Registrar of Companies as mentioned hereunder:

Dividend for FY	*contact Office*	*Action to be taken*
2000-01 and 2001-02	Not Applicable due to non-declaration of dividend	—
1995-96 to 1999-2000	Tata Share Registry Ltd.	Letter on plain paper. In respect of dividend for FY 1995-96, the Members are requested to apply before August 2003.
1978 to 1994-95	Office of the Registrar of Companies, CGO Complex, 'A' wing, 2nd floor, Next to RBI, CBD-Belapur, Navi Mumbai, Maharashtra 400 614 2757 6802	Claim in Form No. 11 of the Companies Unpaid Dividend (Transfer to General Revenue Account of the Central Government) Rules, 1978

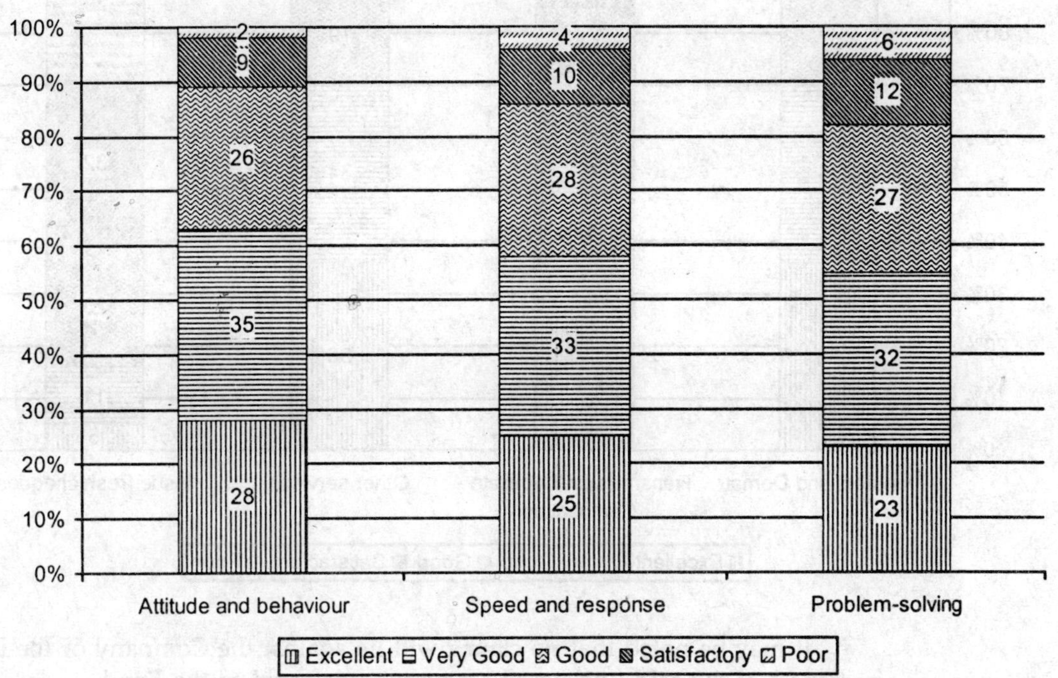

As per the provisions of Section 205A read with Section 205C of the Act, the Company is required to transfer unpaid dividends, matured deposits, redeemed debentures and interest accrued thereon remaining unclaimed and unpaid for a period of 7 years from the due date to the Investor Education and Protection Fund (IEPF) set-up by the Central Government.

Given below are the proposed dates for transfer of the unclaimed dividend to the IEPF by the Company:

Financial Year	*Date of declaration of Dividend*	*Proposed date for transfer to IEPF**
1995-96	July 30, 1996	September 16, 2003
1996-97	July 31, 1997	September 16, 2004
1997-98	July 29, 1998	September 14, 2005
1998-99	August 3, 1999	September 19, 2006
1999-2000	July 26, 2000	September 12, 2007

* Indicative dates, actual dates may vary.

Specific Services by Registrars

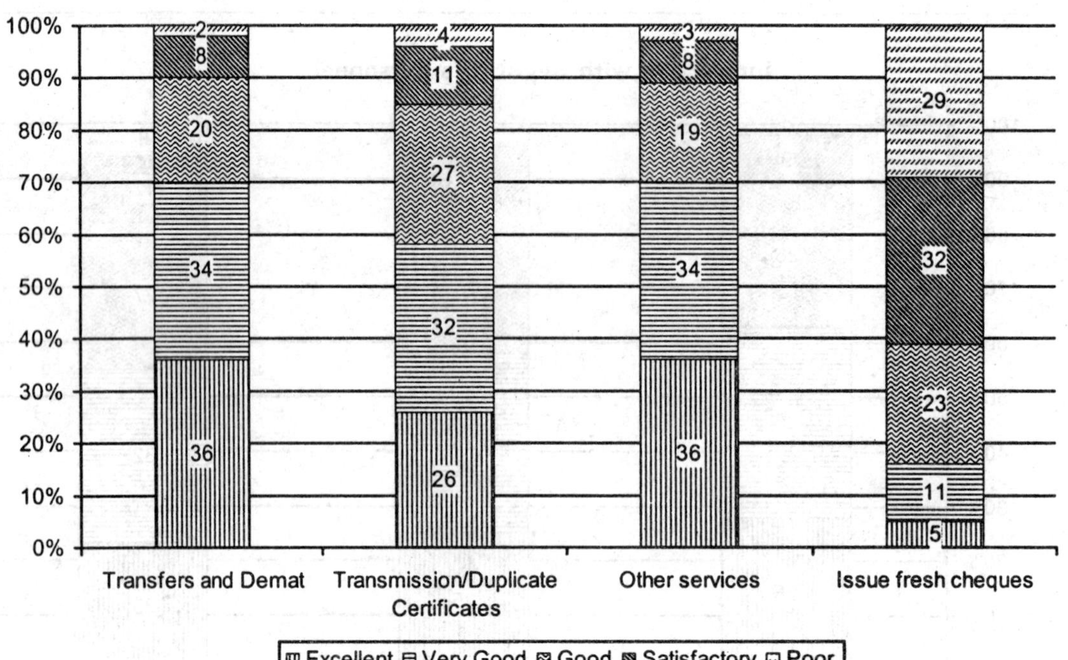

It may be noted that no claims will lie against the Company or the IEPF in respect of the said unclaimed amounts transferred to the Fund.

Amount Transferred to IEPF

The following amounts have been transferred to IEPF of the Central Government as on March 31, 2003:

Particulars	*Amount in Rs.*
Unpaid/unclaimed matured deposit with the Company	41,47,000
Unpaid matured debentures with the Company	3,34,48,898
Interest accrued on the amounts referred to above	81,82,880
Total	4,57,78,778

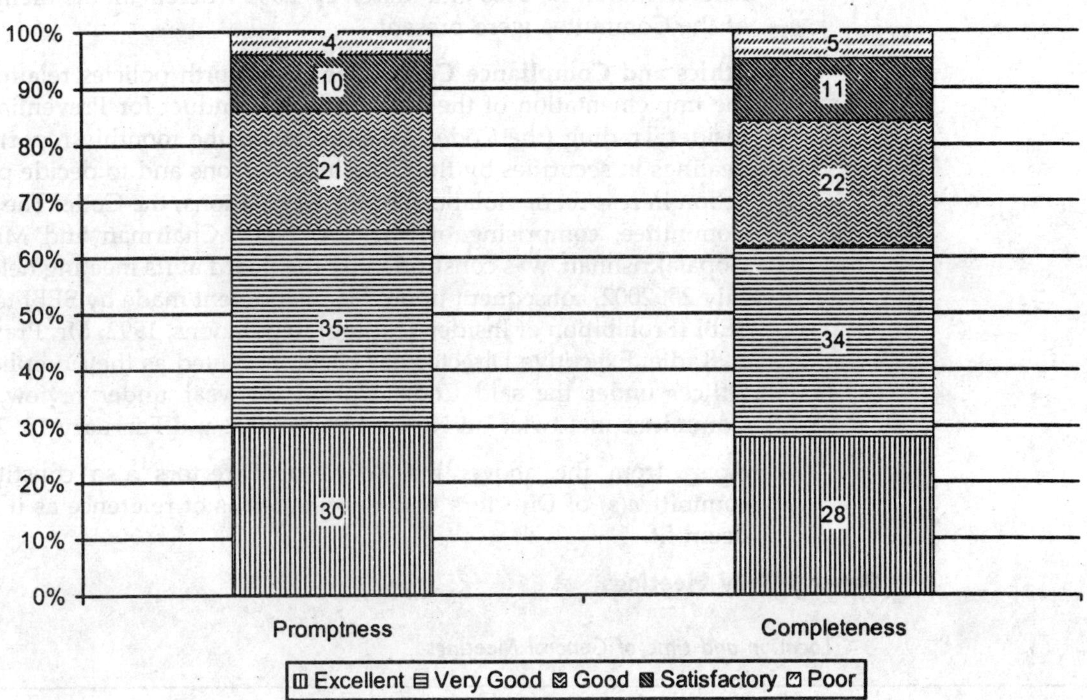

Committee of Directors

In addition to the above committees, the Board has constituted the following committees:

1. **Finance Committee of Directors** to look into matters pertaining to finance and banking transactions, granting power of attorney, property matters and other day-to-day operations of the Company. The Committee also makes appropriate recommendations to the Board on investments, restructuring initiatives and policy-related matters. The Committee comprises of Messrs. Ratan N. Tata, Chairman, N.A. Soonawala, J.K. Setna, R. Gopalakrishnan and Praveen P. Kadle. During the year under review, four Finance

Committee meetings were held on September 11, 2002, December 17, 2002, February 18, 2003 and March 17, 2003 wherein all the Members of the Finance Committee were present and 22 circular resolutions were passed.

2. **Committee of Board** to review revenue and capital expenditure budgets, long-term business strategies and organisational structure of the Company. The Committee comprises of Messrs Ratan N. Tata, Chairman, N.A. Soonawala, J.J. Irani, R. Gopalakrishnan and N.N. Wadia. During the year under review, two Committee meetings were held on March 17, 2003 and March 27, 2003 wherein all the Members of the Committee were present.

3. **Ethics and Compliance Committee** to set forth policies relating to the implementation of the Tata Code of Conduct for Prevention of Insider Trading (the Code), take on record the monthly reports on dealings in securities by the "Specified Persons and to decide penal action in respect of violations of the Regulations/the Code. The said Committee, comprising of Mr. S.A. Naik, Chairman and Mr. R. Gopalakrishnan, was constituted by the Board at its meeting held on July 25, 2002, consequent upon the amendment made by SEBI to the SEBI (Prohibition of Insider Trading) Regulations, 1992. Mr. Praveen P. Kadle, Executive Director has been appointed as the Compliance Officer under the sâid Code. During the year under review, the Committee met twice on November 26, 2002 and February 18, 2003.

4. Apart from the above, the Board of Directors also constitutes committee(s) of Directors with specific terms of reference as it may deem fit.

General Body Meetings

Location and time of General Meetings

Year	*Type*	*Date*	*Venue*	*Time*
2001-2002	AGM	July 26, 2002	Birla Matushri Sabhagar 19, Sir Vithaldas Thackersey Marg, Mumbai -400020	3.30 p.m.
2001-2002	EGM	March 27, 2002		10.00 a.m.
2001-2002	Meeting of the holders of 7% Fully Convertible Debentures	March 27, 2002		11.30 a.m.
2000-2001	AGM	August 14, 2001		3.30 p.m.
1999-2000	AGM	July 25, 2000		3.30 p.m.
1999-2000	EGM	March 28, 2000		4.00 p.m.

All special resolutions moved at the last AGM were passed by show of hands by requisite majority of Members attending the meeting and no resolutions were required to be passed by postal ballot.

Other Disclosures

- During the year under review, besides the transactions reported elsewhere in the Annual Report, there were no other related party transactions with its promoter, directors, management and subsidiaries that had a potential conflict with the interest of the Company at large.
- The Company has complied with various rules and regulations prescribed by stock exchanges, SEBI or any other statutory authority relating to the capital markets during the last three years. No penalties or strictures have been imposed by them on the Company.

Means of Communication

Half-yearly report sent to each household of shareholders	Yes
Quarterly and half yearly results	Published in Times of India/Indian Express and Maharashtra Times/Loksatta (Marathi)
Any website, where displayed	www.telcoindia.com
Whether it displays official news releases and presentations made to institutional investors or to the analysts	Yes
Whether MD&A is a part of Annual Report	Yes

Annual General Meeting

Date and Time	:	July 21, 2003 at 3.30 p.m.
Venue	:	Birla Matushri Sabhagar, 19, Sir Vithaldas Thackersey Marg, Mumbai 400 020
Dividend Payment Date	:	The Dividend Warrants will be posted on or after July 21, 2003
Date of Book Closure	:	July 1, 2003 to July 21, 2003 (both days inclusive)
Financial Calendar	:	Financial reporting for the quarter ending June 30, 2003 (Last week of July 2003) Financial reporting for the quarter ending September 30, 2003 (Last week of October 2003) Financial reporting for the quarter ending December 31, 2003 (Last week of January 2004) Financial reporting for the quarter ending March 31, 2004 (Last week of May 2004) AGM for the year ended March 31, 2004 (Last week of July 2004)

Listing

Presently, the Company's securities are listed on the following 13 Stock Exchanges in India:

1. The Stock Exchange, Mumbai (BSE)
2. National Stock Exchange of India Limited (NSE)
3. Bangalore Stock Exchange Limited*
4. Cochin Stock Exchange Limited
5. Hyderabad Stock Exchange Limited
6. Madhya Pradesh Stock Exchange Limited
7. The Uttar Pradesh Stock Exchange Association Limited
8. The Stock Exchange, Ahmedabad
9. Madras Stock Exchange Limited
10. The Calcutta Stock Exchange Association Limited
11. The Delhi Stock Exchange Association Limited
12. The Ludhiana Stock Exchange Association Limited
13. Pune Stock Exchange Limited

* Ordinary Shares have been delisted.

Specific attention of the Members is drawn to Item No. 8 of the Notice of the AGM and the Explanatory Statements attached thereto, whereby the Company proposes to delist its Ordinary Shares from all stock exchanges, excluding BSE and NSE. With the wide and extensive networking of centres of BSE and NSE, the investors have access to online dealings in the Company's securities across the country. The trading volumes of the Company's securities on the stock exchanges mentioned at (3) to (13) (hereinafter referred to as "the said Stock Exchanges") are on the decline since the past few years as a bulk of the trading is transacted on BSE and NSE. The listing fees paid to the said Stock Exchanges do not now offer commensurate benefits to the Company/its investors and the continued listing on the said Stock Exchanges is no longer required. The Board of Directors at their meeting held on May 27, 2003 have, therefore, decided to apply for voluntary delisting under the SEBI Guidelines on Voluntary Delisting of February 2003 of the Company's Ordinary Shares from all the Stock Exchanges excluding BSE and NSE. Considering that the Ordinary Shares will continue to be listed on BSE and NSE neither the Company nor its Promoters are required to offer exit option to the Members situated in the regions covered by the said exchanges. The delisting would further contribute to the cost reduction initiative taken across various functional areas of the Company. The delisting of the Company's Ordinary Shares from the said Stock Exchanges will not adversely affect any investors including the Members located in the regions where the said Stock Exchanges are situated.

The Non-convertible Debentures and the Warrants allotted with the Convertible Debentures and Non-convertible Debentures issued on a rights basis by the Company would continue to be listed on all the 13 stock exchanges till redemption of the debentures/exercise of the Warrants into shares.

Other Details

The ISIN Nos. for the Company's Ordinary Shares, 11% NCDs and the detachable Warrants are INE155A01014, INE155A07029 and INE155A13019 respectively. The Stock codes of the Company's Ordinary Shares at the BSE is '500570' (rolling settlement) and at the NSE 'TELCO EQ'.

The Company has paid listing fees, as applicable to the respective stock exchanges for the financial year 2001-02, 2002-03 and 2003-04 in respect of its listed securities.

The Global Depository Shares (GDSs) underlying the Global Depository Receipts (GDRs) issued by the Company in the International Market are listed on the Luxembourg Stock Exchange. The GDSs underlying the GDRs issued by the Company in the U.S. Markets are eligible for restricted trading through the Automated Linkages Market of The Nasdaq Stock Market, Inc.

Market Information

Market price data—monthly high/low and trading volumes during the last financial year on the BSE and NSE depicting liquidity of the Company's Ordinary Shares on the said exchanges is given hereunder:

Stock Exchange	*The Stock Exchange, Mumbai*				*National Stock Exchange of India Ltd.*			
Month	*High (Rs.)*	*Low (Rs.)*	*No. of Shares traded*	*Turnover (Rs. in Lacs)*	*High (Rs.)*	*Low (Rs.)*	*No. of Shares traded*	*Turnover (Rs. in Lacs)*
April 2002	138.00	122.10	9662336	12548.57	136.10	123.40	21319385	27694.85
May 2002	147.85	117.25	11202256	14776.63	146.80	119.45	24903880	32971.86
June 2002	159.50	122.00	30499539	44916.71	157.10	125.20	63699920	94110.43
July 2002	165.15	121.80	17450370	26213.72	164.50	124.80	48325203	72967.63
August 2002	140.80	121.15	15681174	20710.61	139.50	123.70	39223123	51814.48
September 2002	144.35	127.00	8714959	11866.13	142.60	128.40	24797445	33652.43
October 2002	145.75	128.80	11730827	16079.83	144.75	129.30	26410649	36200.67
November 2002	170.50	142.30	16282432	25685.32	169.70	143.30	43151381	68175.36
December 2002	173.40	156.40	16617841	26912.80	168.65	157.60	46637736	75514.17
January 2003	167.95	149.00	15391142	24683.54	167.20	151.00	44595679	71510.33
February 2003	168.00	153.00	7450260	12017.59	164.00	156.85	24330753	39269.00
March 2003	165.35	147.75	9035295	14002.91	162.75	150.15	26645915	41424.43

The performance of Company's Stock Price and Market Capitalisation vis-a-vis Sensex and Auto Index

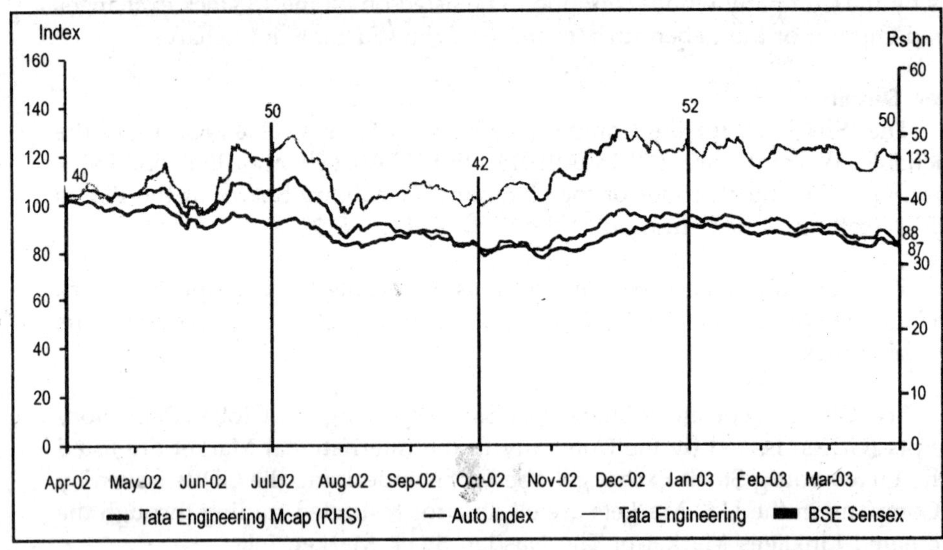

The monthly high and low of the Company's GDRs during the last financial year

(in US $,

Month	*High*	*Low*	*Month*	*High*	*Low*
April 2002	2.78	2.50	October 2002	2.99	2.67
May 2002	2.90	2.35	November 2002	3.51	2.98
June 2002	3.21	2.55	December 2002	3.50	3.27
July 2002	3.38	2.55	January 2003	3.49	3.16
August 2002	2.89	2.55	February 2003	3.44	3.29
September 2002	2.93	2.65	March 2003	3.40	3.16

Source: Citibank N.A., New York as Depository.

Two-way Fungibility of GDRs

On August 23, 2002, the Company signed an agreement with Citibank N.A., New York, Depository for GDR holders supplemental to the Depository Agreements executed by the Company at the time of issue of GDRs in 1994 and subsequently in 1996. Under the said Supplemental Agreement, the Company offers foreign investors the facility for conversion of Ordinary Shares into GDRs within the limits permissible for Two-way Fungibility as announced by the Reserve Bank of India vide its circular dated February 13, 2002.

Registrar and Transfer Agents

Members are requested to correspond with the Company's Registrar and Transfer Agents—Tata Share Registry Limited quoting their folio no. at the following addresses:

(i) For transfer lodgement, delivery and correspondence

Tata Share Registry Limited
Army & Navy Bldg.,
148, Mahatma Gandhi Road,
Fort, Mumbai - 400 001
Tel.: 5656 8484, Fax 5656 8494
e-mail : csg-unit@tatashare.com
website : www.tatashare.com

(ii) For the convenience of members based in the following cities, transfer documents and letters will also be accepted at the following branches/agencies of Tata Share Registry Limited:

Branches

1. 503, Barton Centre, 5th Floor
   84, Mahatma Gandhi Road,
   Bangalore - 560 001
   Tel : 080 - 5320321, Fax :080-5580019
   e-mail : tsrlbang@bgl .vsnl.net.in
2. Tata Centre, 1st Floor,
   43, Jawaharlal Nehru Road
   Kolkata - 700 071
   Tel :033 - 22883087, Fax : 033 - 22883062
   e-mail tsrlcal@cal2.vsnl.net.in
3. Bungalow No. 1, "E" Road
   Northern Town, Bistupur
   Jamshedpur - 831 001
   Tel: 0657 - 2426616, Fax: 0657 - 2426937
   e-mail : tsrljsr@sify.com
4. Plot No. 2/42, Sant Vihar
   Ansari Road, Daryaganj
   New Delhi - 110002
   Tel : 011 - 23271805, Fax : 011 -23271802
   e-mail : tsrldel@giasd 101 .vsnl.net.in

Agent

1. Shah Consultancy Services Limited
   Sumatinath Complex, 2nd Dhal,
   Pritam Nagar, Ellisbridge,
   Ahmedabad - 380 096
   Tel: 079 - 26575094
   Fax : 079 - 26576038
   e-mail : shahconsultancy@hotmail.com

Share Transfer System

- Securities lodged for transfer at the Registrar's address are normally processed within 15 days from the date of lodgement, if the documents are clear in all respects. All requests for dematerialisation of securities are processed and the confirmation is given to the depositories within 15 days. Senior Executives of the Company are empowered to approve transfer of shares and debentures. Grievances received from investors and other miscellaneous correspondence on change of address, mandates, etc. are processed by the Registrars within 30 days. The Company extends the facility of simultaneous transfer and dematerialisation of shares to the shareholders.
- Pursuant to Clause 47(c) of the Listing Agreement with the stock exchanges, certificates, on half-yearly basis, have been issued by a Company Secretary in Practice for due compliance of share transfer formalities by the Company. Pursuant to SEBI (Depositories and Participants) Regulations, 1996, certificates have also been received from a Company Secretary in Practice for timely dematerialisation of the shares of the Company and for conducting a secretarial audit on a quarterly basis for reconciliation of the share capital of the Company.

Distribution of Shareholding as on March 31, 2003

Range of Ordinary Shares	*No. of Shares*	*% to Capital*	*No. of Holders*	*% to Holders*
1 to 100	5852509	1.83	126021	55.26
101 to 500	18577932	5.81	78432	34.39
501 to 1000	10264180	3.21	14469	6.35
1001 to 5000	15376873	4.81	8140	3.57
5001 to 10000	3300904	1.03	478	0.21
Above 10000	266411989	83.31	502	0.22
Total	319784387	100.00	228042	100.00

Shareholding Pattern

Category	*As on March 31, 2003*		*As on March 31, 2002*	
	No. of Shares	*%*	*No. of Shares*	*%*
Individuals	50600739	15.82	49116568	15.36
Companies, Mutual Funds & Trusts	26121666	8.17	23614442	7.38
Tata Group Companies	103007460	32.21	102996528	32.21
Foreign Institutional Investors	45529560	14.24	43458571	13.59
NRIs & Foreign Companies	48320676	15.11	45840974	14.33
Nationalised & Other Banks	396891	0.13	1264954	0.40
Government & Public Financial Institutions	45807395	14.32	53490358	16.73
Total	319784387	100.00	319782395	100.00

Dematerialisation of Shares

Electronic holding by Members comprises 82.29% of the paid up Ordinary Share Capital of the Company held through the National Securities Depository Limited (81.04%) and Central Depository Services (India) Limited (1.25%) as on March 31, 2003.

Outstanding Securities

Global Depository Receipts (GDRs)

Out of 40,320,746 GDRs issued, outstanding number of GDRs as on March 31, 2003 is 19,579,602 (6.12%). Each GDR represents one underlying Ordinary Share. There were no ADRs or convertible instruments outstanding on that date.

Warrants

The holders of 2,55,59,500 warrants including fractional coupons for 11,718 warrants is ued on the Convertible and Non-convertible Debentures on a rights basis are entitled to apply for 1 Ordinary Share of Rs. 10 each per warrant at a premium of Rs. 110 at any time between June 6, 2003 to September 30, 2004.

Securities

Out of the Rights Issue of Convertible and Non-convertible Debentures as on March 31, 2003, 36,042 Ordinary Shares (arising out of conversion of CDs), 14,414 NCDs and 14,418 Detachable Warrants on the CDs/NCDs, being the entitlement on Ordinary Shares which are the subject matter of various suits filed in the courts/forums by third parties for which final order is awaited, are held in abeyance pursuant to Section 206A of the Act.

Plant Locations

Plant Location	*Range of Products Produced*
Pimpri and Chikhali, Pune-410 018	Medium and Heavy Commercial Vehicles (M&HCVs), Light Commercial Vehicles (LCVs), Utility Vehicles (UVs) and Cars
Jamshedpur Town Post Office, Jamshedpur - 831 010	M&HCVs
Chinhat Deva Road, Lucknow - 227 105	M&HCVs, LCVs & UVs
KIADB Block - 2, Belur Industrial Area, Dharwad - 580 007	Project under construction/formulation

Address for Correspondence

Tata Engineering and Locomotive Company Limited,
Bombay House,
24, Homi Mody Street,
Mumbai 400 001.

CERTIFICATE

To the Members of

TATA ENGINEERING AND LOCOMOTIVE COMPANY LIMITED

We have examined the compliance of the conditions of Corporate Governance by Tata Engineering & Locomotive Company Limited, for the year ended on March 31, 2003, as stipulated in Clause 49 of the Listing Agreement of the said Company with the stock exchanges.

The compliance of the conditions of Corporate Governance is the responsibility of the management. Our examination has been limited to a review of the procedures and implementations thereof, adopted by the Company for ensuring compliance with the conditions of Corporate Governance. It is neither an audit nor an expression of opinion of the financial statements of the Company.

In our opinion and to the best of our information and according to the explanations given to us, and the representations made by the Directors and the management, we certify that the Company has complied with the conditions of Corporate Governance as stipulated in Clause 49 of the above mentioned Listing Agreement.

As required by the Guidance Note issued by the Institute of Chartered Accountants of India we have to state that based on the report given by the Registrars of the Company to the Investors' Grievance Committee, as on March 31, 2003 there were no investor grievance matters against the Company remaining unattended/pending for more than 30 days.

We further state that such compliance is neither an assurance as to the future viability of the Company nor the efficiency or effectiveness with which the management has conducted the affairs of the Company.

For A.F. FERGUSON & CO.
Chartered Accountants

A.K. MAHINDRA
Partner

For S.B. BILLIMORIA & CO.
Chartered Accountants

Y.H. MALEGAM
Partner

Mumbai, May 27, 2003

AUDITOR's REPORT

To the Members of

TATA ENGINEERING AND LOCOMOTIVE COMPANY LIMITED

1. We have audited the attached Balance Sheet of Tata Engineering and Locomotive Company Limited, as at March 31, 2003 and also the Profit and Loss Account and the Cash Flow Statement of the Company for the year ended on that date annexed thereto. These financial statements are the responsibility of the Company's management. Our responsibility is to express an opinion on these financial statements based on our audit.

2. We conducted our audit in accordance with auditing standards generally accepted in India. Those Standards require that we plan and perform the audit to obtain reasonable assurance about whether the financial statements are free of material mis-statement. An audit includes examining, on a test basis, evidence supporting the amounts and disclosures in the financial statements. An audit also includes assessing the accounting principles used and significant estimates made by the management, as well as evaluating the overall financial statement presentation. We believe that our audit provides a reasonable basis for our opinion.

3. As required by the Manufacturing and Other Companies (Auditor's Report) Order, 1988 issued by the Central Government of India in terms of sub-section (4A) of Section 227 of the Companies Act, 1956, we enclose in the Annexure a statement on the matters specified in paragraphs 4 and 5 of the said Order.

4. Further to our comments in the Annexure referred to in paragraph 3 above, we report that:

   (a) We have obtained all the information and explanations, which to the best of our knowledge and belief were necessary for the purposes of our audit;

   (b) In our opinion, proper books of account as required by law have been kept by the company so far as appears from our examination of those books;

   (c) The Balance Sheet, the Profit and Loss Account and the Cash Flow Statement dealt with by this report are in agreement with the books of account;

   (d) In our opinion, the Balance Sheet, the Profit and Loss Account and the Cash Flow Statement dealt with by this report comply with the Accounting Standards referred to in sub-section (3C) of Section 211 of the Companies Act, 1956;

(e) On the basis of written representations received from the directors, as on March 31, 2003, and taken on record by the Board of Directors, we report that none of the directors is disqualified as on March 31, 2003 from being appointed as a director in terms of clause (g) of sub-section (1) of Section 274 of the Companies Act, 1956;

(f) In our opinion and to the best of our information and according to the explanations given to us, the said accounts give the information required by the Companies Act, 1956, in the manner so required and give a true and fair view in conformity with the accounting principles generally accepted in India:

(i) In the case of the Balance Sheet, of the state of affairs of the Company as at March 31, 2003;

(ii) In the case of the Profit and Loss Account, of the profit of the Company for the year ended on that date; and

(iii) In the case of the Cash Flow Statement, of the cash flows of the Company for the year ended on that date.

For A.F. FERGUSON & CO.
Chartered Accountants

A.K. MAHINDRA
Partner
Membership No.: 10296
Mumbai, May 27, 2003

For S.B. BILLIMORIA & CO.
Chartered Accountants

Y.H. MALEGAM
Partner
Membership No.: 3242

ANNEXURE II

CORPORATE GOVERNANCE, 2002-03, RELIANCE INDUSTRIES LTD.

Reliance's Corporate Governance Principles uphold its global standing at the forefront of corporate governance best practices. Reliance continues to review its corporate governance practices to ensure that they continue to reflect domestic and international developments to position itself to conform to the best corporate governance practices. It takes feedback into account in its periodic reviews of the guidelines to ensure their continuing relevance, effectiveness and responsiveness to the needs of local and international investors and all other stakeholders.

Principles

Reliance's corporate governance practices focus on the following main principles.

Recognising the respective roles and responsibilities of Board and Management

To establish an effective mechanism for overseeing the affairs, keeping in view the Company's size, complexity, geographical operations and corporate tradition and culture, the Reliance's framework is designed to:

- enable the Board to provide strategic guidance for the Company and effective overseeing of the management;
- define the respective roles and responsibilities of senior executives and officers to ensure accountability; and
- ensure a balance of authority such that no single individual has unfettered powers.

Having a Board of appropriate composition, size and commitment to adequately discharge its responsibilities and duties

To ensure effectiveness of the Board, facilitating efficient discharge of duties and adding value in the context of the Company's circumstances, the Board periodically reviews its composition and size for ensuring a strong element of independence and commitment. Accordingly the Board is structured in such a way that

- it has a proper understanding of, and competence to deal with, the current and emerging issues of the business and the benefit of a variety of perspectives and skills;
- it has the appropriate mix of executive and non-executive directors ensuring Directors' commitment and time to participate in the affairs fully; and
- it can effectively review and challenge the performance of management and exercise independent judgement.

The Directors are elected by the shareholders. However, the Board plays an important role in the selection of candidates for shareholders' approval. Reliance's policy does not prescribe any term limit for Directors, as the term limits, while could help fresh ideas and view points of new entrants, they have the disadvantage of losing the valuable contribution of directors who over the time have developed insight into the Company and its affairs.

Independent verification and safeguarding integrity of the Company's financial reporting

To ensure the truthful and factual presentation of the Company's financial position, the Company has put in place a structure of review and authorisation apart from strong internal audit process. For this purpose, the Board has also constituted an Audit Committee, which is charged with paying particular attention to the management processes supporting external reporting, the performance and objectivity of the internal audit function, and the performance and independence of the external auditors.

Timely and balanced disclosure of all material information concerning the Company

To give investors an equal and timely access to material information, and to ensure that Company announcements are factual, balanced and in compliance with the applicable provisions of law, the Company has put in place a mechanism to ensure that:

- all investors have equal and timely access to material information concerning the Company—including its financial position, performance and governance.
- Company announcements are factual and presented in a clear and balanced way, disclosing both positive and negative information.

Highest Importance to Investor Relations

To ensure long-term shareholder value creation and to promote shareholder participation in corporate affairs, Reliance has established and maintained communication strategies, including a policy for clarity in notices of meetings. Reliance also maintains its corporate website www.ril.com for convenient access by the shareholders to all the material information about the

Company. Reliance's endeavours are to empower its shareholders by:

- communicating effectively with them,
- giving them appropriate information about the Company, and
- making it easy for them to participate in general meetings.

Sound System of Risk Management and Internal Control

To establish and maintain a system of risk management and internal control, the Company has set-up a policy which includes a review of the risk management system, and maintenance of a risk profile (both financial and non-financial risks). Reliance has set-up an effective internal audit function, independent of the external auditors, to review the effectiveness of the risk management system. Audit Committee of the Board oversees the risk management and internal control systems. This system is designed to:

- identify, assess, monitor and manage risks, and
- inform investors of material changes to the Company's risk profile.

Fair Review, Active Encouragement and Management Effectiveness

To ensure consistent effectiveness of the overall management, the performance of the senior executives and officers is subject to review. This includes equipping individuals with the knowledge and information they need to discharge their responsibilities effectively, and reviewing individual and collective performance regularly. Performance evaluation process is fair and transparent and uses both measurable and qualitative indicators.

Efficient Executive Remuneration Policy

The Company has adopted a remuneration policy that attracts and maintains talented and motivated executives so as to encourage enhanced performance of the Company. The remuneration policy envisages a clear relationship between performance and remuneration, including the link between remuneration paid and the overall corporate performance.

Remuneration of managing directors and whole time directors is determined by the Remuneration Committee of Directors within the permissible limits under the applicable provisions of law and is approved by Shareholders. Non-Executive Directors are paid sitting fees within the limits prescribed under law.

Corporate Ethics

Reliance has a defined policy framework for ethical business conduct by its personnel.

The Ethics Policy sets forth, *inter alia*:

- Our Values and Commitments
- Our Code of Ethics
- Our Business Policies
- Our Code of Conduct for Prevention of Insider Trading
- A detailed programme for Ethics Management at Reliance.

These policies support the consistent endeavour to enhance the reputation of the Company.

The *"Values and Commitments"* policy document states that Reliance believes that any business conduct can be ethical only when it rests on the nine core values of Honesty, Integrity, Respect, Fairness, Purposefulness, Trust, Responsibility, Citizenship and Caring.

These values are not to be lost sight of by anyone at Reliance under any circumstances irrespective of the goals that are intended to be achieved. To us, the means are as important as the ends.

In pursuit of these values outlined in the "Values and Commitments" policy document, we are committed to an ethical treatment of all our stakeholders—our employees, our customers, our environment, our shareholders, our lenders and other investors, our suppliers and the Government. A firm belief that every Reliance team member holds is that the other persons' interests count as much as their own.

The "Code of Ethics" and the "Business Policies" are in alignment with Reliance's Values and Commitments. The essence of these documents is that each employee should conduct the Company's business with integrity, in compliance with applicable laws, and in a manner that excludes considerations of personal advantage.

The "Code of Ethics" policy document contains policy on the following:

- Conflict of Interest
- Payments and Gifting
- Receipt of Gifts
- Purchases through suppliers
- Appointment of full-time agents, consultants and representatives
- Political Contributions

The "Business Policies" document contains policy on the following:

- Fair Market Practices
- Inside Information
- Financial Records and Accounting Integrity
- External Communication
- Work Ethics
- Personal Conduct
- Health Safety and Environment
- Quality

The "Code of Conduct for Prevention of Insider Trading" contains policies prohibiting insider trading.

The Company's shares are listed on ten Stock Exchanges in India and GDRs are listed on Luxembourg Stock Exchange. In accordance with Clause 49 of the listing agreement with the domestic stock exchanges and best practices followed internationally on Corporate Governance, the details of compliance by the Company are as under:

1. Company's Philosophy on Corporate Governance

As discussed above, Reliance's philosophy on corporate governance envisages the attainment of the highest levels of transparency, accountability and equity, in all facets of its operations, and in all its interactions with its stakeholders, including shareholders, employees, the government and lenders. Reliance is committed to achieving the highest international standards of corporate governance. Reliance believes that all its operations and actions must serve the underlying goal of enhancing overall shareholder value, over a sustained period of time.

2. Board of Directors

The Board of Directors consists of 13 directors. The composition and category of Directors is as follows:

Category	*Name of the Directors*
Promoter/Executive Directors	D.H. Ambani* Chairman (upto 6th July, 2002) M.D. Ambani** Chairman & Managing Director (from 31st July, 2002) A.D. Ambani*** Vice-Chairman & Managing Director (from 31st July, 2002)

	N.R. Meswani Executive Director
	H.R. Meswani Executive Director
Promoter Non-Executive Director	R.H. Ambani
Non-Promoter Executive Director	H.S. Kohli Executive Director
Independent Directors	M.L. Bhakta Y.P. Trivedi T.R.U. Pai U. Mahesh Rao (Nominee Director—G/C) Dr. D.V. Kapur M.P. Modi S. Venkitaramanan

* D.H. Ambani, passed away on 6th July, 2002.
** M.D. Ambani, Vice-Chairman and Managing Director, upto 3rd July, 2002.
*** A.D. Ambani, Managing Director, upto 30th July, 2002.

Brief Resume of the Directors being reappointed at the ensuing Annual General Meeting, nature of their expertise in specific functional areas and names of companies in which they hold directorship and the membership of the committees of the Board are furnished hereunder:

A. Shri Mukesh D. Ambani holds a Bachelor's Degree in Chemical Engineering from the University of Mumbai and MBA from Stanford University, USA. He joined Reliance in 1981 and sharpened his skills and capabilities under the able guidance of the founder Chairman, late Shri Dhirubhai H. Ambani. He initiated Reliance's backward integration from textiles into polyester fibres and further into petrochemicals. In this process, he directed the creation of 51 new, world-class manufacturing facilities involving diverse technologies that have raised Reliance's manufacturing capacities from less than a million tonnes to nine million tonnes per year. He is credited with having brought about financial innovations in the Indian capital markets. He pioneered India's first forays into overseas capital markets with international public offerings of global depository receipts, convertibles and bonds. He directed Reliance in its efforts to raise, since 1991 around US $ 2 billion from overseas financial markets; with a 100 year yankee bond issue in January 1997 being the high point. He directed and led the creation of the world's largest grass-root petroleum refinery in Jamnagar, India, with a capacity of 5,40,000 barrels a day integrated with petrochemicals, power generation, port and related infrastructure, at an investment of Rs. 25,000 crore (nearly US $ 6 billion). He has steered the Reliance Group to its current status as India's leading textiles—petroleum-petrochemicals-power-telecom player. He is a member of the Prime Minister's Advisory Council on Trade and Industry, Government of India, Council of Scientific and Industrial Research (CSIR), India, Board of Governors of National Council of Applied Economic Research

(NCAER), Advisory Council of Indian Banks' Association and is the Chairman, Board of Trustees of the Indian Institute of Software Engineering, Mumbai.

His Achievements

- Rated No. 1 among the top 50 Power People in the 2003 Power List published by *India Today*, February 2003.
- Ranked 33rd among the Top 50 Most Respected Business Leaders of the World, tops among the three Indian CEOs featured in a survey conducted by Pricewaterhouse Coopers and published in *Financial Times*, London, January 2003.
- Conferred 'Membership Award' by The Textile Association (India), December 2002.
- Conferred 'The Entrepreneur of the Decade Award' by the Bombay Management Association, October 2002.
- Rated as one of 'India's Most Admired CEOs' for the fourth consecutive year in the *Business Barons*—Taylor Nelson Sofres-Mode Survey, July, 2002 and also emerged as one of the Super Six World-class Indian CEOs.
- Recipient of Ernst and Young Entrepreneur of the Year Award-2000.
- Honoured by University Department of Chemical Technology (UDCT), University of Bombay as "Distinguished Alumnus of the Decade", December, 1999.
- Conferred the 'Business of the Year 1997' award by *Business India*, December 1997.
- Recognised as 'Global Leader for Tomorrow' in 1994 by the World Economic Forum, Switzerland.
- Named in 'Time Roster of Young Leaders for the New Millennium' by *Time Magazine*, December 1994.

He is a Director on the Boards of Reliance Europe Limited and Reliance Infocomm Limited. He is Managing Director of Reliance Communications Infrastructure Limited and Chairman of Indian Petrochemicals Corporation Limited. He is also a member of the Shareholders'/Investors' Grievance Committee of the Board.

B. Shri Anil D. Ambani holds a Bachelor's Degree in Science from the University of Mumbai and MBA from The Wharton School, University of Pennsylvania, USA. He joined Reliance in 1983 as co-Chief Executive Officer and sharpened his skills and capabilities under the able guidance of the founder Chairman, late Shri Dhirubhai H. Ambani. He is credited with having pioneered many financial innovations in the Indian capital markets. He pioneered India's first forays into overseas capital markets with international public offerings of global depository receipts, convertibles and bonds. He directed Reliance in its efforts to raise, since 1991, around US $ 2 billion from overseas financial markets; with a 100-year Yankee bond issue in January 1997 being the high point. With an investment of over Rs. 36,000 crores (US $ 9 billion) in petroleum refining, petrochemicals, power generation, telecommunication services and a port terminal in a three-year time frame, he steered the Reliance Group to its current status as India's leading textiles-petroleum-petrochemicals-power-infocom-telecom player. He is a Member of the Wharton Board of Overseers, The Wharton School, USA. He has been nominated by the Government of India as a Member of the Board of Governors of the Indian Institute of Management, Ahmedabad.

His Achievements

- Rated No. 1 among the top 50 Power People in the 2003 Power List published by *India Today*, February 2003.
- Conferred 'The Entrepreneur of the Decade Award' by the Bombay Management Association, October 2002.
- Rated as one of 'India's Most Admired CEOs' for the fourth consecutive year in the *Business Barons.*
- Taylor Nelson Sofres—Mode Survey, July 2002 and also emerged as one of the Super Six World-class Indian CEOs.
- Awarded the First Wharton Indian Alumni Award by the Wharton India Economic Forum (WIEF) in recognition of his contribution to the establishment of Reliance as a global leader in many of its business areas, December 2001.
- Named amongst 'The Power 50—India's 50 most powerful decision-makers in Politics, Business & Finance', *Business Barons,* August 1999.
- Selected by *Asiaweek* magazine for its list of 'Leaders of the Millennium in Business and Finance' and was introduced as the only 'new hero' in Business and Finance from India, June 1999.
- Leading business magazine *Business Barons* included him in its list of 'India's 25 Most Influential Business and Financial Leaders', June 1998.
- Conferred the 'Businessman of the Year 1997' award by India's leading business magazine *Business India,* December 1997.

He is a Director on the Boards of Indian Petrochemicals Corporation Limited, Reliance Europe Limited and Indian School of Business, Hyderabad. He is Chairman and Managing Director of BSES Limited. He is also a member of the Shareholders'/Investors' Grievance Committee of the Board.

C. Shri Nikhil R. Meswani, a Chemical Engineer from University Department for Chemical Technology (UDCT), is the son of Shri Rasikial Meswani (late), one of the founder Directors of the Company. He joined Reliance at an early age and since 1990, he is an Executive Director on the Board of Reliance, with overall responsibility of the entire petrochemicals division. He has contributed to the growth of the petrochemicals division of Reliance to its present position as market leader in India and one amongst the top ten petrochemical companies in the world. Shri Meewani is currently Chairman of Asian Chemical Fibre Industries Federation and President of Association of Synthetic Fibre Industry. He is also a Member of Young President's Organisation (YPO) and a Director of Indian Petrochemicals Corporation Limited.

D. Shri H.S. Kohli was appointed as a Whole-time Director designated as 'Executive Director' of the Company for a period of five years with effect from 1st April, 2000. An M.S. (Chem.), he has wide experience in implementing and operation of Petrochemical complexes. He is working in the Company since 1991 at its Hazira Complex. He is also the Occupier of the Company's factories at Hazira, Patalganga and Jamnagar. Currently he is incharge of the Company's manufacturing division at Hazira. He is also a Director of Reliance Assam Petrochemicals Limited.

E. Shri Yogendra P. Trivedi, an Advocate of the Supreme Court and a Tax Consultant, is a Director of the Company since 16th April, 1992. He has vast experience in finance and taxation. He is a member of various clubs and associations and holding important positions in various fields: Economic, Political, Professional, Commercial, Education, Medical, Sports and Social. He has received various awards and merits for his contribution in various fields. He is also a Director of Safari Industries Ltd., Siltap Chemicals Ltd., Birla Kennametal Ltd., Monica Travels Pvt. Ltd., Sai Service Station Ltd., Zandu Pharmaceutical Works Ltd., Zodiac Clothing Co. Ltd., Ripples Club, Metro Exporters Pvt. Ltd., Clare Mont Trading Pvt. Ltd., Telstar Travels Pvt. Ltd., Trivedi Consultants Pvt. Ltd., and Bloomingdale Estates Pvt. Ltd. He is also a member of the Audit Committee, Shareholders'/Investors' Grievance Committee and the Remuneration Committee of the Board.

3. Board Meetings, its Committee Meetings and Procedures

A. Institutionalised Decision-making Process

With a view to institutionalise all corporate affairs and setting up systems and procedures for advance planning for matters requiring discussion/ decisions by the Board, the Company has defined guidelines for the meetings of Board of Directors and Committees thereof. These Guidelines seek to systematize the decision-making process at the meetings of Board/Committees, in an informed and most efficient manner.

B. Scheduling and Selection of Agenda Items for Board Meetings

(i) The Company holds minimum of four Board Meetings in each year, which are pre-scheduled after the end of each financial quarter. Apart from the four pre-scheduled Board Meetings, additional Board Meetings will be convened by giving appropriate notice at any time to address the specific needs of the Company. The Board may also approve permitted urgent matters by passing resolutions by circulation.

(ii) The meetings are usually held at the Company's Registered Office in Mumbai.

(iii) All divisions/departments in the Company are encouraged to plan their functions well in advance, particularly with regard to matters requiring discussion/approval/decision in the Board/Committee Meetings. All such matters are communicated to the Company Secretary in advance so that the same could be included in the Agenda for the Board Meetings.

(iv) The Board is given presentations covering Finance, Sales and Marketing, and the major business segments and operations of the Company, before taking on record the results of the Company for the preceding financial quarter at each of the pre-scheduled Board Meeting. The Board's annual agenda includes recommending dividend keeping in view the dividend policy, determining directors who shall retire by rotation and recommending appointment of Directors/Auditors, authentication of annual accounts and approving Directors' Report, long-term strategic plan for the Company and the principal issues that the Company expects to face in the future. Board Meetings also note and review functions of its Committees.

(v) The Chairman of the Board and the Company Secretary in consultation with other concerned persons in the senior management, finalise the agenda papers for the Board Meetings.

C. Board Material Distributed in Advance

(i) Agenda papers are circulated to the Directors, in advance, in the defined Agenda format. All material information is incorporated in the Agenda Papers for facilitating meaningful, informed and focussed discussions at the meeting. Where it is not practicable to attach any document to the Agenda, the same are placed on the table at the meeting with specific reference to this effect in the Agenda.

(ii) In special and exceptional circumstances, additional or supplementary item(s) on the agenda are permitted. Sensitive subject matters may be discussed at the meeting without written material being circulated in advance or at the meeting.

D. Recording minutes of proceedings at Board Meeting

The Company Secretary records the minutes of the proceedings of each Board and Committee Meetings. Draft minutes are circulated to all the members of the Board for their comments. The minutes of proceedings of a meeting are entered in the Minutes Book within 30 days from the conclusion of the meeting.

E. Post-meeting follow-up mechanism

The Guidelines for Board and Committee meetings facilitate an effective post meeting follow-up, review and reporting process for the action taken on decisions of the Board and Committees.

F. Compliance

The Company Secretary while preparing the agenda, notes on agenda, minutes, etc. of the meeting(s) and holding and conducting the meetings, is responsible for and is required to ensure adherence to all the applicable provisions of law including the Companies Act, 1956 and the Secretarial Standards recommended by the Institute of Company Secretaries of India, New Delhi.

4. Attendance of each Director at the Board Meetings, last Annual General Meeting and Number of other Directorship and Chairmanship/ Membership of Committee of each Director in various Companies

Name of the Director	*Attendance Particulars*		*No. of Directorships and Committee Membership/Chairmanship*		
	Board Meetings	*Last AGM*	*Other Directorships*	*Committee Memberships*	*Committee Chairmanships*
D.H. Ambani*	0	N.A.	0	0	0
M.D. Ambani	7	Present	4	1	0
A.D. Ambani	7	Present	4	1	0
N.R. Meswani	6	Present	1	1	1
H.R. Meswani	7	Present	0	0	0
H.S. Kohli	6	Present	1	0	0
R.H. Ambani	6	Present	7	1	1
M.L. Bhakta	7	Present	6	6	3
Y.P. Trivedi	6	Present	12	7	2
T.R.U. Pai	5	Present	5	2	0
S. Venkitaramanan	5	LOA	9	4	0
U. Mahest Rao	6	Present	7	10	1
Dr. D.V. Kapur	6	Present	11	5	3
M.P. Modi	7	Present	3	3	2

*D.H. Ambani passed away on July 6, 2002.

LOA—Leave of absence.

5. Number of Board Meetings held and the dates on which held

7 (Seven) Board Meetings were held during the year, as against the minimum requirement of 4 meetings. The dates on which the meetings held were as follows: 23rd April, 2002, 3rd July, 2002, 2nd September, 2002, 30th September, 2002, 31st October, 2002, 20th December, 2002 and 31st January, 2003. The maximum time gap between any two meetings was not more than three calendar months. None of the Directors of the Company was a member of more than ten Committees nor was the Chairman of more than five Committees across all Companies in which he was a Director.

6. Board Committees

A. Standing Committees

The Company has the following Standing Committees of the Board:

(i) Audit Committee

The Board of Directors of the Company has constituted an Audit Committee, comprising four independent, Non-Executive Directors, viz. Shri Y.P. Trivedi, Chairman (having financial and accounting knowledge), Shri S. Venkitaramanan, Shri U. Mahesh Rao and Shri T.R.U. Pai. The constitution of Audit Committee also meets with the requirements under Section 292A of the Companies Act, 1956.

The terms of reference stipulated by the Board of Directors to the Audit Committee are, as contained in Clause 49 of the Listing Agreement and Section 292A of the Companies Act, 1956, as follows:

(a) Oversight of the Company's financial reporting process and the disclosure of its financial information.

(b) Recommending the appointment and removal of external auditors, fixation of audit fee and also approval for payment for any other services.

(c) Reviewing with management the half-yearly and annual financial statements before submission to the Board, focussing primarily on: (i) any changes in accounting policies and practices, (ii) major accounting entries based on exercise of judgement by management, (iii) qualifications in draft audit report, (iv) significant adjustments arising out of audit, (v) the going concern assumption, (vi) compliance with accounting standards, (vii) compliance with Stock Exchange and legal requirements concerning financial statements, and (vii) any related party transactions, i.e. transactions of the Company of material nature, with promoters or the management, their subsidiaries or relatives, etc. that may have potential conflict with the interests of Company at large.

(d) Reviewing with the management, external and internal auditors, the adequacy and compliance of internal control systems.

(e) Reviewing the adequacy of internal audit functions.

(f) Discussion with internal auditors any significant findings and follow-up thereon.

(g) Reviewing the findings of any internal investigations by the internal auditors into matters where there is suspected fraud or irregularity or a failure of internal control systems of a material nature and reporting the matter to the Board.

(h) Discussion with external auditors before the audit commences nature and scope of audit as well as have post-audit discussion to ascertain any area of concern.

(i) Reviewing the Company's financial and risk management policies.

(j) To look into the reasons for substantial defaults in the payment to the depositors, debentureholders, shareholders (in case of non-payment of declared dividends) and creditors.

During the year, the Committee has met 5 times, as against the minimum requirement of 3 meetings. The Statutory Auditors and the Cost Auditors of the Company were also invited to attend the Audit Committee meetings.

Attendance of each Member of Audit Committee Meetings held during the year

Name of Member of Audit Committee	*Attendance particulars (Present)*
Shri Y.P. Trivedi, Chairman	8th June, 2002, 30th September, 2002, 30th October, 2002 and 30th January, 2003
Shri S. Venkitaramanan	23rd April, 2002, 8th June, 2002 and 30th January, 2003
Shri U. Mahesh Rao	23rd April, 2002, 8th June, 2002, 30th September, 2002, 30th October, 2002 and 30th January, 2003
Shri T.R.U. Pai	8th June, 2002, 30th September, 2002 and 30th October, 2002.

(ii) Remuneration Committee

The Board of Directors of the Company has constituted a Remuneration Committee, comprising of 4 independent, Non-Executive Directors, viz. Shri M.L. Bhakta (Chairman), Shri Y.P. Trivedi, Shri U. Mahesh Rao and Shri S. Venkitaramanan.

The Remuneration Committee has been constituted to recommend/review the remuneration package of the Managing/Whole-time Directors, based on performance and defined criteria.

The remuneration policy is directed towards rewarding performance based on review of achievements on a periodical basis. The remuneration policy is in consonance with the existing Industry practice.

Since there was no proposal for enhancement in the remuneration of the Directors, the Committee did not meet any time during the year under review.

Details of Remuneration to Directors for the year

The aggregate value of salary and perquisites including commission payable for the year ended 31st March, 2003 to the Managing Directors/Whole-time Directors is as follows: Late Shri D.H. Ambani, Rs. 4.50 crores, Shri M.D. Ambani, Chairman and Managing Director, Rs. 12.18 crores, Shri A.D. Ambani, Vice-Chairman and Managing Director, Rs. 12.15 crores, Shri N.R. Meswani, Executive Director, Rs. 3.14 crores, Shri H.R. Meswani, Executive Director, Rs. 3.13 crores. The aggregate value of salary and perquisites paid to Shri H.S. Kohli, Executive Director was Rs. 0.27 crore. The above amounts include Company's contribution to Provident Fund, Superannuation or Annuity Fund, to the extent not taxable and Gratuity and encashment of leave at the end of tenure, as per the rules of the Company.

The Company pays sitting fees to all the Non-Executive Directors at the rate of Rs. 5000 for attending each meeting of the Board and/or Committee thereof. The sitting fees paid for the year ended 31st March, 2003 to the Directors are as follows: Shri R.H. Ambani, Rs. 30,000; Shri M.L. Bhakta, Rs. 90,000; Shri Y.P. Trivedi, Rs. 1,15,000; Shri T.R.U. Pai, Rs. 45,000; Shri S. Venkitaramanan, Rs. 40,000; Shri U. Mahesh Rao, Rs. 55,000; Dr. D.V. Kapur, Rs. 35,000 and Shri M.P. Modi, Rs. 40,000.

The Company has paid Rs. 8.65 lacs as professional fees to Messrs Kanga & Co., a firm in which Shri M.L. Bhakta, Director of the Company, is a partner.

(iii) Shareholders'/Investors' Grievance Committee

The Board of Directors of the Company has constituted a Shareholders'/ Investors' Grievance Committee, comprising of Shri M.L. Bhakta (Chairman), Shri Y.P. Trivedi, Shri M.D. Ambani and Shri A.D. Ambani. The Committee, *inter alia,* approves issue of duplicate certificates and oversees and reviews all matters connected with the securities transfers. The Committee also looks into redressal of shareholders' complaints like transfer of shares, non-receipt of balance sheet, non-receipt of declared dividends, etc. The Committee oversees the performance of the Registrar and Transfer Agents, and recommends measures for overall improvement in the quality of investor services. The Board of Directors have delegated the power of approving transfer of securities to the Managing Directors and the Company Secretary.

In pursuance of the Securities and Exchange Board of India (Prohibition of Insider Trading) Regulations, 1992 (duly amended), the Board has approved the "Code of Conduct for Prevention of Insider Trading" and authorised the Committee to implement and monitor the various requirements as set out in the Code.

The Board has designated Shri Rohit C. Shah, Vice-President and Company Secretary, as the Compliance Officer.

The total number of complaints received and replied to the satisfaction of shareholders during the year under review, was 16285. Outstanding complaints as on 31st March, 2003 were Nil. 213 requests for transfers and 1618 requests for dematerialisation were pending for approval as on 31st March, 2003, which were approved and dealt with by 1st April, 2003 and 3rd April, 2003 respectively.

(iv) Finance Committee

The Board of Directors of the Company has constituted the Finance Committee to make recommendations to the Board relating to capital structure and the issuance of securities, review banking arrangements and cash management, and review and approve certain short-term and long-term investment and other financial transactions.

The Finance Committee meets as and when the need to consider any matter assigned to it arises. Time schedule for holding the meetings of the Finance Committee is finalised, in consultation with the Committee Members

B. Functional Committees

The Board may, from time to time, constitute one or more Functional Committees delegating powers and duties with respect to specific purposes. Meetings of such Committees will be held as and when the need for discussing the matter concerning the purpose arises. Time schedule for holding the meetings of such functional committee(s) are finalized in consultation with the Committee Members.

C. Procedures at Committee Meetings

Company's guidelines relating to Board Meetings are applicable to Committee Meetings as far as may be practicable. Each Committee has the authority to engage outside experts, advisers and counsels to the extent it considers appropriate to assist the Committee in its work. Minutes of the proceedings of the each of the committee meetings are placed before the Board for its perusal and noting.

7. Annual General Meetings

Location and time for last 3 Annual General Meetings were as follows:

Year	*Location*	*Date*	*Time*
1999-00	Birla Matushri Sabhagar, 19, Marine Lines, Mumbai 400 020	13th June, 2000	11.00 a.m.
2000-01	Same as above	15th June, 2001	11.00 a.m.
2001-02	Same as above	31st October, 2002	11.00 a.m.

During the year ended 31st March, 2003, there have been no resolutions passed by the Company's shareholders through postal ballot. At the ensuing Annual General Meeting, there is no resolution proposed to be passed by postal ballot.

8. (a) Disclosures on materially significant related party transactions, i.e. transactions of the Company of material nature, with its promoters, the directors or the management, their subsidiaries or relatives, etc. that may have potential conflict with the interests of the Company at large.

None of the transactions with any of the related parties were in conflict with the interest of the Company.

(b) Details of non-compliance by the Company, penalties, strictures imposed on the Company by Stock Exchanges or SEBI, or any statutory authority, on any matter related to capital markets, during the last three years.

SEBI has imposed a monetary penalty of Rs. 4.75 lakhs on the Company for the alleged non-disclosure under Regulation 7(1) of the Securities and Exchange Board of India (Substantial Acquisition of Shares and Takeovers) Regulations, 1997, in respect of acquisition of shares of a listed Company. The Company has preferred an appeal to the Hon'ble Securities Appellate Tribunal against the said order of SEBI and the said appeal is pending.

9. Means of Communication

Half-yearly un-audited financial results

Half-yearly un-audited financial results for the half-year ended 30th September, 2002 were sent to each household of shareholders.

Quarterly results

The quarterly results were published in 'Financial Express' and 'Tarun Bharat', alongwith the official news release, and the detailed presentations made to the media, analysts, institutional investors, etc. were displayed on the corporate website, www.ril.com

The Management Discussion and Analysis (MD&A) is a part of the annual report, and each quarterly official media release.

ANNEXURE III

A TAKE ON MICROSOFT AS A GOOD CITIZEN

JOHN CARROLL*

In honour of my (John Caroll) one-time favourite late-night talk show, I present the top 10 reasons why Microsoft is a good corporate citizen.

10. Microsoft drives computing cost down

With all the rhetoric surrounding Linux and its "free" status, it is often forgotten why consumers (Linux users included) pay so little for computer hardware these days. Not only have Microsoft's desktop efforts led to greater hardware economics of scale, the company has actively worked to drive down hardware prices through standard PC specifications, including simple things like the WinModem.

Though WinModems drive Linux usefulness to distraction, the reason WinModems exist is that they cost less, saving consumers on new PCs.

Furthermore, let's not forget that Microsoft has historically charged far less than its proprietary cousins. Compared to Sun Microsystems' high-priced Unix servers. Oracle's incredibly expensive database and the price combo of Apple hardware with ANY Apple OS, Microsoft products have been an incredible bargain.

9. Microsoft has been instrumental in bringing computing to ordinary people

Although that might be a "negative" for those who don't want to be bothered by hordes of "newbies", non-technical computer users wouldn't be on the Internet if it weren't for hand-holding from companies such as AOL and, of course, Microsoft. Though its marketing and products, Microsoft has done more than any other company to help users find ways to integrate computing into their daily lives.

8. Microsoft employees absolutely love their company

Microsoft regularly is ranked one of the best places to work. Programmes are respected, and creativity is encouraged. Plus, the company pays well to

* John Carroll, In arrangement with www.zdnetindia.com

boot. That leads to one of the lowest employee turnover rates in the industry, even at a time when the company is in the midst of a government suit which has dragged its name through the mud.

7. Microsoft pays loads in taxes

According to information found on Yahoo Financials, Microsoft paid $ 1.288 billion in income taxes for the fiscal quarter ended March 31.

6. Its founder has donated more money to charity than anyone in history

At the last count, Bill Gates, as an individual, has given about $ 22 billion—or just under 26 aircraft carriers— to charity. To put that in perspective, George Soros' donations as an individual total a "merely" $ 2 billion. Andrew Cornegie, the famed philanthropist, gave only $ 3 billion in current dollars over the course of his life.

5. Microsoft creates a computing economy worth far greater than its own net worth

If one counts up all the companies that develop Windows-compatible software (including such industry luminaries such as Oracle and IBM), all the hardware companies that make money selling to Windows users, and all the technicians engaged in writing software for Windows or providing technical support for it, you'll find that there is far more money made from Microsoft products outside of Redmond than is made of it.

4. One of the largest R&D budgets in the industry

In fiscal year 2001, Microsoft spent $ 4.4 billion, a spending total that rose to more than $ 5 billion in fiscal year 2002. R&D benefits us all through technological advancements. Though developing software that is more productive might not seem as earth-shattering as, say, finding a cure for cancer, such advances improve the efficiency of the digital infrastructure upon which we build our lives.

3. Microsoft takes risks

This might seem a strange reason to consider Microsoft a good corporate citizen, but consider the results. How many companies would have the courage—much less the stamina—to take on Sony in game consoles, Palm computing in handhelds, Sun in server operating systems, Oracle and IBM in databases, AOL in Internet access, and practically every wireless phone-maker in existence (Nokia and Ericsson among them) in the provision of operating systems for advanced cell phones? Not many.

Microsoft is the primary competitor to these leading companies in most of these markets, which helps boost quality and innovation. I might be going off on a tangent, but if Microsoft can enter already dominated markets and manage to keep its head above water, why can't other large companies compete in markets Microsoft dominates?

2. A beacon of profitability in a sea of red ink

Microsoft is one of the few companies to have managed to maintain robust sales throughout the current recession. That should matter to those who care about the health of the US economy. And last but not least . . .

1. No accounting scandals at Microsoft

In contrast to all the revenue-padding at Enron, WorldCom and even AOL, Microsoft was prompted by the Securities and Exchange Commission to adjust its past income upwards. So there you have it. My apologies to David Letterman for dragging him into the mother of all greek wars.

Reference

John Carroll, www.zdetindia.com and *Economic Times*, New Delhi.

ANNEXURE IV

BUSINESS FULFILS ITS CORPORATE RESPONSIBILITIES—A CASE STUDY OF HLL

We discuss the role currently played by business and its leaders, and to assess how it should evolve, given the current global context.

Is shareholder value the singular measure of a business capability, success and contribution? Surely not. Recent events like the dotcom bust and events in corporate America have certainly shown that we need to move beyond the mere metric of the stock market. Business has several stakeholders—Employees, Customers, Suppliers, Government, and of course the Community at large, apart from our Shareholders. Each of these groups has different anticipations from us each expects us to make a different kind of contribution. The sum total of these contributions, across all of business, can potentially have a very broad impact on society—and I dare say, even on the nation. This is not only true for India—it is true globally.

I were to share with you our perspective on how we in Hindustan Lever are trying to achieve this across our various constituencies. A key stakeholder for us is the Government. HLL has always believed and practised that "What is good for India, is good for HLL." We were the first company to voluntarily disinvest 10% of the Unilever holding in 1956 to local shareholders. Since then, there has been progressive disinvestment of the Unilever shareholding, essentially to attract local ownership to a point where today only 52% of the company is held by Unilever and the rest by 350,000 local shareholders and financial institutions. Our local shareholding brings us several benefits—it helps us identify very clearly with national interest. It also provides a greater degree of accountability for performance.

Another example is our commitment to growing exports and foreign exchange earnings. We are already one of India's largest exporters with a total export of over Rs. 1500 crores last year, and have been rated a Super Star Trading House for several years by the Government of India. Indeed, we believe that we can grow our exports strongly and sustainably by leveraging on our strengths to source products for other Unilever countries, and also by focussing on areas where India has a natural country advantage like Marine Products.

A couple of years ago, we were the first company to avail of the Government's disinvestment policy with the acquisition of the loss-making Modern Foods. Within a couple of years, we have been able to double its sales, reduce its cost base and bring it to breakeven this year. We believe this is a good illustration of our professional management and of course, the very principles of disinvestment.

We are also collaborating with the Government and other agencies to uplift the general level of social development. Let me give you one example. Not many people know that diarrhoea is the largest cause of children's deaths, accounting for over 2 million fatalities globally each year, 30% of which are in India. The cause is poor hand hygiene—a large number of people do not wash their hands before eating or after personal hygiene practices. The result—germs are transferred from the hand to the mouth and the result is a disaster for human life. In October, we are launching a massive programme in the State of Kerala to educate the population on the need to wash their hands with soap.

Last, but not the least, we take very seriously our responsibility of associating with the Government in various forums, providing information, insight and advice on policy formation and implementation.

Another major stakeholder is the *Community at large*. We have, over the years, established 15 manufacturing units in various backward areas. Many of these were barren lands with no infrastructure when we arrived. It is today a source of great pride to see vibrant factories with skilled manpower, as well as local ancillary industries to support us, contributing to the local economy and prosperity. Importantly, these units are not merely cutting edge in India—they are world class both in quality and cost! Many of these units are also involved in several community initiatives—adult education, running of schools, etc.—and often become a catalyst for social improvement.

Another example of our commitment to the Community is the work we are doing with Self Help Groups in Andhra Pradesh, in partnership with several NGOs. The women in these Self Help Groups can access micro-credit from NABARD and are in search of a viable enterprise model. That is where we come in. We provide them with the opportunity to educate others in the villages on the nutritional and hygiene benefits of our brands and also to retail these.

We are totally committed to protecting our environment PTO. Several initiatives are under way. Our load on the environment has reduced dramatically—specifically, our energy and water requirements have halved in five years. Our plants do not discharge effluents and we are leading efforts towards harnessing water and greening the environment. In our tea plantations, we are working to ensure their sustainability. A good example is the conversion of waste from our workers' homes to natural fertiliser, using vermin composting, thereby reducing our use of chemical fertilisers.

Let me now turn to our *Shareholders*. They are obviously interested in a fair return on their capital. However, I believe our shareholders are not looking for a fast buck with the concomitant risks attached with it. They are interested in steady, long-term appreciation, and we are determined to deliver this—and we have. Over the last five years, we have delivered a growth of 300% to them. Our EVA has trebled over the last five years, growing consistently at over 30% p.a. But they also require transparency. They want information. They want to know how we are managing their company. What is the strategy that is being followed? How well is it being implemented? Who are the key people running it? And it is their right to know—after all, they are the owners. Many see this as an unnecessary intrusion—a burden. At HLL, we welcome this and indeed try and provide as much information as possible. We provide detailed financial updates every quarter. We were amongst the first to lead with segmental reporting. Our Balance Sheet runs into 50 pages and provides all the information we sensibly can. In January 2001, we developed a new strategy to take into account changes in the competitive environment in a more open India. We shared this with all our investors and now regularly review our progress against this. We hold analyst meets very six months, attend investor conferences and of course, meet individual investors as required. We also get them to meet our other senior people, and all that we say is immediately put on our web site making it available to every investor—current or potential. We never brief investors selectively. Our smaller individual shareholders also have several opportunities to access information, including at our AGMs, which are very well attended—the last one had 10,000 people. It is our practice to answer every single question that is raised, even if it means that our meeting often lasts for 6-8 hours.

Let me now turn to another important group—*our Employees*. Of course, we reward them well, and place a great emphasis on linking reward with performance. But What is only a small part of our contract with them. We do believe that people are not motivated by money alone. Their main motivation in working with us is to pursue their own development and growth. In this context, we provide a culture of complete meritocracy. Every individual manager, salesman, factory worker, joins after a very thorough selection process and justifiably feels an enormous sense of pride at being selected. Each manager's contribution in the year is thoroughly assessed against agreed targets and openly communicated to him, including areas of further development. All promotions are on merit. Each opportunity is advertised within the company and any manager who fulfils the required experience criteria can apply. A due selection process is followed—very similar to the one for entry to the company —and the best candidate selected. Each person who is not selected is told why he has not made it. Do people value this? Yes, definitely. Our attrition rate is relatively low at 6-7% p.a. Also, last year, we were rated as the No. 1 employer in a survey of all leading business schools.

I could go on like this about our other stakeholders . . . the Consumers,

Customers, Suppliers, etc. . . . but shall not do so for want of time. Thus far, I have been telling you what we have done to meet the expectations of our various stakeholders. Let me now move to talking about how we have been able to create an *organisation culture of responsibility*.

HLL follows a very *strong Code of Business Principles*—a framework that is available to each of our employees. Every manager is given a copy as he joins and there are several forums at which these are discussed and reiterated. Violation of this code is simply not tolerated. You can make any number of mistakes in a business sense, as long as you learn from them. However, you cannot go against the code. Let me give you some examples that will show you how we enforce this.

A few years ago, the terrorists in North East India threatened the safety of our management unless we provided 'safety money'. It took us virtually no time to decide that we simply could never accede to such a request. Overnight, we decided to close down our plantations and fly our managers and their families to safety. We chartered an Indian Airlines plane and flew it into that area at night, and evacuated all our people under cover of the Indian Army. This, of course, had considerable implications, both in terms of cost and the publicity that we received, but we were simply not prepared to succumb to unlawful demands and operate under threat. We went back into Assam only several months later, when we were assured of the Government's intent and ability to protect our people.

In another case, we were opening a new factory. A Factory Inspector wanted us to employ a person known to him. The individual concerned was tested, but regrettably was not selected as he failed the skills test. We provided feedback, both to the candidate and the Inspector, and offered to re-test him after he had improved his skills base. The Inspector took great umbrage at this and refused to allow us to open the factory on some spurious technical grounds. Every week's delay cost us a lot as our investment was idle, but we stood our ground. We fought the matter all the way up the bureaucratic hierarchy till our stand was upheld.

Recently, we built a new office building of about 30,000 sq. ft. When it was ready, we discovered that we had inadvertently built about 300 sq. ft. extra which was not in the plan. This was, of course, challenged by the authorities who saw in this a way for them to seek favour. It would have been quite easy for us to resolve the matter in some way, but we chose not to do so. We appealed to the higher authorities that this was a genuine mistake. When this was not accepted, we decided to demolish the 300 sq. ft. that was extra so that there would then be no reason for them not to give us an occupancy certificate. The whole process delayed us by a few months, but we were determined to secure occupancy in the right way.

In each of these cases, we have had to bear a short-term cost. This has never impacted our determination to uphold our way of doing business. In general, today, there is a lot of cynicism about whether you can do business in the right way. Our experience is that you can. But only if you are prepared to fight for it. The good news is that once you establish a reputation for being principled, you are not persecuted—your reputation is your armour!

We have also identified and articulated a very clear set of values for the company. Why? Because these values provide a moral framework by which our people can view their own actions. Values also provide a very aspirational environment—they attract like-minded people into the company and help to bind them together. So what are the HLL values?

HLL Values

We expect our managers to live by the values of TRUTH, COURAGE, ACTION and CARING. At one level, these appear very naive words. However, when you think deeply about them, and then apply them to all situations, they have a very profound meaning.

Truth

What is truth? Some call it candour, honesty. What does it give us? Truth helps us acknowledge the problems as they arise, so that we spend the rest of our time dealing with them—not denying them.

Truth helps us to be honest with each other—to tell each other what we really feel, of course, to get truth, you have to be a good listener. We have to be open to feedback and pick up signals.

A very important precursor to truth is trust—and trust comes from knowing each other better. So we encourage our teams to really get to know each other—to spend time together, to eat together, to spend time outside the office together with their families. We are also using 360 degrees feedback throughout the entire organisation to bring about greater openness, greater trust, and greater truth.

Courage

Another value is Courage. Courage is about inner confidence. Courage is about conviction. Courage is about betting. Courage is about saying, "I will do this because it will work." But courage is not recklessness. Courage comes from knowledge. Courage comes from rigour. If you have done your homework, you will have plenty of courage. Courage is also about doing what is not obvious. We have recently decided to focus our attention and resource of key brands in our FMCG businesses. We had two very successful businesses—Seeds and Flavours and Fragrances—both growing and very profitable. A convenient decision would have been to keep them for now, at a time when growth is hard to come by. But we took the courageous decision to let them go—we parted with two highly successful businesses so we could concentrate our efforts on our key brands.

Action

Our third value is Action. This is quite simple. Wars are not won because of the battle plan. They are won in the trenches, on the hills of Kargil, by what people do. So we must move. We must move with great speed. We must move with great precision. We must move with great excellence. Last year, we faced the challenge of putting up additional capacity in a short time. Our teams took an impossible target, and put up 6 factories in different corners of India in just 9 months.

Caring

Last, but definitely not the least, is the value of Caring—caring for each other, for each other's families, sharing the joy of good times, sharing the sorrow of difficult times. Tragedies do happen everywhere. One thing is for sure—the HLL families are secure in the knowledge that they will be taken care of in every eventuality—the very best medical care in the world, a determination to protect the lifestyle of the family and children's education in the event of a premature death. But caring is not being soft. Caring is about really feeling for the other person. Caring is about being honest to a person about his potential, even if the truth is difficult. Caring is knowing that every person has only one life to live and you owe it to him or her to be totally honest.

So these then are the values of HLL. We expect all our managers to live by these. How do we ensure that? We have involved a large number of them in identifying the specific behaviours that best exemplify these values and also those that contradict them in each function. These desirable and undesirable behaviours have been widely publicised throughout the company. Those who live by these values are celebrated-eulogised, written about.

Cultures are built by leaders and driven by the people. I am here reminded of a wonderful story told to me by Prakash Tandon, the first Indian Chairman of HLL. He was once asked as to what qualities he would look for in his successor. He replied unhesitatingly, in one word—"character." Today when we recruit people, we of course look for professional competence, but much more that, we look for people who have integrity. Integrity, because they will have the ability to objectively assess reality and give both good and bad news. We also look for self-confidence. We need people who have faith in themselves, even in the face of immense adversity—people who can and will make a difference, to their organisations and to India.

In conclusion, I would say this. Business leaders can, of course, play a major role in driving shareholder value, but they can do much more. They can build a very positive relationship with all the other stakeholders—and through these wide ranging relationships, they can make a very broad impact on society, and indeed on India. I would also like to say that employees increasingly wish to work in organisations, which, of course, are commercially successful, but in addition, make a positive contribution to society. I have also no doubt that consumers too will increasingly choose brands, not just on the basis of the brand benefit, but on the value systems of the company behind the brand. The interest and appreciation that employees, consumers and shareholders show, in how a business fulfils its corporate responsibilities, helps build a virtuous cycle of greater commitment from the business and greater trust from the stakeholders.

Reference

This an Extract from the Text of the address delivered by Mr. M.S. Banga, Chairman, HLL at the CII Leadership Summit, New Delhi on September 18, 2002. Gratefully acknowledged.

ANNEXURE V

ETHICS IN ADVERTISING

Ethics is a choice between good and bad, between right and wrong. It is governed by a set of principles of morality at a given time and at a given place. Ethics is related to group behaviour in ultimate analysis, thus setting norms for an individual to follow in accordance with the group norms.

Advertising too has ethical values. Advertising communication is a mix of art and facts subservient to ethical principles. In order to be consumer-oriented, an advertisement will have to be truthful and ethical. A hundred years ago the ethical standards of business were different from what is considered appropriate today. Some deception or a little tilt towards the unethical was taken for granted by both buyers and sellers and the credo was 'let the buyer beware'. But as the buyer become more sophisticated, businesses became more stable and pressures for reforms from consumers and government increased advertising practices changed considerably. It is because of the change, which has taken place that the ethical effects of advertising are favourite targets for critics. Ethical standards vary among cultural, religious, racial, age and other groups.

What is Ethical Advertising

Any advertisement that can be termed ethical is one:

- Which contains truth, although not absolute truth but socially accepted standard of honesty as truth.
- Which is right in its approach and claims.
- Which keeps in view social morality.
- Which observes the relevant laws framed to keep the scene ethical.

What Exactly is Unethical Advertising

Unethical advertisements are those:

- Which degrade rival products or substitute products.
- Which give misleading information.

- Which give false information.
- Which conceal important information that vitally affects human life.
- Which make exaggerated or tall claims.
- Which is obscene or immoral.
- Which is against the national and public interest.

After looking into what is ethical and what is not it becomes imperative to find out whether modern Indian advertising is ethical or not. Degrading ads are unethical which speaks ill about rival 'products or brand'. It is obvious that it would result in counter attempts by the rival. The scene is flooded with ads which reflect conflicts between products and brands. Let us look into competing ads in visual media The most striking example is the ad war between the soft drink giants, Pepsi and Coca-Cola. Their rivalry is cut throat, none of them is prepared to let the other improve its market share. Every action follows a counter action.

Obscene or ads resorting to sex can be categorized as unethical. It is very difficult to single out a product category, which doesn't have an obscene ad. There are scores of ads which use women as a sex object just to make more ads more glossy. In the present scenario, what advertising has actually done is that it has opened up the whole area of sex that has been under wraps since centuries in India. Ad men are definitely guilty of beauty abuse, they are more and more inclined to creating erotic or sensuous ads aimed at titillating men.

In the promos of music cassettes and C.Ds, the women models are so seductively clad that they appear to be acting in porno movies. Recently there was news item in a prominent channel that people have shown their concern at the growing sex projections in'Bhangra pops' promos and there has been a strong demand of censorship for such promos.

Ads resorting to untruthful and unverifiable claims too are unethical. Ads offering products and medicines which promises fairness, beauty, loss of weight, hair growth, growth in height, increase in sexual energy, Improvement in health and strength can be placed in this category.

Same is the case with ads of hair growth or increase in height or increase in memory power, they are simply an exaggeration because there is just no way to verify such claims.

Ads of cigarretes and alcohol fall in the category of unethical (in the Indian context. 'Ethic in Indian advertising is passe'. One out of every three ads is resorting to unethical practices. Now the question is, so many unethical ads, what about the legal provisions or regulatory norms? Why not there are provisions of MRTP Act, Consumer Protection Act, Security and Exchange

Board of India, Drugs and Magic Remedies (Objectionable Advertisements) Act and Trade Marks Act. There are codes of Doordarshan, All Indian Radio, Indian Newspapers Society and the Cable TV Networks (Regulation) Act and as an effort of self-regulation there are codes of conducts of both CFBP (Council for Fair Business Practice) and ASCI (Advertising Standard Council of India). Code for Commercial Advertising on Doordarshan suggests 33 Do's and Don'ts for advertisers. MRTP Commission is a statutory body set-up to protect the interest of consumers by preventing restrictive trade practices. CPA has regulatory provisions to be enforced through the redressal of grievance by a three-tier, quasi-judicial machinery, set-up at the district, state and the national levels, known as the District Consumer Disputes Redressal Forum, the State Consumer Dispute Redress Commission and the National Consumer Disputes Redresses Commission respectively. A complaint against misleading or deceptive advertising can be filed in the appropriate consumer court by any consumer or recognized consumers' association of the Central Government or the State Government. The Drugs and Magic Remedies (Objectionable Advertisements) Act seeks to curb undesirable advertisements pertaining to drugs and magic remedies as such advertising was considered to encourage self-medication of harmful drugs. False and misleading advertisement may also attract regulatory measures provided in the Trade Marks Act, 1999. The provisions are intended to prevent the use of fraudulent marks and thereby protect the interest of consumers as well as legitimate businessmen. The Guidelines on advertisements contained in the SEBI (Disclosure and Investor Protection) Guidelines, 2000, provide that an advertisement for the issue of shares, etc. must be truthful, fair and clear and should not contain any statement which is untrue or misleading. ASCI is a voluntary organization of advertisers, advertising agencies and the media. ASCI has adopted the Code of Self Regulation in Advertising, which is intended to control offensive contents of advertisement. ASCI also entertains complaints against advertisements, which are considered by the Consumer Complaints Council (CCC), a 14 member sub-committee consisting of people from various walks of life. Codes for advertising have also been developed by Indian Newspapers Society (INS) and All India Radio but they lack legal backing and are not effectively enforced.

Inspite of these regulations norms and codes for the control of unfair deceptive and misleading advertising in India, the practice continues almost unabated and unethical ads are increasing day by day. The most prominent reason is that consumers are unaware of their rights against unscrupulous businessmen indulging in unethical practices. Along with this there is no censorship at the launching stage. Once an advertisement is launched it can be withdrawn only if complaints are lodged and it is the verdict of the competent authority that the ad is unethical or against the norms specified. As we find that normally people are unaware of the procedure of stopping what they feel is unethical and one has to admit, are complainant and therefore, there is reluctance and very few complaints are lodged with the competent authorities.

The comprehensive legal framework for the control of deceptive, unfair and misleading advertisements can be meaningful only when the *consumers and their organizations assert their right against unethical ads*. The enforcement agencies should make efforts to create the required awareness. Along with creating awareness there can be a Censorship for advertisements, which would see the advertisements to be launched commonly with the norms and provisions which are essential to keep the scene ethical. The NGOs should also make efforts to create the required awareness among the consumers and should help them in their pursuit against unethical ads. Along with it they, themselves should take initiative to stop what they feel is against the interest of the public. ASCI too should ensure that the required awareness about the Codes of Self Regulation in Advertising is created among the practitioners in advertising as well as the consumers.

To conclude, it can be said that advertisements should conform to laws and should not resort to immorality and indecency. Advertisers should fulfil their obligations towards the society. The success of advertising and products depends on public confidence and no practice should be permitted to impair this.

Unethical Approach to Build and Maintain Customer Relationship

Following unethical ways are also normally adopted towards building customer relationship. However, readers must note that these unethical practices are brought to your attention only for creating an awareness and not for application.

Addiction: Creating a sense of addiction to the brand by adding ingradients that are harmful to body and mind, as in the case of beverages, soft drinks, food items, etc.

Fear: Developing a sense of fear in the mind of the customers, that once a brand is continuously used, any brand switchover would cause problems as in the case of cosmetics, food, drinks, medicines, etc.

Imitating: Imitating the attributes of well-accepted brands in an unlawful way.

Promises: Making promises to customers with no intentions to perform.

Commitment: Developing misleading commitments and obligations.

Discrimination: Discrimination on the quality and services among buyers.

Forcing: Making tie-up sales with other highly preferred items.

Rewarding: Extending undue benefits in the forms of cash or equal means of benefit to the members of purchase team in case of industrial organisational purchase.

Insisting on sentiments:	Making use of the faith of the sentiments of customers to the best advantage of the organisation.
Communal Affiliation:	Extending communal affiliation and drawing the attention of customers of selected community.
Negative Publicity:	Making negative publicity to competitors' brand.

Many more unethical ways are also being practised towards building relationship. However, a customer can be retained permanently only by means of quality products and services.

Source: Dr. Anand Sen Gupta, Ashish Kumar Srivastava, Gorakhpur University, Gorakhpur, "Ethics in Advertising is Passe", *Indian Journal of Marketing*. This is an abstract of the article. Gratefully Acknowledged.

ANNEXURE VI

CORPORATE SOCIAL RESPONSIBILITY (CSR) AT GLAXO SMITH KLINE PHARMACEUTICALS LIMITED, INDIA

A company is linked closely to the communities in which it operates locally, nationally or globally. It cannot exist in isolation.
—*Sir Richard Skyes*, Chairman, GlaxoWellcome plc

I. Introduction to CSR

Companies operating in globalised markets are increasingly required to balance the financial and economic considerations of their business with social, community and environmental aspects as well, while building shareholder value.

The socially responsible business is attracting some of the best business minds, as numerous initiatives seek to identify the issues and create the tools to implement programmes at the company level. For different industries, responsible business practice involves different issues.

As Mc Williams & Siegel have said, "Corporate Social Responsibility are actions above and beyond that required by law." The voluntary actions of the companies for the benefit of the community is what CSR is about.

Corporate Reasons for Response

CSR is designed to deliver sustainable value not only to the shareholders but also to the society at large.

According to the CSR Survey 2002 (India) Report, Indian companies see corporate social responsibility as central to corporate action, with "excessive philanthropy" no longer a sufficient response to rising expectations of the society. The above mentioned report surveyed 102 Indian companies and was conducted jointly by the United Nations Development Programme, the British Council, Confederation of Indian Industry and Pricewaterhouse Coopers. The report found that the most important driver for involvement in CSR within Indian industry was the desire to be a good corporate citizen, linked to company as well as product/brand reputation. Improved ties with local communities was also seen as a strong factor.

The authors have surveyed most of the large corporates, both national and multinational, and have observed that corporates undertake CSR activities due to the feeling of community belongingness.

In this article presented a case of an Indian Pharmaceutical Company's responsibility towards the community through its CSR-related activities.

2. Glaxo Smith Kline Pharmaceuticals Limited, India

Gluxo Smith Kline Pharmaceuticals Ltd. is India's leading Pharmaceutical company with a market share of over 6.6 per cent. The company markets a wide range of ethical formulations and is the leader in therapeutic areas of respiratory, dermatology and vaccines, besides having a significant presence in areas of gastroenterology, dietary supplements, and intensive care. Glaxo Smith Kline [GSK] is also the undisputed leader in animal health and fine chemicals businesses. CSR's strategic intent is to become the undisputable leader in its industry—not simply in terms of size, but in how it uses that size to achieve its mission. Through its Global Community Partnerships function and Corporate Donations Committee, GSK partners wish and *supports organisations whose goals and objectives reflect its mission* of improving the quality of human life.

The company has manufacturing units in India, located at Thane, Nasik, Mysore and Bangalore. Operational Excellence is the buzzword at GMS, a new global improvement programme that will drive change, increase efficiency and raise quality standards in every process.

GSK employs over 4000 skilled persons across the country. The company has the largest field force in the industry and a nation-wide network of about 4000 dealers. This gives the company a wide reach across the nation in its efforts to strengthen the hands of the doctor in his fight against diseases. GSK is the largest prescription generator in the indusry.

Glaxo Smith Kline plc is the world's leading research-based pharmaceutical and healthcare company.

A truly global organization with a wide geographical spread, GiaxoSmithlKline has its corporate headquarters in West London, UK. The company has over 1,00,000 employees and supplies its products to 140 markets around the world. It has one of the largest sales and marketing operations in the global pharmaceutical industry.

GSK's global quest is to improve the quality of human life by enabling people to do more, feel better and live longer.

GSK's *community investment programmes* represent a commitment that, as the company builds upon its successes and grows, it will continue to recognise the responsibility of leadership and the strength of partnership.

This commitment is maintained through a blend of innovative and more established philanthropy and sponsorships, and initiatives in global public health.

The company's flagship community programme is its key role in the Global Alliance to Eliminate Lymphatic Filariasis—a 20 year programme to eliminate one of the world's most disfiguring and disabling diseases.

3. GSK's Core Value—We Care

Being a premier pharmaceutical company in the country GSK's core value is to be a good corporate citizen. It is committed to the communities in which it works. Suppinrt to the community through charitble initiatives is the ways through which it invests in society.

To GSK being a good corporate citizen means:

- being proactive in improving the environment,
- participating in and contributing to the well being of the local community, and
- actively contributing to national priorities in health and safety.

At Glaxo Smith Kline, India, the activities towards community development are attached to the Corporate Communications Department. There is also a Community Welfare & Social Activities Department.

Mr. N.Y. Sanglikar, Sr. G.M. states that the organization performs Socially Responsible activities as a sincere attempt to give back to the society what it earns from it. GSK believes that it owes its services to the community.

Mr. Sanglikar stated that the initiatives are mainly towards Women and Children and the focus areas are Education, Hygiene and Health, because, the company believes that the three areas are related and of direct concern to GSK. If there is proper education will one eventually learn to be hygienic, and if one is hygienic will one remain healthy. He adds that the organization facilitates towards educating masses on good practices of healthy living.

The assistance given is always need-based; there is no budget driven expenditure. This implies that there is no planned expenditure towards community development, but an impulsive attempt to uplift the needy whenever it is possible.

4. Programmes undertaken by the Social Work Unit of GSK

Since 1970's the company has been implementing various social responsibility programmes apart from the statutory ones. The following Communities Development activities are carried out:

(a) Child Welfare at Koliwada, Mumbai

In 1979, 'the International Year of the Child', the employees of the heritage company Glaxo India promoted this charitable trust for the development of the financially disadvantaged children deprived of opportunities such as basic education, healthcare and recreation. It aims at promoting the physical, intellectual, emotional and psychological development of needy children. The SSSS runs a Modern Care Centre which provides comprehensive health check-up and treatment.

An initiation of the social workers has enabled rehabilitation of a few mentally and physically challenged children, which was a task beyond the reach of the parents.

(b) Rural Development: Gramin Arogya Vikas Sanstha (GAVS) at Dhondbar Village

The Sanstha (Organization) works in Dhondbar village in Sinnar taluka, Nasik district. Inaccessibility, low literacy level, absence of any NGO and paucity of basic healthcare facilities characterized the village. Ms. Pooja highlighted the fact that before their adoption of the villages, the literacy level was zero, today, many of the adolescents know to read and write. The trust, sanctioned of an amount of 11 crores and the organization ensured that the funds were utilized in the most effective way.

(c) Quality Streets Circle at Worli, Mumbai

In 1990, Glaxo initiated a unique project—Quality Streets Circle (QSC), which is an association of over 25 business establishments located around the Glaxo & Wellcome headquarters in Worli. The objective of QSC is to maintain clean and healthy civic environment in the neighbourhood. It tackles various civic issues through collective action and so far has been successful in removal of some unauthorized construction, widening and beautification of the roads and pavements in the vicinity and installation of post boxes. QSC has developed a positive working relationship with the Mumbai Municipal Corporation, the local ward office.

(d) Glaxo HIV/AIDS Help Line

The company launched a 24 hours phone in help line in October 2000, as a unique and innovative initiative for counseling and dissemination of information on HIV/AIDS to the lay public in Mumbai. A highly trained and experienced team of counselor answers thousands of callers at the help line. GSK's help line was rated as the best help line on the subject in India. The organization provides HIV/AIDS drugs at discounted price.

(e) Positive Action on HIV/AIDS

Positive Action is GSK's long-term, international programme of HIV education, care and community support.

(f) The Fight Against Malaria

GSK has been active in the fight against malaria for many years.

(g) Audio Visuals for Promoting Health Awareness

A series of public health audio visuals on balanced diet, prevention of TB and AIDS, environment protection, primary healthcare for infants and consumer rights and responsibilities have been produced by Glaxo. These are screened for various audiences including voluntary and Government bodies.

(h) Medical Education for Health Professionals

A subsidized teaching aids programme for doctors and health professionals was implemented by GSK.

(i) Science Education Programmes for the Youth.

(j) Product Donations for Humanitarian Relief Efforts

Such donations are made at the request of government and major charitable organisations.

(k) Eco Consciousness

Treating effluent, planting trees and energy conservation form the thrust of this programme. The nature of the company's business points to the generation of effluents. Effluent Treatment Plants (ETP) are in operation at all sites and the treated water is used for gardening. Solid and chemical waste is also disposed off in a way as to protect the environment from damage. Tree plantation is an ongoing process at GSK sites.

(l) Employee Development through Cultural, Social and Educational Programmes.

(m) Employee Involvement

GSK has more than 5000 employees in India, all of whom have been drawn together to assist in the fight against human disease and suffering. Employees are encouraged to take advantage of the company's employee volunteering support scheme.

(n) Helping the Physically Challenged

GSK has been the employer of a large number of disabled persons in all its four factories and has won awards from voluntary bodies and the Government in recognition for the same.

(o) Financial and Infrastructure Support to Voluntary Bodies

GSK supports the needy organizations and causes by way of cash donations, souvenir advertisements and medicines.

GSK's contribution to those affected by natural calamities, like the earthquake at Latur and the cyclone in Gujarat has always been swift.

5. Final Observations and Summary

- Most of the CSR activities revolve around their core business activity, mainly healthcare. GSK's products and business operations therefore focuses on improving the health and quality of life of people throughout the country.
- GSK stresses on the importance of education to lead a healthy life.
- The programme of charitable and community contribution is an aspect of the activity which the company regards as a proper part of its set role in society to be a good corporate citizen worldwide.
- In selecting projects towards social responsibility, equal priority is given to those activities which promote scientific and medical education.
- The presence of a team within GSK to work towards community development explains the organisations' long-term interest in the concept of CSR.

Source: This is an abstract of an article by N.M. Kandop, "Corporate Social Responsibilty" in *NMIMS Journal*, July-December 2003.

ANNEXURE VII

CASE STUDIES ON ETHICS

DON'T STRETCH THE LINE

In the materialistic world that we occupy today, means are becoming less important than the end. The line between right and wrong is thin. It takes a long time to cross the line, but once you do it you are lost for ever. Many a professional who has taken things for granted has got caught unawares, and been disgraced for the rest of his life. You have classic cases of such ruin amongst IAS officers, chairmen of companies, cabinet members and other professionals. You become a vulnerable target, once you cross the thin line. That it is a common practice is no reason for you to follow that is wrong. It is incorrect reasoning. Let me a few examples.

Case Study

I had joined India Pistons as sales manager. A couple of weeks later, the managing director walked into my room and gave me a letter which he wanted me to sign and send to the chairman of the company. I found that the contents did not reflect facts. It also seemed odd that a sales manager who was not a member of the board should write directly to the chairman instead of the managing director. However, I corrected the factual inaccuracies and also mentioned that I was taking the liberty of writing to the chairman directly under the specific instructions of the managing director. When I sent the draft for approval, my managing director rushed to my room and shouted, "I wanted you to sign my letter and not tamper with it." I was forthright in my reply and said, "In the first instance, I do not see any reason why I should write a letter to the chairman. It is your duty to do so; however, though I agreed to follow your instructions, please be clear that I will never make a false statement. You are at liberty to write what you want on your own." I knew that taking such a stand could prove detrimental to my position in the organisation. But my professional integrity was more important. Fortunately, my reply stunned him and he agreed to sign it himself. I had no problem with him thereafter, as he knew that I would not budge on principles or be a party to anything that was wrong.

In the late sixties, the *Indian Express* carried some articles by Shri HVR Iyengar on bureaucracy and the Government. Shri Iyengar recalled an incident when the union minister for industry wanted his secretary to the ministry to review the licence of an industrialist whose application had been rejected. The secretary went through the entire case all over again. Finally, he wrote to the minister that there were no fresh grounds on which they could reconsider the issue and that his original recommendation to reject the licence stood. However, he mentioned that he was prepared to abide by the minister's decision, whatever it may be. The minister had to accept his recommendation and agree to close the file.

A bureaucrat is as much a professional in his own right as an industrial executive. The political interference in the case of government officers is a major issue. While they do not under-estimate the hardship they may have to face by not toeing the line, almost all senior officers agree that they would be in worse trouble if they did something wrong without the written instructions of the superior or the minister.

PRESSURE FROM SUPERIORS

Case Study

Let us consider the example of Gunasekhar, a district forest officer (DFO) located at Visakhapatnam, Andhra Pradesh.

Kannan, a landlord, had encroached into the forest lands of the Government in Andhra Pradesh and various departments of the Government had enquired into the matter. After considerable deliberations, a government order was issued to evict Kannan from the encroached land.

At that time, the minister of forests happened to visit Visakhapatnam, and called the DFO, Mr Gunasekhar, and orally instructed him not to evict Kannan and instead treat the encroachment as a lease. The DFO advised the minister that he had already served notice for eviction as per the government order; however, he would try to see what could be done.

According to government rules, if a written government order is countermanded by the minister, the concerned officer should advise his immediate superior and seek his instructions, with this his responsibility ceases. Accordingly, Mr Gunasekhar advised the chief conservator of forests (CCF) in writing about the oral instructions of the minister which were contrary to the earlier government orders.

> The CCF was angry with the DFO for cornering him instead of following the minister's instructions. He knew there was no way he could allow the encroachment to continue or prevent eviction.
>
> The DFO was a marked man and within a short time some false charges were framed against him to explore the possibility of suspending him. However, the minister and the CCF could not succeed, as Gunasekhar had a spotless record. He was cleared of all the charges after an enquiry and, in due course, got quick promotions. Ultimately Gunasekhar became the chief conservator of forests.

Had Gunasekhar buckled under pressure and fallen into the trap by implementing the oral instructions of the minister, he could have landed himself in trouble, as the action required of him was irregular and the instructions were oral. Probably Gunasekhar had taken a risk by adopting this course of tough action, but if he had compromised it would have been a compromise for all time.

An officer cannot afford to preach, adopting a holier than thou attitude. As there is a constitutional provision for job security for IAS officers, the right approach will be to avoid being a party to any illegal action. By all means be polite, respect the seniors and the minister in charge, but be firm when it comes to falsifying information or acting contrary to government regulations and procedures. While the minister has every right to veto your advice, only when he gives his instructions in writing are you obligated to act on his behalf.

AVOID GOSSIP

Similarly, never be critical of your immediate superior or members of top management and indulge in gossip. This will create all types of problems. You must concern yourself with your work and be "issue-oriented" rather than "person-oriented." Loose talk indicates your immaturity. You must give respect and take respect.

Case Study

> A company held a test to recruit supervisors. The candidate recommended by the chairman of the company was rejected in the normal course as he got single-digit marks in the written test. The chairman was annoyed and wanted to look at the recruiting tests.
>
> The managing director enclosed the recruiting procedures, the test and the answer paper of the candidate; he also stated the reason why the particular candidate was not selected. On seeing these papers, the chairman concurred with the managing director that the company was right in rejecting the candidate.

What do these examples indicate? There is no need for you to be afraid if you are in the right. Never be a party to any false statements. Fear will land you in trouble sometime or the other.

WHY COMPROMISE ALL THE TIME

Case Study

Let me quote a typical case of Kalyanasundaram, a young quality control engineer with five years' experience. He took up the position of chief inspector in a motorcycle factory, reporting directly to the works director, Madhusudhana Rao. Kalyan was competent, knew his job well and was a stickler for quality scrupulously rejecting defective goods. One day the works director called him and said, I will tell you what to reject and what to pass. You cannot hold up production by being too rigid." He replied, "Yes, sir", and was terrified to confront the works director, whose instructions were all oral. If the works director had authorised a deviation in writing, there would not have been any problem. It happened that a few weeks later a bulk consignment worth Rs. 20 lakhs was rejected by the defence ministry as not conforming to the quality standards. There was an uproar and when the works director was hauled up to give an explanation by the board, he simply held the chief inspector responsible for passing the defectives and Kalyan was sacked on the spot.

WHAT DOES THIS CASE TELL YOU?

Even though Kalyanasundaram was innocent, he was taken for a ride by his works director and made the scapegoat. In the first instance, he should never have compromised with quality standards. It is against all principles of commercial ethics. He should have deviated only when authorised to do so by the works director in writing.

Kalyanasundaram learnt his lesson the hard way. When he applies for another job, he should tell his new employees the whole truth about what happened and start with a clean slate. He should ensure that he does not fall into such a trap again.

When you deal with ethics, you must realise that there are many aspects to it.

Case Study

There is the case of Bansilal, a young manager who was on the fast track and was made chief executive of a small factory. He was hardworking but manipulative and over ambitious. He started

> getting involved with unions whose interests were inimical to the long-term interests of the company. A professional cannot be ethical on one issue and unethical on another. Bansilal was ultimately asked to resign. Later he changed two jobs. In every case, what he was concerned with was his personal ego, emoluments and short-term results for quick promotions. He left every company he joined in a shambles before he moved to another job.

Persons like Biharilal are merely time-servers, opportunists and can never build institutions. They are dangerous and companies which want to institutionalise should never touch them.

In industrial relations, whatever may be the union's attitude, no respectable management professional should get entangled with goondaism, framing of false charges, political manipulations, etc. He must be above board and earn the respect of employees and unions as an honest and fair-minded person.

SUCCUMBING TO TEMPTATION IS EQUALLY BAD

Some companies indulge in compensating their employees with emoluments and perquisites outside the tax network. Even if such practices may not be frowned upon and to the advantage of the company, in the long-run, they will prove unwise. The law itself gives you considerable leverage, which you can take advantage of. In ethics, there is no degree. It is an absolute. You are either ethical or unethical. There is no middle ground. During the 45 years of my professional career, I have not once deviated from the right path. I may not be wealthy, but I have no regrets and sleep soundly every night.

Professionals must have the courage of their convictions when they start their career. This will remain with them life-long. Whether it is falsifying travel bills, or travelling by a lower class and claiming upper class fare, or claiming allowance on days you were not on tour, they are all indications of weakness. You are always vulnerable.

Case Study

> There was a sales representative in a multinational company who used to cover Assam and other north-eastem states, where there were few hotels. He printed his own letterheads of fictitious hotels, made false bills, and claimed allowance. When he was ultimately caught, he was dismissed unceremoniously.

Some young men may take this lightly, presuming that a small manipulation does not matter as it would never be detected. It is a false sense of security. Anything wrong that you do is on record. You can be hauled up at any time during your career. Even a slight moral lapse on your part a long time ago may boomerang in such a manner that you lose your job. It is not worth indulging in such petty gains, leave aside major frauds. *Professionalism and lack of ethics cannot co-exist.*

ATTRACTION TO THE OPPOSITE SEX

Another occupational hazard is attraction to the opposite sex at work. We are all human, and it is likely that you may get interested in someone working with you. If you are having an affair, it could become a scandal. If you are married, it will be even worse. It is foolish to think that you can hide such matters. Walls have ears and eyes, and even before you know, it will be a company scandal. Higher the hierarchy, worse will be the impact.

If both of you are serious about the matter, one of you must resign from the company before the matter gets out of hand. Otherwise, it will be a blot on your moral stature and leadership. Generally speaking, it is best to keep away from company employees.

OTHER ISSUES

There are other issues like evasion of tax, excise duty, provident fund, etc. If a company has a dubious reputation, it is much better not to join such a company. If you learn about it only later, be extremely cautious not to get personally involved in such transactions. If threatened, better leave the company than get yourself into deeper trouble later.

SOCIAL RESPONSIBILITY

One of the important issues under debate in the country is social responsibility of business. Let us see how it relates to the role of a manager.

The manager is in the centre of a triangle, with his head roped in by the consumer, one leg by the shareholders and the other by the employees. An effective manager must ensure that all the three maintain a static and dynamic balance. The interests of the consumer are paramount, and, if not fully protected by way of lower prices, better quality goods and effective customer service, the manager will be choked and the business will not survive. Similarly, if the shareholders do not get a fair return on their investments, there will be an uproar. Above all, emoluments of the employees must progressively increase, leading to an improvement in their living standards year after year. Few recognise the dynamics of this process.

You can be sure that an organisation which is successful has taken good care of the consumer's, the shareholder's and the employee's interests. If you are partial to one, it will tilt the balance. Once you have grasped the dynamics, you will serve society's interests better.

Many questions the wisdom of struggling to be sincere in a highly corrupt environment. I have not known of any individual or organisation whose activities have been above board and yet they have not survived. On the other hand, they have been extremely successful. I want to dispel any false notion that it is impossible to carry on business without being corrupt, unethical or above the law. Let me emphasise that how you behave is your personal choice. My advice is: be on the right side and take the rewards legitimately due to you rather than be in the wrong all your life for temporary gains. It is just not worth the price you pay.

THE FAMILY MANAGER

There is a big controversy about the role of the family manager. In the first instance, as majority shareholders, family managers have every right to approve the appointment of the chief executive and other directors on the board. Similarly, dividends and appreciation of the value of shares are legitimate benefits that accrue to them for the investments they make.

The conflict lies in the role that the family managers can play if they get involved in operating management. If any family member has had proper education and training, I am of the opinion that they should not be denied the opportunity to manage the affairs of the company on their own merits. The issue is who judges their competence? We can even give them the benefit of doubt. But once they accept the position of the chief executive or executive director or divisional manager, they must abide by the rules and regulations of the company and the statutory obligations, and be held equally responsible for result-oriented performance, failing which they have no place in the management of the company. No concession should be made on that point.

Even the perquisites, facilities, etc., must be in line with the position he holds. It is here that most family managers fail. They take it for granted that rules do not apply to them; that they can come and go as they please and do what they like. Job security is taken for granted. This undermines the morale in the company and stands in the way of institutional culture.

COMPETENCE—THE ONLY CRITERION

What should be the role of professionals in such a set-up? You must not be person-oriented. Regardless of who holds the higher position, stand up for what you think is right and do not become a sycophant. You must be issue-oriented and must express frank, unbiased opinions, keeping the company's well-being in mind. Through such conduct, a professional earns the respect of everyone. If your approach does not work, by all means you can part as friends.

Case Study

As management consultants, we once had an assignment to turnaround a medium-sized manufacturing company. We asked the promoter if any member of his family was interested in taking

> over the general manager's position. When he said "no", we recruited a young manager with a master's degree in industrial engineering from the US from one of the companies in the group belonging to the promoter. The company, which was running on a loss for several years, had a quick turnaround within a few months and started making profits. The promoter then insisted on having one of his young nephews, Jawahar, take over the affairs of the company. But Jawahar was unwilling to take on the responsibilities of the chief executive. He wished to visit the factory whenever he liked, and give *ad hoc* instructions to the general manager. We felt that such a manner of functioning would damage the long-term interests of the company and affect its stability and therefore dissuaded the promoter from making such a move. However, sometime later, due to pressure from his family members, he buckled and insisted on involving his nephew in the company's managemen' without any accountability or responsibility.
>
> Within a few months, the company again slide down and within a year, it deteriorated to such an extent that the promoters had no alternative but to close down the company.

This case clearly reveals how family managers who are insensitive to their responsibilities could have a devastating effect on the company's future. In a liberalised economy, there should be no distinction between family managers and professionals. Family managers must train themselves to compete with professionals on the basis of merit and occupy positions which they can hold with competence.

As the Indian economy opens up to global competition, unethical issues relating to family management will surface more and more. The earlier the family managers see the writing on the wall and behave themselves, the better it will be for them.

I shall not touch upon political corruption and top management or promoters' involvement for political patronage, since this may not directly concern professionals. In any case, these issues fall beyond the scope of this book. I know of a group which follows a firm policy of keeping away from politicians and the Government and it has not hurt them. There are many groups like that in India. Given the choice, I prefer to grow slowly or not at all rather than solicit political patronage at a price. It will lead to unmanageable situations in no time and you cannot backtrack. You make yourself vulnerable to black-mail and exposure.

SUMMARY

- It is in your interests to start your career on the right track. You must dispel the notion that you cannot get anywhere by being honest.

- Ethical issues arise all the time. You are the best judge. Do not be too sure that you can get away with anything.
- There is no unemployment for hardworking people. The liberalised economy provides enviable opportunities for professionals, who can rise to the highest ranks by sheer merit. Therefore, stand up, hold your head high and do not compromise on principles, regardless of the consequences. It is the only way you can lead a life of dignity.

Source: M.K. Raju, Managerial Success, University Press India Ltd., Hyderabad. Gratefully acknowledged.

Annexure VIII

WIPRO: A RESPECTED COMPANY

Recently, a very famous salesman made an unscheduled visit to the Delhi office of Ranbaxy Laboratories managing director D.S. Brar. Azim Premji's wasn't a courtesy visit; he was there on a business development mission. During the tete-a-tete, Premji made a forceful pitch on behalf of Wipro, besides, of course, assessing Ranbaxy's hardware needs. Later, Brar told a peer how impressed he was with Premji's customer-centric attitude.

He isn't the only one surprised by Premji's visits to customers. Even as late as 1999, Premji would visit shopkeepers around India to gather customer feed-back. By this time, Premji was already a household name, though he hadn't yet earned the sobriquet of the Richest Man in India.

Today, Premji may no longer be able to pound the streets—he calls himself an animal in the zoo. But touching customers directly is still as dear to him as his favourite Vadas. Both habits, incidentally, are a throwback to his Mumbai days.

The *ability to connect with customers* is what is most admired and emulated by the Wipro diaspora—the 100-odd former Wipro-ites who now head businesses in as diverse areas as IT consulting and networking to strategic investment and BPO the world over. (The Wipro diaspora is considered second only to the famous Hindustan Lever alumni, who, at last count, managed more than 220 companies.)

One of the former Wipro employees who swears by Premji is Sridhar Mitta, managing director of Bangalore-based e4e Labs, which mentors and invests in organisations servicing applications on the Internet. A 20-year Wipro veteran (he last served as chief technology officer in 2000), Mitta's respect for Wipro has remained undiminished even after he quit the company. Mitta says he has rarely seen such customer focus driven so hard by the chairman of a company.'In the old days, when a customer was not satisfied, Premji made sure that unless the problem was solved, nobody left the customer premises."

Sudip Banerji, the incumbent Wipro Technologies president (enterprise solutions), agrees: "Premji says if somebody complains, he must get an answer."

In fact, way back in 1981, Premji hired Wipro's first quality assurance manager, who reported directly to the CEO. "The quality assurance manager could overrule the factory manager," says Mitta. That commitment hasn't changed. Five months back, Wipro hired GE's Six Sigma head Anurag Behar as corporate vice-president to determine Wipro's quality standards. Predictably, he reports to Premji.

Former Wipro-ites also believe that Wipro is respected because it is among the few organisations that truly nurture independent thinking. Take Mitta, who as part of Wipro Infotech was involved only in domestic hardware and software maintenance. He had been repeatedly pitching for Premji's permission to export embedded software, which Premji repeatedly denied. In one meeting, Mitta stood his ground. Premji finally relented. Today, embedded software is one of Wipro's greatest strengths.

Says Mitta: "You could go to the chairman and say 'I don't agree' and still your interests would not be harmed. He has the openness to take the idiosyncrasies of all."

Behar, who's just joined Wipro after nine years with GE, says: "At Wipro, the space for dissent and independent thinking is unbelievable. It's usually difficult to listen to thousands of views. So it's a culture shock to me to see how much dissent exists and is listened to."

The organisation has encouraged entrepreneurship by cross-fertilisation of talent and fostering diversity. While former software head Ashok Soota was from compressor manufacturing company Shriram Refrigerators, former Wipro Infotech head N. Krishnakumar was a marketer.

The other fact that every Wipro-ite swears by is Premji's *ethics and integrity*. "Wipro works on a very high integrity platform. That's religiously followed," says Mitta. So much so that the company even today has an unwritten code of conduct of not dealing with the government where the relationship requires bending the rules. Premji's own take on all this: "What keeps respect is integrity. For us, integrity is non-negotiable. It's not just about refusing to bribe . . ., but is about keeping all your commitments—in letter and spirit. Without integrity, there is no respect."

At Wipro, the leader's influence has clearly seeped down the organisation. As the company's diaspora puts it: "Wipro's respect hasn't been demanded, but has been commanded."

ANNEXURE IX

CODE OF CONDUCT FOR EMPLOYEES OF PUBLIC SECTOR UNDERTAKINGS

DO'S AND DON'TS FOR CONDUCT

Do's

1. Do always remember that you are public servants, duly compensated for your services through salaries, allowances, perks, etc., out of the public exchequer'. As such, you are covered under the definition of 'public servants' as incorporated under the Prevention of Corruption Act, 1988 and also under the Indian Penal Code, 1860.

2. Do always keep in mind that as public servants, you are to do 'public duties' and enhance public well-being only and not private duties to benefit certain private people, with vested interests.

3. Do always appreciate that public servants are answerable for any suspected malafide actions on their part. As such, try to distinguish between 'Malafide' and 'Bonafide' actions or decisions. 'Bonafide' is, what is done in good faith, i.e. done with due care and attention. 'Malafide' is its exact opposite.

4. Do try to understand the implications of the words—Conduct, Misconduct and Criminal Misconduct. Briefly, 'Conduct' means the general and uniform behaviour that is expected of a public servant by the employer-organisation. Certain types of behaviour are explicitly shown as misconduct—which may be in the form of omissions as well as commissions 'Misconduct' attracts departmental actions against the public servants, charged with it. 'Criminal misconduct' means the misconduct as has been defined in Section 13 of the Prevention of Corruption Act, 1988, which also amounts to an 'offence' under the Indian Penal Code and a public servant charged with 'criminal misconduct' is proceeded criminally, in the competent court of Law; some examples are—demanding or accepting bribe by public servants, show of undue favour causing 'wrongful loss' to the organisation and/or wrongful gain to the individual(s)/agency(s); joining in criminal conspiracy with

colleagues/subordinates and others to cause undue favour as aforestated, forging of documents/reports; possession of assets/properties in cash or kind or both disproportionate to the known, legal sources of income, etc. etc.

5. Do spread the message that corruption and malpractices by public servants directly or indirectly cost the country heavily as those are discriminative in nature, and as such, are violative of Article 14 of the Constitution of India, which provides for "Equality before Law" and "Equal Protection of Law."
6. Do try your best to combat corrupt practices and wilful violation of the laid down Rules, Procedures and Systems by your subordinates and colleagues as 'Good Citizens' of the largest democracy.
7. Do a periodical self-assessment or self-analysis of yourself as a public servant, a good citizen and a vigilant professional and also about what others think and talk of you.
8. Do understand that 'liberalization of the economy does not imply liberalisation of corruption'. Liberalization and corruption often go together, as amply demonstrated in advanced as well as third world countries. To ensure speedy decision-making in the new environment, make specific suggestions for liberalization of cumbersome Rules and Procedures and then function within those, not outside.
9. Do always remember that you are an employee of PSU—the largest and most performing power utility in the country and that whatever you do, or have to do you will do to keep not only the flag flying high, but to take it to further commanding heights.
10. Do always keep in mind the organisation Vision, Mission and the Objectives. To be world leader and to remain as such, each and every employee of the organisation has to contribute his/her mite through highest standards of integrity, dedication, commitment, competence and impartiality—in a free, fair, fearless and dispassionate manner.
11. Do create a vigilance friendly environment in the organisation, through your own positive, transparent, fair and timely actions. You can make vigilance altogether redundant, thereby.
12. Be cost-conscious, cost-effective and plug all pilferage, wastes and leakages, to be really competitive. Initially, such actions may irritate, but in the long-run these pay handsomely.
13. Take prompt and firm actions to bring the corrupt to book. This will enhance the moral health of the organisation, give extra impetus to the honest and keep the corrupt few under constant pressure. Those on the fence will jump over to your side.

14. Remember always that you are managers and as managers, your duties are to manage men, money, materials, machines and methods in an economic, efficient, effective, excellent and equitable manner.
15. One's actions and decisions in official matters and dealings should be such, as a person of ordinary prudence would usually take in one's own personal business affairs.
16. Keep your image both in public and in the organisation as that of an honest, just, reasonable, fair and friendly public servant.
17. Observe normal courtesies in dealings with the public, subordinates and colleagues.
18. Always take prompt action to redress the complaints or grievances of the people, wherever possible. If you have to say 'no' to somebody, say the same very politely, but firmly.
19. Every executive having supervisory functions is a vigilance officer in respect of persons under his/her charge and the Company's Conduct Rules enjoin upon him/her to take all possible steps to ensure the integrity and devotion to duty of the employees under his/her control and authority.
20. Do acquaint yourself with the basic Laws of the Land, respect the laws and observe them, both in letter and spirit. Remember that ignorance of law cannot be an excuse.
21. Infringement or violation of any law could result in departmental action, apart from other proceedings under the law violated e.g. laws relating to prohibition, bigamous marriages, taking or giving dowry, drugs addiction, giving or taking of bribes, etc.
22. Please verify whether any rules, regulations, policies, guidelines, procedures, practices and functions exist in the organisation about the modalities in which the works of your unit are to be carried out. Some instructions issued from time to time; might have become defunct or redundant. It would be advantageous to consolidate them and uptodate so that clear and unambiguous guidelines are available for following the correct path.
23. If there are no written instructions or procedural guidelines about various types of work/ functions to be performed in your unit and the same are being carried out as per certain practices, it would be desirable to make a humble beginning to streamline those through written procedures. It would definitely help the new entrants to your unit to perform his/her duties properly. This will also help in sharing of accountability on individual decisions. Remember, you cannot escape the accountability tomorrow, by evading it today.
24. The schedule of Delegation of Powers confers considerable

discretion on the executives, at various levels and the company expects the executives to use the discretionary powers judiciously. Proper caution should be taken in the exercise of discretionary powers and as far as practicable, seasonings for the use of discretion in a particular case, in a particular manner should be recorded. Vigilance would not question the use of such discretionary powers, unless there is clear evidence of abuse or misuse of such powers in a 'malafide' way.

25. The Conduct, Discipline and Appeal Rules are the generally uniform guidelines and are not only for keeping the management informed about the personal acquisitions, disposals, etc. of the employees; but are also meant for their protection against allegations made by unscrupulous persons. The disclosures made or permission obtained at appropriate time, as required under the Conduct Rules, would provide you protection against unnecessary allegations at a later date. Even if you have taken advance for the purchase of car, house, etc. from the company, this does not dispense with the requirement of permission or intimation under the Conduct Rules.
26. Follow scrupulously the Conduct, Discipline and Appeal Rules/ Standing Orders as laid down for the employees.
27. Every employee is required to maintain absolute integrity, at all times, under the Conduct Rules. A man of integrity will never listen to any plea against conscience and is always accepted, believed, trusted and befriended by all.
28. Gifts upto a value of Rs. 500 can be accepted from near relatives on occasions such as weddings, anniversaries, funerals or religious functions when the making of a gift is in conformity with the prevailing religious or social practice.
29. Gifts on the occasions listed above from personal friends having no official dealings can be accepted upto a value of Rs. 250. Gifts beyond the value of Rs. 250. A require reporting to the competent authority.
30. On any other occasion, gifts upto a value of Rs. 250 can be accepted by the executives. Any gifts of value beyond this amount require prior sanction of the competent authority.
31. Deposits with the banks, Life Insurance Corporation, or a firm of standing, doing normal banking business do not require any prior sanction or intimation under the Conduct Rules, except where specifically called for.
32. All transactions of movable property beyond the value of Rs. 10,000 have to be reported to Competent Authority, within one month of the transaction (For Supervisors, it is Rs. 5,000). If such

transaction is with a person or firm having official dealing with the employees or his subordinates, the same requires prior sanction of the Competent Authority.

33. Every executive is required to submit a statement of his Immovable and Movable Property on his first appointment. Remember that possession of assets disproportionate to your known/legal sources of income is an offence and your Property Return is going to help you tremendously, if you are faced with any wild allegations of corruption.

34. To submit the Periodical Return of Immovable Property as on 1st January of that year, notwithstanding the fact that the return may be a 'Nil' one i.e. there was no acquisition of immovable properties during the period under report.

35. Keep a good conscience and stick to it. It is a constant friend and will never let you down. Hence decide on what you think is right and stick to it. Please record your reasonings for a particular advice or decision in the file as logically and as clearly as possible.

36. Think well before acting, but when the time of action comes, stop thinking and start acting, for action is the expression of your thoughts.

37. Behaviour is an important tool of success; so, behave cogently, gently, amply, kindly, friendly, cheerfully and boldly. Behave with others the way you expect others to behave with you.

38. Encourage your subordinates to do their best. The inner most expectation of every human being is the "craving to be appreciated." If you want to effect change, and change fast, encouragement is the best tool.

39. Sometimes, you may commit errors. But if you do so, please admit the same gracefully, instead of trying to pass on the responsibility to others. The greatest error one could make in life is to be in fear of committing error.

40. Wherever son, daughter or any member of your family or any other close relative accepts an employment with any private firm with which you have official dealings or with any firm having officials dealing with the Company, apply for the previous sanction of the Competent Authority. Where the acceptance of the employment cannot await the prior permission of the Competent Authority, the employment may be accepted provisionally, subject to the permission of the Competent Authority.

41. If you or any of your relatives is interested in any case or in a contract or in any other matter connected directly or indirectly with your official duties, refer such matter or contract to your official

superior, without any noting from you on the subject.

42. Always obtain the previous sanction of the Competent Authority before you own wholly or in part; any newspaper or periodical or conduct or participate in the editing, publication or management of any newspaper or periodical.

43. Always obtain the previous sanction of the Competent Authority before you participate in a radio broadcast, or contribute any article or write any letter, either in your own name or anonymously, pseudonymously or in the name of any other person to any newspaper or periodical, unless you are satisfied that such a contribution is of a purely literary, artistic or scientific in nature.

44. Do indicate to the Management, if any member of your family is engaged in a trade or business or owns or manages an insurance agency or commission agency.

45. You can accept the full amount of fee for any work done by you, with the prior permission of the competent authority, provided, it is for one time assignment performed.

46. When you take recurring and continuous assignments such as lectures for evening class, part time or other courses, you can get honorarium, fees, etc. up to an amount of Rs. 1,000 per annum only. Where the amount received is beyond Rs. 1,000 per annum, you should deposit 1/3rd of the amount, in excess of Rs. 1,000 with the Company.

47. You must seek and obtain sanction of the Competent Authority before you accept any fee or any pecuniary advantage for any work done by you for any public body or any private person.

48. Remember, each one of you as a public servant is expected to act honestly and faithfully, at all times.

49. Always demonstrate a sense of fair play and impartiality in disposing of cases; it is paying.

50. Avoid seeking and receiving cash donations and advertisements from the Corporation's Contractors/suppliers, etc. even for a good cause lest it should place you under obligations.

51. Dispose of cases promptly and without undue haste.

52. Do intensive monitoring of delays and disposal of files of your department, it helps curbing corruption.

53. Give job rotation to those who are on sensitive desks/positions atleast once in 5 years, lest vested interests should grow.

54. Pay personal and particular attention to compliance of Rules and Procedures; it is an effective method of preventive vigilance.

55. Keep on assessing the strength and weaknesses of the 'Internal Control Mechanism'; this is the surest way to reduce malpractices.
56. Publicise the Rules and Procedures as widely as possible, in simple words and make them less cumbersome; it dispenses with the necessity for 'speed money'.
57. Pay surprise and frequent visits to the places visited by the public; it will give you a good feed-back of the happenings.
58. Remember always that corruption starts in a small way; it would thus be wise to 'press the break' in the initial stage itself.
59. Follow scrupulously all laid down procedures; this will go a long way in eliminating malpractices. In case any deviation is considered necessary in Corporation's interest, get the approval of Competent Authority.
60. Keep a quiet watch over the style of living, types of visitors etc. of the employees posted on sensitive desks/areas/posts; it will help detection of corruption at early stages.
61. Remember, problems start where vigilance ends.

Don'ts

1. Don't be arbitrary and illogical in your decisions. The decisions should be justifiable on all counts.
2. Never delay the decisions and/or movement of files. Delay creates doubt and breeds corruption. Even innocent delays create suspicion in the minds of the people. Please remember that the percentage of mistakes in quick decisions is no greater than in long drawn ones.
3. Don't mix with the contractors and suppliers having dealings with you or your Company and also do not accept lavish hospitality, except to the extent it is necessary for the business of the company. Having regular club associations and social parties with such contractors and businessmen creates suspicions in the minds of public, your colleagues and subordinates, about your integrity; and could result in avoidable complaints.
4. If the case of any person or firm comes up, in which you do have direct or indirect interest, do not hesitate to put up the case to your higher authority pointing out what interest you have with the person or the firm.
5. Do not mix up your personal and official business as far as possible. If it is unavoidable, particularly while on tour, you can take casual leave and do not claim Daily Allowance.

6. Never delay submission of your T.A. Bills. These should be submitted carefully and any excuse that wrong Daily Allowance has been claimed, as the bill was prepared by the Private Secretary, is not acceptable.
7. Never sign the minutes or any other documents back-dated. This may or may not achieve the desired objective, but can certainly land you in difficulties during interrogation, in the event of a vigilance case later.
8. Avoid dealing with firms which do not give full and complete address or detailed particulars. Do go into antecedents of such firms wherever required. Do verify *bonafides* of the firms which furnish addresses like "C/o Post Box No..."
9. Do not be bigamous. Even if you are permitted by your personal law to marry while your spouse is living, you would be violating the Conduct Rules by such marriage, unless you have taken written permission of the Competent Authority and that such a marriage has also got legal sanction.
10. Please avoid giving any statements to the Press, unless you are authorised to do so. If you have something to convey to the Press, use the good offices of the Corporate Communications/PR Department.
11. Do no fail to be fully conversant with the powers delegated to you under Delegation of Powers. Do not unjustifiably put up proposals to higher authorities if the case can be disposed of at your level, under the delegation.
12. Do not, be negligent or lack in devotion to duty any time. Barring *bonafide* mistakes or errors of judgement, if any employee exhibits lack of devotion to duty or negligence, he/she attracts provisions of Conduct Rules.
13. Do not forget to conduct yourself in a manner which enhances the image of the company. This covers not only your actions in your official capacity and position, but also your private life and dealings. For example, if you are found in an inebriated state in a public place, you are liable to be proceeded against for serious breach of Conduct Rules.
14. Do not engage or participate in any demonstration involving incitement to an offence.
15. You are prohibited from engaging directly or indirectly in any trade or business or undertaking any other employment, part time or whole time, without the previous sanction of the Competent Authority.

16. An executive should avoid monetary transactions either directly or through members of his/her family, which places him/them under pecuniary obligation to any person with whom he/she has or is likely to have official dealings.

17. Do not forget to report any acquisition or disposal of immovable property to the Competent Authority in advance. However, previous sanction would be required if the transaction is with a person or a firm having official dealings with the executive concerned, or with his subordinate(s).

18. Do not forget to give prior intimation to the Competent Authority about the construction, including additions and modifications, etc. of immovable property. On completion, a "Valuation Certificate" together with the sources of fund, out of which the cost of construction has been met, should be submitted to the Competent Authority within one month of the completion.

19. Do not give evidence in connection with any enquiry other than judicial or departmental enquiry or enquiry before an authority appointed by Government, Parliament, or State Legislature, without previous permission of Competent Authority, and where permitted to give evidence, do not criticise policy or action of the Government or the Company.

20. Do not communicate information to anybody unauthorisedly, either during service or after leaving service. Do not own, edit or publish any newspaper or periodical without previous sanction of Competent Authority.

21. Do not make statements criticising policies or action of Government or the Company except when the statements made or views expressed are factual, but not confidential in nature, made in official capacity or in performance of assigned duties or views expressed by recognised trade union office-bearers for purposes of safeguarding or improving the conditions of service of the employees.

22. Do not give or take or abet in giving or taking of dowry.

23. Do not take part in the registration, promotion or management of any society, bank or any other company which is required to be registered under the Companies Act or any other Act, or a Cooperative Society, for commercial purposes subject to exceptions, if any, provided in the Conduct Rules.

24. Do not be brash in telling 'no' to anybody for any undue request made by him/her. Try to learn the art of saying 'no' politely, but firmly. A soft answer always turns away the wrath.

25. Do not forget to do your duty as efficiently as you can. Every duty is holy and devotion to duty is the highest form of worship of God.

26. Never use your position or influence directly or indirectly to secure employment for any person related to you, whether by blood or marriage, or to your wife or husband, irrespective of whether such a person is dependent on you or not.
27. Always desist from dealing with any matter or sanction of any contract to any Company or to any person if any member of your family or any of your relatives is employed in that Company or under that person.
28. Do not fail to report to your Controlling/Competent Authority when you apply to be declared; or is adjudged, or declared insolvent by any court of jurisdiction.
29. Do not, yield to temptation or run after petty gains; it does not pay ultimately.
30. Do not live beyond your means; it may be tempting, but dangerous.
31. Do not make any attempt to flout or circumvent or short-circuit the Rules or Regulations, to suit vested interests; it may cost you heavily in the long-run.
32. Do not take any obligation in any form, from anyone; it may boomerang.
33. Do not lean too heavily on your superiors as also subordinates; it may prove costly.
34. Do not allow your family members to use your name for personal gains; it can ruin your reputation. Do not fail to remember: reputation once gone is not retrievable.
35. Do not use your influence for securing any advantage for yourself or anyone related or known to you; it does not speak well of you.
36. Don't exceed your powers—financial and administrative, except in an emergency; it is irregular and gives rise to suspicion.
37. Avoid getting influenced by personal likes and dislikes, whims and prejudices while disposing of the files or cases.
38. Do not relax while you are on supervision duties; this may bring trouble for you and your Company.
39. Avoid misuse of the Corporation's property, i.e. sub-letting of allotted houses, misuse of vehicles, telephones, etc.
40. Do not take part in political activities, such as: (a) being an office-bearer of a political party or an organization which takes part in politics; (b) to take part or assist, in any manner in any movement/ agitation or demonstration of political nature; (c) to take part in an election to any legislature or local authority; and (d) to canvas in any

manner in any election to legislature or local authority.

41. Do not make any unauthorized communication directly or indirectly or part with any information to any other employee or person to whom you are not authorized to communicate or to part with such information, or which may be detrimental to the interests of the Company.

42. Do not accept or permit any member of your family or even a person acting on your behalf to accept any gift which includes free transport, boarding, lodging or other services or any other pecuniary advantage from a person other than a near relative or personal friend having no official dealings with the employee. Even in permitted situations, do not accept any gift in cash or kind, of more than the specified value.

43. Do not accept or permit any member of your family or any person acting on your behalf to accept gifts if the value thereof exceeds Rs. 250 without the sanction of the competent authority.

44. Do not demand directly or indirectly from the parents or guardian of a bridegroom as the case may be any dowry, either in cash or in kind or both.

45. Avoid habitual indebtedness.

REFERENCES

Alan Kitson and Robert Campbell, Macmillan Business.

A. Parthasarathy, Vedanta Treatise, Vedanta Life Institute, IA, Landsend, Dongarsi Road, Malabar Hill, Bombay, India.

Peter Madsen and Jay M. Shafnitz, Essentials of Business Ethics, Penguin Group, USA Inc., 375, Hudson Street, New York.

Amartya Sen, Resources, Values and Development, Oxford University Press.

S.K. Chakraborty, Ethics in Management Integrity at Work, Oxford University Press.

S.K. Chakraborty, Human Values for Managers, Wheeler Publishing.

Joseph A. Petrik and John F. Quinn, Management Ethics, Response Books, Sage Publication Inc.

Peter Prattey, The Essence of Business Ethics, Prentice Hall of India.

S.A. Sherlekar, Ethics in Management, Himalaya Publishing House.

Larue Tone Hosmer, The Ethics of Management, Universal Book Stall (UBS).

Prof. Sorab Sadri, Dr. Dhun S. Dastoor, Ms. S. Jayashree, The Theory and Practice of Managerial Ethics, Jaico Publishing House.

R. Edward Freeman, Business Ethics: the State of the Art, Oxford University Press.

David Murray, Ethics in Organisation, Coopers Lybrand.

David Robinson, Business Etiquette, Kogan Page (I) Pvt. Ltd.

Verne E. Henderson, What is Ethical in Business, McGraw-Hill, Inc.

R.C. Shekar, Ethical Choices in Business, Response Books.

Chartered Secretary, Special Issues on "Business Ethics and Corporate Governance", in September and November, 2003.

Raja Achanta, The Work-Life Balance, *HRM Review*, March 2004.

www.hbs.edu.

www.stanford.edu.

www.globalethics.org.

www.zdetindia.com

INDEX